Peace Psychology

A comprehensive introduction to the rapidly growing research area of peace psychology. Both a topic in its own right and studied within courses on peace studies, conflict studies and subsidiaries of psychology, international relations and politics, peace psychology is a practically and theoretically important area. This textbook covers the whole research literature focusing on studies since the end of the Cold War but also incorporating aspects of earlier literature which retain contemporary relevance. The content includes an introductory chapter outlining the growth of the field and goes on to cover interdisciplinary practice (international relations, education, feminist studies and ethics), primary psychological topics (development, social psychology, psychodynamics and cognition), core topics from peace studies (conflict resolution, crisis management, nonviolence, peacemaking and peacebuilding, specific locations such as the Middle East and sustainable development) and terrorism (threats and victims). This is a unique textbook that will appeal to students and practitioners alike.

HERBERT H. BLUMBERG is a Reader in the Psychology Department at Goldsmiths College, University of London. He has written numerous articles in social psychology and research methods and is the Review Editor and Bibliographer for *Peace and Conflict: Journal of Peace Psychology*.

A. PAUL HARE is Professor Emeritus in the Department of Behavioral Science at Ben-Gurion University, Israel. He has written extensively on social interaction and was the editor of *Sociological Inquiry* as well as the founder and first editor of *Israel Social Science Research*.

ANNA COSTIN is a journalist with Jane's Information Group, London, where she writes and reports on terrorism and security issues.

Peace Psychology

A Comprehensive Introduction

Herbert H. Blumberg, A. Paul Hare and
Anna Costin

CAMBRIDGE
UNIVERSITY PRESS

CAMBRIDGE UNIVERSITY PRESS
Cambridge, New York, Melbourne, Madrid, Cape Town, Singapore, São Paulo

CAMBRIDGE UNIVERSITY PRESS
The Edinburgh Building, Cambridge CB2 2RU, UK

Published in the United States of America by Cambridge University Press,
New York

www.cambridge.org
Information on this title: www.cambridge.org/9780521547857

© Herbert H. Blumberg, A. Paul Hare and Anna Costin 2006

First published 2006

Printed in the United Kingdom at the University Press, Cambridge

A catalogue record for this book is available from the British Library

ISBN-13 978-0-521-83914-3 hardback
ISBN-10 0-521-83914-9 hardback
ISBN-13 978-0-521-54785-7 paperback
ISBN-10 0-521-54785-7 paperback

Contents

Preface

The number of publications concerned with research and practice in the field that has come to be known as peace psychology has been growing rapidly and there are some landmark volumes (which the present work does not in any way replace!), displaying many of the major theoretical and practical contributions – as noted in the Introduction to this book. No prior work that we know of, though, provides a comprehensive review with a usable taxonomy of all of the relevant post-Cold War research. We certainly cannot pretend that the present work cites, much less integrates, *all* of the applicable research – as will be evident from the analysis and figures in the Introduction. We have, however, done our best to fill the need.

Acknowledgements

We would like to thank Sarah Caro for advice on the organization of this volume and Milt Schwebel and Dan Christie for their comments on a draft of the work.

The scope, structure and content of this book

The present volume covers, as far as feasible, the whole post-Cold War research literature for the practically and theoretically important area now known as peace psychology. This area includes a spectrum of topics drawn from psychology and its interfaces with other disciplines insofar as they relate to peace and conflict resolution primarily, but by no means exclusively, in an international context. The area is of widespread interest to practitioners, to academics (there being, for example, a substantial number of university courses in peace studies, including psychological aspects) and to the general public.

Psychology's major contributions to conflict resolution and peace studies are, for the most part, fairly readily retrievable, for instance from the key compendia named below. The breadth of published papers within this area is, however, less retrievable, being dispersed across journals and books covering most of the behavioural and social sciences.

Primary present coverage is of the post-Cold War period from 1990 to 2003. Of course we do not hesitate to cite major earlier work, but to include it comprehensively would be beyond the scope of a single volume. Moreover, pre-1990 classified bibliographic work is already available in a volume compiled by Blumberg and French (1992) and also compilations by B. M. Kramer and Moyer (1991) and Müller-Brettel (1993a). For notes on seventeen early peace psychologists (including Pythagoras and Pavlov!), see Rudmin (1991).

The present volume is intended to provide a comprehensive introduction to research in peace psychology, perhaps offering a synthesis and bibliographic complement to existing compendia of core contributions. In their landmark compendium of peace psychology, Christie, Wagner and Winter (2001) describe the field as covering psychological aspects of direct and indirect conflict (especially at intercultural and international levels), and particularly as covering the means of addressing conflict: peacekeeping and peacemaking – as a response to direct conflict – and peacebuilding, to address and prevent indirect or institutionalized violence. Their collection includes papers by many of the main research-ers and practitioners in the field (for subsequent views of the 'state of the art' see Christie, 2006).

Approximately fifteen years before them, while the Cold War was still unfolding, Ralph White (1986) assembled papers covering the founda-tions of work in this area. Deutsch's (1986) chapter in that volume provides a well-balanced and moving summary of major psychological approaches and contributions. S. Staub and Green (1992), too, gathered key papers covering much of peace psychology. Arguably, Claggett Smith (1971) was the first to assemble a volume of the then major behavioural science perspectives on conflict and its resolution. Authors of earlier work, some of which is represented in Smith's compendium, include Deutsch (e.g. Deutsch and Krauss, 1960), Escalona (1982), Kogan, Osgood (1962), Schwebel (1965) and Sherif (Sherif and Sherif, 1953) – and, in other related fields, distinguished scholars such as Kenneth and Elise Boulding and Talcott Parsons among others. William James, who wrote in 1910 about the moral equivalent of war, has been described as the first peace psychologist (Christie, Wagner and Winter, 2001: 2; Deutsch, 1995).

The compendia named above include within them work by 'key' contributors to peace psychology; among the main contemporary con-tributors, many more, but obviously not all, are represented in papers published in *Peace and Conflict: Journal of Peace Psychology* (the journal of the Society for the Study of Peace, Conflict and Violence: Peace Psychology Division of the American Psychological Association), whose founding and subsequent editors, respectively, are Milton Schwebel (Roe, McKay and Wessells, 2003; Winter, 2003) and Richard Wagner.

The present volume is intended to provide and synthesize a fairly comprehensive set of references related to the topics of peace psych-ology. The reality is probably more modest. Based on the degree of convergence among previous, roughly parallel bibliographic efforts, we reckon that for every two items we have cited, there is probably at least one that does not essentially duplicate material we have otherwise covered, is worth citing and was published in the relevant time span – but that we do not (yet) know about!

Many of the articles and books cited in this volume were read in full. For many others, however, an abstract in a bibliographic database was our primary source of information concerning the relevance of the research for the analysis of psychological aspects of conflict resolution and peace.

The main corpus of material for the present volume was retrieved using the search strategy employed by Blumberg and French (1992) (see below). The retrieved materials were then sorted according to the classification scheme developed by Blumberg (1993, 1998). This scheme, updated for the present contemporary purpose, forms the basis for the table of contents of the present volume.

Contents

This volume does *not* cover general treatments of the various topics (such as aggression and attitudes) but focuses on work that bears on peace and related topics, usually in an international context. Some of the description below is based on Blumberg (1998).

In Part I an introductory chapter describes the growth of peace psychology and delineates ways in which the field can be organized and the material applied.

Part II covers key interdisciplinary work from the interface of psychology and other fields. Political scientists, in particular, have increasingly included psychological variables (relating to perception and to power, for example) among their concerns. In this section we also cover research related to peace education (such as categories included in Deutsch's comprehensive recommendations for effective education for a peaceful world) and a relatively small but important corpus of publications concerned with typically feminist approaches to achieving and maintaining a broad-based peace. A further chapter in this section pertains to historical, religious, philosophical and ethical matters – such as principled nonviolence and threats to professional neutrality.

The chapters in part III cover work from several major areas of psychology. For this section, in particular, the organization follows from extant research.

Developmental psychology covers most core psychological areas but through a specialized filter. Developmental work considers ways of dealing with the effects of war on children and adolescents (as part of general populations and in particular as victims) and also with the rehabilitation of child soldiers. Of special concern is how children's fears of war can be addressed constructively.

Relevant aspects of several core areas – attitudes (within social psychology), psychodynamics (personality), cognition and also aggression – are brought together as parts of a single chapter. The section on attitudes draws on eclectic approaches, but especially those relating to social identity and mutual perceptions of 'ingroups' and 'outgroups'.

Psychodynamics here refers not only to personality and psychopathology but also to aspects of public health, concerning effects both on general populations and on the victims and perpetrators of violence. Much of the work (some of it displayed under 'attitudes' rather than 'psychodynamics' per se) consists of empirical studies of special populations, such as holocaust survivors, war veterans and simply clients in psychotherapy.

Cognition, as such, is the focus of surprisingly little research in peace psychology, but the topics from a variety of other chapters bear on perceptual matters, and these are extracted and covered in the separate chapter on cognition. For example, according to research findings on prospect theory, in making decisions people are more risk aversive for gains than for losses – a cognitive matter that has implications for peacebuilding. This chapter also includes publications concerned with images – of the effects of war, on cooperation and on desired futures. A further section deals with the nature and effects of aggression. This also includes recent work on the (lack of) inevitability of violence and negative conflict.

Somewhat like developmental psychology, research on language and communication – constituting the final chapter in this block – relates to various areas of psychology (and some other disciplines as well) including most facets of peace psychology. In fact this chapter is organized according to (a) links with international relations and other disciplines and (b) primary psychological and related topics.

Finally, some core areas of psychology such as motivation and learning have obvious relevance to conflict resolution and peace but are left out of the chapter titles and headings altogether because, for the most part, relevant research has not been framed explicitly in terms of these fields of psychology.

Part IV concerns psychological aspects of core topics in peace studies. Conflict resolution is central and here emphasizes practice related to international peace but also includes all levels from intrapersonal to international, and covers both theory and practice (such as Pruitt's and Bercovitch and Rubin's findings and recommendations with regard to third-party mediation). A chapter on decision-making and crisis management deals with risk assessment, crisis behaviour (stress and coping), and effective decision-making.

Material on peace movements and on nonviolence is especially varied, covering resources, participants, goals and leadership, and basic values. 'Some themes have centred on the ongoing need for workshops and other forms of training in nonviolent action, peacemaking, and peacekeeping' and on 'applications of direct action to peace-linked concerns such as achieving sustainable development and ameliorating discrimination' based on prejudice (Blumberg, 1998: 26).

This part also includes psychological aspects of peacemaking and peacebuilding in a broad variety of contemporary and also historical international contexts (linking, for example, to attitude- and cognition-focused research covered in Part III).

A substantial literature (and hence a relatively long chapter) focuses on specific locations, particularly (and not surprisingly) the Middle East and also Russia and the former Soviet Union.

Relevant work on sustainable development represents a crucial multifaceted objective associated with addressing structural violence and hence forms the concluding chapter of this section. The research, both theoretical and practical, deals with a variety of problems (including environmental threats, defined broadly) in various arenas, from individual behaviour to large-scale public policy.

Part V includes two chapters on terrorism. One covers terrorist threats (crisis intervention; specific forms of threat; understanding and dealing with terrorists; and interdisciplinary topics) and the other is concerned with victims of terrorism (effects on children; psychodynamic and other effects on adult victims; relevant aspects of crisis intervention).

The former chapter includes, for example, material on antecedents of terrorism and the (situational and dispositional) circumstances under which people are recruited to terrorist groups. It also looks at 'rehabilitation' work, such as Wessells's description of psychosocial assistance for former child soldiers in Angola. The latter chapter includes (topical) work on dealing with trauma, a 'near neighbour' of Macy's despair work (which is noted in chapter 2 and is also relevant to psychodynamic matters in chapter 7). This complements the more global efforts at peacebuilding, covered in chapters 12, 13 and 14 – ranging from peacebuilding to working generally towards a sustainably just and peaceful world.

Search strategy

The search strategy used for retrieving much of the material covered in the present volume is essentially as follows, although it was adapted for different databases (which indexed material in different ways) and time periods.

Freetext searching (where * indicates possible truncation) for:

1. (peace* or disarm* or arms race) OR
2. (nuclear or atom*) followed by (bomb or deterrence or weapon* or war or arm* or threat* or image or freeze*) OR

3. (international) followed by (bargain* or mediat* or negotiat* or nonagressi* or nonviolen* or security or relations or conflict*)

The above strategy is deliberately liberal, retrieving many irrelevant items that were deleted manually. In addition, of course, we have included materials called to our attention from a variety of other sources.

Part I

Introduction

1   Trends in peace psychology*

Herbert H. Blumberg

One important cause to which several thousand psychological publications have been devoted is the pursuit of worldwide peace. For the period up to the end of the Cold War, particularly in the 1980s, Blumberg and French (1992) documented about 1,500 publications in this and closely related areas; and – if one uses a rather wide definition of peace psychology – Kramer and Moyer (1991) and Müller-Brettel (1993a), between them, documented a further like amount.

The present discussion is intended, first, to give a broad picture of the field – rather like a town plan that puts locations in perspective but may show little about the architecture of the buildings and the feelings of the people living there. This 'broad picture' includes delineation of the contents and growth of the area, and consideration of taxonomic schemes for the relevant research. Following that, however, is an indication of some of the major developments and themes included in the research.

Readers who would like to 'zoom in' slightly on the 'town plan' should refer to the earlier section 'The scope, structure and content of this book', to learn how this book's topics are clustered. Those wanting information on a fairly specific topic might, of course, also consult the index.

Arguably the two events occurring between 1980 and 2005 that have had the greatest (direct or indirect) impact on Western foreign policy – and possibly on psychological aspects of peace and international conflict resolution – have been the end of the Cold War (and of the Soviet Union)

---

* This chapter is based in part on: Herbert H. Blumberg (2005, June), Peace psychology before and after September 2001. Presented at the Ninth International Symposium on the Contributions of Psychology to Peace, under the auspices of the International Union of Psychological Science, Portland, OR, USA. The Portland paper was itself developed in part from: Herb Blumberg (2005, February), Overviews of peace psychology. Presented at a Symposium on the Psychology of Peace and Conflict, Goldsmiths College, University of London.

and the terrorist attacks of 11 September 2001 (as regards the latter, see Roy, 2002).

The range of topics covered in relevant psychological research appears to have remained reasonably constant, but the distribution across topics seems to have shifted. Blumberg (1998) concluded that in the two years after the end of the Cold War – compared with preceding years – peace psychology research showed a significantly different distribution across topics, with the difference due to a number of relatively small changes (between 5 and 10 per cent relative increase or decrease in each of half a dozen areas). For instance, research on attitudes, on conflict resolution and on the interface between psychology and international relations tended to increase.

One main concern, here, is to extend this comparison (using three different bibliographic databases) so as to include both an entire decade following the end of the Cold War and also, separately, the years immediately following 11 September 2001.

Research growth

With modern bibliographic databases one can step back from the details of the subject matter at hand in order to examine the ebb and flow, as it were, of virtually all published research – and to infer whether the growth (or decline) of a field is a function of broad, general trends or of discipline-specific or topic-specific ones.

Table 1.1 displays, for each year band used in the present analysis, the overall number of records in the PsycINFO database and the number of articles retrieved by several types of search.

The number of articles added to the PsycINFO database each year has generally grown over the entire period, a matter that must be taken into account when considering the temporal progression of any particular topic. In general the figures show a substantial progressive increase in the number of records added to the database. The lower figure for 2004, as sampled on 1 January 2005, simply reflects a time lag between a work's publication year and its accession to the database. (Table 1.1 is not broken down by document type; but in the case of books and chapters, which currently comprise over 10 per cent of the records, the figures are also lower for 2003, due to longer time lag for accession, and for years prior to the 1990s, due to database coverage.)

The column headed 'peace-psych.' tracks the frequency of peace psychology publications as defined by the main search strategy described and used by Blumberg and French (1992) and carried forward as a main foundation for the present volume. This included, for example, relevant

Table 1.1. *PsycINFO records showing selected words in title or abstract*

PY	N	peace-psych.	psycholog*	peace	terroris*
1970s	270,247	382 (0.141)	24,504 (9.1)	155 (0.057)	23 (0.009)
1980s	427,259	1348 (0.315)	44,629 (10.4)	398 (0.093)	143 (0.033)
1990s	551,731	1728 (0.313)	63,899 (11.6)	520 (0.094)	165 (0.030)
2000	66,329	247 (0.372)	8,681 (13.1)	100 (0.151)	23 (0.035)
2001	72,165	285 (0.395)	8,654 (12.0)	115 (0.159)	53 (0.073)
2002	79,665	363 (0.456)	9,790 (12.2)	123 (0.154)	309 (0.388)
2003	86,001	387 (0.450)	10,854 (12.6)	136 (0.158)	265 (0.308)
2004	46,696	176 (0.377)	5,618 (12.0)	80 (0.171)	215 (0.460)

Tabulations were done on 1 January 2005 and include accession numbers ending with the second week of December 2004.

PY = Publication year of the work abstracted. 'peace-psych.' refers to the search strategy used by Blumberg and French (1992). A star (*) indicates truncation; for example, psychol* includes psychology, psychologists and other words starting with 'psychol'. Figures in brackets are percentages of the row N.

works on peace and disarmament (about half of the retrievals) plus research on international conflict resolution and also some works concerned with nuclear warfare. There is a large, significant increase between the 1970s and the 1980s and a further significant but smaller increase after the 1990s. These increases are not only in absolute terms but also as a proportion of the (growing) number of records added to the database.

Conceivably such increase might be due simply to PsycINFO broadening its coverage beyond psychology's 'usual' boundaries. However, the column tracking instances of words starting 'psycholog' itself in titles and abstracts shows a small progressive significant increase across decades (aggregating 2000–2004 as a prorated 'decade'). This makes it unlikely that the overall temporal increase in total records, and arguably in those concerned with peace research, would simply reflect a broadening of the databases' coverage – except possibly insofar as other disciplines (e.g. political science) include more research on their interface with psychology.

As a cruder but possibly more 'objective' (or 'time fair') index than the composite peace-psych. one, records simply including the word *peace* show a broadly similar temporal increase. That is, for tabulation purposes, use of a composite index that seeks terms such as 'nuclear war' might be more comprehensive but also may show more artificial unevenness over time than a search for just the word 'peace'.

Table 1.2. *Number of SSCI records showing selected words in one or more of: title, keywords or abstract*

Year	N	psycholog*	peace	terroris*
1980s	1,104,518	20,690 (1.87)	2,464 (0.22)	820 (0.074)
1990s	1,347,255	47,127 (3.50)	3,570 (0.27)	720 (0.053)
2000	145,251	6,059 (4.17)	561 (0.39)	89 (0.061)
2001	149,881	6,738 (4.50)	541 (0.36)	145 (0.097)
2002	135,814	6,041 (4.45)	410 (0.30)	465 (0.342)
2003	152,795	6,831 (4.47)	448 (0.29)	482 (0.315)
2004	132,591	5,980 (4.51)	425 (0.32)	623 (0.470)

Notes:
Figures in brackets are percentages of the row N.

Finally, the terrorist threat and, particularly, responses to it represent an important contemporary topic for psychologists concerned with peace and conflict resolution. Table 1.1 indicates that, not surprisingly, work in this area shows a quantum leap starting with 2002. Given typical publication lags for scientific publications, the fact that the increase emerges full-blown in 2002 is itself almost surprising. (The small *drop* from 2002 to 2003 is not statistically significant when one considers only peer-reviewed journal articles – given that books and chapters, which otherwise represent about one-sixth of the psychological works on terrorism, were not yet fully accessed for 2003 in the database.)

Social Sciences Citation Index (SSCI): to consider a wider disciplinary base, one can examine progressions in Thomson ISI's SSCI database of source records. Across decades (counting 2000–2004 pro rata as a 'decade') there is a highly significant increase in the total number of records added ('N'), as displayed in table 1.2.

Records including 'peace' not only reflect this increase but – as with PsycINFO – show an increasing proportion of the total records. (This is notwithstanding that SSCI not surprisingly covers fewer psychology journals than PsycINFO and, in particular, has not covered *Peace and Conflict*, the most important journal of peace psychology.) In principle this could reflect some combination of: increased number of journals concerned with peace studies, increased coverage of such journals and increased interdisciplinary interest in relevant phenomena.

Likewise, words starting 'psycholog' also show, across decades, an increasing proportion of total records – with potential rationales similar to those for peace.

Table 1.3. *Number of WorldCat book records showing selected words*

Year	N‡	psycholog*	peace	terroris*
1970s	1,212,490	27,786 (2.29%)	4948 (0.41%)	868 (0.07%)
1980s	1,719,615	33,939 (1.97%)	7126 (0.41%)	2303 (0.13%)
1990s	1,875,677	48,619 (2.59%)	9532 (0.51%)	3316 (0.18%)
2000	189,335	5,740 (3.03%)	1106 (0.58%)	542 (0.29%)
2001	171,426	5,378 (3.14%)	1115 (0.65%)	1053 (0.61%)
2002	156,060	5,110 (3.27%)	1172 (0.75%)	2111 (1.35%)
2003	126,005	4,847 (3.85%)	1098 (0.87%)	1703 (1.35%)
2004	75,517	3,650 (4.83%)	746 (0.99%)	1131 (1.50%)

Notes:
Search limited to books known to be held in at least five libraries. A record is included if the given word is among the key words of a record, including title, author, subject and source phrase.
Figures in brackets are percentages of row 'N' entry.
N‡ Shows Library of Congress book records added for the publication year span. This index is broadly comparable to the 'kinds' of records of current concern and are tabled rather than acquisitions for the entire database (which includes, for example, more dissertations) or for a major academic university library (such as the University of Michigan, which has a smaller sample size) but with both of which it is nevertheless very highly correlated.

Records concerned with terrorism show the familiar large increase starting with 2002 and this is foreshadowed by a relatively small but significant increase between 2000 and 2001 – i.e. in manuscripts *predating* 11 September 2001.

WorldCat: OCLC FirstSearch's WorldCat database (which holds over 50 million catalogue records) was used in order to track similar progression of books, including works that are not necessarily academic. As shown in table 1.3, clearly both 'psycholog' and peace show the now-familiar progressive increase over the 1970s, 1980s and 1990s. Books on terrorism, too, show a progressive increase that is especially marked between the 1970s and the 1980s and, of course, more recently reaching a peak (or plateau) in 2002.

Peace psychology taxonomy

The distribution of retrieved records across various categories within peace psychology (as retrieved mainly from PsycINFO) is displayed in table 1.4. The taxonomy used for the categorization and the assignment of records to the various categories have previously been shown to be reasonably valid and reliable insofar as, respectively, (a) there is good

Table 1.4. *Peace psychology: relative frequencies of publications*

Category	Pre-1990	1990s	2002–2004
Introductory			
General	5.3%	2.6%*	3.2%
Interdisciplinary practice			
Government	13.5%	6.4%*	5.5%
Education	4.1%	2.5%*	6.8%*
Primary psychological topics			
Children & adolescents	11.3%	8.0%*	3.9%*
Psychodynamics; mental health	12.0%	4.5%*	5.8%
Attitudes	13.2%	3.8%*	1.9%
Cognition and images	4.6%	6.5%	1.3%*
Peace & environmental studies			
Conflict resolution	7.6%	22.9%*	16.1%*
Peace movements, etc.	5.1%	3.3%*	2.3%
Peacemaking, history	6.0%	7.0%	13.2%*
Middle East	–	5.0%	5.5%
Other specific places	–	9.7%	14.8%*
Sustainable development	–	4.5%	1.6%*
Additional			
Miscellaneous	4.3%	0.2%*	2.3%
Other[a]	12.2%	13.0%	15.8%
Sample size[b]	1591	1080	310

Notes:

For these tabulations, post-1990 records and the bulk of pre-1990 records (from Blumberg and French, 1992) are from PsycINFO.

– indicates 'not tabulated separately'.

The years 2000 and 2001 are not included in the post-1990s column, and hence omitted from the table, so that the final column reflects only works published after 11 September 2001. Terrorism is the subject of a separate search strategy as delineated in previous tables.

[a] Due to small frequencies, several (nevertheless important) categories from Blumberg and French (1992) are here collapsed among 'other'. These (with specific frequencies for pre-1990, 1990s and 2002–3, respectively, shown in brackets and with '–' indicating topics not separately delineated) are as follows:

a. Introductory: Bibliographic (14, –, –);
b. Interdisciplinary practice: Feminist (16, 21, 9), Philosophy and religion (44, 19, 8) and Anthropology (–, 10, 2);
c. Primary psychological topics: Aggression (20, 21, 7) and Media and language (–, 17, 6);
d. Peace studies: Effects of conflict and war (41, 10, 6), Emergency decision-making and Risk assessment (54, 17, 5), Genocide (6, 25, 6) and Sustainable development (–, 49, 5).

Note that most of these categories have large, general literatures in their own right.

[b] Approximately 10% of the entries in each column refer to additional categories for multi-coded records. The actual numbers of unique records for each of the columns are 1472, 979 and 274 respectively.

*$p < .01$ for shift from immediately previous column. The decrease for Government and for Peace Movements in the 1990s, however, would not be statistically significant if one adjusts the figures for records 'moved' to the three categories newly used in the 1990s.

concordance between the present system and another one independently developed by other researchers and (b) the records classified into each category have been shown (using computer-generated comparisons) to use discriminable lexicons (Blumberg, 1993).

What changes have been taking place in the field? The sheer number of publications is greatest in the areas related to peace and environmental studies. Work related to conflict resolution continues to provide the largest amount of research, though this has diminished of late partly due to the relative decrease in laboratory studies in 'well-mined' research areas of coalitions, bargaining and interdependence games. Peacemaking, and research related thereto, have burgeoned in the new millennium with (for example) increased instances of United Nations interventions in intercultural – often intranational – disputes. There has been a concomitant rise in peace-psychological research focused on particular, often crisis-ridden locations.

In describing changing patterns of research, it would probably be a mistake to dwell on the smaller shifts over time, even though some of these are statistically significant. Some of the changes, however, seem clearly to merit at least brief comment, as follows: (a) the increasing current recognition of the importance of peace education (which showed a dip following the widespread perceived diminution of nuclear threat); (b) the progressive decrease in research concerned specifically with children and adolescents, largely through the apparent disappearance of widespread concern about how to address children's fears of nuclear annihilation, which continued to some extent into the 1990s – similar considerations are associated with the relative fall, in the 1990s, of concern with government, with psychodynamics and with attitudes (see e.g. Schatz and Fiske, 1992); and (c) the more puzzling recent near-disappearance of relevant explicit research on cognitions and images, which had already previously seemed to be an 'under-researched' area. Of course cognitive processes are combinatorially involved in much of the research in all areas of peace psychology; and a substantial portion of the work that formerly dealt explicitly with cognition and images was concerned with apocalyptic impressions of the aftermath of nuclear war.

Christie, Wagner and Winter's 2 × 2 classification

We have chosen a near-disciplinary taxonomy to organize the present volume because, empirically, it seems to provide the most convenient way of organizing the large volume of research being introduced.

Probably conceptually superior, though, is Christie, Wagner and Winter's (2001) classification, described briefly in the introductory section on the scope of this book. Their 2 × 2 scheme distinguishes between direct and structural/institutional violence and, for each, examines psychological aspects not only of the violence itself but also ways of addressing that violence.

Although there is a spectrum rather than a sharp line between them, structural differs from direct violence in that it tends to kill people indirectly (through the effects of poverty and discrimination, for instance), kills slowly, inflicts somatic deprivation rather than injury, and is commonplace, impersonal, chronic, continuous, often difficult to observe and 'unintentional' (Christie, Wagner and Winter, 2001: 9).

Likewise, peacebuilding (addressing structural violence) differs from peacekeeping and peacemaking (addressing direct violence) in that it emphasizes social justice, tends to be proactive and ubiquitous, and typically represents a 'threat' to the status quo (Christie, Wagner and Winter, 2001: 11).

This scheme cuts across the one used in the present volume largely as follows. Developmental, psychodynamic and mental-health research covers all of the categories but is concentrated on delineations of direct violence. Included are studies of child soldiers (and prevention and rehabilitation), of the impact of war on children, and of children's attitudes towards hostilities – also, as concerns adults, the ubiquity of conflict, how it can be ameliorated, and studies of people in (or from) war-torn and conflict-ridden areas. The bulk of the papers focusing on the Middle East and other specific places emphasize conflict and crises, but many are also concerned with the three other Christie–Wagner–Winter categories: ameliorating conflict and, going beyond that, depicting and addressing structural violence.

Some of our categories fall rather squarely within the two quadrants for addressing, respectively, direct and indirect violence. The psychological research on government, for instance, could in principle cover any of the quadrants but in fact much of it is concerned with the prevention or diminution of conflict. Work concerned with peace movements and peacemaking, and the majority of papers on conflict resolution, also focus on addressing direct conflict.

The bulk of research on peace education, attitudes, cognition and sustainable development relates to addressing structural violence, that is, to peacebuilding.

Some general considerations

Some of the work in peace psychology seems too 'general' to fall within specific chapters of the present volume but does introduce the 'flavour' of contemporary research classified into the chapters that follow. Some relatively broad-spectrum work considered in the sections below relates to: the *Transcend* method of conflict resolution, a panoply of contributions, an interdisciplinary note, cognition and government, violence and nonviolent problem-solving, and various other behavioural science contributions.

Conflict resolution

Several approaches have, to a relatively great extent, transcended the categories described above. One of these, appropriately called the *Transcend* method, scans and analyses conflict solutions in order to favour those that provide creative, workable, expeditious solution packages that do more than 'tidy up' after a conflict and that moreover are consonant with environmental sustainability (Galtung, 2004: 180). (Galtung 'founded' the distinctions between direct and indirect violence.)

Panoply of contributions

In a remarkably concise but thorough (and well-referenced) presentation of psychology's contributions to peace and nonviolent conflict resolution, Wessells (2000) considers war, violence and conflict mitigation and resolution. Although war between nations has traditionally emphasized power struggles, resource scarcity and environmental degradation amplify social pressures that lead to ethnopolitical wars. Particularly with the 'splintering of states' in the post-Cold War era, damaged intergroup relationships foster a host of negative psychological dynamics, with objective elements (such as oppression) and subjective ones (such as Serbs and Croats each selectively perpetuating cultural memories of being victimized). Perceptual biases and manipulated public opinion (such as the fomenting of enemy images) exacerbate situations.

Psychological processes also underpin an array of violence, from interpersonal to intercultural, some of it following from the structural violence of deprivations and of cults of sexism and militarism.

Legal systems, according to Wessells, provide a limited but useful means of mitigating conflict at all levels from interpersonal to international. Beyond law are a variety of situation-dependent tools such as diplomacy, negotiation, mediation and arbitration, interactive problem-solving, cooperation on superordinate goals, and graduated unilateral initiatives. (These are described elsewhere in the present volume.) Although formal agreements may 'manage' a dispute, conflict resolution usually requires changed relationships (such as may be achieved by interactive problem-solving workshops – see below). 'Psychology also has much to contribute to tasks of conflict prevention' (Wessells, 2000: 530), partly through some of the aforementioned tools as well as peace education, broadly defined.

An interdisciplinary cautionary note

The present volume, including this chapter, gives prominence to research within 'interfaces' between psychology and other disciplines. A persuasive case can be made, though, that effective efforts towards peace and justice must go beyond the interfaces and actually marshal material from *within* a variety of disciplines (in addition to psychology) such as economics, political science and anthropology (for anthropological research, see e.g. Fry, 2005).

Pilisuk and colleagues (Pilisuk and Zazzi, 2006; Pilisuk, Zazzi and Larin, 2003) document – with moving, graphic detail – the systemic violence, including revolution, that has taken place in a number of countries (more than would popularly come to mind) as part of some-times hidden systems that resonate with, for example, American political and economic interests.

Pilisuk, Zazzi and Larin (2003: 137) summarize their thesis as follows: 'Psycho-cultural values of power, masculine domination, acquisition, and development provide a worldview with hegemonic intensity and little tolerance for alternatives . . . An elite group of military and corporate officials have sufficient power to act without fear . . . A global economy pushes natural resources . . . toward multi-national conglomerates . . . People displaced from prior sources of livelihood . . . sometimes fight back with either violent or non-violent activities . . . Powerful strategists . . . respond to these challenges with propaganda and military action . . . Enemies are created by the government with the help of the mainstream media . . . Suppression of enemies by force or disenfranchisement leads to a cycle of violence' (see original for supporting citations).

The described systemic forces are clearly not effectively democratic nor, of course, ideologically totalitarian, but they do seem to be relentlessly self-interested. Pilisuk et al. suggest that work done within disciplines, including psychological contributions towards addressing direct and structural violence, is singularly important but may best be pursued with an awareness of the larger, multidisciplinary picture.

With very different details, an analogous plea for interdisciplinary (and psychological intradisciplinary!) awareness can be made for various contingents within peace psychology – counselling professionals, for instance (Hoshmand and Kass, 2003; see also, Moeschberger and Ordonez, 2003).

Cognition and government

Robert Jervis (1994), writing before the American presidency of George W. Bush, suggested that the post-Cold War might call forth, and would certainly need, leaders (and concerned citizens) showing particularly great cognitive complexity to deal with a world requiring empathy, trade-offs and a tolerance for ambiguity.

Rather prophetically, Jervis noted some practical dangers of psychological biases whereby, for instance, leaders (and people in general) tend to be risk-acceptant in order to recoup losses – for example, to strike outward in times of crisis, thereby possibly exacerbating matters. Developed countries would, he suggests, try to spread their values abroad. He points out that leadership can make a significant, if not decisive, difference. 'We can see this in the way the Cold War ended: not all national leaders would have followed the path that Gorbachev did (which is not to say that he realized where his steps would take him)' (Jervis, 1994: 776).

Violence, nonviolence and problem-solving

MacNair's (2003) volume on the psychology of peace provides an introduction to some of the ground covered by Christie, Wagner and Winter's (2001) collection and uses a structural scheme that overlaps with their taxonomy described above. The scheme includes four complementary pairs of themes: causes and effects of violence, causes and effects of nonviolence, solving problems by constructive conflict resolution vs. nonviolent 'people power' and, finally, public policy as contrasted to private peaceful lifestyles.

All of these she describes in terms of their psychological underpinning. Nonviolent approaches, for example, use humanizing rather than dehumanizing language. Neither victims nor perpetrators are 'blamed'. And agendas for truth and justice are assertively, but not aggressively, followed.

Behavioural science contributions

Drawing on decades of experience both (a) in formulating social psychological theories related to social influence and conflict resolution and (b) in developing practical workshop strategies for facilitating solutions to regional international problems, Herbert Kelman (1991) has summarized behavioural science perspectives on war and peace (cf. Beer, 2001). He points out that, as forms of human behaviour, war and peace can be studied scientifically but must be viewed from a systems approach, which considers the dynamic interplay of a variety of factors. Although international relations research tends to be normative, in examining the conditions for avoiding war and promoting peace, an important part of the origins of such conditions rests in psychological phenomena.

Peace does not – he adds – mean the absence of conflict, which can be part of a creative struggle towards truth, but it does mean the absence of violent conflict. The relevant goal is a *livable* peace associated with security and with human rights. One must pay special attention to a global society with multiple actors, to avoiding long-term systems conducive to war (arms competition) and to the possibility of questioning one's assumptions about international systems.

Kelman concludes that behavioural science contributions to peace research emphasize: (a) macro-processes of international relations (e.g. correlates-of-war research) to test propositions about nation-states; (b) micro-processes of national and international behaviour (such as social psychological aspects of decision-making in crises and the formation of public opinion) – the study of which complements and challenges 'realist' (power-based) approaches; and (c) alternative approaches to security (including third-party mediation at all levels) that broaden one's views of states and of war, peace and foreign policy (cf. Levinger, 1998).

Among current directions, according to Kelman, behavioural methods represent an accepted approach to conflict resolution. In particular, promising procedures of Interactive Problem Solving (IPS) have been based on the work of John Burton (1969, 1979), who influenced Kelman further to develop some of the relevant methods. The informal problem-solving workshops (different aspects of which are discussed in chapters 9, 13 and 14) rest on assumptions that, in order to reverse escalatory conflictual social interaction, conflict resolution requires an expanded range of information processes and a broad view of the goals of negotiation.

Emphasis is placed on mutual assurance and positive incentives for de-escalation, negotiation and conflict resolution. These contributions represent themes that run through much of the research covered in the present volume.

Additional studies

For additional relevant work set in a general context see: 2003 Gold Medal (2003) on Ethel Tobach's contributions; A. Anderson and Christie (2001) on cultures of peace; Boody (2003; see also, Glad,

1990a) for an optimistic historical perspective; Cairns and Lewis (2003) for a very concise review of peace psychology; Dawes (2001) on liberation; Fogarty (2000) on sociological and peace-science contributions to understanding war and peace; Kimmel (1995) on sustainable development; Klineberg (1991) on psychological influences on international decision-making and public opinion; F. Rose (2000; see also, Houlihan, 2002) on discrepant perspectives such as between environmentalists, labour (workers) and peace activists; Schwebel (1999) on preventing violent conflict; Wagner (1993) on positive vs. negative approaches to peace; Wessells (1993) on psychological (cognitive, emotional and social) obstacles to peace.

For history and changing conceptions of political psychology's contributions to peace, see Smith (1999); see also: Barber (1990); Deutsch (1999); Feshbach (1999); Grawitz (1990). See also: R. Anderson (2004); Christie (2003); de Souza (2003); Fishbein and Dess (2003); Richmond (2004, reviewing works by Ian Clark and by Rob McRae and Don Hubert); Williams (2004).

Summary and conclusion

Research in peace psychology has grown progressively to the extent that the total output from the whole of the 1970s is roughly comparable (with regard to *number* of publications in PsycINFO) to just a year's output in 2003. Although abstracted research in psychology as a whole has also increased dramatically over the period, this general increase is far outstripped by the growth of psychological work related to peace and conflict resolution.

Likewise, articles in the social sciences (as indexed by the source indexes of the *Social Sciences Citation Index*) and book output (as indexed by OCLC FirstSearch's WorldCat database) have both increased since the 1980s, and work in psychology and in (overall) peace studies have more than kept pace with this expansion (that is, they have grown at a faster rate) – though the increases are not as dramatic as for peace psychology.

The increases in research related to conflict resolution and to peacemaking have been especially pronounced. Also, since the end of the Cold War and the demise of the Soviet Union, studies concerned with particular nations and regions have proliferated ('replacing' many of those that formerly would have dealt with more 'global' politics in a bipolar world). Research on terrorism has also increased very markedly, as one might expect, but the start of the dramatic increase *predates* September 2001.

Studies concerned with primary psychological topics such as those dealing with young people, psychodynamics, mental health, and attitudes – a significant portion of which dealt with fears about nuclear war and with Cold War mirror-image perceptions – have shown a *relative* decline.

The chapter concluded by describing a fairly heterogeneous mixture of topics that seem too 'general' to be confined exclusively within subsequent chapters and which introduce some of the 'flavour' of contemporary research in peace psychology.

Part II

Interdisciplinary practice

2 Government policy and international relations

Herbert H. Blumberg

Research related to conflict resolution and peace that combined psychological factors with political or economic ones was relatively uncommon before the 1990s. Research in international relations might dwell on power politics, for example, and economic paradigms might describe strategies for achieving maximum profit as a function of wholly rational choices. Such work has yielded valuable findings – for instance, two bargaining parties are likely to achieve maximum joint profit if even one of them successively explores resolutions at the frontiers of diminishing profit. It has become increasingly common, however, for such research to be genuinely interdisciplinary and to take account of social, cognitive, motivational and other psychological factors (see, for example, Etheridge, 1992).

The present chapter covers research related to ethnopolitical violence, social psychology and personality, core concerns of international relations (including aspects related to interpersonal relations and motivation), deterrence and arms control, democracy and alliances, and the United Nations and other international bodies.

Ethnopolitical conflict

Among the key factors that determine whether ethnopolitical (often intrastate) violence is likely to escalate are ingroup identification coupled with what Deutsch (1986) has called a malignant (spiral) process of hostile interaction. Such negative processes can be reversed, but only with difficulty, and tend to 'attract' conflict in a variety of sectors or 'functional areas' (which can be remembered by their 'MIGR' initials), including *Meaning* and values (e.g. based on religious differences), interpersonal *Integration* (friendship choices), *Goal-attainment* (motivation and group leadership for getting on with tasks at hand, possibly embracing violent political subcultures) and *Resources* (including information and media manipulation as well as economic assets) (cf. Chirot and

Seligman, 2001). Thus affected areas may well include all four ('MIGR' or 'LIGA') Parsonsian sectors (Hare, 1983).

Addressing societal schisms is, as already noted, difficult but possible. Deutsch (1986) summarized a variety of palliative measures derived largely from psychological theory and research. One classic example of a relevant paradigm is Osgood's (1962) Graduated Reciprocated Initiatives for Tension Reduction (GRIT), sometimes described as an 'arms race in reverse', whereby one party to hostilities announces a series of diverse, limited tension-reducing initiatives, which persist but evolve in magnitude according to the degree to which they are reciprocated. The value of 'GRIT' has been established by both laboratory research (e.g. Betz, 1991) and 'real-world' examples.

Suedfeld (1999) has provided some classification schemes for ethnopolitical violence in order to facilitate both intervention and research. Relevant aspects include degree of state sponsorship (e.g. official vs. populist persecution) and the strength and nature of the forces involved (e.g. persecution, suppression and terrorism).

Like Chirot and Seligman, Niens and Cairns (2001) emphasize the pivotal explanatory power of social identity (SI), giving examples from Northern Ireland and elsewhere. They suggest that SI subsumes understanding derived from authoritarian personality theory (increased group identity may be associated with conformity and authoritarian aggression), relative deprivation theory, and the contact hypothesis. According to Allport's (1954; see also, Hewstone, 2003) contact hypothesis, interpersonal contact can foster a common group identity (that bridges ethnic subgroups) when it takes place with the support of authorities and is on an equal-status basis between members of different groups that all contribute towards a common goal (as manifest in the research not only of Allport but also of Sherif, Pettigrew and many others). Interventions may of course impact differently on different parties, as happened in a field intervention designed to promote contact between Australian and international students at an Australian university (Nesdale and Todd, 2000).

Intergroup accommodation can apply to relations between large as well as small groups (Gurr, 2000). Helping victims of ethnopolitical and other forms of violence to work through their despair can be palliative (Macy, 1983). When the political climate is favourable, as in a post-dictatorship period in Chile, psychologists can work with the victims of oppression in order to help re-establish a peaceful, just society (Lira, 2001). Differences may well persist but third parties, in particular, can help former opponents to deal with them constructively (M. H. Ross, 2000). It may be of particular generalizable use to teach *methods* of successful handling of disputes (Pruitt, Peirce, Zubek, McGillicuddy and Welton, 1993).

Social psychology and personality

Social psychology may be construed as ranging from group dynamics (the 'social' end of social psychology) to social cognition (the 'psychology' end), with the study of communication and attitude change (described immediately above) linking the two. Research on the contact hypothesis is associated with group processes but the processes depend on social cognition, that is, how groups of people perceive one another. Attitudes that impact on peace and justice are of course linked to both group processes and interpersonal (including intergroup) perception.

Well-established social-psychological principles of communication and attitude change are, one would expect, applicable to social interaction related to international conflict resolution. These principles, described eloquently by McGuire (1985), include (for example): (a) properties of the communication link (such as a source that is expert and trustworthy, a persuasive message that is pitched at an optimal level of motivation and that 'inoculates' recipients against counter-arguments) and (b) successful negotiation of the 'hurdles' inherent in an information-processing paradigm. Attitude and behavioural change follows when recipients are exposed to a relevant message (the first hurdle), attend it, agree with it, are influenced by it, code it for future use, retrieve and apply it. Although the opportunity cannot always be found for applying these attitude-change principles in large-scale conflicts, the principles themselves, at least, are fairly straightforward.

Communications may effect influence by means of techniques within any of the aforementioned 'MIGR' sectors, such as the values (M) and norms (I) inherent in diplomacy and negotiation, and the various degrees of compulsion (G) and economic influence techniques (R), where the relative effectiveness of various techniques may systematically differ with the situation (Leng, 1993a – though Leng does not refer specifically to Parsonsian analysis).

Like communication and attitude research, group dynamics and other aspects of small group research may be applicable to understanding political tensions. Such applicability has been documented in a series of case studies – emphasizing psychodynamic principles – assembled by Ettin, Fidler and Cohen (1995). For a more general view of small group research related to conflict resolution and cooperation, see review linked to Blumberg, Hare, Kent and Davies (in press). The development and maintenance of interparty trust – by means of open communication, for example (Majeski and Fricks, 1995) – is especially important, according to much of this literature (Larson, 1997).

Laboratory-based studies of group dynamics have included hundreds of studies concerned with cooperation, competition and various political and other processes. These have used three experimental paradigms, among others, modelling coalitions, mixed-motive games (such as Prisoner's Dilemma) and bargaining (see, for example, Hare, Blumberg, Davies and Kent, 1996: chapters 9 and 10). Although approaches to understanding political phenomena related to conflict have expanded our understanding, a consensus as to their validity has not yet emerged. Variants of game theory take account of repeated interactions and varied goal structures but do not necessarily predict outcomes better than do classical paradigms based on power and other phenomena (R. W. Stone, 2001).

Social cognition research, the remaining major area of social psychology, is rich with findings of clear relevance to conflict resolution and peace. Typical among these are the widespread (but by no means universal) biases against 'outgroups'. Derived from these are the 'mirror-image' perceptions, described by Bronfenbrenner (1961) and eventually others, whereby both of two (or more?) hostile parties, such as the United States and the Soviet Union during the Cold War and concomitant arms race, may attribute their own actions and weaponry as benign and defensive and the other party's as aggressive.

Although the absolute positivity–negativity of other countries' actions and words are of obvious importance, the levels *relative to expectations* may set the pace for reciprocity. No doubt this is a manifestation of Helson's (1964) classic, general theory of people being sensitive to changes, or deviations from 'adaptation level'. Thus a slightly benign overture from a sworn (national or group) enemy may, as it were, invite reciprocation. (If such an overture has been prompted by a third party, moreover, there may be less fear of it being taken as a 'sign of weakness'.) In determining the course of interaction between nations, degree of over- or under-reciprocation may be more important than the absolute levels of positivity–negativity. Degree of reciprocation, in turn, may depend in part on the mutual attributions of the countries (or other entities – Castano, Sacchi and Gries, 2003) concerned, as delineated by attribution theory (Bogumil, 2001).

Attribution theory, which forms an important part of social cognition research, suggests that the perceived cause of a party's action will be attributed to the party's *disposition* rather than the *situation* to the extent that the action is low consensus (in the same kind of situation, other parties act differently), low distinctiveness (in similar situations the same party acts in the same way) and consistency (the pattern is reasonably stable over time) (H. H. Kelley and Michela, 1980). Moreover, people (including national policy-makers) tend to be biased towards dispositional attributions, especially if the other party is 'distant' (such as the leader of an alien culture or state) (cf. Jones, 1990). Among other probable 'biases' is a reluctance of democratic regimes to use force against other similarly democratic nations (Geva and Hanson, 1999). This is discussed in more detail below.

Links between personality and effective political action can be explored at the 'content' level of the attributes of known political leaders or at a more abstract, higher order level (or somewhere in between). Feldman and Valenty (2001) follow the former approach, profiling major twentieth-century leaders from a variety of countries.

As an example of the latter approach, a very plausible prediction based on organizational findings is that effective leadership, associated with good outcomes for all parties concerned, is likely to be characterized by the following profile of traits: moderately (but not unconditionally) positive, moderately dominant (assertive but not aggressive) and moderately task-oriented (Koenigs, 1996). In terms of the contemporary view that most variance in personality is accounted for by five factors (the 'big five'), this profile corresponds to being fairly conscientious, extroverted and open, and agreeable and low on neuroticism (Blumberg, 2001).

Although international crises tend to invoke rather simplistic chauvinism, policy-makers who are fairly flexible and high on integrative complexity tend to be associated with better outcomes for all concerned (Janis, 1986; Tetlock, 1988). For some detailed, relevant considerations, see Tetlock (1998).

For an astute discussion of the application of social psychological principles to nationalism and issues of war and peace, see Druckman (2001). For other applications of group dynamics and personality to political conflict see: Battegay (2000); Chafetz, Abramson and Grillot (1996); Singer and Hudson (1992b).

'Core' topics

Not surprisingly, topics from a variety of quarters broadly within 'political psychology' bear strongly on conflict resolution. Kressel's (1993) compendium deals, for example, with culture and knowledge, cognition and consciousness, personality and leadership, media effects, public opinion and what Kelman has described as sanctioned massacres. For more recent coverage of the considerable achievements in understanding relevant phenomena – but with a fuller critique and real-world application of this understanding still largely remaining to be done – see Monroe (2002) and see also Kressel's (2003) review of this coverage.

Two major occurrences since 1950 that might well impact on international relations and world peace are of course the demise of the Soviet Union and, as discussed in chapters 15 and 16, perceptions about the threat of terrorism. Apparently the end of the Cold War and concomitant shifts in international boundaries and configurations have resulted in a substantial number of changes both in the perceptions held by elite policy-makers and in research perspectives; but nevertheless, most beliefs and research perspectives have remained relatively consistent in 'overall structure' (Koopman, McDermott, Jervis, Snyder and Dioso, 1995; Blumberg, 1998).

Apparently accurate forecasts of trends in international relations entail a combination of scepticism, integrative complexity, and an awareness of basic major trends – though the conditions that favour each perspective are not yet known (Tetlock, 1992). Ripley (1993) discusses some basic tenets of research into foreign policy decision-making, among which are the importance of elite policy-makers and how they themselves define a situation. For additional research on governmental decision-making, see chapter 10 on crisis management, chapter 12 on groupthink and on the Cuban missile crisis and chapter 13 on specific locations.

How situations are defined may follow from ethnocentric identifications (as noted above), particularly in the aftermath of economic or other crises; ethnocentrism may itself be rooted (and manifest) partly in rigid upbringing of children (Mack, 1993; see also classical conceptions of authoritarianism – Adorno, Frenkel-Brunswik, Levinson and Sanford, 1950).

Power and motives   Apparently, when a country is not directly involved in a conflict, policy-makers' views about that conflict tend to be based on situational or 'systemic' criteria rather than their own country's domestic matters (Mowle, 2003). Strategic interests (e.g. relating to East–West power), though not economic interests as such, are associated with US intervention in Third World internal wars in the 1945–1989 period (Yoon, 1997). Decision-making in times of crisis does, moreover, tend to be influenced by domestic matters such as economic climate and the proximity of national elections (Wang, 1996; see also, Clark, 2001).

Changes in the relative power of belligerent states constitute a strong predictor of war (Werner, 1999), though this depends to some extent on data measurement and analysis (de Soysa, Oneal and Park, 1997). At a different – broader international systemic – level, a neural network model was especially accurate in predicting interstate conflict (Schrodt, 1991).

Power rivalries are themselves more likely to end during periods of 'capability deconcentration' (whereby, for example, a particular techno-logical process spreads to multiple countries) (Colaresi, 2001). That is, great-power rivalries such as Austria–France and Austria–Ottoman are embedded in an international system of constraints; using carefully considered operational definitions and multivariate statistics, Colaresi confirmed that wars and other systemic shocks, not necessarily directly involving the rival powers, tend to lead to systemic flux that makes rivalry termination more likely than at other times.

It seems likely to be context-dependent as to whether a 'realist' view (that parties seek relative gains) or a 'liberal' one (that absolute gains are sought) predominates (cf. a laboratory experiment by Rousseau, 2002); further research is needed to articulate the relevant contextual features.

Additional research For other psychological contributions to the study and understanding of central facets of international relations see: Chiozza and Choi (2003); Chiozza and Goemans (2003); Collyer (2003, reviewing work by Glenn Paige); Crocker, Hampson and Aall (2003); Fordham (2004); Geva, Mayhar and Skorick (2000); Kressel (2003, reviewing Kristen Monroe's political psychology collection); Pettigrew (2004); Shenkar and Yan (2002); Singer and Hudson (1992a); M. B. Smith (1991); Taliaferro (2004); van Oudenhoven and van der Zee (2002); Wilkenfeld and Kaufman (1993).

Deterrence and arms control

Although it represented one of the main research arenas for studying deterrence, the effects of nuclear deterrence under various conditions during the Cold War are still unclear (Tetlock, McGuire and Mitchell, 1991). A strategy of deterrence does carry known and obvious risks, such as the potential for disastrous misperceptions (Glad, 1990a).

Certainly under at least some circumstances (where it reduces the likelihood of a threat), 'reassurance' is preferable to 'deterrence' and less risky (J. G. Stein, 1991). Mutual military build-ups are, not sur-prisingly, associated with conflicts escalating (Sample, 1998; see also, Downs, 1991). Nonetheless, deterrence seems deeply rooted in human experience, apparently having emerged separately in the Eastern and Western hemispheres thousands of years ago (Cioffi-Revilla, 1999). Paradigms have, though, been developed for evaluating both the desirability of the terms of arms control treaties and compliance with these terms (Weissenberger, 1992).

Arms control   The contemporary post-Cold War period has been viewed as presenting an opportunity to control the international arms trade (Bellany, 1995), which has been implicated in exacerbating hostilities. The potential of 'third parties' (discussed in other contexts above) in preventing war has so far been only partially realized (Wallensteen, 1991). Consonant with 'GRIT' procedures, discussed above, are de-escalation processes in general, which need to be 'tuned' to particular organizational, national and circumstantial contexts (Kahn and Kramer, 1990). Building acceptable verification processes into arms control was crucial during the Cold War (Arbatov, 1991) and remains so.

The success rate of unilateral initiatives and the likelihood of reciprocity among adversaries may sometimes be low and the effectiveness of initiatives in general seems to be very dependent on context (Druckman, 1990). Given this, one of the clear needs for further research is the systematic exploration of contextual effects.

For additional research related to deterrence, arms races and arms control, see: Davidson and Newman (1990); Etheridge (1992); Sutton and Kramer (1990).

Democracy, alliances and aftermath of the Cold War

Partly because of the tendency for democratic regimes to resolve conflicts nonviolently at least among themselves (which is itself the subject of some of the research noted immediately below), the process of democratization has been studied in detail both at a larger economic level and at the 'micro' level of specific processes that can be subject to mathematical modelling (Kuglet and Feng, 1999).

Although the causal linkages remain somewhat equivocal, a multivariate study of democratic governments in the twentieth century found a clear negative correlation between the proportion of people voting and the likelihood of initiating disputes (Reiter and Tillman, 2002). Given experimental results (among undergraduates) that public support for the use of force depends on the regime of the antagonist, Mintz and Geva (1993) conclude that one reason why democracies do not fight each other is the lack of political incentives for doing so. Far from it being a transient or constant phenomenon, moreover, the inclination of democratic states to remain at peace with one another increases over time (Cederman and Rao, 2001). In the post-Cold War period, at least in the 1990s, no

Western nations were among those seen as somewhat hostile by a sample of American college students (Sulfaro and Crislip, 1997). Paradoxically, democratic regimes may tend to be targets of international violence, possibly because the turnover in their administrations elicits a perception (and sometimes a reality) of their being less likely to retaliate (Gelpi and Grieco, 2001). Partly as a result of the compounding (at different system levels) of the various phenomena mentioned above, Gleditsch and Hegre (1997) conclude that democratization begins with an increased – but gradually diminishing – probability of war (with non-democratic states).

There are of course individual differences among democratic states in their likelihood of initiating force. Ireland and Gartner (2001) have developed a 'veto player' theory, supported by findings that conflict initiation is more likely in larger democracies, those with minority governments, and those without allies.

Pilisuk (2000) provides a salutary reminder of the need to monitor and modify major systems within democracies in order to encourage universal participation. Saunders (2002) adds that research into building peaceful, just, democratic societies requires truly interdisciplinary work.

Alliances

Findings about international alliances that do occur seem more complex and far-flung than the robust tendency for democracies not to fight each other. For some matters, such as alliances and trade, results may depend heavily on one's research design, whereas for others (e.g. related to democracy) results seem more general (Bennett and Stam, 2000).

Using a substantial dataset of pairs of states in the nineteenth and twentieth centuries, Lai and Reiter (2000) conclude that after 1945, similar regimes (whether democratic or totalitarian) were more likely to form alliances and that the findings depended on a variety of variables such as proximity, threat and culture.

Not surprisingly, alliances form when it is to both parties' advantage, with regard, for example, to risks, such as a common threat, or to savings, such as realizable from a mutual border that no longer needs monitoring (Sandler, 1999).

Findings from laboratory studies of coalition formation have provided seemingly clear insights, such as (to take just one example) related to the paradoxical strength of 'pivotal power' where a small party holding a balance of power needed for a coalition to be successful may command premium rewards (Hare, Blumberg, Davies and Kent, 1994: 244–8).

The reality for international alliances, however, includes an arguably 'richer' setting, with substantial dependence on (for example) cultural factors (Fedor and Werther, 1995). For additional research on international (including corporate) alliances, see Bruton and Samiee (1998) and Palmer and David (1999). Once alliances – including those that have a bearing on peace and conflict – do form, nations usually (but not always) honour their terms (Leeds, Long and Mitchell, 2000).

American–Soviet relationships, the Cold War and its aftermath

Several studies suggest that, during the Cold War, American and Soviet actions were variably but robustly predicted by comparative reciprocity – the tendency, discussed above, for parties to respond to another's words and actions *relative to expectations* (Patchen and Begumil, 1997). Overlaid on expectations based on consistency and reciprocity are individual differences whereby those American leaders who were most suspicious of the Soviet Union are more suspicious of other countries as well and feel that the post-Cold War world remains especially dangerous (Murray and Meyers, 1999). One would expect such views to be associated with general authoritarianism (as documented initially by Adorno, Frenkel-Brunswik, Levinson and Sanford, 1950).

American–Russian relations since the Cold War have of course improved but have perhaps also become variable and equivocal (cf. J. Haslam, 1991; Herrmann, 1994). Whether a particular leader affects policy related to peace and conflict apparently depends on contextual factors. Content analyses of speeches by American presidents George H. W. Bush and Bill Clinton showed the latter to be more flexible and cooperative, but these differences were more relevant to action choices when the country's power position was favourable and strategic interests were absent (Walker, Schafer and Young, 1999; see also, Lebow, 1995).

In post-Soviet Russia, too, policy has reflected different – overall ambivalent – attitudes, including initial cooperation with the West on economic and security issues, and (by contrast) nationalist and Eurasian perspectives (Shiraev, 1999). For additional viewpoints (based on Cold War data) about approaches that are likely to encourage humane post-Cold War policy, see Nissani (1992).

International organizations

The prevention of armed conflict, as advocated by the United Nations and regional international organizations, represents a singularly important 'emerging norm' (Ackerman, 2003), taking a place alongside not only peacekeeping and other mediatory approaches to managing direct conflict (Bercovitch and Rubin, 1992) but also peacemaking and peacebuilding, which represent antidotes to structural violence (Christie, Wagner and Winter, 2001).

As one might hope, international law itself is often viewed as a force for peace as well as justice, through a variety of mechanisms including the values and goals of statehood (Cooper, 1999) and the salutary effects of communication (Frederick, 1993; cf. English, 2001).

One would hypothesize that many of the mechanisms described in this chapter would apply to the work of international organizations – for instance, preventing ethnopolitical violence by acting in all four 'MIGR' areas, articulating superordinate goals as prescribed by the contact hypothesis, and facilitating states' constructive actions and views at all stages of information processing. Although more research is clearly needed as regards psychological aspects of the work of international organizations, their role in maintaining and establishing peace in intercultural as well as international matters is obviously crucial (Miall, Ramsbotham and Woodhouse, 1999).

Summary and conclusion

Research in international relations has increasingly taken psychological factors into account. Ethnopolitical hostility is best addressed before it becomes associated with a societal 'cleavage' involving a variety of sectors. In such a cleavage the same two 'sides' may differ, for example, in ideology, leadership, resources and friendship networks. Such schisms can nevertheless be ameliorated by a variety of means such as initiatives that reduce tension, counter despair constructively and favour *common* security and welfare.

Such positive efforts may benefit from applying known principles of effective communication – for instance, using media, personnel and message content in ways that maximize mutual trust and encourage awareness of any self-serving biases which may, for instance, negatively distort people's perception of their 'outgroups'. It is generally helpful to encourage flexible rather than rigid (low integrative complexity) thinking within this context. Third parties who combine neutrality and expertise may of course prove beneficial to 'de-escalation' processes, which usually need to be 'tuned' to specific circumstances. As an example of partly context-specific findings, since 1945 similar regimes (whether democratic or totalitarian) have been more likely to form alliances amongst themselves but the findings depend on a variety of variables such as proximity, threat and culture.

One major research need is to track further the generality of known findings, so that our understanding of psychological aspects of the 'politics of peace' includes greater awareness of contextual effects. Particularly crucial, perhaps, is to apply relevant findings to enhance the role and ability of international organizations to augment peace, justice and societies' sustainability.

3   Education

Herbert H. Blumberg

Peace education is crucial for transforming the thinking and values of students with regard to social interdependence and social justice, as Coleman and Deutsch (2001: 223) have pointed out. A majority of publications on research about peace education seem concerned mainly with secondary-school level materials though some concentrate on primary school and some on post-secondary and general materials. There are nevertheless a very substantial number of actual college and university courses – as well as those designed for younger ages – that are concerned with peace studies and conflict resolution, including psychological and other aspects (see, for example, the websites listed at the end of this chapter).

Coverage in this chapter is necessarily rather selective. Readers may also wish to consult Bodine and Crawford (1998), Harris and Morrison (2003) and Salomon and Nevo (2002; Christie, 2004).

Pre-secondary level

The few pre-secondary-school studies emphasize the importance of promoting a 'positive' peace rather than just the curtailing of violence; this includes raising consciousness about peace and discussing appropriate problem-solving (Tabachnick, 1990; see also, C. E. Johnson and Templeton, 1999; Vandenplas-Holper, 1990). The importance of a comprehensive programme has been emphasized, even if some features – such as using children's stories to promote peace in the classroom – are more prominent only in particular instances (V. G. Morris, Taylor and Wilson, 2000).

Detailed analyses of children's conceptions of war and peace and of applications of peace education to both school climate and curriculum have been assembled by Raviv, Oppenheimer and Bar-Tal (1999; see also, Oppenheimer, 1996). Avery, Johnson and Johnson (1999), for example, discuss the instructional processes that facilitate children's motivation to understand war and peace and to deal constructively with conflict (see also chapters 8 and 9 for a description of Johnson and Johnson's work on constructive controversy in cooperative learning and chapter 12 for applying this approach to peacemaking education).

Clayton, Ballif-Spanvill and Hunsaker (2001) reviewed 30 primary school curricula related to violence prevention, conflict resolution and peace. They developed criteria for selecting the best such programmes based on: theoretical foundations (M), population diversity (I), enhancing self-worth (G), skills (R) and teacher training. We have added 'MIGR' initials in brackets because these categories reflect, as it happens, the more general need to attend all four functional areas: meaning and values (M), interpersonal integration (I), motivation and goal-direction (G) and economic and information resources (R) (Hare, 1983).

Even younger children from at least the third primary grade onward benefit from weekly or fortnightly open meetings to discuss topics of importance to the group (Emmett et al., 1996). It will come as no surprise to readers familiar with works such as *Summerhill* (Neill, 1960) that such meetings foster attainment in all four of the aforementioned sectors including promoting values conducive to peace and conflict resolution. Moreover, in a controlled study, children as young as infant reception level (kindergarten and upward) benefited from a PeaceBuilders violence prevention programme covering social competence and reduced aggression (Flannery, Vazsonyi and Liau, 2003).

Secondary school level and undifferentiated

Deutsch has provided a thorough consideration of peace education and aptly summarizes suggestions for key components (Deutsch, 1993). These relate to cooperative learning, training in conflict resolution, constructive incorporation of materials into ordinary school curricula and the value of centres for resolving within-school disputes.

Several variants on these four themes have been put forward (see, for example, Ediger, 2003 and Nation, 2003). LaFarge (1992) emphasizes teaching social responsibility, which – in addition to Deutsch's emphases – delineates community building and environmental and global education. Several questions that sometimes remain 'behind the scenes' are raised by Harris (2003): for example, What research might suitably evaluate peace education? How can peace education be resourced and nonviolent culture encouraged? Positive effects may be realized 'by teaching culture-specific examples of the dangers of violence and of how relevant strategies can address problems. Possible techniques include trauma circles, peer counselling and support groups to help young children manage grief, fear, and anger' (Harris, 2003: 348).

Harris notes the existence of hundreds of relevant curricula in many different languages.

One of the most comprehensive works on psychological and other aspects of peace education is no doubt Salomon and Nevo's (2002) compendium. Salomon (2002) himself focuses on how such education can be adapted to different cultures and applied to intractable conflicts. Although they have common theoretical roots, peace education in intractable regions and areas of ethnic tension may focus on changing mindsets towards the 'other' groups; whereas in regions of relative tranquillity, emphasis may be directed towards raising awareness about peace concerns. Much empirical work is still needed, according to Salomon, to evaluate the effectiveness of different interventions (some of which are more drastic than others) and to distinguish between outcomes with participant satisfaction and those with desirable behavioural change; both are welcome but the latter are especially important and the two tend to be uncorrelated.

In particular, can peace education address the documented psychological phenomena demonizing and dehumanizing others (S. Shapiro, 2002)? Shapiro suggests the crucial importance of educating for democracy: providing for multicultural education to 'hear the voices of the excluded' – including use of textbooks portraying genuine social justice, help in construction of broad cultural identities and emphasis of the value of recognizing both cultural differences and also human similarities.

According to E. Staub (2002), some major aims of peace education are: to understand and address the human tendency to devalue 'them' (outgroups); to promote peaceful rather than destructive (aggressive) conflict resolution; to learn the origins of violence; and, particularly in some settings (e.g. Rwanda), to train community group leaders. Such training ideally entails ethnically mixed groups, promotes the realization that bystanders to violence who do nothing may thereby encourage perpetrators, and also provides experiential elements and provision for filling people's basic needs (cf. Burton, 1979). An ethic of caring can, it seems, be built into school communities, serving to decrease violence within the schools and in society as well (Thurston and Berkeley, 2003). There is of course a fuzzy line between war studies (a seeming preoccupation within mass media) and peace studies. The links between the two have been discussed by Firer (2002).

Multicultural education, as it relates to conflict resolution and peace, is a theme running through many of the above-cited papers and, not surprisingly, a focus of research and practice in its own right. D'Andrea and Daniels (1996), for example, suggest that curricula should include a clearly defined multicultural component, recognizing difference and similarities both within and between groups. Their recommendations are set partly in terms of cognitive development theories.

The guidance is, however, also consonant with Langer's (Langer, Bashner and Chanowitz, 1985) well-controlled research demonstrating that even general mindfulness training among school children – e.g. 45 minutes a week for a fortnight devoted to a programme of tasks such as naming several solutions to a variety of 'problems' – can dramatically reduce prejudice against people with disabilities, for instance, enabling children to see the disabilities as affecting specific functions (positively or negatively) rather than tainting the disabled person.

The value of conciliatory multicultural education has been analysed in the context of Northern Ireland and elsewhere by Alan Smith (2003) and Cairns (1996) and, in an Israeli–Palestinian context, by Bekerman (2002). Hones and Cha (1999) discuss the value of peace education among immigrant children.

Morrell (2002) suggests that violence in schools worldwide can best be understood and addressed from a gendered perspective and suggests that most discourses on violence moralistically stand in the way of addressing social inequalities that underlie much of the violence. As if to anticipate this view, Brock-Utne (1990), in examining gender issues in peace education by interviewing feminist and 'traditional' mothers, found a wide spectrum of environmental and social pressures on sons to conform to male stereotypes. Indeed, as Schwebel (2003) eloquently indicates, the arrangement of three essentially separate school systems in America itself fosters structural violence.

As if to complement Morrell's analysis, Lanir (1992) suggests that education that presumes children to be democratic, rational and tolerant may be overly positivist. According to this analysis, one essential component of peace education is to teach children to enrich their construct systems so as better to understand and 'experience' others' situations. This view is at least consonant with research by Janis (1986) and Tetlock (1988) on the advantages of parties' high integrative complexity in terms of the outcomes of crises.

Post-secondary and general

Dugan (1991) has emphasized the need not just for peace education but for maintaining links among education, research and action. As if to take Dugan's advice, Davidson and Versluys (1999) report a controlled laboratory experiment demonstrating that training in cooperation and problem-solving really does increase success on various outcome measures.

As regards the links between pedagogy and practice, L. L. Nelson and Christie (1995) emphasize the need not only to heighten awareness of peace research as part of a traditional approach to psychological and other curricula but also to incorporate values of political efficacy into the pedagogy itself. Using a Conflict Resolution Strategies Checklist, L. L. Nelson, Golding, Drews and Blazina (1995) found that instruction about approaches to problem-solving elicited student essays that incorporated a wider range of strategies (e.g. third-party involvement and non-punitive influence as well as negotiation and force). Ronald J. Fisher (2003) has prepared a curriculum for a professional postgraduate training programme for trauma relief and conflict resolution in ethnopolitical warfare.

For additional approaches, see: Alvarez and Cabbil (2001), on the application of social work to multicultural communication and social change; De Vita (2000) on inclusive communication in business management studies; Kowalewski (1994) on the pacific effects of teaching about war; Vincent and Shepherd (1998) on Internet-based roleplay simulations to teach Middle East politics and, with it, a more general understanding of international relations; and Wronka (1993) on human rights curricula. For Woolf's social psychological approach to peace education directed against political and interpersonal violence, see Howe (2004).

In their survey of courses in political psychology – a near neighbour of peace psychology – Sears and Funk (1991) found that most major political science departments in North America did offer (mainly new) courses which, however, tended to focus only on part of the field, typically either mass behaviour or personality or international relations.

An interesting comparison of how negotiation is taught in law, business studies, public policy planning and international relations shows similarities but also some key differences related to the nature of the disciplines (Fortgang, 2000).

A study of psychology teachers at American colleges and universities found that few psychology courses were dedicated to links with peace, war and international relations, but that a majority of respondents – especially those who were tenured (!) or had favourable attitudes towards nuclear disarmament – had at least discussed relevant issues in their classes (Murphy and Polyson, 1991).

Peace education may be defined more broadly so as to address structural violence, for instance, by sharing literacy and consciousness-raising among oppressed peoples. For moving examples of such work, see Freire (1972), Freire, Freire and Macedo (2000), www.paulofreireinstitute.org and Illich (1973). The concern is 'with education not in the narrow sense of "schooling" but in the broadest sense of people learning and feeling what is important to their lives' (Blumberg, 1977: 5).

Summary and conclusion

A wealth of material on peace education covers all levels from primary to post-secondary. Research on primary-level curricula has provided detailed analyses of children's conceptions of war and peace and of instructional processes that facilitate children's motivation to deal constructively with conflict in order to achieve a 'positive' peace.

Research related primarily to secondary education provides a wealth of techniques and sensible advice about fostering cooperative learning and an understanding of peace and conflict resolution applicable both within school and outside at a variety of levels from interpersonal to international – and criteria for adapting materials to a variety of cultures.

Peace education can address psychological phenomena of demonizing members of other cultures, can promote peaceful rather than destructive (aggressive) conflict resolution, and can serve to train community group leaders even in adverse circumstances. Multicultural education can stress mindfulness of both the differences and similarities that contribute to the richness of human experience. A gendered perspective helps broaden peace education so that it concerns not only direct violence but also the structural violence implicit, for example, in institutionalized poverty and prejudice.

Websites and indexes of peace education curricula

www.uwm.edu/Dept/Peace/pec.html
www.crinfo.org/menu/education.jsp
www.peacejusticestudies.org/publications.php (gives link for ordering *Global directory of peace studies and conflict resolution programs*, 7th ed., 2006, San Francisco (5th floor, University Center, 2130 Fulton St., 94117-1080, USA): PJSA).

4   The feminist approach

Anna Costin

This chapter looks at both feminist methods of conceptualizing and initializing peace, and the effects of conflict on women and girls. The feminist approach is distinct from other conceptual approaches in its philosophy and analysis and is one that has often been overlooked or marginalized in peace studies.

Understanding the feminist approach to peace psychology

Feminist analysis is a system of thought that analyses the world through the experiences of women as subjects. McKay (1995) states that although interdisciplinary feminist analyses of conflict, violence and peace have produced a substantial body of research, feminist perspectives in peace psychology are only just starting to be discussed. The greater focus of peace psychology has been on the international field and security studies, where women psychologists' input has been limited. Obviously, if women do not publish their studies as much as men, they will be less visible. This is further compounded if they choose not to involve themselves in international activism. Feminist scholars in other disciplines, such as international relations, have also discussed the marginal involvement of women (e.g. Tinckner, 1992).

McKay (1995) argues that there is a need for gendering in peace psychology, as it has disregarded gender differences and needs to balance its patriarchal assumptions by including the perspectives of women. McKay and Mazurana (2001) state that gendered thinking highlights substantial differences between female and male perspectives. An example of how peace psychology is not adequately gendered is how we think about war and peace: when asked to think about who dies and gets hurt, most people – both men and women – follow patriarchal thought by identifying soldiers, who are mostly men. In reality most casualties are civilians, the majority being women and children (B. Levy and Sidel, 1997; United Nations, 1996). A further example is the image

37

we have of peacemakers. Many people have images of high-profile male politicians, but not many people know about the instrumental women peacemakers. Women's activities at community level are extensive and long-standing.

McKay (1995) argues that both feminism and peace psychology have in common a commitment to eliminate coercion, domination and oppression of all people. She argues that peace psychology has inherited the biases present in other areas of the discipline: people who are not Western, white and male have been marginalized. Parlee (1991) argues that the predominantly logical positivist approach of psychological research has directed itself to concepts that focus on actions, thoughts and feelings, devoid of any context, so feminist perspectives in peace psychology have not been adequately incorporated into its practice. McKay argues that while some women's voices have been heard in peace psychology, the majority have been silenced by the patriarchal structures on psychological science and practice.

As a group, women have had little influence in contributing to the parameters of peace psychology. For example, in mixed-sex peace groups, women have often been denied substantive roles, relegated to being organizers and supporters (Brock-Utne, 1985). McKay (1995) argues that the andocentric biases in psychology must be examined. Peace psychology and feminism share common values. An example given by McKay is that feminists and peace psychologists have common beliefs about the centrality of dialogue and cooperation as opposed to violent confrontation and dominance. Roberts (1984) calls for the interpersonal violence towards women by men to be better incorporated into the discipline's focus, with links drawn between power relationships and violence. Within peace psychology, violence is more frequently discussed in terms of interstate conflict. Dorsch, Livingston and Rankin (1991) argue that violence during war, on the streets and in the home have similar characteristics.

McKay (1995) offers some steps for how we can redress the gender balance in peace psychology:

1. Become informed about feminism and feminist perspectives.
2. Read about women's experiences with militarism.
3. Become more aware of the relation between domestic and political violence.
4. Work for the equal representation of women, when designing conference proceedings.
5. Use women's – and men's – full names in papers to render their work visible.
6. Seek women's involvement in peace-related research projects.

In relation to the concept of power, Bunch (1987) argues that integrative power is the closest to feminist perspectives of power, and is associated with energy, strength and effective interaction, as opposed to manipulation, domination and control. Reardon (1993) identifies feminist criteria for global security as sustainability of the earth and the meeting of basic human needs; this is very different from andocentric definitions. The concept of the enemy is seen differently by women and men. Brock-Utne (1994) posits that women have a global connection with other women, often thinking of each other as mothers and daughters. A theme that unites many women's peace groups is their special relationship to motherhood and emphasizing the polarity between giving life and taking it away (Alonso, 1993). Regarding conflict resolution, Wheeler and Chinn (1991) observe how traditional approaches focus on compromise between opposing groups rather than consensus. McKay (1995) argues that there are many opportunities for feminist analyses to guide the development of effective ways of conflict resolution.

Mazurana and McKay (1999) state that a question of particular importance to feminist peace psychologists is the extent to which states, NGOs and grassroots organizations emphasize human processes like reconciliation and restoration of relationships, in their peacebuilding. The authors found that peacebuilding within women's grassroots organizations promotes relational behaviours, healing of psychological wounds and reconciliation. They also emphasize the centrality of psychosocial and basic human needs, such as food, shelter and safety, far more than do governments, NGOs and the United Nations. The UN Platform For Action (PFA), adopted in 1995, provides a blueprint of peacebuilding for many women's groups. McKay and Mazurana (2001) state that many sections of the PFA address issues of central importance to peace psychologists including violence against women and the human rights of women. It is of great importance to feminist peace psychologists as it identifies strategies that can be implemented throughout the world to improve the status of women.

Psychological theories applied to the feminist perspective of conflict and peace

In psychological research, sex-role theory is the common model for explaining gender differences in attitudes and behaviours towards war. Feminist research puts forward several alternative theories: feminist psychoanalysis, feminist moral theory, and social constructionism. M. J. Johnson and Newcomb (1992) examined each of these theories for its utility and limits. They argue that social constructionism is a useful way of conceptualizing the intersections of gender and war. This theory integrates a feminist psychoanalytic formulation of gender differences in personality and moral development with a theory of social and power structure.

Abu-Saba (1999) examined human needs theory in the role of women's peacebuilding movements in Lebanon, a country that has seen much violence. Human needs theory is based on the satisfaction of human needs for security, identity, well-being, self-determination and promoting human rights. McKay and de la Rey (2001) argue that although women's instrumentality in peacebuilding is acknowledged globally, gendered meanings of peacebuilding are not very well understood. In a study on South African women they found that for their subjects, peacebuilding is a process; relationship building is crucial to its effectiveness and meeting basic human needs underlies its success. The importance of relationships in women's peace movements is also underlined by Brooks et al. (1992), who argue that women's psychological development takes place within a relational context.

Testing women's attitudes to peace and war

Caprioli (2000) tested the relationship between state militarism and domestic gender equality. The study concludes that international relations research has found that women leaders advocate more peaceful foreign policies than men and that domestic gender inequality leads to greater use of state military violence. Using the Militarized Interstate Dispute dataset he tested these findings and stated that the results confirmed that domestic gender equality has a pacifying influence on international relations. However, this could be due to underlying societal values, thus suggesting a questionable causal relationship.

Tessler, Nachtwey and Grant (1999) undertook a cross-national survey in the Middle East. The societies studied were Israel, Egypt, Palestine, Kuwait, Jordan and Lebanon. In contrast to studies in Europe and the United States they found that there was no statistically significant relationship between gender and attitudes towards international conflict. The authors hypothesized that characteristics of the conflict to which attitudes relate may be more significant than regional attributes in determining the validity of the women and peace hypothesis.

Bourne, Sinclair, Healy and Beer (1996) examined the influence of a peace treaty between two hostile nations on decisions about retaliation against one nation's transgression. Results showed that the guiding principle for men seemed to be justice and an eye for an eye. The guiding principle for women seemed to be preservation of the relationship established in the treaty.

Women and violence

Across cultures, women are traditionally seen as pacifists, seeking to build and maintain a peaceful society through reconciliation. Men, on the other hand, are commonly seen as warriors, ready to initiate conflict in order to resolve an issue. The majority of research on peace and conflict supports these commonly held beliefs. However, it is important to understand that this is not always the case. In the Middle East, for example, women have martyred themselves as suicide bombers – committing violence against both themselves and others. Likewise, Israeli women complete military service in the army, as do men. In many countries there are women who willingly join the military to fight for their country. It is untrue therefore to state that all women universally reject conflict and political violence.

Effects of conflict on women

McKay (1998) states we now have a greater understanding of how armed conflict is gender-specific and acknowledges that women and girls are targeted in war tactics.

Much research on the effects of political violence on females comes from studies of refugee communities. The 1996 UN Machel Study estimated the vast majority of refugees to be women and children – around 80 per cent (United Nations, 1995). Women and children are vulnerable to sexual assault when in transit and during resettlement. In refugee camps they are frequently assaulted due to family breakdown and lack of protection. The Machel Study calls for improved security and well-designed camps that can improve women's physical and psychological health. Gender bias compounds camp problems because in many countries men eat first, so starving women and children stay alongside well-fed men (Ashford and Huet-Vaughn, 1997). Comas-Diaz and Jansen (1997) found that many refugee women cope with their grief through creative transformation. They also found that women's resistance groups and the contributions of such groups to the peace process embody female forms of empowerment.

McKay (1998) reviewed the gender-specific effects of armed conflict on women and girls that are highlighted in the 1996 UN Machel Study on the impact of armed conflict on children. She argues that because women are usually the primary care-givers, when war affects them, it affects their children too. As men leave to take part in combat, women are increasingly charged with maintaining the social fabric of their communities. Furthermore, during and after war, women are central in providing a sense of family and supporting children recovering from war-related trauma. They also serve important roles in nurturing reconciliatory values in their children (El-Bushra and Piza Lopez, 1994). Yet, McKay (1998) argues, the discussion of children in war zones is often in isolation from the experiences of women who care for them.

Seifert (1993) states that women are tactical targets of special significance because of their essential roles within the functioning of the family. Two of the most traumatic consequences are sexual exploitation and gender-based violence. Other gendered effects happen following girls being recruited as child soldiers, girls and women becoming refugees and when reproductive health services are unavailable. The Machel Study challenges policy-makers to place greater attention on increasing women's capacities in order to more effectively protect children's physical and psychosocial health.

McKay (1998) states that the Machel Study recognizes rape as a deliberate weapon in war, used to terrorize populations and force the enemy to flee. Swiss and Giller (1993) point out that as well as pregnancy and the risk of sexually transmitted diseases including HIV/AIDS, women and girls must also suffer the shame, humiliation and other psychological consequences of rape and sexual assault. Human Rights Watch/Africa (1996) noted that they might avoid seeking medical treatment for fear of being judged. Suicide rates are high.

Tompkins (1995) found that the psychological trauma of rape during war emanates from the destruction of a woman's sense of control over her body and her life. If the rape results in pregnancy, women may be psychologically traumatized and unable to have normal sexual or child-bearing experience (S. Fisher, 1996). Fisher acknowledged the central importance that reproduction holds in the continued existence of the psychological identity and ethnic identity of a group. Women forced to bear the child of their aggressor suffer major physical, psychological and spiritual injury. McKay (1998) states that the long-term psychosocial effects of rape are hard to heal and are often ignored when post-conflict communities focus on reconstruction. Women and girls who have been sexually assaulted may benefit from cleansing rituals, which are community-based. Swiss and Giller (1993) note that many cultures concentrate on healing the relation between the psychological and social aspects of being, rather than on intrapsychic processes, as in the Western model of psychotherapy. Swiss and Giller posit that situating the sequelae of rape in a cultural and political framework helps expand the therapeutic potential for overcoming the trauma.

The Machel Study states that prosecution of the perpetrators of war rapists rarely occurs. Brunet and Rousseau (1996) argue that impunity leads to important psychological implications as it contributes to phenomena like silence and denial, shame and guilt, and being stuck in the past.

Nikolic-Ristanovic (1999) took the study of the effects of political violence on women one step further by studying violence against women in areas of war that were not directly influenced by the conflict. The study found that violence towards women increased in these areas too, citing as its cause the criminalization of society and inappropriate formal social control that occur in time of war. The research indicated that militarism and nationalism – the contradictions to democracy – increased the vulnerability of women. Likewise, McWilliams (1998) discusses some of the issues faced by victims of domestic violence during the troubles in Northern Ireland. She highlights the way in which such violence can be hidden and justified during political conflict.

Girl soldiers

It is not only boys who are recruited as child soldiers. Although fewer in number and given gender-specific responsibilities, girls are recruited, either voluntarily or through coercion, into fighting forces too. Mazurana, McKay, Carlson and Kasper (2002) state that between 1990 and 2002 girl soldiers were participating in fighting forces in 54 countries, including Uganda, the Democratic Republic of Congo and Sri Lanka.

A Save the Children report, published in April 2005, found that more than 120,000 girls and young women have been abducted and pushed into conflict. They often serve as cooks, and care for the wounded. This report and the Machel Study found that almost all of these girls and young women are forced to submit themselves sexually to paramilitary forces. Even those not recruited into the ranks of militant groups may be forced to have sex with male soldiers as a means of protecting their families and for economic survival. Reunification with families may be difficult too. Due to cultural attitudes, girl soldiers who have been sexually abused may find it hard to remain with their families and have no prospects of marriage. They may eventually turn to prostitution. The arrival of peacekeeping forces often leads to increased prostitution. For example, in Mozambique in the early 1990s adolescent girls were recruited into prostitution by UN peacekeeping soldiers (McKay, 1998).

Mazurana, McKay, Carlson and Kasper (2002) looked at girls in fighting forces and contended that gender-specific physical and psychological impacts both during and after armed conflict must be recognized so that both genders receive effective help. The authors argue that little is currently understood about girls' experiences, due to an almost exclusive research focus on boys. Programmes to rehabilitate them into peaceful society and heal more quickly from both physical and psychosocial trauma are hardly ever developed. The authors caution that girls should be viewed within the context of their specific fighting force, the larger socio-political context of that conflict and the roles they carry out.

Mazurana et al. argue that the psychosocial effects of being a girl soldier must take into account the physical effects as well. They argue that psychologists must integrate the emotional, mental, psychological and physical health of war-affected children, and be aware that girls will have different health effects from boys. They cite as an example the severe emotional effects that accompany reproductive health problems – often resulting from sexual assault – as well as sexually transmitted diseases, including HIV/AIDS. Acute embarrassment and psychological distress can occur when menstruation cannot be properly managed, and becomes public, such as when sanitary supplies and washing facilities aren't available. Wardell and Czerwinski (2001) reported that even women in the United States military can have difficulty managing personal hygiene when in hostile environments. During pregnancy and childbirth, girl soldiers – who may be impregnated through either consensual sex or rape – often suffer complications that are accompanied by psychological distress.

In El Salvador and Cambodia girls in militia groups were given the option of abortion or having their child raised by peasants until they reached fighting age, when they would be reclaimed by the fighting forces (Coalition, 2000). Children conceived as a result of rape may be branded children of hate or bad memories, and suffer from having this identity. World Vision (1996) reported that the misery following rape can be compounded by taunts from males who label the women as used products. Many cannot face the prospect of marriage, which can result in social stigma in many countries. Efraime (1999) noted that if they do marry, some have found bonding with their babies difficult. The United Nations Children's Fund, Liberia (1998) reported that with the ending of the war, the vast majority of girls in fighting groups were left to fend for themselves, and often ended up in camps for internally displaced people. Mazurana et al. conclude that girls continue to be marginalized in reintegration programmes for child soldiers and that psychologists working with such children must increase their gender sensitivity to improve the efficacy of psychosocial healing methods.

Additional studies

For additional relevant information see: Badekale (1994); Brooks et al. (1992); Caprioli and Boyer (2001); Cohn and Enloe (2003); Fish and Popal (2003); Gerber (2004, reviewing work by Goldstein); Helms (2003); Leppanen (2004); McKay (1996); Molyneux (2004); Norsworthy (2003); Norsworthy and Khuankaew (2004); Oyama (1997); Shadmi (2000); Skjelsbaek (2003); Stevanovic (1998); Wetzel (1992); Wylie (2003); Youngs (2003).

Summary and conclusion

Consciously understanding the close relationship between feminist values and peace psychology is an important step in building a more inclusive approach for the discipline (McKay, 1995). This will have implications both academically and in applied areas. McKay (1998) concludes that the differential psychosocial effects of armed conflict upon men and women, boys and girls must be investigated and appropriate healing methods developed. She states that if children are to be protected, women must be protected from gender-specific violence and supported in their own psychological healing.

5   Philosophy, ethics and religion

Herbert H. Blumberg

Peace psychology has links with a surprisingly wide array of disciplines, partly because information and the setting of peace-related priorities in any discipline are typically mediated by perception and other psychological processes. This is true for some of the scientific aspects of armaments and more obviously so for, say, the philosophical meaning of peace among both principal policy-making 'actors' and the general public. Within the arts, these links pertain – among other disciplinary perspectives – to philosophical, ethical, religious and historical matters and are concerned with topics such as historical interpretations, principled nonviolence and threats to professional neutrality.

In principle, a research literature within peace psychology could also analyse the salutary effects of drama, music and other artistic endeavours. With some exceptions, however (e.g. Bruck, 1993; Hendershot, 1999; Hunt and Benford, 1994; Kapitan, 1997; Warner, 2001; Yawney, 1995), references to these in the recent behavioural sciences literature have been mainly incidental, so we can do little more here than note the importance, in principle, of such approaches, with regard to addressing indirect (institutionalized) as well as direct conflict.

Some of the material on the interface between psychology and disciplines within the arts is dealt with in part IV. The present chapter is mainly concerned with some philosophical, ethical and religious matters.

Quasi-philosophical considerations

S. M. Mitchell, Gates and Hegre (1999), basing their mathematical paradigm partly on precepts of Immanuel Kant, have confirmed that war tends to be followed by democratization, which in turn acts to diminish the likelihood of subsequent wars. One would expect such a system to lead to more peace and democracy in the world. The likelihood of democracies to remain at peace with each other, at least, has been well researched (see chapter 2).

The possibility (or likelihood) remains open, however, that unpredicted changes (e.g. diminished resources and resulting chaos or constructive responses or both) due to developments outside the system being mathematically simulated in Mitchell et al.'s work may, as it were, change the nature of the world. There may be at least a weak (analytical) parallel here with Roger Brown's (1965) explanation that Homans (1950) was correct that social interaction (task and social), proximity and friendship all potentiate one another – but nonetheless, due to external changes in the system, human interaction has not converged towards a 'uniform sugar syrup'.

The specific theme of 'embracing the other' has been the subject of multidisciplinary studies of altruism, such as found among non-Jewish rescuers of Jews during World War Two (S. P. Oliner, 1991a; P. M. Oliner, Oliner, Blum, Krebs and Smolenska, 1992). Indeed, altruism has been described as one of the 'antidotes' to war (S. P. Oliner, 1991b). For now-classic research on altruism – including early experimental findings that positive behaviour (even something as simple as smiling when paying a garage attendant) elicits positive responses – see P. Sorokin (1954: 58–60).

General research on altruism and prosocial behaviour – within philosophy much less across disciplines – is beyond the remit of the present volume, but interested readers are referred to the following work and references cited therein: S. G. Post, Underwood, Schloss and Hurlbut (2000); see also, Blumberg, Hare, Kent and Davies (in press, chapter 4 by Kent on behavioural compliance); Kapur and Chong (2002); Kent (1983); Hare, Blumberg, Davies and Kent (1994: 91–100).

Various authors describe a universal imperative for people to take responsibility for a wide range of global crises and to carry out the necessary 'inner' (psychic) and 'outer' (social/political) work (Dalai-Lama et al., 1993).

An examination of the links between 'personal philosophy' and a variety of personality traits found that – as one might predict – efforts towards nuclear arms control were associated with a set of internationalist and other interrelated values such as trust, low authoritarianism and high integrative complexity (Barron and Bradley, 1990).

The boundaries among psychology, philosophy and ethics remain somewhat 'fuzzy' (cf. the contemporary journals *Behavior and Philosophy*; *Journal of Theoretical and Philosophical Psychology*; *Philosophical Psychology*; *Philosophy, Psychiatry and Psychology*). Psychology itself has some of its roots in philosophy, including the philosophical study of ethics. In the early twentieth century William James (1910, 1997) discussed the human need for a 'moral equivalent of war' that would preserve the order and discipline associated with militarism but without resort to actual warfare.

More recently others (e.g. Roach, 1993b) have discussed the connections between culture (including mythology) and war, including how mass media portrayals of war affect women and minority groups. More subtly, perhaps, mass media tend to promote cultural imperialism and *not* – as meaningfully as they ought – a peaceful global society, an imbalance that Roach's compendium advocates redressing.

Human 'innate aggressiveness' has of course been called into question by scientists and non-scientists alike, for example in the Seville Statement on Violence (Adams et al., 1990). Goodman and Hoff (1990) are among those who have argued against the innateness of human aggression. They do, however, discuss the untoward consequences of maintaining a philosophical view about war's inevitability. Noting findings of pervasive denial and fatalism, they discuss educational and other strategies for achieving more constructive and positively critical views.

One might hypothesize a 'rally effect', whereby the public will militaristically unite to support their nation's head of state during political crises. Close analysis of 193 'militarized interstate disputes' between 1933 and 1992 involving the United States, however, failed to find a substantial or significant overall effect, but did find that such 'rallies' depended on White House rhetoric, framing by mass media and bipartisan support (Baker and Oneal, 2001).

Field lore suggests that militarized interstate disputes are likely to arise out of moral obligation, material interests and leaders' perceptions. The reality seems more complex, as manifest in American policy elites' responses to various scenarios (Herrmann and Shannon, 2001). In particular, participants typically used a logic of 'utilitarian consequences' to explain their decisions. Decisions were not, however, systematically affected by the adversary's power nor by the political or isolationist orientation of the respondent.

Mikula and Wenzel (2000) have analysed the meaning and effects of 'justice' in the context of social conflicts and have indicated that labelling a particular resolution of international conflict as 'just' can render it more acceptable.

Ethics

In a rather more direct application of psychology and ethics to issues of warfare, Linn (2001) discusses Kohlberg's research relating moral judgement to combatants' actions in My Lai-type situations.

Integrity ('sincere' and 'honest') does seem to be viewed as one of the most valued traits (with interpersonal understanding closely following) – and 'phony' and 'liar' the most derogated (slightly even worse than cruel) (Deaux, Dane and Wrightsman, 1993: 85; N. H. Anderson, 1968). Hiebert (2003) provides a salutary reminder, however, that integrity does not guarantee that right and wrong have been assessed accurately, that integrity can cause rather than resolve conflict, and that integrity's effectiveness is limited by one's power.

It might, almost, go without saying that standards of ethics vary cross-culturally. Pitta, Fung and Isberg (1999) offer some advice about managerial guidelines – for smaller American companies doing business in China – that would seem to have broad applicability for intercultural relations. They suggest that reducing the potential for ethical conflict requires knowledge, not only about contemporary ethics and expectations but also as regards their historical foundations within particular cultures.

For a broader treatment of ethics in the context of psychological development see Lapsley and Narváez (2004). For consideration of the links among ethics (including the roles of medical personnel), human rights violations and international law, see Sorensen (1992).

Theology

Although 'theology' may be seen as too narrow a term to subsume it, a sense of the unity of humanity, of earth's ecology and indeed of the universe represents a theme found in many treatments of the psychology of social responsibility (e.g. more than a few of the diverse selections included by S. Staub and Green, 1992; by Christie, Wagner and Winter, 2001; and a collection of five articles on sustainable development introduced by Oskamp, 2000b).

In a survey of respondents representing various fundamentalist Christian churches, non-fundamentalist churches, and non-church sources, Kierulff (1991) found that an 'Armageddon theology' was associated (at the time) with belief in the likelihood of American–Soviet nuclear war, its survivability and a willingness to use nuclear weapons. Decades earlier, Thrall and Blumberg (1963) found broadly similar findings, including strong associations, within the American Protestant clergy, among fundamentalism, political conservatism, reactionary views with regard to nuclear weapons, demographic variables (such as being located in the south-central regions of the United States) and an authoritarian personality.

The relationship of Christian fundamentalism with nuclear threat and apocalyptic thinking seemed to be mediated by additional variables. In-depth research by Strozier and Simich (1991) indicated that black fundamentalism did embrace concerns about nuclear war and 'end-time' imagery but nonetheless retained the idea of people's power to act, whereas white fundamentalism was more fatalistic.

Although two of the four plausible scenarios leading to wide-spread nuclear war (Calder, 1979) have effectively disappeared – direct American–Soviet counterforce and confrontation starting between East and West Germany – two have not: accident and proliferation. Blight (1992) argues that there is now a particular danger from relative com-placency over the matter. (One notes widespread concern about weapons of mass destruction but, for instance, inadequate funding for securing the former Soviet Union's dangerous materials.)

In any case, the links among religiosity, authoritarianism and militar-ism no doubt remain widespread. Tibon and Blumberg (1999), for instance, found a cluster of just such associations with attitudes, among Israeli university students, towards peace processes.

One effort of clear contemporary importance is to address mutual misperceptions of Western and Islamic approaches, in general and also as they relate to psychological and religious aspects of peace (see K. H. Reich and Palouzian, 2002, in their introduction to a special journal issue on the topic 'From Conflict to Dialogue: Examining Western and Islamic Approaches'). A variety of common misperceptions about Islam have been delineated particularly clearly on a Public Broadcasting Company web page ('What are some typical misperceptions . . .?', 2004).

Tessler and Nachtwey (1998) found cross-cultural support for a dis-tinction between a political-religious dimension (political Islam being associated with unfavourable attitudes towards peaceful resolution of Arab–Israeli conflict) and a personal-religious dimension (religiosity and piety being unrelated to such attitudes).

One possible constant in the psychology of religious ideology is belief in a just world (Lerner, 1991). Substantial research related to equity theory indicates that people typically feel that rewards generally ought to be distributed equitably; depending on contextual norms, this can mean that rewards should be equal or else proportional to effort or to need. One commonly held view among religiously observant people may well be that rewards and punishments *are* distributed equitably – a manifest-ation of belief in a just world. A corollary of these findings is that innocent victims are often doubly penalized, once for being victims and again for being treated as if they must have done something to deserve their fate (see, for example, Hatfield, 1983). Lerner argues, moreover, that the theme of justice (discussed above) may play a central role in human activities, even more so than other values.

Likewise, it may be especially challenging to curb aggression that is initiated or sustained on grounds of pursuing a 'just war' (regardless of whether such justification is genuine or represents a pretext). Indeed, among the four Parsonsian functional areas described in chapters 2 and 12, behaviour underpinned by Values is generally the most difficult to shift. Difficult but not impossible – capable of yielding, for instance, to 'challenges' or influence from a majority or a persistent, flexible minority (for an introduction to social influence see, for example, Baron and Byrne, 2006; for recent findings see, for example, Blumberg, Hare, Kent and Davies, in press, chapter 4).

Consideration of psychological-religious factors in peace might seem incomplete without brief consideration of the 'Maharishi' effect. Notwithstanding telling criticisms of the methodology (e.g. Abelson, 1995; Schrodt, 1990), Orme-Johnson, Alexander and Davies (1990) maintain, for instance, that participants in transcendental meditation in Jerusalem reduced tensions in Lebanon.

Most psychological research on 'inner peace' arguably lacks relevance to international conflict resolution. Leyden-Rubenstein (2001) contends, however, that inner peace, attainable by spirituality even in the face of adversity, is a prerequisite for world peace. Dyer (2003) suggests that there is a spiritual solution to every problem. Nepstad (2004) discusses the differences, related particularly to worldviews, that distinguish peaceful religious movements from violent ones (see also, Wellman and Tokuno, 2004).

In a volume touching on the full remit of the present chapter, Mustakova-Possardt (2003) describes the underpinnings of a peaceful world as being constituted by a just international morality, by religious tradition as exemplified, for instance, by the Baha'i faith, and by a critical consciousness representing an attainable universal human goal. Dudley, Bankart and Dockett (2003) put forward a broadly similar view with regard to Buddhism. They emphasize our ability as psychologists, as Buddhists, or simply as thoughtful human beings of any or no major faith to help, at least, in bringing about peaceful solutions to 'terror, fear, and ethnic warfare'.

Summary and conclusion

Peace psychology's links with philosophy and theology are diverse and arguably unsystematic. Studies of altruism confirm the tendency for positive behaviour to elicit more positive behaviour, hence underpinning the value of a universal imperative for people to take personal responsibility for ameliorating crises.

The inevitability or 'innateness' of human aggression has been called into question by both scientists and non-scientists. Belief in such inevitability – by policy-makers or the general public – may, however, tend to be self-fulfilling. Merely labelling a particular resolution of international conflict as 'just' can render it more acceptable. Various strategies may help to reduce dogmatic militarism.

Integrity appears to be one of the most valued of human traits. Standards of ethics vary cross-culturally, however; to reduce the potential for conflicting ethics requires particularly broad knowledge.

Although fundamentalism may by definition be dogmatic – for example in documented links between Christian fundamentalism and apocalyptic thinking – the relationship varies and seems moreover to be mediated by additional variables. The links among religiosity, authoritarianism and militarism no doubt remain widespread. Misperceptions – for example, about 'just wars' or the inevitability of human aggression or concerning the similarities and differences between Western and Islamic approaches – remain prevalent and seem unlikely to disappear of their own accord. Various authors have, however, suggested that a growing awareness of the 'unity of humanity' may facilitate successful action for a just peace and sustainable society.

Part III

Primary psychological topics

6   Developmental issues: children and adolescents

Anna Costin

Children are a vulnerable group in society, especially those societies that are experiencing war and conflict. This chapter looks at their under-standing of and attitudes towards peace and war and the effects of conflict upon them.

Young people's attitudes and understandings of war and conflict

Even at a very young age – around five or six years – children have developed an understanding of the meanings of war and peace. In a study of Dutch children with a mean age of six years Hakvoort (1996) reported that concrete factors like friendships and the absence of quar-rels dominated peace images; weapons, soldiers and the after-effects of war dominated war images. Children at this age did not have an abstract level of reasoning regarding peace. However, as Hakvoort and Oppen-heimer (1999) state, the exploration of the developmental pathways for conceptions of war and peace, and strategies for attaining peace, is an area of research that has been theoretically underdeveloped. Hakvoort and Oppenheimer (1998) reviewed studies that address the developing understanding of children's comprehension of peace and war. They found that there is no overall consensus about the meaning of these two concepts. Different cultural settings yield different results. Further-more there is ample evidence that results are dependent upon the study design and upon variables such as age and gender of the subjects. The authors argue that variables such as social institutions and socialization agents are rarely empirically supported.

Haegglund (1999) calls for the necessity to broaden the theoretical scope in the empirical research in this area, by including the social level in models of analysis. Haegglund argues that stating that there is a link between peer relationships and children's understanding of war and peace – found to be a common observation in studies – is trivial, and that to remove such trivia one must discuss the socio-cultural theoretical approaches that allow for a deeper elaboration of this link.

In a study that yielded optimistic results for the future, Myers-Bowman, Walker and Myers-Walls (2003) studied American and Yugoslavian children's concepts of the enemy. They found that a common theme was that the enemy was seen as someone bad but that children recognized that there were two sides to a conflict. They conclude by stating that the children generally showed great optimism that enemies could become friends.

Jagodic (2000) studied the attitudes towards war of children who had experienced war in their country. A revised version of Punamaki's 1987 Attitude Scale towards War and Peace and the Questionnaire on Children's Stressful and Traumatic War Experiences were administered to a cohort of 230 11–14-year-old Croatian children; results were compared to those of 185 Israelis and 128 Palestinians who had been assessed eighteen years earlier at ages 9–13. The study found that Croatian children generally have a negative attitude towards war but exhibited strong support for their country's fight for freedom. Gender, age and war experiences affected the subjects' attitudes – perhaps more so than cultural or geographic factors. The study found a greater similarity between Croatian and Israeli subjects than between the attitudes of both Croatian and Palestinian subjects and Israeli and Palestinian subjects.

Covell, Rose-Krasnor and Fletcher (1994) assessed school-aged children's attitudes to strategies for peace, in response to the Gulf War. They found that younger subjects cited government rather than individuals as having responsibility for attaining and maintaining peace; older subjects were more likely to state that there should be no intervention in conflicts between other countries. Age differences in strategies for establishing peace between individuals were found to be greater than age differences in beliefs regarding establishing peace between countries. But there does seem to be some developmental maturation with regard to both kinds of views.

Two moral orientations in reasoning about moral dilemmas have been identified in previous research: an orientation to rights, fairness and justice and another based on care, compassion and concern for others and the self. To investigate the association of political violence and ethnic conflict with children's preferred moral orientation, Garrod et al. (2003) conducted two studies in Bosnia and Herzegovina, the first with 10–12-year-olds and the second with 6–8- and 9–11-year-olds. In the first study, children's solutions to dilemmas involving animal characters were most likely to reflect an orientation to care and concern rather than to justice and fairness. In the second study, children who responded to stories involving humans were even more likely to offer solutions from the care perspective than those who heard stories about animals. No consistent gender differences were found. The results were generally similar to those from North American samples; however, the content of Bosnian children's responses reflected their experiences with displacement and their concerns about the role of physical power in conflict resolution. Of course, as with instrumental and expressive traits and as with tasks and social skills in leadership, fairness and care personally represent separate (but possibly positively correlated) dimensions, and these separate scores would underlie the difference between them.

Jones (2002) found that adolescents in Bosnia who had lived through the recent war there were more likely to have high scores of psychological trauma if they were more engaged in searching for the meaning of the war. Searching for meaning appeared to be associated with sensitivity to the political environment, and feelings of insecurity about possible future war. The more avoidant methods of coping with political violence appeared to be protective. This finding is broadly inconsistent with some of the earlier research elsewhere, and the author argues that these methods need further investigation. Possibly there is an 'optimal level' of confrontation or sensitivity.

In Croatia-based research, art therapy is among the treatments proposed for war trauma in children – though children have been found to be surprisingly resilient in developing their own coping strategies (Barath, 2003). There is nevertheless the possibility of a high incidence of post-traumatic stress disorders (T. M. McIntyre and Ventura, 2003).

Muller-Brettel (1993b) found that, in relation to children's attitudes to war and peace and their anxieties, coping with anxiety as well as understanding political developments depends not only on the social-cognitive development, but on the existence of social structures, that allow the development of emotional bonds and activities to make a discussion possible on those problems corresponding to the children's developmental stages.

McLernon, Ferguson and Cairns (1997) compared the attitudes of 14–15-year-olds in Northern Ireland to conflict and conflict resolution before and after the 1994 ceasefire announcements. A questionnaire was administered to 56 youths seven months before and 61 youths three months after the ceasefire. Overall, responses indicated the perception of war shifted from a strong emphasis on one-sided conflict instigated by a national leader before the ceasefire to a more generalized view of war in terms of war activities, negative consequences of war, and mutual conflict between countries. Although the proportion of adolescents who said the country was at peace did not change significantly after the ceasefire, the percentage who expressed ambivalent feelings about the status of Northern Ireland in terms of peace increased significantly. This suggests that, at the time of this study, many young people had not fully accepted the reality of the peace process.

Ferguson (2000) compared levels of just world beliefs held by Protestant and Catholic 16–18-year-olds in Northern Ireland before and after the 1994 ceasefire. He found that the Protestant sample held stronger just world beliefs than the Catholic sample and that the introduction of peace to Northern Ireland strengthened just world beliefs in both groups. Religious discrimination was suggested as the cause for the weaker beliefs in the Catholic teenagers, while the increase in just world beliefs after the ceasefire was attributed to an increased hope for peace in Northern Ireland.

Juhasz and Palmer (1991) interpreted adolescents' attitudes to peace. They found that skills in interpersonal relations were viewed as essential for attaining peace and that responsibility for peace was seen as resting with the individual, family, society and political leaders.

Bickmore (1999) presents a case study, based in one Grade 4 and 5 classroom with a diverse population of 33 students, showing how a curriculum focusing on the concept of conflict was tied tightly to social studies and other subject area learning goals, and woven around instances of global as well as interpersonal problems. Specifically, the analysis focuses on the processes and subject matter through which students developed understanding about conflict and conflict resolution. Complex social or political material, which is frequently avoided in the elementary classroom, served to strengthen the curriculum's conceptual framework and to provide entry points for diverse students to comprehend the sources and management of conflict. Bickmore presents analysis of descriptive vignettes, selected to represent evidence of curriculum process and content and students' developing understandings of conflict. Her findings substantiate the idea that young children are indeed able to handle complex political and international conflicts. In fact, their conceptual sophistication for handling interpersonal conflicts seems to be enhanced by making sense of these intergroup conflicts, in the context of social studies and across the curriculum.

Attitudes to nuclear war

Columbus (1993) found that adolescents who held logical-positivist attitudes – as opposed to social-constructionist attitudes – more strongly endorsed the view that nuclear weapons deter war and that the impact of a nuclear attack would not be so devastating. Subjects who held social-constructionist attitudes were more inclined to endorse a nuclear weapons ban.

In a study that looked at the reactions to the nuclear threat on American sixth, seventh and eighth grade school children, Christie and Hanley (1994) found that older subjects had lower fear levels but greater levels of powerlessness and futurelessness. After an educational unit on the subject of nuclear war, levels of fear decreased and optimism about preventing nuclear war increased.

In a cross-national comparison conducted in the early 1990s, Dodds and Lin (1992) state that teenagers in the US, Eastern Europe, Western Europe and New Zealand have consistently rated death of a parent and nuclear war as their greatest concerns about the future. However, Chinese subjects reported nuclear war as a much more remote concern and therefore more survivable.

Freeman (1991) examined the attitudes towards nuclear war of intelligent young people (mean IQ 135) in Britain. Those with higher IQs were more inclined to believe in possible destruction.

Jerome and Lewis (1996) examined the relationship between anxiety and threat of nuclear war in adolescents receiving inpatient treatment for conduct disorder and comorbid depressive disorder and learning difficulties. Subjects from the normative control group were more likely to express anxiety over nuclear war than the clinical group. There was no significant correlation between emotional stability and fears over nuclear war in either group.

Children and adolescents as peacemakers

Verbeek and de Waal (2001) looked at peacemaking among groups of European American preschoolers. They found that the contexts in which conflicts occurred affected peacemaking as did the relationship of the opponents – friends vs. non-friends. One of the single most important predictors of peacemaking was preconflict interaction between opponents. This illustrated subjects' concern with the continuity and integrity of their social interactions with peers.

Bonta (1997) posits that children in the world's nonviolent societies are raised to be hesitant and fearful about the intentions of others, in order that they internalize nonviolent values and never take peacefulness for granted. He states that in these societies children lack competitive games and that although they are much loved, by the age of two or three they are made to feel no more special than others. These societies devalue achievement as it leads to competition and aggressiveness, which leads to violence. Bonta states that they have internalized their peaceful, cooperative values so that their psychological structures are compatible with their nonviolent beliefs.

Regarding the opportunity that young people have been given to contribute to peacebuilding in Northern Ireland, Horgan and Rodgers (2000) found that young people have not felt part of the political process in the past. The authors identify ways in which young people in Northern Ireland can be more involved in political structures following the 1998 Good Friday Agreement.

Hetsroni (1998) investigated whether high school peace activists remained as different from their age cohorts later in life. The subjects were two groups of former Israeli high school seniors who had signed protest letters in the 1970s and 1980s respectively, against Israel's lack of efforts to make peace with the Palestinians. The findings of the study show that they remain as left-wing and pacifist now – in 1998 – as they did when they were student activists, although they were generally less politically active than they had been.

Crary (1992) evaluated the effects of a peer mediation programme (PMP) organized and conducted in a large, culturally diverse, urban middle school. Crary's survey looked at 125 student disputants (Grades 6–8) and 23 faculty and staff members. Results indicate that the PMP had high levels of utilization, individual case resolution, and satisfaction with outcomes. Faculty responses also indicated that the amount of conflict on campus was lowered while the PMP programme was in effect.

On a dispute resolution project in Australian schools, Soutter and McKenzie (1998) report that during 1994, the New South Wales Department of School Education, in collaboration with the Community Justice Center, developed a dispute resolution project for students in secondary schools. The project was piloted in fifteen schools selected on the basis that a teacher was willing to be trained as a community mediator. The establishment phase of the project was evaluated by Walsh, whose findings were positive. However, the five-month time frame did not allow adequate time for definitive impact outcomes. A qualitative evaluation of the implementation stage was carried out in September 1996, followed by quantitative analysis at the beginning of 1997. Soutter and McKenzie discuss the results of the entire evaluation and the issues arising, which have relevance for those setting up such programmes.

For adults, culture is one of the variables that will influence the use of violence or nonviolence in social situations. This is also true for children. Butovskaya (2001) studied a group of 6–7-year-old Kalmyk school children during their free play time at school. The Kalmyk are a group of Mongol people living chiefly in the north-east Caucasus and north Sinkiang. She observed that within the first minute of a post-conflict period, aggressors initiated affiliative interactions twice as often as targets did. While boys were supported by other group members 2.8 times more often when they were the aggressors, the opposite was true for girls. Targets were always supported by close friends of the same sex. The absolute level of reconciliation among these Kalmyk children was much higher than Russian or American children. Another set of studies was conducted in Italy, Kalmykia, Russia, Sweden and the US. Butovskaya, Verbeek, Ljungberg and Lunardini (2000) report that in each culture a significant percentage of young children (ages 2–7) do make peace with their opponents following a conflict-induced separation. The authors note the differences and similarities in children's peacemaking across the different cultures and age groups.

Mattaini and Lowery (2000) are keen to construct cultures of non-violence in schools. They have developed a toolkit for 'Peace power' that they propose can be adapted for local school programmes to structure systemic changes in maintainable ways (see also Mattaini, 2001).

Child soldiers

It has been estimated in a number of different reports and studies that there are currently around 300,000 children who are actively participating in on-going or recently ended conflicts around the world. (The number of conflicts varies on a month-by-month basis and depending on different criteria.)

As Mendelsohn and Straker (1998) note, there have not been many quality psychological studies on the psychosocial impact of armed conflict on child soldiers. Much material is generally journalistic or anecdotal. This is due to difficulties in accessing child soldiers for the purposes of research.

In the majority of cases, child soldiers are under 15 years of age (Mendelsohn and Straker, 1988). Pearn (2003) profiles a typical child soldier as a boy between the ages of 8 and 18 years, bonded into a group of armed peers, almost always an orphan, drug or alcohol addicted, amoral, merciless, illiterate and dangerous.

Mendelsohn and Straker (1998) reviewed key findings of the Graca Machel Study (United Nations, 1996) in relation to child soldiers. Children may be conscripted by both government and opposition forces. Recruitment may be coercive or abusive. Wessells (1997) argues that a child's involvement in military conflict can never be entirely voluntary. Mendelsohn and Straker state that children may feel they have no choice but to participate in warfare in order to gain employment, self-esteem, exact revenge for the death of relatives or merely in order to survive. The authors state that the Machel Study suggests that child soldiers need to be reinstated within their communities as children and given assistance in developing prosocial attitudes and behaviours. Regarding psychosocial recovery programmes, family and community centred approaches may be more beneficial than clinical approaches, and should use local religious and cultural methods. Difficulties in implementing psychosocial recovery programmes include a lack of consensus between the beneficiaries of the programmes and the broader community and between funders and recipients.

Several authors (Boothby, 1986; Macksoud, Dyregrov and Raundalen, 1993; Wessells, 1997; Wessells and Monteiro, 2003) have found that former child soldiers experience a range of traumatic stress symptoms, requiring a variety of psychosocial remedies and programmes for reintegration into society. Mendelsohn and Straker also state that children who have actively participated in conflict situations may be better able to cope with the situation, have greater resilience and a commitment to an ideological belief system that may help them process their experiences. However, participation in violence is often associated with the experience of guilt, which is found to be a risk factor for increased severity and chronicity of post-traumatic stress reactions (Pynoos, Steinberg and Goenjian, 1996). A major risk is that the moral development of child combatants may be arrested (Boyden, 2004) and, in particular, they may come to be dominated by a fear of violence from those in superior positions, and furthermore, they may not be able to control their aggressive impulses. Wessells (1997) states that this may lead to their involvement in further violent episodes. Studies that paint a more optimistic picture include McWhirter (1983) who argued that due to the influence of the church and the essentially traditional nature of the society, there was no growth of anti-social behaviour amongst young people. Straker (1992) found that in a study of South African township youth involved in violence, only a small number were involved in anti-social activities. Age and developmental level are important factors when evaluating potential effects of violence on child soldiers; literature on traumatized children suggests a complex interaction between development and trauma (Pynoos, Steinberg and Goenjian, 1996).

Dickson-Gomez (2002) explored the long-term effects of children's active participation in the war in El Salvador. She examined four young adults who had fought with the guerrilla army as children. She found that traumatic experiences were even more devastating when they occurred early in childhood as they destroyed the ability to build basic trust in competent and nurturing care-givers. Adolescent soldiers behaved in ways that they did not feel were morally correct and they were not given the chance to develop autonomy and to learn adult peacetime roles.

Hernandez and Romero (2003) explored the impact of guerrilla life in adolescent peasant girls coerced into joining the rebel army in Colombia. They highlight the continuum of patriarchal practices that make girls specific targets of sexual exploitation within rebel fighting forces.

Certain aspects of child soldiers' participation may be positive. Dodge (1991) recognized that abandoned or displaced children in Uganda were adopted by National Resistance Army officers and were given a home, food, clothing and shelter. Martin-Baro (1994) noted other positive aspects such as a sense of purpose and order and enhancing friendship and solidarity.

The impact of violent conflict on psychological development

There is a wealth of research on the psychosocial effects of political violence on young people, in many different conflicts around the world and at different times. The research outlined below is categorized by special circumstances and the geographical location of the conflict in question.

General

Wessells (1998a) gives a general review of the 1996 Graca Machel/ United Nations study on the Impact of Armed Conflict on Children, commissioned to assess the impact of the many intrastate conflicts which kill mostly civilians, inflict extensive psychological damage and displace masses of people, and led by the wife of former South African President Nelson Mandela and Mozambique's former First Lady and Minister of Education, Graca Machel. He summarizes the study as presenting a holistic picture of the assault on children from direct violence and from the structural violence associated with poverty, malnutrition and inadequate health care. It looks at issues of physical attack, landmines, sexual abuse, separation from parents, recruitment into military organizations and stress of care-givers among other factors. Wessells states that the study shows unequivocally that armed conflict places large numbers of children at risk medically, psychologically and socially. Because children in war zones are affected emotionally by the interacting stresses of war and poverty and have never known a peaceful society, they will have problems in making effective transitions to peace and developing attitudes and behaviours conducive to nonviolence.

Winter (1998) argues that although the 1996 Machel Study contributed to our understanding of the psychosocial impacts of war on children, it did not link children's distress to the environmental destruction caused by war. Winter posits that damaged habitats lead to children's psychological and physical harm, through displacement, disease, soldiering and landmines.

Raundalen and Melton (1994) suggest interventions for ameliorating the horrors of war for children in conflict zones. These include maintaining as stable an environment as possible, maintaining daily routines and giving attention to health care.

Buried trauma and secondary traumatization

McCarthy and Davies (2003) posit that negative childhood attachment related experiences, brought on by World War Two, may have adversely affected the way in which those children – now older adults – function in old age. They also look at the clinical implications of assessing and treating older adults, based on this argument.

Rowland-Klein and Dunlop (1998) discuss research that suggests the influence of genetic factors on normal and pathological personality traits in children of Holocaust survivors. They report that these people possess traits that may in part be biologically inherited. These features may have helped their parents survive the horror of the Holocaust but at the same time may be maladaptive during peacetime in modern society.

Van Ijzendoorn, Bakermans-Kranenburg and Sagi-Schwartz (2003) addressed whether survivors of the Holocaust were able to bring up their children without transmitting their own past trauma. A meta-analysis of 32 samples revealed no evidence of the influence of parents' traumatic Holocaust experiences on their children. Secondary traumatization emerged only in clinical participants who were traumatized as a result of other factors.

P. T. Joshi and O'Donnell (2003) argue that the violence of war and terrorism often leads to a multi-tiered cascade of negative events and these affect children in an orchestrated whole-organism response.

Refugee children

K. Miller (1998) writes that as civilians have increasingly been intentional targets in conflict, rather than incidental victims, there has been a sharp increase in the number of children directly exposed to the atrocities of warfare and forced into exile either internally or externally. There is a large body of research on the adverse physical and psychological effects that displacement and exile have on children's well-being (e.g. Boothby, 1988; Felsman, Leong, Johnson and Felsman, 1990).

A distinction can be made between refugees – people who have been forced to leave their country – and internally displaced people, forced into internal exile because of violence in their home communities. Refugees come under the protective jurisdiction of the United Nations High Commissioner for Refugees (UNHCR). The internally displaced live without any official protection, often in squalid conditions (Dodge, 1991; United Nations High Commissioner for Refugees, 1997). Many refugees find safety by going abroad; internally displaced communities often face the risk of on-going persecution (Falla, 1988).

Much of the psychological research on children displaced by political violence is based on work with families living in countries of permanent resettlement; however, the vast majority of displaced people are not headed for permanent resettlement (Miller, 1998).

Miller (1998) reports that due to fear of being denied refugee status and deported, many potential asylum seekers opt for undocumented exile. For such families there is the persistent fear of discovery and deportation (Aron, 1988).

There are numerous studies that have highlighted the psychological vulnerability of unaccompanied refugee children (e.g. Boothby, 1988; Felsman, Leong, Johnson and Felsman, 1990). Research has found the importance of keeping families together to reduce trauma and distress. Kinzie et al. (Kinzie, Sack, Angell, Manson, Clarke et al., 1989; Kinzie, Sack, Angell, Manson and Rath, 1986) studied unaccompanied Cambodian refugee children living in the United States. They found that the strongest predictor of distress in these studies was not the level of exposure to traumatic events in Cambodia but whether or not the children were living with relatives in the US.

In children's centres – which care for unaccompanied or orphaned children – the lack of consistent individual attention may place young children at risk for stunted cognitive and emotional development, and even failure to thrive (Boothby, 1988; Bowlby, 1982, 1988).

Protective factors that promote resilience in children in refugee camps have been found to be supportive relationships with trusted adults (Melville and Lykes, 1992), the presence of primary schools staffed by community members and the re-creation of normality in camps (K. Miller, 1994). Lustig et al. (2004) reviewed stressful experiences and stress reactions of refugee children and adolescents. Child and adolescent refugees suffer from significant conflict-related exposures. Reactions to stress may be mediated by belief systems, social relations and coping strategies. The authors call for more research on interventions, particularly on efficacy and cultural relevance. Interventions that have an impact on multiple ecological levels require further development and evaluation.

The importance of local culturally grounded interventions is being increasingly seen as important by aid workers in this field, as opposed to being obstacles to Western psychiatric practices (Boothby, 1988, 1996; Dawes, 1997). K. E. Miller (1998) states that a promising approach to recovery and adaptation is the training of lay mental health workers to work as para-professionals within their communities (e.g. Boothby, 1996). Using people from the same culture as those whom they will assist is more likely to be well received by the communities.

The Balkans

Goldin, Levin, Persson and Hagglof (2003) looked at the difficulty of 'capturing' war trauma in children. They studied Bosnian refugee children who had resettled in Sweden and using the Harvard Trauma Questionnaire (HTQ) compared clinician assessments, child self-reports and parental reports. Parent and clinician reports showed marked group similarities but differed with regard to individual children. Parent and adolescent assessments correlated significantly on total exposure but differed on specific events. The authors conclude that the HTQ functions well as a standardized measure, but a Bosnia-specific scale would increase greater validity and capture social class differences in child war trauma.

C. E. Taylor (1998) hypothesizes that a major cause of the recurring cycles of war between ethnic and religious groups is buried psychological trauma in childhood. According to Taylor, the psychological trauma of Serbs, who were children during World War Two and suffered Croat atrocities during this period, re-emerged in adulthood after being triggered by an opportunity for revenge. The author also cites the events in the Punjab following the independence of India and Pakistan.

The Middle East

Chimienti and Abu Nasr (1993) collected information on the mental health of children living under Lebanon's conditions of war. Factors that affected the impact of war-related stressors on young children included gender, age, previous trauma, classroom behaviour, reactions of significant adult models (mothers) and ambivalent feelings about war.

A study of the effects of the stress of war on Palestinian and Israeli Arab adolescents was carried out by Elbedour, ten Bensel and

Maruyama (1993). They found that as war stress increases, so does psychopathic symptomology. Palestinian adolescents in Gaza had the highest rate of psychopathology but the Israeli Arab adolescents, although less involved in the conflict, also bore emotional problems. In a partial follow-up study Elbedour (1998) examined the psychological well-being and self-esteem of Palestinian adolescents from Gaza, Israeli Bedouin Arab and Israeli Jewish adolescents before and after the 1994 signing of the Israeli–Palestinian Autonomy Agreement. Results demonstrated that psychopathology was significantly higher among Palestinian youth than both other groups. Palestinian youth had the lowest self-esteem levels – with no difference between both other groups. Despite the long period between the administration of the first and second measurements, and the changing conditions after the 1994 accord, there was little evidence of change in distress levels.

Traumatic experiences among Palestinian children were recorded by Qouta, Punamaki and El-Sarraj (1995) noting the relations among the level of traumatic experiences, degree of active participation in the intifada (violent uprising between Palestinians and Israelis), cognitive capacity, and emotional well-being among 55 male and 53 female Palestinian 11–22-year-olds in the Gaza Strip. Results showed that the more traumatic experiences the children had and the more they participated in the intifada, the more concentration, attention and memory problems they had. Traumatic experiences also increased neuroticism and risk-taking, and intifada participation was associated with decreased self-esteem. The highest level of neuroticism was found among active boys who were exposed to many traumatic experiences. They concluded that children's active participation in the intifada could not protect them from developing emotional problems, as was originally assumed.

In a related study, Qouta, Punamaki and El-Sarraj (1995) noted the impact of the peace treaty on psychological well-being. Acceptance of the peace treaty and participating in subsequent festivities mitigated the negative impact of the traumatic experiences.

Qouta, Punamaki and El-Sarraj (2003) assessed the prevalence and determinants of PTSD among Palestinian children aged 6–16. Results showed that 54 per cent of the 121 children suffered from severe PTSD, 33.5 per cent from moderate PTSD and 11 per cent from mild or doubtful levels. Girls were more vulnerable than boys – 58 per cent suffered severe PTSD, and none scored on the mild or doubtful levels. The child's gender and age, mother's education and PTSD symptoms were significant; exposure to traumatic events was only a slightly significant predictor of PTSD symptoms. The most vulnerable to intrusion symptoms were younger girls whose mothers exhibited a high level of

PTSD symptomology. The most vulnerable to avoidance symptoms were children who had personally been targets of military violence and whose mothers had a higher level of education and had higher PTSD scores.

Thabet and Vostanis (2000) established rates of PTSD in children on the Gaza Strip who had experienced war trauma. Twelve months after an initial assessment, during the peace process, children were found to have decreased PTSD levels. PTSD reactions tend to decrease in the absence of further stressors.

Girls in Israel were found to have greater anxiety levels than boys as a result of the 1991 Gulf War, in a study conducted by Ronen, Rahav and Rosenbaum (2003). The gender effect appeared only for older children (sixth and tenth grades).

Klingman (2000) examined the response of children in the Golan Heights to the ambiguous situation during the continuing peace talks between Syria and Israel over a possible evacuation of the area's settlers. The results indicate that social support, living in smaller settlements, religiosity, and defensiveness predicted better coping. Less social support and high emotional expressiveness predicted increased anxiety.

Shamai (2001) found that the emotions experienced by parents in a situation of political uncertainty – among Israeli families living in the occupied West Bank – were, according to the parents, experienced by their children as well. Furthermore, the children were perceived as having more negative emotions. Systemic analysis showed that children are often a channel of expression for their parents' emotions.

Northern Ireland

Muldoon and Trew (2000) examined the experience of negative life events among children in Northern Ireland, including conflict-related events, in relation to behavioural competence and global self-worth. The findings suggested that children reporting less behavioural competence have a greater likelihood of having experienced conflict-related events. Lower global self-worth was linked to experience of non-conflict-related negative events.

McLernon and Cairns (2001) asked Protestant primary school children from areas with both high and low sectarian violence and from an area in England to draw pictures of peace and war. The authors found that Northern Irish children emphasized peace as the absence of war more than English children did and that boys demonstrated a greater knowledge of war than did girls. However, they did not find that children from the high violence area of Northern Ireland emphasized more the concrete aspects of war such as weapons and soldiers. (For similar research using American children, see Walker, Myers-Bowman and Myers-Walls, 2003.)

Various studies, conducted largely in Northern Ireland, suggest that children's experiences of on-going conflict lead to externalizing behaviours such as thrill-seeking (Cairns, 1996; Muldoon and Cairns, 1999). There is also some evidence that suggests that young people exposed to high levels of political violence have lower levels of moral maturity (Ferguson and Cairns, 1996).

Rwanda

Veale and Dona (2002) state that there has been a significant increase in the number of psychosocial interventions following ethnopolitical violence. They critically examined the contribution of these interventions to the wider development agenda of rehabilitation. In relation to Rwanda, Veale and Dona undertake a psychological analysis of the contributory factors to genocide, in order to outline the political and cultural context in which psychosocial interventions operate. An analysis of psychosocial interventions for children demonstrated that the implications of social status and power are rarely looked at before psychosocial interventions are implemented. Their paper concludes by analysing what a human rights framework can contribute to relating psychosocial work more centrally with broader political analysis.

South Africa

In a study of the effects of exposure to political violence upon South African children during the apartheid era Dawes (1990) found no simple relationship between exposure to violence and psychological disturbance or endorsement of violent conduct by children. Attempts to understand the psychological effects of exposure to such violence need to take into account interlinked factors such as type of political violence, the child's developmental level and the support available in the family and community.

South America

Llanos et al. (2001) determined the effects of political violence on emotions in 11- and 12-year-old Colombian children. They found that children exposed to localized violence present more intense and long-lasting reactions to fear, but not to anxiety and anger. This leads to a constant hypervigilance and alarm condition. In children exposed to localized violence who cope well with menacing social stimuli, fear leads to a more useful emotion for survival because children experiencing it are able to build a repertoire of preventive responses that allows them to safeguard their existence.

United States

Garbarino (1995) compared the experiences of children growing up in war zones around the world with those of American children growing up in chronic community violence. International action often brings change in war zones, and the opportunity for peace, but in violent communities in America the war never ends. Garbarino states that this can cause developmental damage and lists strategies that the clinician can use to develop an agenda for action.

The deployment of fathers with the US military was found to lead to disruptions in families' ability to maintain supportive relationships (M. L. Kelley, 1994). Wives of servicemen sent to the Persian Gulf War reported less family nurturance and cohesiveness and more internalizing and externalizing behaviours in children, than in families where the father's deployment was routine.

Additional studies

For additional relevant information see: Alexander and McConnell (1993); Christie, Wagner and Winter (2001, especially chapters 10, 11 and 27); Garbarino and Bedard (1996); Hakvoort and Haegglund (2001); Jensen (1996); Klingman, Goldstein and Lerner (1991); Korol, Green and Gleser (1999); Langley (1997); Leavitt and Fox (1993); McLernon and Cairns (1999); Muldoon, Trew and Kilpatrick (2000); Shaw (2003); Shoham (1994); Sluzki (2002).

Summary and conclusion

Children and adolescents have been found to hold a range of attitudes and conceptual understandings of peace and conflict, across age ranges and cultures. A range of psychological responses and effects upon developmental process have been identified. It is essential to understand the effects of conflict upon this group – the next generation of voters, leaders, fighters, activists and decision-makers – and develop therapeutic interventions where appropriate.

7 Theory and practice related to primary psychological topics: attitudes, psychodynamics, cognition and images, and aggression

Anna Costin and A. Paul Hare

The topics comprising this chapter are empirically among the main 'core' psychological topics covered in the behavioural sciences literature with implications for international peace. Each of these areas of psychological study is looked at in turn.

Attitudes

General

Bar-Tal (1997) identifies three categories of variables that determine stereotypic contents and their intensity and extensiveness: (a) background variables (the history of intergroup relations, political-social climate, economic conditions, behaviour of other groups, characteristics of the outgroup and nature of intergroup relations); (b) transmitting variables (political-social-cultural-educational mechanisms, family's channel and direct contact); and (c) the mediating factor of personal characteristics (values, attitudes, personality, motivations and cognitive styles).

Earlier proposals for the reduction of intergroup prejudice were based on the 'contact hypothesis' that an increase in social relationships between the members of the ingroup and outgroup would be important. However, Brewer (1997) notes that the apparent instability of cooperative arrangements among ethnic groups in the international area can be understood by noting her concept of 'optimal distinctiveness' which provides an explanation for this instability of superordinate groups in terms of competing needs for inclusion and differentiation. In the long run she suggests that groups can maintain both distinctiveness and mutual cooperation. However, Gaertner, Dovidio and Bachman (1996) still maintain that intergroup bias and conflict can be reduced by factors resulting from contact between members of the ingroup and outgroup, that transform members' cognitive representations of the membership from two groups to one more inclusive social entity.

S. A. Haslam, Turner, Oakes, McGarty and Hayes (1992) question the long-held view that stereotypes are fixed, rigid and resistant to change. Based on their research on attitudes of Australian university students towards Americans during the Gulf War, they conclude that social stereotyping is 'context dependent' since it varies with social contextual manipulations related to the hostilities. Data supporting the idea that attitudes are context dependent are also found in a study by Hirshberg (1993a) recording the consistency and change in American perceptions of China.

In line with a long-standing hypothesis concerning attributions (Raven and Rubin, 1983: 103–18), university students attributed helpful US military interventions to the nation's nature, while a harmful intervention was more likely to be blamed on some outside force (Hirshberg, 1993b).

Kloep (1991) investigated the attitudes of 260 Swedish 9th graders in nine different schools towards four countries: Sweden, Germany, the US and the USSR. Students were given a semantic differential to measure their attitudes. Twenty-four variables were formed. The USSR received significantly more unfavourable ratings on nearly all variables than the other countries, which received mainly favourable or neutral ones. The USSR was rated as 'enemy', while the other countries were rated as 'friends'.

On effects of contact, conflict and social identity on interethnic group hostilities, Tzeng and Jackson (1994) examined the effect of contact, conflict and social identity theories of intergroup hostilities on three outgroup hostility components (behavioural intentions, affective reactions and cognitive evaluations) across three ethnic ingroup samples (whites, blacks and Asians). Each of the 484 undergraduates took two forms of the survey concerning two other outgroups. The general proposition of each theory was tested separately for three ethnic groups, and for the total sample. In general, the postulation of the three theories was supported by the research: undergraduates having more unfavourable contact experiences, higher ingroup bias (ethnocentrism), or higher perceived intergroup conflict with the outgroup members were significantly more negative towards members of other ethnic groups. Each theory was validated to some degree for one or more ethnic groups, and some theories exhibited more power than others, depending on the types (components) of hostility and ethnic groups.

Hare, Al Ashhab and Kressel (2003) gave questionnaires to 120 Israeli Jewish university students and 197 Palestinian university students and other adults during the early phase of the intifada in 2001. On the questionnaires, consisting of 26 SYMLOG personality traits that have been translated into Hebrew and Arabic, respondents were asked to rate the frequency with which a typical Israeli Jew, a typical Palestinian, and an ideal mediator would exhibit each of the traits.

When the mean ratings made by each side were compared, both sides agreed on some traits: for example, Jews are more dominant, managerial, selfish, cynical and less obedient and self reliant, but disagree on others: for example, each side saw itself as more sociable, funny, warm, persistent, likeable and contented. Each side saw the ideal mediator as friendly and task-oriented; however, the Jewish respondents rated the ideal mediator as three times more friendly than the ideal mediator rated by the Palestinian respondents.

For additional research see: on American conflictive US–USSR relations as a case of group beliefs, Bar-Tal (1993); on theory-driven versus data-driven decisions about international crises, Hawkes and Stasson (1991); on international political attitudes, Hurwitz and Peffey (1999); on international perspectives on prejudice and racism, Jackson, Brown and Kirby (1998); on beliefs about international security and change in 1992 among Russian and American national security elites, Koopman, Shiraev, McDermott, Jervis and Snyder (1998); on collective identity orientation, patriotism and reactions to national outcomes, Kowalski and Wolfe (1994); on the influence of the press on national images for Japan and US, Luther (2002); on perceptions and misperceptions of the conflicts in Israel and South Africa, M. Moore and Tyson (1990); on attitudes and opinions, Oskamp (1991); on changing American attitudes towards the Soviet Union, Richman (1991); on how nuclear risks are 'marketed' to the public, Rossin (2003); on competing values in Israeli public opinion, Shamir and Shamir (1996); on Polish attitudes towards other nations, Siemienska (1994); on reducing intercultural anxiety through intercultural contact, C. W. Stephan and Stephan (1992); on US and Canadian attitudes towards international interaction involving a double standard, Tobin and Eagles (1992); on asymmetrical international attitudes related to linguistic similarity and size of country, Van Oudenhoven, Askevis-Leherpeux, Hannover, Jaarsma and Dardenne (2002).

Personality traits

Cynical people are more likely to endorse a principle of isolationism and oppose cooperative form of intervention in other nations' problems (Brewer and Steenbergen, 2002).

The trait of authoritarianism was found to be negatively associated with peace supportiveness. In a study of the attitudes of Jewish Israeli students towards the Middle East peace process Tibon and Blumberg (1999) found that the pro-peace individual is generally less authoritarian-conformist, less aggressive and is generally non-religious. For group beliefs, it was suggested that certain characteristics of the group such as socialization practices and social structure might account for the personality features that co-varied with the beliefs.

Tibon (2000) used a psychodiagnostic projective method for measuring, in young Israeli males, the personality trait called integrative complexity – a factor connecting cognitive traits to attitudes towards conflict resolution and seeking compromise during negotiation. It was found that subjects low in integrative complexity tend to rely more on competitive and less on cooperative tactics than those high in it. The author argues that in future studies of complex group decision-making, this approach could be used as a support system in the group negotiation process.

Doty, Winter, Peterson and Kemmelmeier (1997) found a consistent set of relationships between right-wing authoritarianism and aggressive support for US policy during the Persian Gulf crisis and the Gulf War. Their opinions tended to be low in complexity, high in certainty and brief.

Nuclear war

Arias, Soifer and Wainer (1990) offer a psychoanalytic interpretation of why there is a common disavowal of the dangers of nuclear war. They suggest that this attitude results from three aspects of culture: (a) the passion to annihilate; (b) the idealization of technology; and (c) the cult of the beyond (the presumed post-nuclear life). The result is a narcissistic fiction that is taken for reality.

In contrast, those who fear both conventional and nuclear war hold values that are related to dominant themes in their culture. Boehnke and Schwartz (1997) report that for German university students the fear of war was greater for those who expressed concern for others (universalism and benevolence) and those who emphasize the preservation of the social order (security and conformity) (the classic concern about German culture). For Israeli students the fear of nuclear war was greater for those who attributed greater importance to values that legitimate self-enhancement (power and achievement) (hutzpah). For both groups fear was greater for females than males, a finding that the authors attribute both to a stereotype response bias and to role socialization.

Rabow, Hernandez and Newcomb (1991) assessed the quality and ex-tent of nuclear fears and beliefs among 288 college students (48 per cent male) from the US, UK and Sweden, using the Nuclear Attitudes

Questionnaire (NAQ) developed by M. D. Newcomb. Confirmatory factor analyses revealed that the factor structure was similar across the three student groups. Mean differences were found on the NAQ scales by sex and nation. Women indicated more nuclear concern, more fear for the future, less denial, less nuclear support, and more nuclear fear than did men. Swedish students expressed less nuclear concern and fear for the future than did their counterparts. Nuclear denial was not evident in the three samples. Interaction effects between sex and nationality were also found. The NAQ scales were significantly correlated with a measure of nuclear salience.

Peterson, Lawrence and Dawes (1990) examined Australian students' attitudes to nuclear weapons. Men expressed stronger support for nuclear weapons. Authoritarian law-and-order attitudes predicted support for nuclear weapons for both men and women.

Other variables related to attitudes towards nuclear war include: the positive relationships between world-mindedness and anti-nuclear activism for college students in ten countries (Der Karabetian, 1992), and between less dogmatism and higher developmental levels of representation of parents and of representation of a foreign country (Herr and Lapidus, 1998).

Additional survey data concerning beliefs and feelings about nuclear war, reasons for lack of involvement in anti-nuclear activities, and strategies to increase activism are given by Fiske (1992). We note that Susan Fiske received an American Psychological Association Award for Distinguished Contribution to Psychology in the Public Interest for her research work on stereotyping and beliefs about nuclear war (Award for Distinguished Contribution, 1992).

For additional research related to nuclear weapons and war see: on value conflict, value justification, and attitudes towards nuclear weapons for Canadian college students, Kristiansen and Matheson (1990); on attitudes towards nuclear disarmament of university students and activists in Europe and America, Larsen et al. (1992), and in the US, UK and Japan, Mayton and Furnham (1994); on attitudes of Native American and Caucasian US adolescents, Mayton and Sangster (1992); on differences in activism related to attitudes about nuclear arms compared with environmental problems, Nemiroff and McKenzie-Mohr (1992).

War with conventional weapons

Variables related to the attitudes towards war with conventional weapons are similar to those towards nuclear war. For German university students, attitudes are related to the amount of anti-war knowledge

(Cohrs and Moschner, 2002). In the US, university students who are mastery-oriented towards the news and have a high degree of perceived competence at understanding the news are more likely to seek the news and become involved and think about social issues (Griesinger and Anderman, 1997). For American students, right-wing authoritarianism was associated with support for US policy during the Gulf War (Doty, Winter, Peterson and Kemmelmeier, 1997). Nelson and Milburn (1999) also report that militaristic attitudes were also related to religious/social authoritarianism and social dominance orientation for US university undergraduates.

Jayaratne, Flanagan and Anderman (1996) examined the attitudes of American college students to the Persian Gulf War, as a function of gender and the amount of exposure to television coverage of the conflict. Results indicated that males were more likely to believe that casualties were necessary and to think military censorship justified. Women reported feeling more anxious and depressed about the war and less energized. A significant relationship between exposure to news coverage and support for the war was found for women living on the residential campus.

Grussendorf, McAlister, Sanstroem, Udd and Morrison (2002) developed a 'Peace test' to measure 'moral disengagement' in support for war, which they tested in 21 countries. Moral disengagement is a cognitive process used by people to make excuses for inflicting suffering on others while maintaining a clear conscience. They suggest that the test can be useful in evaluating educational efforts to increase support for peace.

Peffley and Hurwitz (1993), comparing models of attitude constraint in foreign affairs, found that general foreign policy orientations were more stable over time than specific policy attitudes and that more general orientations played an important role in anchoring specific policy preferences.

For additional research on attitudes towards war, see: on civilian treatment, S. G. Levy (1995); on the political economy evaluations and attitudes towards peace among Palestinians and Israelis, Nachtwey and Tessler (2002); on beliefs about war, conflict and peace for children and adolescents in Israel, Raviv, Bar-Tal and Koren-Silvershatz (1999); on local losses and individual attitudes towards the Vietnam War, Gartner, Segura and Wilkening (1997).

Genocide

Genocide represents an extreme case of negative attitudes towards an outgroup or minority such that there is an attempt to eliminate members of the outgroup. In a search for some of the factors related to genocide, du Preez (1997) compared the case of genocide in Rwanda with the results of the change in regime in South Africa where genocide or great violence might have been expected to occur but did not. The crucial difference between the cases appeared to be the difference between splitting and dividing groups. Whereas in Rwanda the Tutsi and Hutu were systematically split since the Belgians used the Tutsi as surrogates to dominate the Hutu, in South Africa there was no systematic use of surrogates and hence no malignant splitting of the indigenous population. The technique of rule in South Africa was by division, which did not focus rage on any indigenous group.

As a method of attitude change in the second generation after genocide, I. Maoz and Bar-On (2002) describe group meetings where descendants of Jewish Holocaust survivors and descendants of Nazi perpetrators are brought together to share life stories and to reflect on them. The same approach, focusing on 'reflect and trust', is also used with members of other groups as part of a process of reconciliation involving both victims and victimizers.

In an article on the origins and prevention of genocide, mass killing and other collective violence, E. Staub (1999) observes that life conditions give rise to scapegoating and ideologies that identify enemies and lead one group to turn against another. Conflict between groups and self-interest are additional instigators of group violence. Discrimination and limited violence can escalate into mass killing or genocide. The passivity of bystanders may allow this process to unfold. The prevention of future violence may require healing of psychological wounds due to past victimization, reconciliation and the resolution of conflict between antagonistic groups. See also E. Staub (1996, 2001). For comments on Staub's article see: J. M. Post (1999), R. W. Smith (1999), Weine (1999) and Wessells (1999).

Hare (1995) provides a review of the literature on attitudes related to race and ethnic conflict. Among the many examples, two are discussed in some detail. Regarding images of whites and blacks in South Africa in the 1950s and 1960s, the members of the black population might have become the object of genocide but they provided the necessary labour force. Regarding the values held by German and Jewish Israeli university students in relation to their ability to 'work through' their attitudes towards consequences of the Holocaust, those students whose value position was on the positive side of the attitude space and midway between an authoritarian and a humanitarian position were more likely to be successful in 'working through'.

For additional research on genocide or its aftermath, see: on the widening circle of genocide, Charney (1994); on multigenerational perspectives on coping with the Holocaust experience, Bar-On et al. (1998); on counselling with Holocaust survivors, Hassan (1998); on psychoanalytic contributions to Holocaust studies, Jucovy (1992); on treating Holocaust survivors, Kaslow (1990); on healing the wounds of the Mahantdori after the Cambodian holocaust, Kuoch, Miller and Scully (1992); on recalling the Holocaust, Kraft (2002); on horrendous death and health, Leviton (1991); on psychological reactions to incidents of political mass killing, S. G. Levy (1999); on the individuation process and the capacity for intimacy of adult children of Holocaust survivors, Mazor and Tal (1996); on Holocaust messages from the past, Mor (1990); on an encyclopaedia summarizing the fundamentals of genocide scholarship, Mork (2003); on understanding the Holocaust in connection with unique historical events, Scharfenberg (1990); on the trauma of the Holocaust and the ability to speak out, Schindler, Spiegel and Malachi (1992); on the aetiology of human destructiveness, Solomon, Greenberg and Pyszczynski (2003); on genocide, war and human survival, Strozier and Flynn (1996); on children of the Holocaust as memorial candles, Wardi and Goldblum (1992). See also: Arons (2003); Bar-On (2003, reviewing Suedfeld's collection, *Light from the ashes*); Bastien, Kremer and Kuokkanen (2003); Bolton (2003).

Psychodynamics

Freud (1922) wrote that all human behaviour stems from the interaction between Eros – the life instinct – and Thanatos – the death instinct. Through the concept of displacement, the energy of Thanatos is directed away from the self, towards others. This concept of self-directed destruction is one of the most controversial in psychoanalytic theory. While rejected by many psychodynamic psychologists, the idea that aggression stems primarily from instinctive drives has generally been supported within psychoanalytic research (but see also, Solomon, Greenberg and Pyszczynski, 2003).

Causes of conflict – are we capable of peaceful behaviour?

Samuels (1993) advocates that the inner journey of analysis and psychotherapy and the political convictions of the outer world are linked. He lays bare the hidden politics of the father, the male body and of men's issues generally.

Schmidt (1993) posed the question of whether people are capable of peace or are driven by a natural disposition to resolve conflict through confrontation. He states that peace can only be achieved by those who are inwardly at peace and not attached to the attitude named by Adler as masculinity protest. Schmidt argues that peace is not only conflict-free harmony, but also the acknowledgement of the equal worth of other people.

Stevens (1995) promotes the Jungian approach to understanding war. He states that agreement about the universality of warfare is compatible with Jung's theory of archetypes as part of the human collective unconscious. Young men's predisposition to aggressive pursuits is a biological propensity that is mediated by archetypal structures in the psyche. Stevens argues that peaceful international relations can be facilitated by the conscious awareness of archetypally determined patterns of intergroup conflict and a collective decision not to pseudospeciate – negatively characterize – other nations.

Rangell (1991) discusses the intrapsychic mechanisms that render the acquisition of enemies inevitable to human relations. He advocates that only total composite psychoanalytic theory, including formulations of object relational and intrapsychic conflict, can examine both group and individual psychopathology. The roles of the led in strengthening the leader are stressed in leading to the final psychic states of severe group psychopathology.

Gillibert (1993) states that the twentieth century has witnessed a culture of extermination, through different episodes of genocide, and that this is due to instinctual contradiction. He argues that the aporia of instincts, unresolved by narcissism, leads to repetition of the exterminable. He asks whether the theory of instincts can account for nihilism, genocides and the atom bomb, and concludes that it can only in part.

Redfearn (1990) suggests that avoiding the intrapsychic clash of opposites might contribute to the concrete danger of world destruction. The author explains that in analysis, an atomic bomb dream signifies a conflict of opposing drives, which, in the context of an analytic situation, tends to lead to the resolution of the conflict. Redfearn suggests that this is significant to real socio-political situations.

Steinberg (1991) examined the roles of shame and humiliation during the Cuban missile crisis, as determinants of the behaviour of Kennedy and Khrushchev. The author argues that both leaders had a failure of self-esteem that led to feelings of shame, humiliation, narcissistic rage and aggressive behaviour. The aggression is a way of increasing feelings of self-worth.

Both Kennedy and Khrushchev used the power of their countries as an instrument of aggression to try and mend their self-esteem. The conclusion drawn is that putting political leaders in positions of humiliation may lead to a desire for revenge and consequently warfare.

Intergenerational transmission of trauma

Using a psychoanalytic framework, Apfel and Simon (2000) posit that the pressure for aggression is not civilization versus instinctual expression, but the pressure for each generation to transmit its own traumatic experience on to the next generation.

Looking at the psychological forces that underlie Turkish–Greek relations, Volkan and Itzkowitz (2000) suggest that generations of Greek and Turkish people have included mental representations of past glories and humiliations as part of their national identities. They argue that collective narcissistic injuries are never properly mourned, so they turn into feelings of victimization. The authors argue that these intergenerationally transmitted traumas have led to violent outbreaks in Turkish–Greek relations.

Nuclear annihilation

Ribas (1993) suggests that the deterrence of global atomic annihilation has eliminated any outlet for the projection of destructive impulses.

The psychological fallout of the nuclear threat has not disappeared with the end of the Cold War, according to Wangh (1994). He argues that the psyche is still torn between Thanatos and Eros – the death and life instincts – and this leads to self-destruction. He postulates that the current trend of denying the danger of global nuclear annihilation correlates with narcissistic withdrawal into the self. However, given the development of the so-called war on terrorism in recent years, this theory has to be interpreted as meaning that in times of a nation lacking a significant enemy, its people still require an outlet for their natural self-destruction. This is also postulated by Demause (1992), who argues that in 1992 the US sought a leader with a confrontational mood, as they had been deprived of an enemy following the end of the Cold War and the Gulf War.

Ameliorating violence

The founding father of Rational Emotive Therapy, Albert Ellis, posits that RET can facilitate the acquisition of more peaceful attitudes and behaviours. He argues that RET can increase negotiation, compromise and altruism and help to overcome prejudice and hostility. RET uses emotive-experiential methods to help people achieve peaceful human relationships.

Albeck, Adwan and Bar-On (2002) describe how telling the story of personal experiences in a small group made up of members from opposing sides of intractable conflicts can help work through some of the on-going intergenerational effects of political violence. The concept of 'working through' underlines the rationale for this method of psychotherapy. This method has been adapted for use in South Africa, Northern Ireland and Palestine-Israel.

Additional studies

For additional relevant information see: Bracher (1998); Byles (2003); Edelman, Kersner, Kordon and Lagos (2003); Edelstein and Gibson (2003); Fisher (2003); Fuhr and Gremmler-Fuhr (2003); Graves (2003); Kernberg (2003); Kroth (1992); Lifton (1993); M. W. Morris, Leung and Lyengar (2004); Offerman-Zuckerberg (1991); Ognjenovic, Skorc and Savic (2003); Olweean (2003); Palmer (2003); Pappas (2003); Quintana and Segura-Herrera (2003); Richter (1996); Saunders (1998); Volkan (1999a); Volkan (1999b); Withers (2003).

Cognition and images: war effects, cooperation and the future

Perception

Ziller, Moriarty and Phillips (1999) measured the tolerant personality, or universal orientation, of American college students' responses to real and romanticized photographs of the Gulf War. Results showed that those who were most universally oriented perceived the real photographs – that depicted death, destruction and suffering – as the most defining photographs of war.

Stringer, Cornish and Denver (2000) compared students' preferences for places within Northern Ireland following two and a half years of peace, compared with those collected during a prolonged period of intergroup conflict eleven years before. They found that a relatively short period of peace had a significant effect on perceptions. For Protestants, the link between perceived violence and other judgements has weakened, and for Catholics it has practically disappeared. The implication is that, for Catholics at least, participants' attitudes have shifted towards peacetime thinking. The authors conclude that rapid changes in locational perceptions can occur in post-conflict societies, and that groups may differ in their rate of change.

According to Bar-Tal and Jacobson (1998), as individuals evaluate the level of security via cognitive processes, the outcomes are subjective. They argue that beliefs about security are formed on the basis of the perception of the threat in the environment with which the individual perceives a difficulty in coping. The authors conclude that while military, political and economic events are real, they have to be perceived in order to become part of the individual's reality. Events that are external have to be subjectively interpreted by the individual. This approach gives special importance to political psychology in studying security problems.

A shift in the paradigms of socio-political thinking is occurring, altering the collective reconstruction of reality in people's minds (Kohr and Raeder, 1991). This is based on catalytic events in reality, that become contextual symbols which govern the structural connection of interpretations.

American subjects tended to recall stereotype-consistent information about the nation's self-image, relating to international intervention (Hirshberg, 1993b). Hirshberg claims that this is due to cognitive biases in national perception.

Kaplowitz (1990) presents a psychopolitical theory of international conflict in which national self-images and perceptions of enemies are analysed as determinants of various types of conflict-related behaviour. A typology of conflict-related strategies from totalism to conciliation takes into account both manifest aims and latent attitudes.

Kemmelmeier and Winter (2000) investigated the effects of perspective taking on perceptual distortions of conflict, using perceived power motivation as an unobtrusive measure of perceived threat. They found that subjects cued into the perspective of a military officer from one side of the conflict had greater levels of distortion than those cued into the perspective of a historian. They also found that taking the perspective of a mediator did not reduce perceptual distortion, suggesting distance to the conflict as an important factor for reducing threat perceptions.

Cognitive complexity

Walker and Watson (1992) suggest that the cognitive mapping technique might be useful in investigating the cognitive complexity of political leaders, in relation to crises that end peacefully compared to those that do not. Bonham (1993) argues that cognitive mapping can be made into a practical tool for negotiators to use throughout the negotiation process.

He argues that because it is intuitively understandable, the technique can be used by diplomats to assess differences in assumptions as they attempt to reach cognitive convergence and concrete agreements. Bonham claims that this technique is an improvement over intuitive analysis and reveals the structure of thinking about a problem, showing which factors actually impact on judgement. Through cognitive mapping, negotiators can construct more complex cognitive structures and alternative ways of looking at a problem.

Santmire et al. (1998) assessed the impact of cognitive complexity on group decision-making. They found a positive relationship between the level of homogeneity in cognitive complexity among decision-makers and the achievement of positive outcomes in crisis negotiations. See also Campanella (1993) for a discussion of the analyses of international affairs developed from the cognitive mapping paradigm.

Janis and Mann (1992) argue that it is necessary to clarify the nature of the debate regarding the merits of complexity and simplicity of decision-making procedures in international affairs. They argue that drawing a contrast between simple and complex decision-making processes is not particularly helpful for evaluating the effectiveness of different procedural strategies for making major policy decisions. Janis posits that one such strategy – vigilant problem-solving – that is moderately complex will lead to better outcomes than those that are either less or more complex. The author calls for research to determine under which conditions this strategy is effective. (See also R. M. Kramer, Meyerson and Davis (1990b) for a discussion of the role of cognitive processes relating to an international security dilemma.)

Prospect theory

Prospect theory was developed by Kahneman and Tversky (1979, 1990) to understand decision-making under conditions of risk. Jervis (1992) suggests that prospect theory has implications for political decision-making. The theory posits that people tend to be risk averse for gains and risk acceptant for losses. This explains observed patterns in deterrence and the origins of wars, and suggests why states are less likely to behave aggressively when doing so would produce gains, than when it might prevent losses. Methodological problems in proving inferences of prospect theory for international situations are discussed. McDermott (1992, 1998) also supports the role of prospect theory in relation to political risk-taking.

McInerney (1992) uses prospect theory to explain the behaviour of the USSR towards Syria in 1966 and 1967. She demonstrates that the

Soviets were risk acceptant in order to avert the loss of the incumbent Syrian regime. It is argued that the Soviets defined the situation in the Middle East as including a socialist-oriented Syria aligned with the USSR against the West. For a further discussion of the role of prospect theory in international relations, see Milburn and Isaac (1995).

Boettcher (1995) tested the strength of prospect theory in international relations in a study with undergraduate students. Results provide support for prospect theory, but also indicate that decision theorists need to be more concerned with the manner in which probabilistic information is conveyed to and discussed by decision-makers.

J. S. Levy (1992) evaluated the contribution of prospect theory to the understanding of international relations. The author examined conceptual and methodological problems that complicate the theoretical and empirical application of the theory to international behaviour. The problems include: generalization from laboratory experiments, the assessment of probability and risk and the preventive war problem. He states that when applying the theory to empirical cases the researcher must show that the empirical behaviour is consistent with the theory and that the behaviour cannot be adequately accounted for by a rational choice model that posits the maximization of the expected value.

Additional studies

For additional relevant information see: Beck (2002); Fischhoff (1991); Janis (1996); Jones and Remland (1993); Kohr (1991).

Aggression

This chapter section addresses research on aggression in relation to political violence and conflict. For a general overview of theories on aggression, refer to any comprehensive psychology textbook, or one that deals specifically with general human aggression.

What is aggression, in terms of political violence?

G. Kemp (2001) states that with regard to international relations there is not much consensus – either within or across cultures – on the definition of an aggressive act. He suggests that the reason behind this failure may have relevance to a broader understanding of human aggression.

Nordstrom (1998) contends that the realities of war are quite different from the public presentations of war, in the media, literature and formal military texts. This has encouraged a number of myths about human aggression to hold sway, in both academia and with the public. The author suggests that a new form of empiricism is required for studying such difficult, dangerous and complex phenomena as political aggression and peace-building.

Defending the role and extent of aggression in conflict

De Rivera (2003) claims that the achievement of peace rests on an understanding of aggression, violence and evil, but that we must go further than looking at what is usually classed as pro-social behaviour and include the use of aggression in a struggle with violence and evil. He states that aspects of aggression may be necessary for the achievement of peace.

Feshbach (1990) discusses the relationship between individual psychological factors and attitudes towards military action, concentrating on the role of aggression in determining these attitudes. Feshbach found that evidence from research on violence and the concepts of nationalism and patriotism indicates that predispositions other than aggression may account for attitudes towards war.

Ember and Ember (1994) contend that war is more likely when a population has a history of unpredictable disasters that destroy food supplies. People often go to war to take resources that will protect them from future scarcity. The authors claim that while socialization for aggression in boys significantly predicts more war, it may be that such socialization is a *consequence* of war. Such a stance is supported by Pilisuk (1998) who cites the global economy as a source of diverse manifestations of structural violence, due to its role in increasing disparities between rich and poor.

Aggression and conflict

Mesquida and Wiener (1996) posit that male coalitional aggression is a reproductive fitness-enhancing social behaviour. Whilst not increasing the welfare of an entire population it is likely to increase the fitness of the coalition participants. The study argues that the age composition of the male population should be taken as the critical demographic factor in determining a nation's tendency towards peace or violence. Analyses of periods of collective aggression since the 1960s indicate the existence of a consistent correlation between the ratio of males aged 15–29 years per 100 males aged 30 and over and the level of coalitional aggression.

Fry (1992) examined differences in aggression between two Zapotec communities in Mexico. Data revealed significant intercommunity differences in children's play and serious aggression, which corresponds to intercommunity differences in adult behaviour. This supports the hypothesis that different social learning environments contribute to the maintenance across generations of divergent ideologies and patterns of social interaction, related to peacefulness or violence. Fry suggests that studies of violence that neglect social learning influences may be providing only partial explanations.

Guerra, Huesmann and Spindler (2003) investigated the effects of witnessing community violence on aggressive cognitions, in children living in urban neighbourhoods in the United States. The findings suggest that witnessing community violence has an effect on children's aggressive behaviour through both imitation of violence and the development of associated cognitions as children get older.

Ramirez and Richardson (2001) examined aggression and reconciliation from a cross-cultural viewpoint. They maintain that social representation is connected to the role of culture in influencing situations that result in anger, and in establishing the appropriateness of anger expression that is engaging in some form of aggression in these anger-eliciting situations.

Tiffany and Tiffany (2000) assert that understanding control balance provides the tools for learning responsible behaviour, and finding alternatives to violence in all its forms, including war. They use experienced control theory to illustrate how control varies as a function of different contexts.

Human needs theory

Christie (1997) discusses how human needs theory can explain why needs for security and identity are often prevailing factors in interstate wars and destructive identity conflicts. He explains how structural violence occurs when political and economic structures systematically deprive need satisfaction for certain parts of society. When economic deprivation occurs, the need for well-being is not met, resulting in deficits in human growth and development. Politically, structural violence provokes the systematic deprivation of the need for self-determination. Six propositions on direct and structural violence are put forward, including the proposition that a just and sustainable peace will at the very least require the equitable satisfaction of human needs for security, identity, well-being and self-determination.

E. Staub (2003) contends that some conditions in the lives of individuals can be construed as fulfilling universal human psychological needs. The constructive fulfilment of these basic needs promotes caring and positive helpful relations; their frustration leads to a tendency towards hostility and aggression. Staub advocates that inducing a culture change that promotes harmony and peace will lead to a reduction in intergroup violence. The author claims that, optimally, such a change would incorporate the healing of past wounds, the creation of positive ideologies, reconciliation and the creation of a shared collective memory, education promoting peace and the development of collective caring in children.

Additional studies

For additional relevant information see: Beck (2002); Hinde (1993); G. Kemp (2000); Patchen (1993); Sanson, Prior, Smart and Oberklaid (1993).

Summary and conclusion

The core areas of attitudes, psychodynamics, cognition and aggression are interrelated. A number of different theories and models have been put forward to explain peaceful and non-peaceful thoughts and behaviour. By looking at studies from all four areas it is possible to understand how complex internal processes, shaped by our environment, affect our tendencies towards peaceful and violent behaviour on an individual, group and societal level and how world events affect our attitudes, psychodynamics, cognitions and levels of aggression.

8 Language and communication

Herbert H. Blumberg

Studies of communication seem to touch on many, perhaps most, of the areas of peace psychology – particularly as regards interdisciplinary matters and primary psychological topics. Language characteristics impact on intragovernmental and especially intercultural and international relations, on the framing of peace education, on the diction of feminist approaches and on how wars are 'sold' to the public. The ascribed meaning of concepts such as *war* and *peace* may inform our understanding of socialization and of adults' attitudes in particular cultures. Rhetoric may reveal the psychodynamic properties of perceptions of (say) weaponry. Accordingly the present chapter has an organization that is rather similar to that of this book as a whole.

In volumes cross-cutting the aforementioned topics, Korzenny and Ting-Toomey (1990; Ting-Toomey and Korzenny, 1991) collected a variety of theoretical and applied studies relating to cross-cultural contrasts of interpersonal communication and (among other things) conflict resolution. Theories of communication for peace need to take account of the special nature of various forms of discourse, for example: (a) the language of diplomacy – which is highly salient to all parties and must be tactful – in partial contrast to less formal 'track two' diplomacy in which parties' real needs may be shared (see discussion of Kelman's work described in chapter 14, below); (b) the need, in general, for not only power but also trust to be implicit in diplomacy discourse at all levels; and (c) the need for communication to overcome various 'hurdles' in people's information-processing paradigms if change (such as reversing malignant spirals of hostility) is to be effected. Ting-Toomey and Korzenny's compendium also provides a variety of apt examples whereby an understanding of culture-specific discourses can often help in achieving reconciliation and agreements.

International relations and government

Goffman (1955) pioneered studies of 'face-work' in which subtle gestures and comments help smooth the 'fabric' of social interaction. The concept of face-work applies, also, to East–West discourse, where different expectations may confound mutual understanding. Scollon and Scollon (1994) point especially to differences in emphasizing relationships vs. information, to the degree of hierarchy in interpersonal roles, and to the ways in which roles are verified.

Even if policy-makers (and others) are unable to take others' viewpoints in international relations, sometimes because of language barriers, they should at least be very aware that confounding differences may exist (Scheer, 1996). The opposite 'problem' of too little diversity may also exist, whereby historically important differences in perspective have been 'homogenized' by communication in a unified global infrastructure (Mowlana, 1996).

Within-group communication may foster either cooperation or competition between groups – a distinction of obvious importance for intercultural and international discussions and one that can be elucidated in laboratory studies – for example, using an intergroup prisoner's dilemma game (Goren and Bornstein, 2000). Increased provision for group members to communicate with one another generally fostered increased participation and cooperation both within *and* between groups, though the latter depended on whether sessions were designated as cooperative or not. Expressions of competitive motivation were not necessarily associated (positively or negatively) with competitive *behaviour*. 'Even highly competitive teams often realized that it is in their own interest to cooperate with the out-group' (Goren and Bornstein, 2000: 717).

As Gallois (2003) has pointed out, intercultural communication is not merely interpersonal communication writ large nor even writ large with additional discrepancies. Successful communication between cultures may require special training as regards miscommunication in particular contexts and moreover may require an awareness of the social and political motives held by the parties concerned and of the ways in which truly accurate communication might sometimes *exacerbate* difficulties.

Governmental and other intergroup communication   Primarily with regard to within-nation government settings, Kendall (1990) has delineated a broad spectrum of areas elucidated by communications research – for instance, news generation, voting and executive leadership, as well as relevant aspects of interpersonal and international discourse.

As an example of communications research related to international governmental and other contexts, Qureshi (1998) has described the distributed computer-based communication system used by a network of international agencies and has analysed procedures for supporting such networks. (For a summary of general psychological research on distributed communication systems, see Blumberg, Hare, Kent and Davies, in press, chapter 7 and cross-references from there.)

Jarvenpaa and Leidner (1999) go beyond the communications system itself to describe the 'challenges of creating and maintaining trust' in virtual, globally distributed teams that, as it were, transcend space, time and culture. From a laboratory simulation of such teams they conclude that trust is rather readily developed but is fragile.

For additional research on intercultural communication and related topics see: Duncan (2003); Hogenraad (2003); Macnamara (2004); Monge and Matei (2004); and Patrikis's (2003) review of May's work on language and minority rights.

Constructive controversy   Of particular value and relevance is D. W. Johnson and R. I. Johnson's (2000; cf. Gomes de Matos, 2000) delineation of constructive controversy, a prescriptive procedure for resolving perspective-based conflicts in a democratic setting whereby both (or all) parties are aware of their differences and (using research-based guidelines) seek acceptable, creative settlement.

Although one may typically think of controversy as inherently negative, searches for scientific truth are built on constructive controversy. And groups working on problems with intergroup or interpersonal implications, too, have been found – in a variety of studies – to have better quality decision-making when using 'concurrence seeking' procedures. Such procedures, according to D. W. Johnson and R. I. Johnson, ideally incorporate the following properties. Participants:

1. Have the opportunity to propose courses of action that they believe will solve the problem under consideration.
2. Form advocacy groups.
3. Research their position and prepare a persuasive presentation to convince all others of the position's validity.
4. Present the best possible case for its alternative course of action to the entire society.
5. Engage in an open discussion characterized by advocacy, refutation and rebuttal.
6. Reverse perspectives and positions by presenting one of the opposing positions sincerely and forcefully.
7. Strive to create a synthesis that subsumes the various positions being advocated or, at the very least, that integrates the best information and reasoning from all points of view, and a vote is taken in which the majority rules. (Johnson and Johnson, 2000: 297–8)

Johnson and Johnson go on to consider how to socialize new generations into use of constructive discourse. They describe, moreover, various practices in political discourse, some of which are, by the standard presented, legitimate (such as presenting reasoned arguments and viewing issues from all perspectives) and some illegitimate (such as personal attacks on opponents or short-term focus on self-interest). Clearly some situations will provide a challenge to constructive approaches (and some cultures – as might be inferred from other parts of the present chapter – may have different norms), but it remains salutary to have a concrete, empirically tested paradigm for preferred ways of proceeding.

Other disciplines

In a study that bridges (a) globally distributed computer-mediated communication and (b) peace education, Zong (2002) provides essentially a case study of the possible role of such technology in helping teachers to incorporate awareness of global consciousness into their teaching.

Insofar as 'the means should mirror the ends' where feasible, one might imagine that peace education would itself take place in conditions fostering the 'contact hypothesis'. According to the contact hypothesis, intergroup prejudice is reduced if the following conditions are met: members of different groups work and learn together under equal-status conditions, all parties can make positive contributions and those in authority endorse the arrangements (see chapter 2). As a partially alternative view of the relevant 'end goals' – and rather in contrast with the contact hypothesis, however – Glazier (2003) suggests that a major aim of communication that takes place during peace education should not be prejudice reduction per se but rather 'cultural fluency' and cross-cultural salience and awareness. Glazier bases her findings partly on a detailed study of a bilingual bicultural Arab/Jewish school in Israel.

Turning to studies that bear on historical and philosophical matters, Casmir (1997) provides a collection of detailed discussions of the evolved view that ethical behaviour should be built into the framework of intercultural and international communication. Casmir notes that cultures, morals and ethics do differ and change, and that scholars of intercultural communication can help make change maximally beneficial to all concerned. One difficult but essential lesson about intercultural differences, and the tone of intercultural communication, concerns the perils of ethnocentrism and the difficulty of many people realizing that typically we are as 'caged' as exotic peoples, and they are as 'free' as we are (Bradford J. Hall, 1997).

Mass media, especially, have had a role in shaping contemporary, sometimes partisan views of wars and of peace – views that have often been in stark contrast to feminist and other progressive values (Roach, 1993a; see also, for example, Ottosen, 1994). Even within a given population (such as students attending a Slovenian university) and over a period of only a few years, sampled views on the 'meaning' of concepts such as peace, war and capitalism may vary quite noticeably (Pecjak, 1993).

Primary psychological and related topics

The connotations of 'peace', 'no war', 'war' and 'defence' have also been studied in the context of attitudes and images of the effects of war. Martini and Krampen (1990 [English abstract, *PsycINFO* record accession number AN 1992-87556-001]; see also, Krampen, Jirasko, Martini and Rihs-Middel, 1990) noted the cross-cultural variability – across five European countries – of these concepts' meaningfulness, concreteness and imagery. As Pierce, Lovrich and Dalton (2000) also concluded: not surprisingly, area of residence such as living near to a facility producing nuclear weapons – within the United States and to a lesser extent within Russia – can markedly affect respondents' claimed knowledge levels about the potential consequences of weaponry production in their countries.

The psychodynamics of weapons-related diction was described lucidly in Cohn's (1987) analysis of sexual metaphors that have been used in descriptions of nuclear bombs and warfare. Hendershot (1999) discusses the captivating sexuality attributed to the Bomb in a variety of 1950s media, including musical lyrics, novels and cinema. She suggests that the metaphors helped people to manage the fear of highly traumatic prospective events.

In a perhaps lighter vein, the impact of 'international cultural phenomena' such as Disneyland Paris can apparently be managed by careful use of metaphors (Aupperle and Karimalis, 2001).

Cooperation and violence reduction   The evolutionary development of communication under cooperative and competitive conditions has been modelled by Noble (1999), with 'signalling' becoming evolutionarily more costly in competitive situations. The work, based broadly on evolutionarily adaptive animal behaviour, may help to provide baselines regarding conditions that favour cooperative human communication and moreover as to whether the 'signals' embedded in such communication are expected to be subtle (uncostly) or blatant.

An arguably more immediately practical example of reducing conflict and making peace in interpersonal and intercultural relations is given in Hones's (1999) analysis of, in effect, third parties fostering understanding of difficulties, implicit in the 'narratives' of members of bilingual schools. By contrast, Mosco (1993) analyses the technologically advanced communications resources used by the military-industrial complex and advocates making information technology 'literacy' available to all and integrated with peace education (as both a topic and a means of communication).

As a final, further contrasting example, A. McIntyre (2000) provides a moving commentary about participatory action research among urban street youth – who face both violence and peace in diverse forms – enabling them to give voice to their own concerns and become authorities at dealing with their own lives.

Summary and conclusion

Language use and communication properties bear on most areas of peace psychology. In international relations, problems may arise due to subtle (or blatant) cultural differences in the 'meaning' of different concepts. Special training may be useful to surmount such problems. Principles of Johnson and Johnson's 'constructive controversy' help parties to use differences in language and culture in a positive way.

Discussion between opposed groups, in peace education and other settings, is more likely to evolve harmoniously if it follows the principles of Allport's well-established contact hypothesis. According to this view, intercultural groups should work together under equal-status conditions, where all parties can make positive contributions and with the positive sanction of those in authority. A goal of 'cross-cultural fluency' among participants may be as important as harmonious outcomes. Overall, a broad spectrum of communications research testifies to the importance of analysing discourse at all levels and in a wide variety of ways, in order to facilitate both peace and justice.

Part IV

Core topics in peace and environmental studies

9 Conflict resolution

A. Paul Hare

The chapter begins with references to books and articles that provide a general introduction to conflict resolution, an overview of research, or a focus of some aspect of theory, method or application. This is followed by a review of research on the influence of culture on conflict management since many conflicts involve individuals from different cultural backgrounds and there is a concern about the extent to which models developed in the West apply in other parts of the world.

Negotiation, as a method of conflict management in international, national and intergroup disputes, is treated extensively, including techniques that support international negotiation, training, research methods and some research on problem-solving and decision-making, since negotiation is one form of problem-solving.

The next topic is mediation, also with reference to international, national and intergroup disputes, including techniques supporting international mediation and community mediators, with some comments that would also apply to negotiation, on the possibility of using conflict constructively.

The next section focuses on aspects of conflict and various methods for resolving conflict, especially bargaining, that have been investigated using laboratory experiments, surveys, simulations, activities and games. The chapter ends with a brief review of research on conflict in small groups.

Introductions and overviews, general

Books   Several books provide introductions to methods of conflict resolution and surveys of research. The focus may be on conflicts within a community, or a country, or between countries, or all of these.

In his book on *Conflict mediation across cultures: pathways and patterns*, Augsburger (1992) explores variation in conflict and proposes a shift from an interpersonal approach to an international approach in resolving disputes. He examines interpersonal and group conflicts and provides a comparison of conflict patterns within and among various cultures: situational patterns versus cultural, individual versus communal and direct versus indirect.

In their edited collection of chapters on *Cultural variation in conflict resolution: alternatives to violence*, Fry and Bjoerkqvist (1997) bring together descriptions from different academic disciplines and cultures and nations to facilitate comparisons and synthesis. They emphasize three overall themes: that alternatives to violence do exist, that conflict resolution is a cultural phenomenon, and that by studying conflict resolution in different cultural settings it should be possible to enhance the repertoire of alternatives to violence and discover general principles of conflict resolution. In a chapter on 'Conflict life cycles Occident and Orient', Galtung (1997) points out how conflicts are individualized in the West and viewed socially-collectively in the East.

Bercovitch and Rubin (1992) edited a book with the title *Mediation in international relations: multiple approaches to conflict management* in which they provide accounts of international mediation by private individuals, academic scholars, official government representatives, regional organizations, small and large states and transnational and international organizations. In his introductory chapter on 'The structure and diversity of mediation in international relations', Bercovitch (1992b) notes that mediation is a dynamic process taking place within a political context, which affects, and is in turn affected by, the practice of mediation. In their chapter on 'Overcoming obstacles to effective mediation of international disputes', Susskind and Babbitt (1992), evaluate a sample of attempts at international mediation to identify the preconditions for effective mediation.

The characteristics of informal mediation by private individuals are described by Hare (1992) with an example from Cyprus. Kelman (1992) describes the method of problem-solving workshops that he has used in intercommunal and international conflicts. Singapore Ambassador Tommy Koh's approach in mediating at the Third United Nations Conference (in 1978) on the Law of the Sea is described by Antrim and Sebenius (1992). Amoo and Zartman (1992), as an example of mediation by regional organizations, describe the activity of the Organization of African Unity (OAU) in Chad. As an example of mediation by a transnational organization, Princen (1992) presents the case of the Vatican. Jonah (1992) describes the military talks at Kilometre Marker-101 during the Middle East dispute as an example of United Nations intervention in an international conflict. An account of small state mediation in the Iranian hostage crisis is given by Slim (1992). Touval (1992) describes superpowers as mediators.

In *The handbook of conflict resolution: theory and practice* – a comprehensive 'landmark' volume – Deutsch and Coleman (2000), as editors, present theories and practices underlying the constructive resolution of conflict and offer essential guidelines for understanding conflict processes as well as for finding win-win solutions for conflicts of all sorts – interpersonal, intergroup and international.

In an edited book on *Organizations and nation-states: new perspectives on conflict and cooperation*, Kahn and Zald (1990) explain how organizational theory and research can help to understand and improve relations between nations. They also show how insights from the study of international relations can enrich our understanding of important organizational processes, such as how high-stakes decisions are made under pressure. They conclude that the main new facts in international affairs can be expressed in a single phrase: the decision to cooperate. For further consideration of the relationship between international cooperation/conflict and interdependence, see Pevehouse (2004).

In *War and reconciliation: reason and emotion in conflict resolution*, Long and Brecke (2003) provide an examination, in eleven case studies, of the impact of reconciliation on restoring and maintaining peace following civil and international conflicts. For the civil war cases they note that successful reconciliation is associated with a process of national forgiveness, not merely negotiated settlement. All successful cases followed a four-step pattern of public truth telling, justice short of revenge, redefinition of identities of former belligerents, and a call for a new relationship. However, on the international level, successful reconciliation was not a part of a forgiveness process. Reconciliation was successful when it was associated with a signalling process – an exchange of costly, novel, voluntary and irrevocable concessions in negotiating a bargain.

For their book on *Social psychiatry and world accords*, J. Masserman and Masserman (1992) asked one or more leading authorities in each of 24 nations to write chapters on how the social sciences could contribute to the resolution to indigenous and international ethnic, economic, cultural and political conflicts. The chapters deal with the roots of each country's internal travails, their transnational extensions and the use of psychosocial methods for promoting international collaboration.

For a review of a book on the nature of peace studies see Miall (2002). Rubin, Pruitt and Kim (1994) have published a second edition of their book on social conflict and D. M. Taylor and Moghaddam (1994) a second edition of *Theories of intergroup relations: international social psychological perspectives*. In the edited work on *Behavior, society, and international conflict, Vol. 3*, Tetlock, Husbands, Jervis, Stern and Tilly (1993) survey social science research relating to nuclear war aggression, and other topics such as decision-making, negotiation and domestic influences on foreign policy, that are indirectly relevant to the potential for international conflict. For a review of Bartos and Wehr's (2002) manual providing an overview of conflict management, see Mussano (2004).

In an edited book on *Conflict between people and groups: causes, processes, and resolutions*, Worchel and Simpson (1993) collect chapters to present a 'showcase: of theory and research from several different academic fields by scholars possessing diverse perspectives'.

Articles and book chapters   In addition to books, there are journal articles and book chapters that also provide overviews of conflict resolution and related areas of peace research. Bercovitch (1996) analyses data on international conflict management from 1945 to 1990 and examines the factors that contribute to the success or failure of mediation. A comparison of the positivist and constructivist interpretations is provided by Cobb (1991). Coleman (2003) describes a meta-framework for the analysis of protracted, intractable conflict. Roger Fisher (1994) asks if it is better to deter, compel or negotiate in international relations and discusses the reasons why negotiation is superior to compellence. Gaerling, Kristensen, Backenroth-Ohsako, Ekehammar and Wessells (2000) introduce a special issue of the *International Journal of Psychology* on psychological contributions to international negotiations, conflict prevention, and world peace. Helm, Odom and Wright (1991) reviewed *Psychological Abstracts* from 1980 to 1985 to record the main categories of dispute-resolution. Kozan (1997) describes three models of conflict management: confrontational, harmony and regulative (see also Ohbuchi and Suzuki, 2003). The psychology of international conflict is discussed by Tetlock, Hoffmann et al. (1993) and Tetlock (1997).

Introductions and overviews on aspects of the field

In addition to the books, articles and chapters that provide a broad overview of conflict resolution there are those that focus on some aspect of theory, method or application (see also chapter 12).

Books   On conflict resolution as an academic discipline (application from Middle East), see Dane (1992); on roles of scientists, de Cerreno and Keynan (1998); on negotiation as an instance of decision-making, Mullen and Roth (1991); on theory and research in conflict management, Rahim (1990); on origins of violence (book reprint),

Rapoport (1995); and on complex problem-solving, Sternberg and Frensch (1991).

For reviews of more books, see: on a relational model of conflict management, Custance (2002); for the Cold War era, Aall (2002), reviewing works by Hoffman, by Lipschutz, and by Stern and Druckman; and on conflicts and identities, Opotow (2003).

Articles On constructive conflict management, Boardman and Horowitz (1994) and Deutsch (1994); a framework for social psychological analysis, Dovidio, Maruyama and Alexander (1998); on teaching materials, Friedman (2002); an assessment of state of the art, Kleiboer (1996); on cross-cultural analysis, Leung and Wu (1990); on psychological concepts used in studying conflict, Milburn (1998); on relevance of prospect theory, Milburn and Isaac (1995); on use of game theoretic concepts, Munier and Rulliere (1993); on social conflict, Pruitt (1998); on common security, R. R. Rogers (1991); on interpersonal and international levels of conflict, Rubin and Levinger (1995); on conflict, negotiation and peace, Rubin (1992); on cooperative and competitive goals and conflict, Tjosvold (1998); and on the peace process at its culmination: the reconciliation elections, Pagani (1998).

Culture and conflict management

Problems with cross-cultural analysis in conflict management behaviour as a result of applying Western theories and measures to non-Western cultures are noted by Weldon and Jehn (1995). As if in response, Brett (2000, 2001) has developed a model of the way in which culture affects negotiation processes and outcomes. In a book entitled *Negotiating globally: how to negotiate deals, resolve disputes, and make decisions across cultural boundaries* she provides a general framework to help negotiators manage cultural differences whenever they appear at the negotiating table (Brett, 2001). She gives practical advice for closing deals: how to get information and how to manage power.

Miyahara, Kim, Shin and Yoon (1998) explored how Japanese and Koreans may differ in their preferences for different conflict management styles, focusing on the importance attached to conversational constraints such as: (1) concern for clarity; (2) concern for minimizing imposition; (3) concern for avoiding hurting the hearer's feelings; and (4) concern for avoiding negative evaluation by the hearer. Five hundred and thirty-four undergraduate students in Japan and Korea participated in the study. The students were provided with descriptions of the three conflict situations and were asked to rate the perceived importance of each constraint in each conflict situation. The main findings indicate that Koreans are more collectivistic in conflict communication than Japanese. Different processes of conflict management seem to operate in the two cultures: Japanese focus more on clarity constraint, while Koreans focus more on social relation constraints (avoiding imposition to the hearer or loss of face).

Ting-Toomey, Gao et al. (1991) tested S. Ting-Toomey's (1988) theory on conflict face-negotiation by examining the relationship between face maintenance dimensions and conflict styles in Japan, China, South Korea, Taiwan and the US. Nine hundred and sixty-five college students from all five cultures answered questionnaires measuring face maintenance and conflict styles. Results are summarized as follows: (1) culture influences both face maintenance dimensions; (2) culture influences conflict styles; (3) overall, face maintenance dimensions served as better predictors to conflict styles rather than conflict styles to face dimensions; (4) variates dominated by other-face maintenance are associated strongly with variates dominated by the avoiding, integrating and compromising styles. Ting-Toomey and Kurogi (1998) provide a model for training for facework competence in intercultural conflict.

Culture, other   On ethnic and cultural issues, see Emminghaus, Kimmel and Stewart (1997); on culture and negotiation, the Chinese case, Faure (1999); on the need to adapt the US-based view of conflict to other cultures, Faure (1995); on cultural perspectives, Kimmel (1994); on comparing cultures with an intrapersonal grid, Pedersen (1993) and erratum (Pedersen, 1994); on Chinese and American conflict in a multi-cultural organization, Yu (1995); and on styles of negotiation, Brazilian and American, Pearson and Stephan (1998). For cultures of peace and anthropological perspectives see: Boehm (2003); De Rivera (2004a, 2004b); Fernandez-Dols, Hurtado-de-Mendoza and Jimenez-de-Lucas (2004).

Different countries, different problems   In Central and South Pacific, Barnes (2002); in Africa, Blake (1998); for restorative justice in Navaho peacemaking, Bluehouse and Zion (1993) and Leftoff (2003); in the Philippines, Montiel (1995); on historiography and Islamic vocabulary, Hjaerpe (1997); on a South African case study, Jones and Bodtker (1998); on preventing ethnic violence in Macedonia, Marks and Fraenkel (1997); on managerial conflict management in five countries, van Oudenhoven, Mechelse and de Dreu (1998); and on people's conciliation in China, Xu (1994).

Negotiation in international and national intergroup disputes

Bar-Tal (2000) notes that intractable intergroup conflicts require the formation of a conflictive ethos that enables a society to adapt to the conflict situation, survive the stressful period and struggle successfully with the adversary. The formal termination of such a conflict begins with the elimination of the perceived incompatibility between the opposing parties through negotiation by their representatives – that is, a conflict resolution process. But this is only part of the long-term reconciliation process, which requires the formation of peaceful relations based on mutual trust and acceptance, cooperation and consideration of mutual needs. The psychological aspect of reconciliation requires a change in the conflictive ethos, especially with respect to societal beliefs about group goals, about the adversary group, about the ingroup, about intergroup relations and about the nature of peace. In essence, psychological reconciliation requires the formation of an ethos of peace, but this is extremely difficult in cases of intractable conflict. Bar-Tal suggests that political psychologists can and should work to improve the state of knowledge about reconciliation, which until now has received much less attention than conflict resolution.

Druckman, Martin, Nan and Yagcioglu (1999) carried out statistical analyses of 30 cases of international negotiation. Their results supported Ikle's 1964 typology of five types of negotiating objectives: extension, normalization, redistribution, innovation and side effects. They also identified a sixth objective: negotiations concerning multinational regimes. Each type of negotiation had a relatively distinct profile based on such aspects of negotiation as the number of parties and issues, bargain strategies, media exposure, stability of the process and types of outcomes.

For an analysis of the relationship between government structure and the externalization of domestic conflict, Gelpi (1997) examined 180 international crises. He found that democratic leaders responded to domestic unrest by diverting attention by using force internationally while authoritarian leaders were more likely to repress unrest directly.

For an examination of the perceptions of power asymmetry on the outcome of international negotiation, Rubin and Zartman (1995) analysed nine cases. They concluded that outcome is as much a matter of perception as is power. Weaker parties seemed to derive power from their ability to draw on a broad range of resources. Most of the cases showed that power position is not an accurate indicator of the power of the parties going into negotiation or of their perception of the power relationship. The act of negotiation itself tends to balance power asymmetry.

For an analysis of the relationship between a manoeuvre-oriented military strategy, such as the German blitzkrieg of World War Two, and the outbreak of international conflict, Reiter (1999) noted the initiation and escalation of militarized interstate disputes for a sample of states from 1903 to 1992. He found that states with manoeuvre strategies were significantly more likely to initiate disputes in general, although not disputes that escalated to the use of force. However, dispute participants with manoeuvre strategies were significantly more likely to escalate a dispute to war if the adversary employed a military strategy that emphasized attrition.

Leng (1993b) performed a quantitative analysis of the effectiveness of reciprocating influence strategies in 40 real-world militarized interstate crises (MICs). His findings suggest that the success of reciprocating strategies in MICs is related to (1) withholding cooperative initiatives until after the reciprocating party has demonstrated its resolve, (2) using 'carrot-and-stick' influence attempts and responses combining firmness with flexibility and (3) overcoming ambiguity through overt communication of intentions. Reciprocating influence strategies were most likely to be employed by democratic states defending the status quo or following a change in the status quo in their favour through a fait accompli. When reciprocating strategies were employed against different types of influence strategies, the outcomes were consistent with the intersection of the decision rules of the influence strategies employed by the two sides.

On the function of laughter and joking, Adelswaerd and Oeberg (1998) present an analysis of the distribution and function of laughter in three different types of authentic international negotiations, in which both native and non-native speakers of English took part. All the instances in the corpus were identified where one, some, or all of the participants could be heard to laugh or pronounce a phrase laughingly. The analyses focused on when the participants laughed, what the participants laughed at and how the participants laughed – jointly or unilaterally. The analyses indicate first that laughter works as a discourse boundary device; second, that laughter signals what topics are important or less important, sensitive or less sensitive. Third, earlier findings that unilateral laughter, as opposed to joint laughter, is more frequent with participants who are at a disadvantage were confirmed. By contrast, according to a study by Beersma, Harinck and Gerts (2003), insults may magnify conflicts.

For additional perspectives in intergroup disputes, see: on attributional theory, Betancourt (1990); on ripeness, Coleman (1997); on signalling versus balance of power interests, Fearon (1994); on post-conflict peacebuilding, Gonzalez Posse (1998); on threat leading to policy decisions dominated by emotion, C. Gordon and Arian (2001); on a transformational approach, Kingsbury (1995); on questions about the transformational approach, C. Mitchell (2002); on domestic political vulnerability and international disputes, Leeds and Davis (1997); on differences between interpersonal and international conflict, Levinger and Rubin (1994); on the psychological approach to international negotiation focusing on actors rather than outcomes, Rubin (1991); on virulent ethnocentrism and conflict intractability, Sandole (2003); on nations with reliable allies being more likely to go to war, Alastair Smith (1996); on diplomacy and ethics, Belay (1997); and on domestic policies and diplomatic constraints, Pahre (1997). Of possible relevance is the study on hostage negotiations, Donohue, Ramesh and Borchgrevink (1991). For counter-intuitive implications of negotiation and other puzzles related to conflict resolution, see Druckman (2003).

See also: Adair (2003); Brown et al. (2003); Donohue (2003); Druckman (2004); Hoobler (2003); Olekalns and Smith (2003); Olekalns, Brett and Weingart (2003); Putnam (2004); Schei and Rognes (2003); P. J. Taylor and Donald (2003); Wanis-St. John (2003).

On techniques supporting international negotiation

Bonham (1993) recommends 'cognitive mapping' to identify the factors that have an impact on judgement so that negotiators can construct richer, more complex cognitive structures and alternative ways of looking at a problem.

Boudreau (2003) argues that a conflict between groups can be lessened by the explicit affirmation by one group of the other group's identity, including past pain, defeats and collective losses.

H. Burgess and Burgess (1996) developed 'constructive confrontation', in the context of large-scale public policy and international conflicts, as a strategy for approaching intractable conflicts that are not ripe for resolution. Empowerment and recognition and a focus on constructive processes rather than recognition are the primary goals.

A web-based computer assisted tool for diagnosing progress in international negotiation is provided by Druckman, Ramberg and Harris (2002; see also, Kelman, 1999b). Focusing on flexibility in negotiation, the program consists of questions divided into five categories: issues, parties, delegations, situation and process. The questions track to variables, shown in published studies that influence flexibility. Answers to questions are processed according to algorithms that include weights derived from the results of a statistical meta-analysis of bargaining studies.

In a book entitled *Bridging cultural conflicts: a new approach for a changing world*, LeBaron (2003) introduces mindful awareness, cultural fluency and conflict fluency as tools for decoding and moving through intercultural conflicts and for deepening and integrating change. She calls the process 'dynamic engagement'.

For additional approaches, a game theoretic analysis of behavioural issues of rationality in international interaction is provided by C. Langlois and Langlois (1999) and analytical and informational tools that support practical negotiators are assessed by Spector (1997).

Training

Brubaker and Verdonk (1999) present experiences of two consecutive training seminars and follow-up activities organized by the non-governmental organization, Search for Common Ground, based in the US and Angola.

Feeney and Davidson (1996) investigated the validity of the Conflict Resolution Model (described by E. H. Wertheim et al. in 1992). They provided training for conflict resolution for a group of adult volunteers and compared them with untrained volunteers in three types of dyads (trained-trained, trained-untrained and untrained-untrained) who were asked to work together to solve a problem on which they had conflicting views. The trained volunteers displayed greater levels of cooperation, appropriate assertiveness, active listening, brainstorming of creative options and agreement on win-win solutions.

Mandell and Fisher (1992) describe the design and content of a graduate-level course in international problem-solving. The course uses case examples of protracted conflict resolution to illustrate the limits of international mediation and focuses on alternative methods of pacific third-party intervention. Students are taught to distinguish between conflict management and conflict resolution and are urged to investigate socio-psychological explanations of intergroup conflict and conflict resolution.

Davidson and Versluys (1999) evaluated the effects of short periods of training in cooperation and problem-solving, two major components of Littlefield, Love, Peck and Wertheim's (1994) Conflict Resolution Model. Eighty undergraduates were either trained or not trained in each component in a two by two factorial design. During the evaluation phase, each trained participant interacted with an untrained one to make a joint recommendation on an issue about which they held opposing views. The discussions were videotaped and rated blind by two independent raters on five process measures (developing expectancies, active

listening, appropriate assertiveness, identifying interests and brainstorming) and an outcome measure related to agreement. Training in each
component significantly improved success on the outcome measure,
raised scores on the related process measures and generalized to at least
some of the other process measures. The only exception was brainstorming, where training was successful only in the group that also received
cooperation training.

For additional information concerning training, see: for an analysis of
negation pedagogy across four professional fields, Fortgang (2000).

Research methods

Various research methods are presented for use in the analysis of international and national conflicts. See: on content analysis, Druckman
and Hopmann (1991); on discourse analysis, Grimshaw (1992); on
analysis of kernel images and rhetorical visions with an example of the
controversy over spearfishing in Wisconsin, Bradford J. Hall (1994); on
pairwise comparisons of concessions with examples of negotiation concerning carbon dioxide emission reduction in Poland, Brazil and the
Netherlands, Lootsma, Sluijs and Wang (1994); on a framework for
conceptualizing structured encounters between members of groups in
conflict with an example of encounters between Jewish and Palestinian
teachers, I. Maoz (2000); on a framework for analysing pre-negotiation
processes with an example from the Middle East peace talks in Oslo,
Watkins and Lundberg (1998); on an intervention role grid that can
be used to analyse the dispute resolution functions that third parties
can perform, Watkins and Winters (1997); and on scenario analysis as
a means of exposing hidden assumptions in multicultural conflict,
Weisinger and Salipante (1995).

Problem-solving and decision-making

Abstracts of several articles and a book indicate sources that may be
helpful as background for research on problem-solving and decision-
making. See: on behavioural decision theory applied to two areas
of political science research: voting behaviour by the mass public and
foreign policy decisions by political elites, Lau and Levy (1998);
on decision-makers in international teams, Prieto and Arias (1997); on
decision-making under conditions of conflict, Radford, Hipel and
Fang (1994); on deciding to negotiate with villains, Spector (1998);
and on problem-solving as applied to solving ill-structured problems in

international relations, Voss, Wolfe, Lawrence and Engle (1991). See also, Euwema, Van de Vliert and Bakker (2003).

Mullen and Roth (1991), in a book entitled *Decision-making: its logic and practice*, cover a wide range of decisions involving probabilities, causality, sampling, risk, stress and competition, from personal decisions about medical treatment to negotiation strategies.

Mediation in international and national intergroup disputes

Bercovitch (1992a) discusses strategies and behaviour in international mediation. All international mediators (individuals, states or institutions/organizations) operate within a system of exchange and influence, the parameters of which are determined by the communication, experience and expectations of the disputants and the resources and interests of the mediators. While it is customary to describe mediator behaviour in terms of pre-ordained roles, role classification provides only one dimension along which mediation can be categorized. A three-fold classification of mediation strategies (communication, formulation and manipulation) offers the best taxonomy for international mediation. Each mediation should be evaluated in terms of criteria significant to its efforts rather than objective criteria. See also, Bercovitch and Kadayifci (2002).

Based on a survey of 257 disputes for the period 1945–86, Bercovitch (1991) concludes that the interrelationships between contextual variables (nature of the parties, of the dispute and of the mediator) and process variables (mediation strategies) affect mediation outcomes in international disputes. In 1991 he noted that successful mediation would require the development of a taxonomy or framework of mediation and identification of the variables that affect the adversaries' decision-making, choice and behaviour. Continuing on the same theme, Bercovitch and Houston (2000) added to their original dataset so that they now had data for 295 international conflicts from 1945–95. Based on multivariate analysis, they suggest that the conditions of the mediation environment and the identity of the parties in conflict are the most significant influences on the mediator's choice of strategy.

Wilkenfeld, Young, Asal and Quinn (2003) reviewed research on mediation as a means for mitigating or at least minimizing the potentially turbulent and violent consequences of international crises. Two main research questions were explored: (1) Does mediation in general affect the dynamics and outcomes of crisis negotiations? and (2) Does the impact of mediation vary in accordance with mediator style? Data were drawn from the International Crisis Behavior dataset and from experimental work with human subjects. The historical data revealed that mediated crises are more typically characterized by compromise among crisis actors, are more likely to end in agreements, and show a tendency towards long-term tension reduction. The experimental research confirmed the relationship between mediation and the achievement of agreement and also revealed that mediation leads to crises of shorter duration and to greater satisfaction by the parties with the outcome. A manipulative mediation style is more likely to yield favourable crisis management outcomes than is a more restrictive facultative style.

For additional perspectives on mediation, see: on ethical dilemmas in international mediation, Touval (1995); on ethical considerations in unofficial third-party intervention in interethnic and international conflicts, Rouhana (1995); on another way to consider unofficial third-party intervention, Saunders's (1995) comments on Rouhana's article.

Culture   Carnevale and Choi (2000) suggest that culture can play a positive role in the mediation of international disputes. Cultural ties between the mediator and one or both of the disputants can facilitate mediation by enhancing the mediator's acceptability to the parties and enhancing the belief that the mediator can deliver concessions and agreements. Moreover, a mediator who is closer to one side than the other can be effective when the mediator acts in an even-handed fashion. For restorative justice in Navaho peacemaking, see Leftoff (2003).

Culture, other   On problems with mediation in Poland, Olszanska, Olszanski and Wozniak (1993); and on community mediators in China, Wall, Sohn, Cleeton and Jin (1995).

On techniques supporting international mediation

Problem-solving workshops   Kelman (1992, 1999b) recommends an interactive method of informal mediation in the form of problem-solving workshops. It is an academically based, unofficial third-party approach, bringing together representatives of the parties in conflict for direct communication. The third party typically consists of a panel of social scientists, some of whose members possess expertise in group process and international conflict, and at least some familiarity with the conflict region. Unlike many mediators, Kelman's third parties do not propose solutions and unlike arbitrators they do not impose solutions. They try to facilitate a process whereby solutions will emerge out of the interaction between the parties themselves.

One example are the Israeli–Palestinian problem-solving workshops where over a period of twenty years politically influential Israelis and Palestinians have met in private in small groups with a focus on promoting change in the larger system (Kelman, 2001; see also, Kelman, 1997). Kelman discusses five ways in which the workshop group serves as a vehicle for change at the macro level: by functioning as a microcosm of the larger system, as a laboratory for producing inputs into the larger system, as a setting for direct interaction, as a union across lines of conflict, and as a nucleus for a new relationship.

C. Mitchell (1999) comments that Kelman's 'track two' unofficial problem-solving approach may not be appropriate for 'track one' negotiation that is conducted in an adversarial manner. J. G. Stein (1999) also sees problems if the workshop method were used for official negotiation and recommends distributive bargaining. Lumsden and Wolfe (1996) describe the evolution of the problem-solving approach over a 25-year period. Ronald J. Fisher (1998) also describes the method of interactive conflict resolution that takes place in small intensive workshops facilitated by impartial third-party consultants. He notes the need for more trained professionals, adequate funding and a secure institutional basis (Ronald J. Fisher 1993). For more on track one and track two diplomacy, see Chataway (1998).

Peace Brigades   Some activities that are not directed initially to international negotiation may provide experience with some aspect of a conflict which can later be used in international negotiation. This was the case in the third-party activity between Greeks and Turks on Cyprus, described by Hare (1992), where members of the mediating team had had previous experience with the World Peace Brigade, a forerunner of Peace Brigades International. Coy (1993), in an article on 'Protective accompaniment: how Peace Brigades International secures political space and human rights non-violently', examines the nonviolent interpositioning efforts of Peace Brigades International (PBI). He focuses primarily upon the Guatemala programme where he sketches the developments leading to the founding of the Guatemala project, and proceeds to an examination of the various social and political dynamics at play in PBI interpositioning between people at risk and those who might harm them for political reasons. He argues that PBI's use of 'First World' nonviolent escorts for endangered 'Third World' human rights and political activists is a creative, and ultimately helpful, use of the privileges that accrue to citizens of First World nation-states. He suggests that this sort of transnational citizen peacemaking can be an important first step in breaking the hegemonic grip of the nation-state in international affairs.

On community mediators and mediation

Welton, Pruitt, McGillicuddy and Ippolito (1992) conducted an observational and interview study investigating the role of caucusing (private meetings between the mediator and a disputant) in community mediation. Results from 73 self- or court-referred cases at two mediation centres indicate that mediators are more likely to caucus when disputants have a history of escalation, are hostile towards each other during the hearing, and fail to engage in joint problem-solving. Caucus sessions discouraged direct hostility between the disputants but encouraged indirect hostility. There was also evidence that caucus sessions fostered disputant flexibility and problem-solving between the disputant and the mediator. However, no relationship was found between the occurrence or nature of caucusing and the likelihood of agreement or the quality of the mediated outcome.

Grosh, Duffy and Olczak (1995) analysed 27,852 community mediation cases from New York state to determine who uses the community mediation process and what role ethnicity and gender of the disputants play in the process. Analysis of archival data demonstrated that, consistent with predictions from criminal justice research, whites were underrepresented in mediation relative to blacks and Hispanics, and that females were more likely to participate in mediation as claimants than men. Both ethnicity and gender were related to the type of dispute, degree of violence, intimacy between disputants, source of referral and mediation outcome. Additional analysis, taking into account the source of referral, education and income level of the claimant, did not fully account for the observed ethnic or gender differences.

For additional research on community and general mediators, see: on problems faced by government agencies when acting as mediators, Purdy and Gray (1994). See also Weiss (2003).

Conflict: starting, stopping and using constructively

For an analysis of constructive controversy, D. W. Johnson, Johnson and Tjosvold (2000) integrate theory, research and practice on constructive controversy and its role in conflict in interpersonal, intergroup, organizational and international contexts and in constructive conflict management. In well-structured controversies, participants make an initial judgement, present their conclusions to other group members, are challenged with opposing views, grow uncertain about the correctness of their views, actively search for new information, incorporate others' perspectives and reasoning into their thinking and reach a new set of conclusions. This process significantly increases the quality of decision-making and problem-solving, relationships and psychological health. Although constructive controversy occurs naturally, it may be consciously structured in decision-making and learning situations. This involves dividing a cooperative group into two pairs and assigning them opposing positions. Engaging in the constructive controversy procedure skilfully provides an example of how conflict creates positive outcomes.

In a series of controlled studies, D. W. Johnson and R. I. Johnson (1995) demonstrated not only that conflict resolution procedures can be taught successfully – within a nine- to fifteen-hour programme – in a wide range of schools but also that participants can generalize peacemaking procedures to non-school settings (see also, chapter 12).

For additional references on conflict, see: on studying and addressing conflict, Cheldelin, Greenberg, Honeyman and Volpe (2002); on ending conflicts in international disputes by synchronizing the political, military and economic elements of power, Clarke (1993); on the meaning of reconciliation, de la Rey (2001); and on image of 'settlement' when settlement is followed by additional eruptions of conflict, Honeyman (2001).

National/intergroup, additional research

The references in this section are listed alphabetically by author: on using metaphors to facilitate cooperation and resolve conflict, Aupperle and Karimalis (2001); on possible approaches to international negotiation: strategic moves, power, persuasive debate and game theory, Dupont and Faure (1991); on communication approaches to resolving ethnonational conflict, Ellis and Maoz (2003); on intergroup competition and attitudes towards immigrants and immigration based on perceived competition for resources, Esses, Jackson and Armstrong (1998); on techniques for a negotiator to be able to convey concepts using non-verbal tools, Faure (1993); on negotiations throughout history to document how outcomes are determined, Freymond (1991); on the importance of the perceived relationship between two parties as affecting their conception of a conflict situation, Greenhalgh and Kramer (1990); on models of arms control and arms reduction, Hopmann and Druckman (1991); on domestic politics and international negotiations in terms of two-level games, Iida (1993); on Asia-Pacific cases of constructive conflict management when culture can provide a positive resource rather than a barrier, Jandt and Pedersen (1996); on a moral evaluation of holding hostages and nuclear deterrence, Kavka (1991); on parallels between marital conflict and the political Arab–Israeli conflict wherein each new trauma or injury is a reminder of the original experience, Lachkar (1993); on a programme of intervention for promoting community cohesion in response to conflict with an example from the Golan Heights, Israel, Lev-Wiesel (2002); on the dynamics of humiliation as a core agent in conflicts that escalate into cycles of violence, such as terrorism and genocide, where parties feel humiliated and entitled to retaliate, Lindner (2002); on an error of citation in an earlier article on bargaining among nations as it is affected by culture, history and perceptions of regime formation, Lipschutz (1993); on narrative of conflict and change (case study of fishing rights for tribal peoples in northern Wisconsin), Metzger, Springston, Weber and Larsen (1991); on negotiating international norms concerning violence against women, the work of the Inter-American Commission of Women, Meyer (1998); on a time series case study of reciprocity and the domestic–international conflict nexus during the 'Rhodesian problem', 1957–79, W. H. Moore (1995); on peacebuilding and reconciliation with Israeli–Palestinian examples, Nadler (2002); on the psychological contribution to understanding escalation and de-escalation including belief in win-lose outcomes, failure to carefully analyse the situation, the egocentric nature of each side's perceptions, communication problems and attributional errors, Peck (1990); on the legal perspective on international negotiations, Powell (1991); on contributions of applied systems analysis to international negotiation, Raiffa (1991); on intergroup perception, Rothbart (1993); on the constraining power of the international status quo as it relates to the dispute power of the system, Senese (1997); obituary for Irving Janis whose work focused on attitude change, stress and coping, 'groupthink', conflict resolution in personal decision-making, and international crisis management, M. B. Smith and Mann (1992); on lack of understanding of local actors and motivations, Talentino (2003); a case study of two health care teams in conflict with a de-escalative intervention involving exchanging distorted group images, van de Vliert (1995); on game theory and the politics of the global commons, Ward (1993); on institutionalized conflict resolution that emphasizes a short-term solution rather than paying attention to the underlying reasons for the conflict and long-term societal change, Welsh and Coleman (2002); on seven questions to be asked before attempting armed intervention: the international character of the intervention, exploration of nonviolent alternatives, 'winability' of the conflict, estimating probable resistance of those fighting in 'self-defence', international repercussions, prevention of a bigger war later, and demonizing the enemy, White (1995); and on regional conflict resolution in terms of exchange and cost-benefit, Zartman (1991).

Aspects of conflict

For a study of conflict emergence and escalation in international dyads, Kinsella and Russett (2002) examined whether the conditions affecting initial expressions of hostility are similar to those affecting militarized disputes. Analysing dyadic interactions (of politically relevant dyads) during the years 1951–91, they confirm Kant's belief that all states are subject to the realist conditions of interstate competition that makes disputes likely, but that liberal influences, if present, can constrain the escalation of such disputes to war. Several influences on the conflict process have non-monotonic effects over the range of state behaviour. Geopolitical factors affect the opportunity for conflict more at lower levels of the conflict process, when less information is available regarding acceptable settlements and actors' resolve, than at higher levels. Factors affecting willingness gain importance as the conflict process unfolds because they facilitate the flow of information relevant to the on-going dispute. The proposition that democracy and interdependence encourage diplomatic conflicts as signals of resolve is not supported.

By adding linkage politics to the prisoner's dilemma, Lohmann (1997) extends the basic repeated prisoner's dilemma to allow for the linkage of punishment strategies across issues (issue linkage) as well as decentralized third-party enforcement (player linkage). The concepts of issue and player linkage are then synthesized to develop the notion of domestic–international linkage, which connects trigger strategy punishments across games played over different issues by different sets of players. In a two-level game, domestic and international cooperation may be reinforced by a punishment linkage; a defection in the domestic game may trigger a breakdown of international cooperation and vice versa. She also examines the conditions under which the incentives to cooperate are stronger at the domestic level than at the international level and vice versa. With domestic–international linkage, the credibility surplus on one level spills over to offset the credibility deficit on the other level. Finally, she provides conditions under which governments are better off delinking domestic and international issues.

For an analysis of relational demography and perceptions of group conflict, Pelled (1996) assessed on an individual level of analysis the linkages among individual demographic dissimilarity, perceived intragroup emotional conflict and perceived group performance. A questionnaire was given to 233 members of 42 blue-collar groups. Stepwise hierarchical blocked regression analysis showed that both gender and tenure dissimilarities were positively associated with perceived intragroup emotional conflict, and that demographic dissimilarities were indirectly related to individual ratings of group performance. Unexpectedly, race did not have a significant relationship with perceived emotional conflict, and no significant relationship between members' perceptions of intragroup emotional conflict and group performance. Findings suggest that the perception of emotional conflict is a process by which relational demography may indirectly affect members' confidence in the group.

Pruitt and Olczak (1995) examine the resolution or amelioration of severe, seemingly intractable conflicts – the kind that grind on and on. They use an eclectic and multimodal approach in the form of a systems model, which traces social conflict to changes in five modes of human experience. They discuss seven classes of remedies that alter one or another of the five underlying modes, thus helping to ameliorate conflict and examine how and when these remedies should be invoked, in a discussion of diagnosis, sequencing and synergy. Most of the points are illustrated by examples from two realms of theory and practice where the literature is particularly rich: marital conflict and international conflict. For the sake of simplicity, they talk in terms of two parties to conflict. Their analysis can be applied to multilateral conflict as well as using the MACBE (motivation, affect, cognition, behaviour, social environment) model: a systems approach.

Regarding power asymmetry, Rouhana and Korper (1997) note that some methods of unofficial intervention in protracted intercommunal conflict have not considered the possible impact of power asymmetry on the dynamics of conflict and on strategies for third-party intervention. Members of conflicting parties in facilitated unofficial meetings may hold divergent views on the primary intervention goals and the appropriate level of conflict analysis within the meetings. These differences may stem directly from the asymmetrical power relations between their communities. As a result, third parties face the dilemma of satisfying seemingly irreconcilable goals for the intervention. This article analyses the dilemma by examining participants' goals in a series of workshops conducted by the Van Leer Jerusalem Foundation, which consisted of three- to five-day meetings between Arab and Jewish educators. From this analysis, it is concluded that by not adequately attending to the power relations between the groups in conflict, third parties may unwittingly side with the goals of the high-power group. This article highlights the need to focus on power asymmetry in the design and conduct of such interventions.

Models for resolving conflict

This section of the chapter, as well as the next four sections, only provides a list of articles with a brief indication of content.

For models for resolving conflict, see: on a strategic negotiations model, Kraus and Wilkenfeld (1993); on a model for interpersonal, intergroup and international conflicts, Littlefield et al. (1993); on a game-theoretic model for evaluating third-party intervention in intrastate conflict, Carment and Rowlands (1998); on a model for conditions for disarmament, Engelmann (1994); on bargaining models, Cross (1991); on an episodic model of power, Nikolopoulos (1995); on a model for intra-alliance bargaining, Papayoanou (1997); on the role of faith in cross-cultural conflict resolution, Said and Funk (2002); on a model for crisis stability, Seidman (1990); on a game-theoretic approach, Seo and Nishizaki (1994), with risk assessment, Seo and Sakawa (1990); on models of conflict resolution in Japanese, German and American cultures, Tinsley (1998); on a game-theoretical analysis of sanctions, Tsebelis (1990); on a theory of economic sanctions, Lacy and Niou (2004); and on a model, Bazaar, for automated negotiation, Zeng and Sycara (1998).

Bargaining, (negotiations) general

On win-win solution, Brams and Taylor (1999); on fair division, Brams and Taylor (1996); on dimensions of international negotiations, Druckman (1997); on international negotiation, Kremenyuk (1991a, 1991b); on international business negotiations, Phatak and Habib (1999); on multiple meanings of trust, W. Ross and LaCroix (1996); on metaphors for understanding international negotiation, Sergeev (1991); on international trade talks, Sjoestedt (1991); on impact of time pressure on negotiations, Stuhlmaker, Gillespie and Champagne (1998); and on international bargaining with two-sided domestic restraints, Tarar (2001).

Bargaining support (web and computers)

A web-based system for the support and conduct of negotiation is described by Kersten and Noronha (1999). The primary uses of the system are training and research on cross-cultural differences in decision-making and the use of computer support in negotiation conducted at universities and training centres.

The basic definitions underlying a graph model for conflict resolution to support negotiation are reviewed and the techniques for analysis and interpretation are discussed by Kilgour, Hipel and Fang (1994).

Bargaining, other

On Japanese 'ningensei', Goldman (1994); on cultural scripts, Kumar (1999); on effects of culture on buyer–seller negotiation, Mintu-Wimsatt and Gassenheimer (2000); on negotiating in a complex world, Watkins (1999); see also, Watkins and Rosegrant (2002); on sources of power in coalition-building, Watkins and Rosegrant (1996).

Interorganization (labour) disputes

Aquino (1998) on deception during negotiation; on mediation control techniques, Baker and Ross (1992); for British international trade inter-mediaries, Balabanis (1998); on arbitration and risk-taking, Bigoness and DuBose (1992); on personal qualities of mediators, Bowling and Hoffman (2000); on three models, Donohue and Roberto (1996); on breaking a stalemate, Downie (1991); the case of International Harvester and the UAW, Friedman (1992); on arbitrator exchangeability, Marburger (1994); and on intercultural negotiation in international business, Salacuse (1999).

Laboratory experiments and surveys of bargaining

For this review I have brought together research based on laboratory experiments or surveys of bargaining using university students as sub-jects. Although results using students may well reflect gender, ethnic, cultural and personality differences that exist in the wider society, where the results are applied, there are usually no significant age or status differences between students. Also student groups are usually composed of members who are only meeting for the first time for a classroom period or less in time and are presented with a task for which they have no training. The traditional warning is 'caveat emptor'.

For some examples of cases where the research results may well apply in the larger society, Polkinghorn and Byrne (2001) examined the rela-tionship between gender and religious affiliation and preferred conflict styles of student participants living in and attending universities in the stressful contexts of South Africa, Israel, Bosnia-Herzegovina and Northern Ireland. Three hundred and thirty-eight students (aged 17–57 years) completed questionnaires concerning beliefs about conflict, peace-making and violence and also reported preferences among conflict styles of avoidance, accommodator, controller, compromiser or collaborator. They found that gender and religious affiliation significantly affected the type of engagement in conflict. Religious students strongly preferred to use accommodation as a conflict style.

Cai, Wilson and Drake (2000) explored culture's effect on behaviours and outcomes in intercultural negotiation and examined how those effects are moderated by role. Eighty US and international students took part in a previously developed (by D. G. Pruitt in 1981) negotiation task and completed C. H. Hui and H. C. Triandis's (1986) individualism-collectivism scale. Negotiation interactions were coded for information sharing, offers and distributive tactics. They found that a negotiation dyad's collectivism is positively associated with higher joint profit. The effects of culture on both communication behaviours and joint outcomes, however, differed by role of the negotiator. In particular, seller collectivism had larger and more consistent effects on communication behaviour and joint profit than buyer collectivism. Their results sup-ported a 'culture in context' perspective of negotiation that takes into account negotiator qualities, contextual and structural features of the negotiation, and mediating processes, in addition to cultural values.

For a cross-cultural study of Mexican and Norwegian negotiators, Natlandsmyr and Rognes (1955) examined relationships between cul-ture and outcome in contract negotiations and analysed how negotiation behaviour mediates between culture and outcome. Sixty Mexicans and Norwegians participated in a negotiation simulation with potentially integrative outcomes. The study included twelve Mexican dyads, twelve Norwegian dyads and six cross-cultural dyads. The two aspects of out-come were joint benefit and distribution of benefit between negotiators, and the two aspects of process were progression of offers and verbal communication. Results indicate an effect of culture on integrative results but not on distribution of benefit. Process differences found were related to the progression of offers over time and not to verbal communication.

On social-emotional and task behaviour   For any form of social interaction, which would include bargaining, two distinct but related aspects of interaction have been identified. One aspect involves social-emotional behaviour and the other task behaviour. Of the various di-mensions of social-emotional behaviour that have been identified, the

two that account for more of the variance and are most frequently reported are the extent to which a group member is dominant (has power)
or is friendly (affiliative, integrating). For task behaviour there are several variables that might be considered, including the problem-solving
process or the level of creativity of the product; the function of the task in
providing economic rewards in the form of resources is the variable that
is identified more often. Some examples of social-emotional variables
follow.

On a motivational-conceptual model of conflict escalation, Peterson,
Winter and Doty (1994) present a model suggesting that international
conflicts escalate to violence when countries (1) express higher levels of
power motive imagery, (2) exaggerate levels of perceived power motive
imagery in communications and statements from the 'other' side and
(3) express still higher levels of power motive imagery as a result of such
exaggerated perceptions. The model focuses on the role of power and
affiliation motive in escalation and is supported by three studies. In
studies one and two, 149 undergraduates wrote replies to one of two
versions of the same letter taken from two different conflict situations.
Study three explored conditions that affect the exaggerated perception
of power motive imagery of the other side. One hundred and fifty-five
undergraduates highlighted important points of a letter from a real
crisis, under neutral conditions and under conditions arousing power
motivation. The role of psychological variables in escalating conflicts to
violence is discussed.

Mannix (1994) conducted two studies examining the effects of power,
distribution norms, and the scope of future interaction on small group
negotiation. Three hundred and fifteen graduate-level business students
participated in a three-person negotiation exercise in which they had to
reach agreements between two or three players to receive resources. In
study one, the effects of power position, dominant distribution norm and
expectation of future interaction on the distribution of resources were
examined. In study two, the effects of power position, type of need and
scope of future interaction on the distribution of resources were examined. In both studies, power interacted with distribution norms to affect
individual outcomes of small group negotiators. Overall, results indicate
that people care about and use a variety of factors in addition to power
positions to determine resource allocations (see also, Mannix, 1993).

John K. Butler (1994) investigated the causal effects of conflict styles
on outcomes of a negotiation with fully integrative (win-win) potential.
Participants were 444 graduate and undergraduate students who
enacted a negotiating roleplay. While negotiators using the integrating
style were more effective than those using the dominating style, they

were no more effective than those using obliging or avoiding styles. There were no differences in either equality or equity of outcomes across the four styles. Integrating-style negotiators were the most efficient, but there were no differences in efficiency across the other three styles. Pursuit of self-interest and pursuit of other-interest interacted in their prediction of effectiveness. Pursuit of self-interest led to equality, and pursuit of self- and other-interest enhanced efficiency.

Trubisky, Ting-Toomey and Lin (1991) examined the influence of individualism-collectivism and the personality variable of self-monitoring on the conflict communication styles of 212 Anglo-American and 231 Taiwan undergraduates. Based on S. Ting-Toomey's (1988) conflict face-negotiation theory, members of an individualistic culture (IC) were predicted to use dominating, integrating and compromising conflict styles more than members of a collectivistic culture (CC). Members of a CC were predicted to choose obliging and avoiding conflict styles more than members of an IC. Consistent with predictions, Taiwan undergraduates used an obliging style and an avoiding style more than US undergraduates. Inconsistent with the predictions, the Taiwanese undergraduates used integrating and compromising styles more than the US undergraduates. Self-monitoring was related to the dominating style of conflict.

Two additional studies provide related information in that one deals with cohesion and the other with interpersonal skills. On simulation of intergroup conflict, Rempel and Fisher (1997) examined the impact of perceived threat and cohesion on the ability of groups to solve problems in a situation of social conflict. The self-reports and behaviours of 31 groups of college males were studied within a comprehensive, strategic simulation of intergroup conflict. The simulation was based on both a value conflict and an economic competition over scarce resources. A coding scheme for group problem-solving was created based in part on I. L. Janis's (1972) seven symptoms of groupthink. Change scores were calculated over different points in time to assess the relationships among perceived threat, group cohesion and dysfunctional group problem-solving. Large increases in perceived threat were significantly related to decrements in problem-solving effectiveness regardless of whether cohesion was stable or increased. Groups who reported high and increasing levels of cohesion experienced a decrement in problem-solving regardless of the increase in perceived threat, while groups who showed small changes in cohesion demonstrated decreased problem-solving under high perceived threat. The results were consistent with Janis's model of groupthink and Ronald J. Fisher's (1990) eclectic model of intergroup conflict.

Watson, Haines and Bretherton (1996) investigated the effects of interpersonal communication process variables (individual interpersonal negotiator skill level and dyadic negotiator relationship) on the product outcome of a simulated international conflict negotiation. Thirty-two Australian university students formed the negotiating dyads with actors who were trained to present either high or low interpersonal skills. The students then completed questionnaires on beliefs about aggression and relationship, a discrimination test of interpersonal skills, and an intentions form. Results show that the levels of the actors' interpersonal skills affected negotiator relationships and negotiator relationships affected behavioural intention. The students' interpersonal skills were significantly correlated with beliefs about aggression.

Turning to the task side of negotiation   Fukushima and Ohbuchi (1996) examined the antecedents and effects of the multiple goals theory and tested the multiple goals hypothesis, i.e. social goals would be activated even in resource conflicts. One hundred and seven Japanese college students were presented with hypothetical scenarios of re-source conflicts caused by economic issues. Four situational variables (resource cost, familiarity between persons, the other person's manner and the other person's tactics) were presented in the scenarios. In addition, a set of scales to measure four different goals (relationship, identity, justice and resource) were included, as well as two types of mitigating tactics and two types of confrontational tactics. Results supported the hypothesis. It was also found that familiarity activated relationship goals, which increased mitigating tactics and compliance, but decreased confrontational tactics. Further, it was found that a resource cost activated resource goals, which increased both tactics, but decreased compliance.

Most of the research on goals deals with the distribution of economic resources where gain and losses become important and payoffs may be high or low. Some examples follow.

Blumberg (1997) conducted two studies, using pairs of subjects, comparing three strategies for resource accumulation: unilateral ('GRIT'-like), bilateral (mutual agreement) and free choice. A third study explored why participants were very ready to take resources from their partners, even when it was against the interests of both parties. Using 40 undergraduates experiment one was carried out in England while the Soviet–Western arms race was still in progress; experiment two (144 undergraduates) was done in the US in the post-Soviet era. Although the second study incorporated penalties for taking points from one's partner, results were similar in both studies. On average, both players in all three strategies accrued about the same number of 'weaponlike' resources. In particular, the GRIT-like strategy fared as well as the bilateral-agreement strategy, even though it did not require mutual agreement. Marked individual differences under all conditions were examined. Twenty-four undergraduates in experiment three were less likely to take their partners' resources if pairs' common goals were explicitly manifest in joint rewards.

Brett, Pinkley and Jackofsky (1996) conducted an experiment to compare alternatives in dyadic negotiation noting the influence of goals, self-efficacy and alternatives on negotiated outcomes. They found that negotiators with a best alternative to the negotiated agreement (BATNA) obtain higher individual outcomes and a larger percentage of the dyadic outcomes than individuals without a BATNA. Their study observed whether three mechanisms related to a BATNA, an alternative, a specific goal and self-efficacy, independently or in combination, influence outcomes. The participants in the experiment were 326 MBA students. Six of the eight combinations resulted in higher individual outcomes. An alternative coupled with a goal of self-efficacy resulted in a higher percentage of dyadic outcomes and higher impasse rates.

De Dreu, Emans and van de Vliert (1992) investigated the influence of own cognitive and other's communicated gain or loss frame on negotiation behaviour. Research has shown that negotiators are more cooperative when they code their prospective outcomes as gains (gain frame) instead of as losses (loss frame). It is argued that frames are communicated and that negotiators are influenced not only by their own frames, but by others' communicated frames as well. This proposition was tested on 141 undergraduates using a two by three design, manipulating the negotiator's own frame (gains/losses) and other's communicated frame (gains/losses/not given). Results suggest that a negotiator's (cognitive) frames develop and change as a function of their opponent's communicated frame. When two negotiators have different frames, the gain framed negotiator adopts the other's loss frame more readily than vice versa.

On bargainer framing, Lim and Carnevale (1995) examined whether framing negotiator payoffs in terms of gains or losses affects a mediator's behaviour towards negotiators when the mediator has no personal frame. The use of a mediator presents a critical test between an explanation of framing effects based on bargainers' underlying preferences for risk and a simpler explanation based on the psychophysical properties of perceived gains and losses. A computer-based experiment was conducted in which 127 male college students acted as mediators between two disputants (computer programs) in an integrative bargaining task.

As predicted, students proposed settlements of higher joint value when both disputants had loss frames than when both had gain frames. Moreover, within mixed framed disputes, students' proposals favoured the loss-framed bargainer over the gain-framed bargainer.

On high stakes and acceptance behaviour in ultimatum bargaining, Munier and Zaharia (2002) studied whether an increase in the monetary stakes by a factor of 50 influenced individual behaviour in a simple ultimatum bargaining game. Results of the within-subject experiment (124 college students in Romania, 62 college students in France) show that, contrary to current wisdom, lowest acceptable offers stated by the responder were proportionally lower in the high-stake condition than in the low-stake condition. This result may be interpreted in terms of the type of utility functions that characterize the subjects. However, in line with prior results, an important increase of the monetary stakes in the ultimatum game had no effect on the offers made by the proposer. Yet, the present research suggests that the reasons underlying these offers are quite different when the stakes are high.

The last sets of laboratory experiments deal with aspects of the personalities of the individual involved. Are they cooperative or competitive, more concerned for themselves than others, or high in interdependence? On motives and cognitions in negotiation, O'Connor (1997) investigated how motives were related to information exchange (IEX) and how IEX, in turn, affected perceptual accuracy and outcomes. One hundred and seventy-six psychology students participated in a face-to-face simulated bilateral negotiation. Cooperatively motivated dyads followed an IEX route to settlement, whereas individualistic dyads shared little information. Moreover, while IEX was related to perceptual accuracy for cooperative dyads, this was not the case for individualistic negotiators. The effectiveness of this settlement route varied when different kinds of issues were considered. While integrative issues were likely to be settled through IEX, common-value (compatible) issue outcomes were determined in large part by negotiators' first offers.

As a test of responses of cooperators and competitors in a simulated arms race, B. Stone, Jones and Betz (1996) classified 40 undergraduates by social value orientation as cooperators or competitors played a six-choice prisoner's dilemma game in which a simulated participant employed a strategy of graduated and reciprocated initiatives in tension reduction (GRIT) in a simulated arms race. Both groups responded cooperatively to the strategy. Social values may be a less reliable predictor of behaviour in situations where there are a wide range of choices than in situations that require a totally cooperative or competitive choice.

On a two-person social dilemma, Van Lange and Liebrand (1991) examined a dilemma characterized by the conflict between the pursuit of one's own versus collective benefits in two experiments with 70 Dutch participants and 71 American undergraduates. Considerably more co-operation was expected from a person perceived as highly moral than from another perceived as low on morality. This effect was not moder-ated by individual differences in social value orientation. In addition, students with prosocial value orientations, as well as those with individu-alistic and competitive orientations, cooperated considerably more with a person perceived as highly moral than with another person perceived as low on morality. This suggests that individuals who are predisposed to choose non-cooperatively in social dilemmas are willing to cooperate if they are quite confident that the other is truly cooperative and has good intentions. Results were stable across the two countries.

For a study of social identity theory, Derlega, Cukur, Kuang and Forsyth (2002) argue that intergroup relations are more competitive and discordant than relations between interacting individuals. Social identity theory suggests that this discontinuity should be greatest among individuals who identify strongly with their ingroup. To test this predic-tion, 306 university students from countries with collectivistic and indi-vidualistic cultures completed a measure of self-construal. They were then asked to identify how they would respond to a conflict, either with another individual, between their group and another group or between their country and another country. Participants responded more nega-tively to intergroup and international conflicts than to interpersonal conflicts. Self-construal, however, moderated this effect. Controlling for country of origin, students who were high in interdependence en-dorsed threat more and acceptance of the others' demands less in an international conflict than in an interpersonal conflict. Those low in interdependence differed less in their endorsement of conflict resolution strategies in an international versus an interpersonal conflict.

Janssen and van de Vliert (1996) suggest that concern for the other's goals is the key to (de-)escalation of conflict. They described the features of the cooperation-competition model and the dual concern model of motivational orientation to conflict, followed by an assessment of the similarities and differences of both models. They argue that self-concern and other-concern have a very different relationship with cooperative-ness and competitiveness, in the sense that other-concern rather than self-concern is the discriminating factor between a cooperative and a competitive motive. Based on the dual concern model, it is argued that this difference in other-concern clarifies why cooperators, compared to competitors, behave more de-escalatory and less escalatory. This proposition was confirmed in a scenario study and in a simulation experiment among 156 Dutch undergraduates.

Some of the other negotiation variables that have been studied in the laboratory include individual participation, ripeness and noise. Goren and Bornstein (2000) examined two qualitatively different routes to 'peace' in a controlled laboratory setting to gain a better understanding of the conditions that give rise to one process or the other. The intergroup prisoner's dilemma game was played by 120 college students repeatedly in an attempt to distinguish the dynamic process associated with reciprocation at the intergroup level from that resulting from adaptation at the individual level. Results show that when players were not allowed to communicate with one another, they gradually learned that it does not pay to participate, but when within-group communication was allowed, the overall effect was to increase individual participation. However, it was found that this effect varied greatly in later stages of the game. In some cases, intragroup communication eliminated individual participation and rewarded the members of both teams with the mutually cooperative outcome, but in other cases, it intensified the intergroup conflict to its maximal level of full participation.

Coleman (2000) argues that disputant 'ripeness' is a state and a process of critical importance to the resolution of seemingly intractable conflict. Fostering ripeness is often a primary goal of those who attempt to intervene. He presents a typology of interventions for promoting ripeness in highly escalated, protracted conflicts and investigates the distinct effects of four different types of intervention strategies on the commitment of disputants to make peace. The model defines a state of ripeness at the individual psychological level as a high level of commitment by a party to change the direction of the normative escalatory processes of the relations towards de-escalation. Results from 62 graduate students (aged 22–60 years) indicated that process-oriented interventions targeted at removing resistance obstacles to peace were more effective at fostering ripeness than outcome-oriented interventions aimed at driving constructive change. See also, on ripeness, Grieg (2001).

As part of a prisoner's dilemma experiment, Signorino (1996) simulated the effects of asymmetric noise on the emergence and maintenance of cooperation in international politics. 'Noise' was modelled by allowing for some probability p that a player's implemented move was not what was intended, e.g. the probability that an intended cooperative move would be implemented as a defection (Signorino, 1996: 162).

Results show that positive and negative asymmetric noise have very different effects on strategy performance. For forgiving strategies, positive noise provides a stimulus out of perpetual defection or unsynchronized retaliations, but also opens them to exploitation. For provocable strategies, negative noise triggers unsynchronized retaliations or perpetual defection, although this may be tempered by generosity and contrition. The effects of neutral noise reflect the signature of each asymmetric noise type. Of the strategies examined, contrite tit-for-tat (CTFT) is generally one of the best performers in both homogeneous and heterogeneous systems. Moreover, one generally sees the evolutionary models moving from heterogeneous bilateral interaction to cooperative norms of behaviour, often including or even dominated by CTFT.

Laboratory experiments and surveys of bargaining, other

See: on the culture-negotiation link in business negotiations, Drake (2001; see also, Drake, 1995); on situational levers of negotiating flexibility, Druckman (1993); on visibility and negotiating flexibility, D. Druckman and Druckman (1996); on risk propensity and conflict behaviour in dyadic business negotiation, Ghosh (1993); on the alternative negotiator as the invisible third at the table, Giebels, de Dreu and van de Vliert (1998); on development of conflict resolution styles and conflict type, Grace and Harris (1990); on imagined ideological differences in conflict escalation and resolution, Keltner and Robinson (1993); on information exchange, toughness and integrative bargaining, K. E. Kemp and Smith (1994); on overconfidence in buyer–seller negotiation, Lim (1997); on multilateral cooperation in an iterated prisoner's dilemma, Pahre (1994); on complainant–respondent differences in procedural choice, Peirce, Pruitt and Czaja (1993); on perceptions of ethical business negotiation, Mexico and US, Volkema (1998); on experimental evidence concerning cognitive aspects of security decisions, R. M. Kramer, Meyerson and Davis (1990a); on interactants' perceptions of an interpersonal conflict, Hale, Bast and Gordon (1991); on ambiguity and conflict management strategy regarding the success of a venture, Ritov and Drory (1996); and on simulation of a conflict in business negotiation, Conlon and Ross (1992).

Simulations of bargaining

Simulating mixed-motive negotiation, M. A. Boyer (1999) describes a classroom simulation that is designed to provide the social science instructor with an active learning method for teaching a variety of abstract concepts found in various social science fields. It is also a way for students to understand the concepts of mixed-motive negotiations without necessarily having to decipher the often heavily formal theoretical constructs found in much of the literature on negotiation and bargaining. The simulation is assisted by a spreadsheet model used to generate payoffs for the student negotiators. Many of the substantive applications discussed are taken from international relations because of the author's disciplinary background, but others include issues regarding the stability of coalitions in legislative bargaining environments, the mix of conflictual and cooperative motives existing across parties in labour negotiations, and considerations of fairness and justice in negotiated settlements.

As regards simulation modelling in political science, Paul E. Johnson (1999) describes a variety of simulation projects and points out the strengths and weaknesses of simulation in contrast with other methods of research. The strength of simulation research is that it is naturally suited to modelling projects that include a large number of autonomous, interacting agents. Statistical and formal methods of analysis have made contributions in these areas, but there is good reason to believe that simulation can go further. This point is explored in several contexts, including social choice theory, individual-level simulation models, international relations, the prisoner's dilemma game and more general agent-based models of multiperson interaction.

Activities

For storytelling, Albeck, Adwan and Bar-On (2002) describe how telling the story of one's personal experiences in a small group comprised of members from opposing sides of intractable conflicts can help work through some of the on-going intergenerational effects of violence. The concept of 'working through', which underlies the rationale for using this method, is reviewed. This storytelling approach was developed by the members of TRT (To Reflect and Trust). It was initially composed of German descendants of Nazi perpetrators and Jewish descendants of Holocaust survivors. The original members met annually for four to six days at a time, and in recent years have been joined by others actively working to reduce tensions in the current conflict areas of Northern Ireland, South Africa and Palestine–Israel. The guidelines for dialogue work in such groups which have evolved from the TRT encounters are presented and discussed, with examples of how they have been adapted for use in the Northern Ireland and Palestinian–Israeli contexts. See also, Bar-On (2002).

Games

On balance of power, Chapin (1998) presents the 'balance of power game', a simulation that teaches participants about the nature of the international system of states by requiring them to represent and control countries. The main objective for each is to survive. Participants must decide what course of action they will adopt for their representative countries: to engage in war, to negotiate international agreements, to form alliances, or to take some other course of action. The simulation helps students learn about the balance of power, international law and cooperation. The simulation is most effective when followed by a critical debriefing.

Aiello (2001) describes the 'Pantanella Shish-Mahal', a simulation game on the topic of interethnic conflict for the creation of promoting multiculturalism and peace.

Conflict in small groups

A. Joshi, Labianca and Caligiuri (2002) note that multinational companies create international teams to pool global talent and meet organizational goals. But the many differences among team members are fertile ground for conflict. While traditional conflict management techniques gather all team members together to resolve or minimize conflicts, geographic dispersion greatly increases the time, money and disruption to daily workflow activities necessary to bring multinational teams together. Joshi et al. use a social network perspective to identify and prioritize conflicts to increase team effectiveness, allowing management to focus on the most critical conflicts first. Further, they show that the most critical conflict might not be between headquarters and country subsidiaries, but between two country subsidiaries.

Regarding parents and friends as intervenors, Keashly (1994) examined the relationship between the role of the intervenor (parent or friend) and the importance of criteria for subsequent intervention, while taking into account the nature of the dispute. She interviewed 20 women and 16 men (mean age 25 years) who talked about a dispute involving friends, and 23 mothers and 15 fathers (mean age 35.4 years) who talked about helping their children manage a dispute. Participants were interviewed using a semi-structured format consisting of several parts. Only those criteria which reflected the different structure and vulnerabilities of the parent–child and friendship relationships (creating future learning and ensuring continued liking of intervenor) were directly related to intervenor role. Other role differences were a result of intervening in different disputes. Results suggest that decisions regarding how to intervene are also influenced by the broader dynamics and norms of the intervenor–disputant relationship.

For an analysis of strategic choice in everyday disputes, Keating, Pruitt, Eberle and Mikolic (1994) assessed the incidence, order of occurrence and correlates of strategies used in ordinary interpersonal conflicts. A variety of strategies were identified in interview-based chronologies of such conflicts among 38 male and 46 female undergraduates; 39 other undergraduates who were interviewed in an earlier pilot study provided data for developing the coding system. In the main study, verbal confrontation with the adversary was the most common strategy and usually preceded other approaches. Efforts to arrange mediation and arbitration were extremely rare, although third parties were approached for other reasons (e.g. for advice, for support) in most cases. It was possible to distinguish complainants from respondents in 61 per cent of the cases. Respondents used more problem-solving and apology strategies than did complainants; complainants used marginally more pressure tactics.

Porter and Lilly (1996) note that research linking conflict to performance has usually focused on strategic or executive teams. They examined task-performing project teams. They present an overall model for team performance which includes relationship characteristics such as commitment, trust, conflict and task processes. They propose that conflict, which may be quite beneficial for strategic teams, is more likely to hinder than help performance in project teams. Their structural model is tested using data from 464 students in 80 teams working on a new product introduction case project. Their findings support the view that (1) commitment and trust have only an indirect relationship with team performance and (2) conflict and task processes are key explanatory variables directly related to team performance.

Pinkley (1992) examined the relationship between disputants' interpretation of an on-going conflict (i.e. dimensions of conflict frame), their conflict management objectives, expectations regarding settlement, and features of the dispute context. Fifty undergraduates and the individuals with whom they were having a conflict were asked to describe the conflict they shared. Each student's conflict description was given a score for each of the dimensions of conflict frame (i.e. relationship vs. task; emotional vs. intellectual; compromise vs. win). Results suggest that conflict frame scores relate to features of the dispute context. Secondary results suggest disputants with a relationship perspective are more concerned about procedural issues while those with a task frame focus on distributive goals.

Conflict in small groups, other

See: on non-verbal communication and conflict escalation, Jones and Remland (1993), and on escalation as a reaction to persistent annoyance, Pruitt, Parker and Mikolic (1997). For conflict management among organizational teams, see Tjosvold, Hui and Yu (2003).

Summary and conclusion

During the period covered by this review several books have been written or edited that can serve as introductory texts on conflict resolution for university courses or for practitioners involved in conflict situations. Much of present-day research in peace psychology is done in the United States. Caution is recommended when attempting to apply the results to other cultures, especially regarding conflict situations, where cultural variables, such as the concern for clarity or maintaining 'face' in Eastern countries, are very important.

The small sample of research on negotiation in international, national and intergroup disputes presented in this chapter includes a variety of topics, including observations that: the formal termination of intergroup conflicts begins with the elimination of perceived incompatibility between the parties; different types of negotiation profiles can be identified that depend upon the objectives, the number of parties and issues, bargaining strategies, media exposure, stability of the process and types of outcomes; democratic and authoritarian leaders use different methods to deal with domestic unrest; the act of negotiation tends to balance power asymmetry; and in interstate disputes military strategy can play an important role.

A number of techniques have been developed to support international negotiation including 'cognitive mapping', affirmation of group identity, 'constructive confrontation', algorithms provided by a web-based computer tool, 'dynamic engagement', training and the use of a problem-solving and decision-making approach.

Mediation in international, national and intergroup disputes combines communication, formulation and manipulation where the conditions of the mediation environment and the identity of the parties in the conflict are the most significant influence on the mediator's choice of strategy. Mediated crises are typically characterized by compromise. Culture can play a positive role if there are cultural ties between the mediator and one or both of the disputants. Methods that support international mediation are problem-solving workshops and peace brigades. Community mediation often involves private meetings between the mediator and a disputant. Ethnicity and the gender of the disputants play a part in the mediation process in relation to the type of dispute, degree of violence, intimacy between disputants, source of referral and mediation outcome.

Conflict at any level can be used constructively if the conflict is well-structured so that participants have an opportunity to re-evaluate their initial judgements and actively search for new information and incorporate the others' perspectives and reasoning into their thinking. For international conflicts, all states are subject to interstate competition that makes disputes likely, but liberal influences may be able to avoid escalation to war. A model, based on a linkage of politics to the 'prisoner's dilemma', indicates conditions when governments are better off delinking domestic and international issues. At work, both gender and tenure dissimilarities are positively associated with perceived intragroup and emotional conflict. A model, based on a systems approach, will include the variables of motivation, affect, cognition, behaviour and social environment and take into account the power relations between the groups in conflict. This is only the beginning since there are many books, chapters in books, and journal articles proposing additional variables to consider in resolving conflict, especially through bargaining.

Much of the research on bargaining is conducted using laboratory experiments and surveys with university students resulting in generalizations which may not apply to the wider society where there are significant age and status differences and resolution of the conflict will have a major impact on those who are engaged in the conflict. However, as a place to begin, we can note some of the conclusions that have followed from these research methods. Regarding culture, religious persons prefer an accommodation as a style of conflict reduction, a value on collectivism is associated with higher joint profit, and culture may affect the integration of the parties in conflict but not the distribution of benefits.

Data from undergraduates regarding social variables deal primarily with power and affiliation: exaggerated images of power on either side of a conflict can lead to escalation to violence; relative power affects the distribution of resources; negotiators using an integrating style were more effective than those using a dominating style; Taiwanese prefer an obliging and avoiding style more than Americans; increased threat and group cohesion lead to decrements in problem-solving effectiveness; and the negotiators' interpersonal skills are important.

On the task side of negotiation: social goals are activated even in resource conflicts; for resource accumulation a unilateral strategy fares as well as a bilateral strategy; negotiators with a 'best alternative to the negotiated agreement' obtain higher outcomes; when two negotiators have different frames the gain framed negotiator adopts the other's loss frame more readily than vice versa; mediators propose settlements of higher joint value when both disputants have loss frames than when both have gain frames; and the lowest acceptable offers stated by a responder are proportionally lower in a high-stake condition than in a low-stake condition.

Based on findings from laboratory experiments dealing with aspects of the personalities of the individuals involved: cooperative individuals share more information on the route to a settlement than those who are individualistic, although value orientation may be less important if there is a wide range of choices; more cooperation is expected from persons perceived as highly moral; more negative reactions can be expected to intergroup and international conflicts than to interpersonal conflicts; and concern for the other's goal is the key to de-escalation of conflict.

Some of the other variables that relate to negotiation are individual participation (when people are allowed to communicate they will), ripeness (the best time is when individuals are highly committed to change) and noise (when an individual does something that was not intended).

The last few paragraphs of the chapter described simulations of bargaining, activities and games that may help to understand conflict, and some research about conflict in small groups of members of multinational teams, with friends and families, in everyday disputes, for strategic and executive teams and among pairs of students.

10 Emergency decisions, crisis management and the effects of conflicts

Herbert H. Blumberg

The present chapter is primarily concerned with the effects of conflicts and how to deal with these effects: some general considerations; ethnopolitical warfare and trauma; projected impact of catastrophic war; and some theoretical, general and specific aspects of risk assessment and conflict management. Although the larger goal for many psychologists is contributing to a just and sustainable society that is free from violent conflict, contemporary reality apparently dictates a need to deal constructively with strife and its aftermath.

In an extensive treatment of the psychology of war, LeShan (2002) considers not only the actual planning for wars and psychological indicators for their early prediction but also how to plan for the peace that follows and relevant implications for the 'war on terror'.

He notes that no single theory accounts for war in general and moreover that popular intuitive rationales are often fallacious – for instance, that harsh peace treaties are followed by a peace of especially short duration, that leaders typically use war to divert attention from domestic problems, that one of the warring parties is necessarily 'to blame', or that all wars follow from a single cause (which may, depending on the theory one espouses, be seen as human nature, economic stridency or the nature and structure of social groups). Anti-war actions, whether or not in the service of any theory, do not seem to have put an end to war. One can (as LeShan does) chart the differences in perception and experience that are typical of peacetime and prewar and wartime – which show different 'constructions of reality'.

Clearly one way of avoiding the negative effects of war is, as far as possible, to prevent war in the first place. A broad range of preventive structures and procedures may be salutary, coupled with an awareness that abolition of long-standing social institutions is at least possible, such as the (relative) abolition of slavery (LeShan, 2002: 125). Michael Howard (according to Leatherman, 2002) analyses, particularly, some historical, philosophical and religious understandings that may aid the pursuit of peace. Howard notes that war may be as old as humanity whereas contemporary-style serious peace efforts are no more than two centuries old.

Media presentations of war can also be used constructively to enhance the quest for – and understanding of – peace (see also, chapter 8). Terry (2002), for example, uses the war film *No man's land* to put forward a psychodynamic view that to acknowledge our violence may help to redirect destructiveness in productive ways (see also chapter 7 for additional research related to psychodynamic approaches).

One question that arises is whether civil wars (for instance) are best negotiated by partisans or third parties. Although relatively few post-1945 civil wars have been successfully ended by negotiated settlement, Olson and Pearson (2002) conclude that – as regards the negotiator's partisan vs. independent background – success depends on a conflict's specific circumstances but is most likely to follow from repeated attempts for negotiation, in the presence of external military intervention and action by a major power.

Sandole (2003) provides a cautionary note that third parties (and, where relevant, the international communities supporting them) should really be immersed in an appreciation of the historical and psychic background that contributes to conflicting parties' respective identities – and they may need to draw on a variety of theoretical perspectives and multitrack diplomacy efforts, as well as on common sense. (For example, the international community needs to heed early warnings of genocide – as it failed to do in Rwanda – to reinforce armed prevention of atrocities before introducing 'softer' forms of conciliation.) Otherwise, their efforts may make matters worse.

An additional relatively general concern arising from war and its aftermath is how best to provide for the needs of refugees. As Vernez (1991) pointed out even in the early 1990s, worldwide refugee movements have increased dramatically and beyond the scale of international assistance in addressing refugees' material and psychological needs.

Ethnopolitical warfare and resultant trauma

The increased recognition, among psychologists and mental health professionals, of the need to learn how best to deal with war trauma among civilians is exemplified in a collection of papers edited by Krippner and McIntyre (2003). Their selections cover assessment, intervention, peacemaking and – importantly – holistic integration of psychological approaches that recognize ethnic and gender issues. Even a chapter suggesting essentially that a primary cause of war is people's repressed fear of death (because, as experimentally documented, salience of one's mortality leads to cognitive and behavioural discrimination on the basis of social identity) concludes that a cultural emphasis on human similarities and a conscious facing of the fear of death may be salutary (M. R. Solomon, Greenberg and Pyszczynski, 2003), a conclusion surprisingly similar to that of LeShan described above.

In considering the psychological dimensions of war, Glad (1990b) also brings together considerations of crisis management in 'conventional' and (continuing to remain relevant) possible nuclear warfare. Among the perspectives represented, Quester (1990a) provides a rather more global-level analysis of the psychological and other effects of bombing on civilian populations and of the prospect that a major nuclear war could or could not be largely limited to non-civilian targets. He reminds readers that the likely dire effects would be at all levels – not just physical but also societal, social-psychological, interpersonal and familial – and at the very least would have concomitant worldwide political and migration implications.

The effects of ethnopolitical warfare on children and their families is the special focus of Ekblad's (2002) chapter in Stout's (2002) edited volumes on the psychology of terrorism – which themselves deal with public conceptions, clinical aspects, theoretical perspectives and peace-building responses for prevention. Covering both state-sponsored and non-state-sponsored terrorist phenomena – and recognizing that children and girls may be at particular risk – Ekblad provides an integrative paradigm suggesting the value of simultaneous consideration of working at a variety of social-system levels, ranging from individuals and families to national policies (see also, chapters 15 and 16, and the discussion in chapter 6 on rehabilitation of child soldiers).

The circumstances under which post-traumatic stress disorders follow from wartime conflict are, not surprisingly, very diverse, and simply delineating the breadth of these – as does one of the contributions to Lundeberg et al.'s (1990) compendium – represents a worthwhile accomplishment because it may help pave the way for tailoring remedies to particular contexts. The circumstances include considering (for example) the potential effects of weapons of mass destruction, the coordination of physiological and psychological monitoring of stress, and follow-up studies of Holocaust survivors and of torture victims.

A relatively subtle cause of on-going post-traumatic stress disorder is the possibility that the stress, for example war experiences among veterans, holds positive as well as negative 'meaning' for the concerned parties; effective treatment thus may in part entail helping victims to develop a new self that somehow does incorporate positive features of (for example) a 'warrior identity' (Bradshaw, Ohlde and Horne,

1991). The recommended process is perhaps similar to Sarbin's 'self-reconstitution' that represents a final stage of a wide variety of dramatic social enactments (Hare and Blumberg, 1988: 92–5).

A proper full review of the literature on dealing with trauma is beyond the scope of the present chapter. Readers may also wish to consult, for instance, information about Dane and others' work at the Institute for the Victims of Trauma (www.microneil.com/ivt/), about Joanna Macy's (1992) despair workshops (see also, www.joannamacy.net) and work growing partly from the tradition of the learned helplessness literature (Chirot and Seligman, 2001). See also: Brock (2002); Graessner, Gurris and Pross (2001); Kalmanowitz and Lloyd (2005); Schein, Spitz, Burlingame and Muskin (2005); Shalev, Yehuda and McFarlane (2000); Veer (1998); Webb (2004); Webber, Bass and Yep (2005).

Potential impact of catastrophic war

Notwithstanding the arguably reduced post-Cold War likelihood of a nuclear world war, the assessment of risks and of potential effects and responses for such a war continues to merit consideration (see also, chapter 5's section on theology). Within Glad's compendium, noted above, Katz (1990) has joined those who have delineated the disastrous scope of potential damages and the psychological and physical costs of dealing with them: these range from outcomes where there is at least the survival of some intact basic societal structures to those having only the mere survival of groups of individuals but not necessarily any of the underpinnings of modern society.

A variety of factors determine whether particular individuals remain concerned about wars involving weapons of mass destruction (and how people are likely to deal with these concerns). Many of the factors, as described by French (1991b) – particularly including the nature of individual and collective motivations (which tend to be aligned with popular rather than empirically derived assessments of risk) – continue to remain relevant. French (1991a) has also discussed the problems inherent in various possible responses to catastrophe and the particular value of nonviolent international conflict management.

Prediction of responses to events as catastrophic as nuclear war is of course highly speculative, though not wholly beyond a degree of rational estimation (Sederberg, 1990); of special note, severe events seem likely to increase the uncertainty of 'good' decision-making taking place (see e.g. Janis's work, noted in chapters 2, 3 and 12).

The physical consequences of such events may be bad enough, but – to judge by the nuclear/radiological accidents and Hiroshima/Nagasaki attacks that have actually taken place – there is also a sometimes-ignored but likely negative effect in the form of widespread *fears* of (invisible radiological) contamination (Salter, 2001). According to Salter, for every actually contaminated person in a radiological accident, terrorist attack or war, there may be hundreds who suffer apparently similar psychosomatic effects such as severe anxiety, psychic numbing and disorganized behaviour. For a description of actual radiation-induced performance deficits and correlates, see Mickley and Bogo (1991).

Lipton (1991) suggests that one especially productive use of people's fear of nuclear war, and no doubt of other highly destructive events, is to mobilize it in the service of individual empowerment and the prevention (rather than endurance) of catastrophe.

Risk assessment

Theoretical matters Whether precautionary activity is merited in a given circumstance can be estimated, and moreover a (fallible) estimate can be made as to the robustness of the calculations. Indeed, a risk-decision model developed by DeKay et al. (2002) provides for assessment disagreements among parties, and for possible conflict-resolving procedures, in deciding whether a preferred course of action is to avoid an activity, engage in it, or obtain additional (possibly research-based) information.

One particular property of risk assessment that relates to long-term crises (such as environmental problems that challenge sustainable development) has to do with 'discount rates', whereby it is worth something simply to be able to have a reward sooner and also worth something to be able to postpone a course that is costly to one's self (cf. Nevin and Fuld, 1993). Responses to the 'greenhouse effect' that threatens increased global warming represent one such example (see also chapter 14 on sustainable development); as Schelling (2000) indicates, the cost of abatement will need, for some time, to fall mainly on developed countries whereas rewards will accrue to all, but especially to the future more-developed descendants of those presently in undeveloped nations.

Of course people's perceptions of risk may have at least as much effect on public policy as expert assessments do. Papers in a collection edited by Slovic (2000) describe new ways of measuring popular perceptions of risk and discuss (among other things) specific examples, risk education, relevant aspects of democracy and trust, and suspicion of technology.

One important property contributing to the riskiness of a decision is its reversibility. In some cases a sub-optimal decision may be taken because it is seen to avoid irrevocability – for instance, evacuating everyone from the vicinity of a possible nuclear accident because of a (possibly incorrect) concern that evacuation represents a 'now or never' decision (Pauwels, van de Walle, Hardeman and Soudan, 2000).

Ronan and Johnston (2001) have demonstrated the value of risk education among children as a way in which communities can probably also increase their general resilience against major hazards. Elements of such education include specific knowledge (e.g. related to managing emergencies), procedures for realistic risk assessment, and increased communication between children and care-givers.

For an example of the role of social and media processes in amplifying risk, see Flynn, Peters, Mertz and Slovic's (1998) analysis of media and attitudes related to the 1989 FBI raid of the Rocky Flats nuclear weapons production plant near Denver – which, perhaps not surprisingly, led to protracted and on-going negative views regarding the plant.

Applications   Mediation represents one means of mitigating the risks inherent in potentially violent international crises. Both extensive 'real-crisis' correlational data and experimental research confirm that mediation significantly increases the likelihood of agreement and of satisfied parties and shortens the length of crises (Wilkenfeld, Young, Asal and Quinn, 2003). Using the International Crisis Behaviour project dataset (see also, Hewitt, 2003), Wilkenfeld et al. found that a 'manipulative' mediation style was especially likely to have favourable results. (For additional research on mediation, see e.g. Blumberg, Hare, Kent and Davies, in press, links to conflict resolution research.)

Close analysis of international response to complex humanitarian emergencies suggests that aid may be diverted by combatants, and peacekeeping may be diverted by some parties, but that aid and peace-keeping, operating together, may be robust at preventing both kinds of counter-productive result (McGinnis, 2000).

Although there has been only weak support for the intuitively plausible view of links between successive crises between the same adversaries or rivals, Colaresi and Thompson (2002) – who, too, used the International Crisis Behaviour project dataset – conclude that a war or other crisis does indeed increase the likelihood of repeated similar events between the same parties. Thus it is not unreasonable to pay special attention to ways of preventing such 'repeat occurrences'.

There has been increasing recognition of the need for psychological and other support not only for victims of crises but also for aid workers (Hurlburt, 2002). Such support may include provision for security, adequate communication facilities, preparation for cultural differences and means for addressing loneliness and fear.

Although one may tend to think of actual crisis management as being especially relevant outside of Western countries, Lagadec (2002) describes problems arising in complex societies such as France. Lack of adequate responses to crises may sometimes be a reflection of insufficient provision for coordination among relevant agencies or departments.

Although American military action directed by security concerns has commonly been framed in terms of peace and justice, M. J. Butler (2003) explores the possibility that such latter concerns genuinely transcend (or are aligned with) rhetoric rather than, for instance, being covers for (real enough) economic motives. Using logistic analysis to estimate the empirical effect of various factors on the likelihood of American military intervention in a given situation, Butler found that the major factors, among those measured, were US property or persons seized in a crisis (which increases the odds of intervention by a factor of 27!), an authoritarian or military regime as a crisis actor (odds ratio of 5). Controlling for three factors increased the effect of the other significant variables – a US ally involved as an actor, the then Soviet Union involved as an actor and geographic location (as an index of regional hegemony), the effect of the first two of these three being highly significant statistically. In other words, military intervention seemed typically to represent a complex balance in decision-making.

Indeed Devine's examination of US involvement in five post-1900 wars leads him to conclude that Americans do see themselves as a peaceful people who would not initiate hostilities but who entered each war with a belief that it was necessary, even if risky, in order to realize a perpetual peace (Griffiths, 2002). There may of course be alternative perceptions of a given reality including a view that substantial excessive American aggressive intervention has taken place, sometimes covertly, in a large number of settings since 1900.

It remains unclear how best to calculate the extent to which such beliefs are illusions in any given instance and, accordingly, how to prescribe and effect possibly more rational courses of action.

Summary and conclusion

Understanding the parameters related to onset of war may help in the quest for its prevention. The abolition of an institution such as war may prove difficult but is by no means impossible. Efforts to end (or prevent) particular major conflicts should be based on a detailed understanding of their cultural context or else such efforts may be especially likely to be unproductive.

Dealing with ethnopolitical conflict and responding to the needs of trauma victims represents the subject of a substantial, largely recent literature. Concern is with both state-sponsored and non-state-sponsored ethnopolitical warfare. Children and women may be particularly at risk of becoming innocent victims.

The likelihood of a major nuclear or other similarly catastrophic war is seen to have diminished with the end of the Cold War but is not negligible. Such risk makes especially important the routinization of nonviolent international conflict management, including (but not limited to) efforts linked to the United Nations.

Risk assessment – and education as to how risks may be assessed – may help people to prepare more realistically for crises and discount exaggerated publicity about particular hazards. Risks of international conflict may be mitigated by mediation; where applicable, it may be especially effective if peacekeeping and aid can be made available concurrently.

11 Nonviolence and peace movements

A. Paul Hare

For this chapter we first review research on the characteristics of persons who endorse nonviolence, some of the ways that this disposition can be measured and some of the ways that people can be encouraged to adopt this approach. Not everyone who is disposed to behave nonviolently as an individual is motivated to join some kind of nonviolent social movement. Thus the second part of the chapter provides a review of research on the circumstances that move people to take action and on the characteristics of effective peace movements.

Nonviolence

A general introduction to nonviolence is provided by Kool (1993) in an edited book on *Nonviolence: social and psychological issues*. He notes that the multidimensional attributes of nonviolence (e.g. justice and caring) are too complex for the existing overly simple models of psychology. The book examines several of the psychological issues that are related to nonviolence: rules of war and nonviolent action, transforming myths, moral concerns and exclusion, power orientations, obstacles to peace and variations across cultures (see also, Mattaini, 2002).

An edited book by Danieli (2002) discusses, develops and advocates specific policies and practices to enable peacekeepers, humanitarian aid workers and the media in the midst of crises to serve effectively and safely. The book includes suggestions for pre-mission selection, assignment and training, support during the mission and post-mission assistance and counselling. The chapter by Downie (2002) on peacekeepers and peacebuilders under stress notes that in contrast to military peacekeepers, civilians on peacekeeping missions have received little support before, during and after a mission. For a discussion of nonviolent alternatives to political violence, see Lampen (2002). For a comprehensive bibliography with insightful introductions, see Carter, Clark and Randle (2006).

Individual measures of nonviolent dispositions

Mayton, Susnjic et al. (2002), using *Psychological Abstracts* as a database, provide a review of some of the tests that have been developed to measure nonviolent dispositions: Elliott's 1980 Pacifism Scale; Hasan and Khan's 1983 Gandhian Personality Scale; Kool and Sen's 1984 Nonviolence Test; Johnson et al.'s 1998 Multidimensional Scales of Nonviolence; and Mayton et al.'s 1999 Teenage Nonviolence Test. They recommend the use of these measures in peace psychology research.

Values and dispositions of nonviolent individuals

Mayton, Diessner and Granby (1996) investigated differences between individuals predisposed to nonviolent methods of conflict resolution and those predisposed to violent means. Two questionnaires were completed by 167 adolescents and undergraduates (aged 16–49 years) to assess nonviolent personality predispositions: Kool and Sen's 1984 Nonviolence Test and S. H. Schwartz's 1992/1994 Values Questionnaire. Respondents who expressed predispositions to engage in nonviolent strategies for conflict resolution placed higher priorities on the values within the universalism and benevolence value types, providing support for Gandhi's philosophy of nonviolent action. They also placed higher priorities on the restraint of actions, inclinations and impulses likely to upset or harm others than did the violent group. In a similar study, Mayton, Peters and Owens (1999) also report that the high school and college students in their sample who are predisposed to nonviolence also value universalism and benevolence. This is contrasted with those who favour militarism and who are characterized by valuing self-enhancement types of power (i.e. social power, wealth, preserving public image), achievement (i.e. successful, capable, ambitious) and hedonism (i.e. pleasure, enjoying life).

For additional research on nonviolence, see: on nonviolent action, Mayton (2001b); on the philosophy of Gandhi, Mayton (2001a), Steger (2001); on Gandhi as example for social workers, Walz and Ritchie (2000); on why nonviolent peacemaking is important now, A. T. Nelson (1992); on mourning and nonviolence, Judith Butler (2003); on nonviolent interpositioning efforts of Peace Brigades International in Guatemala, Coy (1993). For a review of Tom Hasting's extensive text on nonviolence, see Gandhi (2004).

Peace movements

Mann (1993) examines several factors that affect the success or failure of social movements in producing social change. The factors include social movement organization, mobilization of resources and protest ideology and tactics. He notes that public opinion has an important mediating role in determining success or failure.

McAdam and Su (2002) conducted a time series analysis to address the relationship between anti-war protests and US Congressional voting on war-related roll calls during the Vietnam era, 1965–73. Using protest event data coded from the *New York Times* and counts of roll call votes generated from Congressional voting data, they tested for three specific mechanisms: disruptive protest, signalling and public opinion shift. They expected that extreme forms of disruptive protest would have a direct positive effect on Congressional voting. While results were some-what mixed with respect to all three mechanisms, the most extreme threatening forms of protest (e.g. those featuring violence by demonstra-tors and/or property damage) simultaneously increased pro-peace voting while depressing the overall pace of Congressional action. The reverse was true for more persuasive forms of protest (e.g. large demonstrations) which appeared to increase the pace of voting while depressing the likelihood of pro-peace outcomes. But cf. actions by Gandhi and King.

For additional research on peace movements, see: in the Basque country, Funes (1998); on socialism and pacifism in Sweden, Moerk (1995, 1997); on citizen diplomacy programmes, Molander (1991); on resistance and the cultural power of law, Merry (1995); on resistance in the resistance movement, M. Bastian and Bastian (1990); on peace movements in an abeyance environment, Kendrick (2000); on new social movements and resource mobilization, Klandermans (1991); on the lack of data that might be used to compare the experiences of members of peace movements with those of military peacekeeping units, Weerts et al. (2002); on American culture as addicted to violence, Harak (1992); on how an anti-nuclear test activist group in the US asserted an alternative understanding to that provided by government, Bazerman (2001); on a case study of grassroots peace organization with regard to coordination, motivation and group identification, Bettencourt (1996); on UN efforts to build cultures of peace, Brenes and Wessells (2001); on realistic versus less realistic peace activism, Lowenstein (1990); on what moves the peace movement, Schwebel (1993); on checks on national leaders, Shuman (1991); on a workshop for activists, Wollman and Wexler (1992).

Participation in peace movements

Protection motivation theory   Axelrod and Newton (1991) surveyed 283 peace activists, defence industry workers and psychology students to evaluate the usefulness of 'protection motivation theory' for predicting the extent and direction (disarmist vs. deterrentist) of respondents' efforts to prevent nuclear war. Protection motivation theory centres on a fear appeal communication that is an attempt to influence or persuade through threat of impending danger or harm. This type of communication initiates a cognitive appraisal process that involves: (a) the noxiousness or severity of the threatened event, (b) the probability of the occurrence of the event, (c) the efficacy of a recommended coping response and (d) self-efficacy expectancy. These cognitive processes mediate the effects of a fear appeal by arousing protection motivation, an intervening variable that arouses, sustains and directs activity to protect the self from danger.

Regression analysis showed that the protection motivation model did account for a significant proportion of the variance in disarmist behaviour and that extending the model to include a measure of the belief of the inevitability improved the model's predictive power. The model did not predict deterrentist advocacy. Axelrod and Newton suggest that activism in support of nuclear deterrence may be a response to a perceived threat from an 'enemy' rather than a response to the threats represented by nuclear weapons and preparations for war.

As a possible extension of Axelrod and Newton's views, further thought on the steps in 'protection motivation' suggests that they are the same as those involved in any assessment of an actual or potential change in the situation that a person needs to respond to. Suppose you are at work, about to return home at the end of the day. You see clouds and hear thunder. You might then appraise (a) the noxiousness or severity of the threatened event, (b) the probability that the storm will break before you get to the railway station, (c) the efficacy of taking a newspaper to hold over your head, or of taking an umbrella if available, or of venturing out into a refreshing shower or staying in your office until the storm is over, and (d) your self-efficacy with regard to whether you can do any of these things.

To draw on the four Parsonsian functional sectors described in chapters 2 and 12: steps (a) and (b) deal with the definition of the situation (Meaning), step (c) the equipment and skills required to deal effectively with the event (Resources) and step (d) with whether or not you can do what is necessary, play the part (Integration). What is left is to do or not do (Goal attainment), hence the whole process 'mediates' the response.

Other approaches   Edwards and Oskamp (1992) examined issue salience, perceived efficacy and social support as components of activism within the anti-nuclear war movement. Mail questionnaires were completed by 511 members (average age 53 years) of two anti-nuclear war social movement organizations. They found that each of the three variables predicted a significant independent portion of the variance in activism.

Klandermans (1993) provides a framework for comparisons of social movement participation. He notes that explanations for different levels of participation in social movements involve the societal, movement and individual levels. At the movement level there are four dimensions that may help account for the differences in participation between movements: the magnitude of mobilization potentials, the composition of multiorganizational fields, organizational characteristics and action orientation. He illustrates the framework with examples from the Dutch peace movement.

For additional research on people who participate in peace movements, see: on perceptions of perceived threat and belief in collective control, McKenzie-Mohr, McLoughlin and Dyal (1992) and McKenzie-Mohr and Dyal (1991); on the extent of reasoned action and protest motivation among Japanese adults, Ito (1998). For a review of James Bennett's compendium on peace movement organizations and programmes in North America and of Steve Breyman's history (including contemporary relevance) of peace movements in West Germany and elsewhere, see Hastings (2004).

Individual motivation and experience

Gomes (1992) assessed the surveys of 74 peace activists (aged 14–80) in terms of their most frequent rewarding and stressful experiences. The community of fellow activists was cited as both the most rewarding and the most stressful aspect of being a peace activist. The meaningfulness of peace work emerged as the second most common reward, and success in achieving goals was the third. Failure to achieve goals was the second most stressful experience.

Ajzen (1988: 132–3), in his book entitled *Attitudes, personality, and behaviour*, provides a theory of planned behaviour. The central factor is an individual's intention to perform the behaviour of interest. There are three conceptually independent determinants of intentions: attitude towards the behaviour, subjective norm and the degree of perceived behavioural control. The third factor refers to the perceived ease or difficulty of performing the behaviour and it is assumed to reflect past experience as well as anticipated impediments and obstacles. As a general rule, the more favourable the attitude and subjective norm with respect to a behaviour, and the greater the perceived behavioural control, the stronger should be the individual's intention to perform the behaviour.

Hinkle, Fox-Cardamone, Haseleu, Brown and Irwin (1996) propose a model of grassroots activism based on an integration of concepts from the intergroup relations literature and a modification of Ajzen's theory of planned behaviour. Their model emphasizes identification with grassroots organizations and perceived efficacy as important variables moderating the effects of other constructs (including perceived conflict, ingroup relative deprivation and ingroup biases) on intentions regarding overt grassroots action.

Fox-Cardamone, Hinkle and Hogue (2000), using a modified version of Ajzen's theory of planned behaviour, examined anti-nuclear behaviour. They asked college students to complete a questionnaire measuring their anti-nuclear attitudes, their perceptions of support for taking anti-nuclear action and their perceptions of efficacy in this arena. The students were then given an anti-nuclear behavioural intentions questionnaire and several opportunities to engage in various anti-nuclear actions. Regression analysis supported Ajzen's model to the extent that attitude emerged as a significant predictor of anti-nuclear intentions and behaviours. Models incorporating behaviour-specific attitude measurements accounted for more variance than did models using more general attitude measures towards nuclear war or weapons.

Hetsroni (1998) conducted a follow-up study of persons who were peace activists when they were in high school in Israel. In school they formed a discrete body of students. Hetsroni wondered if they were still different from their age cohorts. The participants were 39 of approximately 150 former Israeli high school seniors who, as two separate groups, signed protest letters in 1970 and 1987, expressing dissatisfaction with the government's unwillingness to make further efforts to make peace with the Arabs. At the time of the survey, in the mid-1990s, most of the petitioners still considered themselves to be leftists and still held pacifist views. The gap between the petitioners and their peers from the same demographic backgrounds remained the same, although the petitioners were less politically active than before. Compared with American anti-war student activists, they had similar academic backgrounds in liberal arts, and were involved in similar occupations in arts, journalism, welfare services and education but not many in engineering and business.

Concerns with nuclear weapons, personal control beliefs and social responsibility values may contribute to the determination of anti-nuclear activism beyond the effects of attitudes and attitude strength (Horvath,

1996). One hundred and seventy-two undergraduates (mean age 22 years) completed questionnaire measures on anti-nuclear activism, anti-nuclear concerns, social responsibility, anti-nuclear attitude and attitude strength. The results indicated that concerns about the nature of nuclear weapons, perceptions of personal control and social responsibility values accounted for a larger portion of the variance of anti-nuclear activism than attitudes and attitude strength combined.

Hunt and Benford (1994) examined 'identity talk' in several peace movement organizations from 1982 to 1991. They found that identity discourse concretizes activists' perceptions of social movement dramas, demonstrates personal identity, reconstructs individual biographies, imputes group identities and aligns personal and collective identities. They describe six types of identity talk: associational declarations, disillusionment anecdotes, atrocity tales, personal political reports, guide narratives and war stories. The stories revolve around the themes of becoming aware, active, committed and weary. Hunt and Benford conclude that identity alignment is a key theme of activists' talk and has crucial implications for understanding micro-mobilization processes.

Oskamp, Bordin and Edwards (1992) investigated the background and motivations of peace activists by conducting semi-structured individual interviews with 21 members (aged 29–70 years) of Beyond War, an American peace activist organization, in 1986. Most of the activists had professional backgrounds and twelve had been involved in activist causes before the peace movement. Almost all reported an experience or event that was instrumental in their becoming involved in the peace movement, such as wartime experiences or particular books, films or speakers. Almost all saw the peace movement as a moral issue, were optimistic about the prospects for achieving peace, were highly motivated for further involvement in the movement and reported strong support from their families.

For additional research on individual motivation: on case studies of the lives of two women activists, Ostrove (1999); on the implications for self-verification theory for social movement participation, Pinel and Swann (2000); on a depressive crisis experienced by members of West German peace and environmental-protection groups, Hilgers (1990); on reasons why nonviolent sympathizers of the Dutch peace movement do not become more active, Oegema and Klandermans (1994); on ways in which professionalism can inhibit or erode, substitute for, or facilitate volunteer activism, Kleidman (1994); on relation between intragroup dynamics and attempts to mobilize peace movements, Hubbard (1997).

Summary and conclusion

People who endorse nonviolence, compared with those who endorse violence, place a higher value on values of universalism and benevolence and higher priorities on the restraint of actions, inclinations and impulses that are likely to upset or harm others.

During the Vietnam era in the US, peace protests had a mixed effect on Congressional voting on war-related roll calls. Protests involving violence or property damage increased pro-peace voting while depressing the overall pace of Congressional action. The reverse was true for large, nonviolent, demonstrations.

People who participate in activism in support of nuclear deterrence may be responding to a perceived threat from an 'enemy' rather than a response to threats represented by nuclear weapons and preparations for war. They believe that protests are salient, effective and involve social support. It helps if the social movement is well organized.

For those involved in peace movements the community of fellow activists, with whom they engage in 'identity talk', is rewarding. They are more likely to take part in this form of 'planned behaviour' if some key experience motivated them to become involved in the peace movement.

12   Peacemaking, wars and crises

Herbert H. Blumberg

How to address both direct and institutionalized violence represents one of humanity's major concerns. The sections of the present chapter pertain to the nature of war (including ethnic and intrastate conflict), historical perspectives, peacekeeping and stressors on peacekeepers, bargaining and diplomacy, and peacemaking and peacebuilding.

The nature of war

Arguing that the cultural basis for war should be examined statistically rather than assumed, Henderson (1997) examined the relationships among cultural factors, proximity and the onset of interstate war (using data for pairs of nations from 1820 to 1989). Cultural factors had a particularly strong impact on the likelihood of war, with the most dangerous dyads being 'religiously dissimilar, territorially contiguous [i.e. neighbouring], and ethnically similar pairs of states' (Henderson, 1997: 666). For discussion of a variety of theories regarding the origins of warfare in primitive societies – including the view that war evolved as a male-coalitional reproductive strategy – see van der Denner (1995).

Some justice in the world is evident in White's (1990) finding that, since 1914 at least, aggressor nations have usually lost in terms of their own self-interest. This has mainly been because of unexpected (albeit predictable) resistance by the victims and intervention by other countries. That is, aggressors typically misperceive such matters. They are, however, correct if they assume that they will be more likely to prevail if the target fails to receive third-party help. The net result may be a tendency towards small wars against the relatively defenceless (Gartner and Siverson, 1996).

Another seemingly persistent example of biased perception is the assumption that bombing civilian populations will inevitably undermine morale and that (even if it does) governments will thereby be moved to surrender (Quester, 1990b).

Moerk (2002) argues that 'unavoidable entry into war' may often be scripted. Examining precursors of wars such as the Pacific component of World War Two, he gives the example of a Japanese script that fleets threatening the homeland must be destroyed, combined with a United States script of (arguably) placing ships as bait for attack (cf. McFarland, 2000). Scripted themes in the examples include avenging a real or fabricated attack, the need for a vengeful response to be greater than the initial attack and the acquiescence of Congress and the American public to presidential manoeuvring.

As one might have imagined, democratic states have been more likely to enter wars early rather than late in an election cycle, regardless of who initiated the war (Gaubatz, 1991). Gaubatz argues that the result may, however, have resulted in (eventual) war being more likely or more severe than it might otherwise have been (see also, Raulo, Gleditsch and Dorussen, 2003).

In cases of acknowledged egregious violations of human rights, though, what forms of intervention are justifiable? Examining the first major superpower intervention subsequent to the Cold War, Kelman (1995a: 117) describes ten psychological assumptions that 'short-circuited' decision-making prior to the 1991 Gulf War:

(a) The rejection of negotiation, (b) the fear of 'rewarding aggression', (c) the concern about not being the first 'to blink' in a confrontation with the enemy, (d) the use of unbalanced cost-benefit analysis, (e) the neglect of the human costs for the enemy, (f) the indulgence in self-glorification, (g) the stigmatization of dissent, (h) the call for rallying around the flag, (i) the stress of overcoming the 'Vietnam Syndrome', and (j) the rhetoric of the New World Order.

Many of these items represent an almost prototypical list of things to *avoid* in order to foster good decision-making. These also resemble the properties of Janis's (1989; Janis and Mann, 1977) groupthink (see Blumberg, Hare, Kent and Davies, in press, chapter 8, for further discussion, indicating that the context-specific balance of importance among the elements in groupthink requires even more research than has already been carried out). Broadly similar concerns have of course been expressed with regard to the 2003 Iraq War or to the planning for its aftermath – e.g. the Statement on the Iraq War (2003, drafted before the event).

As will be evident from the presentation so far, psychology-linked research on war in general is fairly eclectic, drawing (for example) on evolutionary psychobiology, on scripts and schemas, and on cognitive biases.

As a methodological note: improved predictive power for a paradigm covering the progress of conflict can sometimes be achieved by a relatively straightforward adjustment. For example, the termination date of an enduring rivalry seems better indexed by a combination of a conflict-free period and consonant publicly available documents and statements rather than by just a conflict-free period (Bennett, 1997).

After brief consideration of psychohistorical analysis, the discussion turns to positive ways of responding to conflict – peacekeeping, peace-making and peacebuilding.

Historical perspectives

Peace psychology is informed by a variety of publications related to wars and crises, perhaps particularly those of the twentieth century. According to Runyan (1993), psychohistory can contribute to various disciplines at a variety of levels from the individual (or possibly intraindividual) to international. One recurrent feature is the (sometimes opportunistic) attempted curtailment of civil liberties during wars and other crises and the need to find a balance between freedom and safety (B. Levin, 2002).

Another feature has been described as the tendency for stakeholders – related to nuclear production, for instance – to use historical matters to support their preferred ideological narratives (B. C. Taylor and Freer, 2002). Attention to individual perceptions may contribute to under-standing the bases for broader policies, as in: (a) linking a meeting between Eisenhower and Kennedy to American anti-communist policies (Greenstein, 1994), (b) analysing the discourse that apparently enabled Los Alamos scientists to rationalize about the development of the atomic bomb (B. C. Taylor, 1990) or (c) linking childhood trauma of Roosevelt and others to wartime planning (McFarland, 2000).

Equally, media coverage and public response – as with regard to the bombing of Hiroshima and Nagasaki – may help one to understand the unfolding of subsequent policy, e.g. with regard to nuclear threat in subsequent years (P. Boyer, 1996). Psychological study of adaptation among war survivors, too – including studying the eventual interaction of geriatric difficulties and trauma from war and blast – goes back at least to research regarding Hiroshima survivors (Vasconcelos, 1992).

Even more comprehensive recent studies of some of the key decision-makers in the Cuban missile crisis have revealed it to be still more dangerous than was appreciated at the time (Blight and Lang, 1995; Wessells, 1995). Kennedy and Khrushchev were arguably more flexible and concerned about averting war than may be commonly appreciated, but nonetheless there were misperceptions of Cuban views, and these led to dangerous Soviet and American misunderstanding of the situation. (For an appraisal of the historical dynamic contraposition of peace and war, see Sluzki's (2004) review of Howard's analysis.)

Even literary analysis may help in the understanding of historical precedent: the novel *Huckleberry Finn* may be viewed as delineating an earlier period from a post-Civil War perspective in a manner parallel to some contemporary views of the Cold War era (Mauro, 1997). There may have been a need to 'clear the air' in the aftermath of the American Civil War, revealing a parallel contemporary need to leave behind the threatened mutual destruction of the Cold War. Will the same be true eventually for the 'war against terrorism'?

Peacekeeping

Peacekeeping, of course, has played an increasingly important part in dealing with the aftermath of war and with conflict in general. The role of UN peacekeeper has expanded dramatically in recent years beyond the traditional situation of being invited in, as it were, to help maintain an agreed post-conflict situation. The psychological needs of peacekeepers, as well as civilian residents, in areas where (for example) violence remains rife must be addressed. Two especially comprehensive compendia on psychological aspects of peacekeeping have been edited, respectively, by Langholtz (1998b) and by Britt and Adler (2003b; Adler and Britt, 2003).

History and precepts   Langholtz's work provides a temporal span: early psychological thought applied to peacekeeping, the founding of the UN, the generally selfless peacekeeping ethos, conflict resolution, and the post-Cold War period of smaller conflicts, new agendas, and a call for new and more varied psychological considerations (Langholtz, 1998a).

In contemporary instances, there may well be no peace for the peacekeepers to keep – to use McManus's (2004) phrase – but there may still be a prior concern with meeting civilian biological needs (complementing aid organizations), a major objective of providing a psychological climate fostering conflict resolution (see also, the section below on peacemaking) and a variety of additional factors to be considered (Wessells, 1998b).

In the 'newer' forms of peacekeeping, peacekeepers may be deployed without the consent of participants and regardless of national sovereignty (if conditions are severely deteriorated), and they may need to use measures to avert escalation and hasten (rather than maintain existing) reconciliation (Langholtz and Leentjes, 2001; cf. Langholtz,

1998c). Impartiality, however, remains a key precept, even in a long-standing operation having a clearly military ethos (Segal, 2001). Some 'lessons learned' include the need for a clear mandate, sufficient personnel and other resources (including adequate intelligence and publicity), a plan for an acceptable political outcome, and adequate political motivation for achieving comprehensive agreements – perhaps by breaking complex operations into achievable parts. These lessons are reminiscent of Roger Fisher's (1964) advice for 'fractionating conflict' and parallel the four Parsonsian 'functional' sectors described generally by Hare (1983) and others such as Reagan and Rohrbauch (1990).

Impartiality requires peacekeepers who are low in ethnocentrism, a matter related not only to selection (possibly self-selection) but also to training in cultural awareness and arguably in mindful learning (Kimmel, 1998; see also, Langer, Bashner and Chanowitz, 1985, as described in chapter 3).

Boniecki and Britt (2003) give specific training suggestions derived from social psychology, e.g. fostering superordinate goals, providing concrete information about local populations, increasing empathy and generally following the lessons from the 'contact hypothesis'. The relevant findings about contact, following Allport's (1954) analysis and predictions, hold that prejudice is reduced when members of different groups work face-to-face with the positive sanction of authority under conditions where all can usefully contribute on an equal-status basis. For additional considerations as regards selection and training of both civilian and military peacekeepers, see Kidwell and Langholtz (1998).

Psychological factors affecting peacekeepers may relate to: (a) the environmental area – the need for carefully selected peacekeepers to operate far from their own culture and language and to act impartially whilst de-escalating conflicts (preferably while wearing a 'protectively' distinct uniform) in a wide variety of often difficult and changing circumstances for which there cannot have been specific training; (b) training, tactfully emphasizing *non*-aggressive robust performance; (c) violations, where it is advantageous if individual peacekeepers are aware of the nature of likely problems, such as disputes or misperceptions arising from nation formation, colonial legacy, Cold War legacy, religion and socio-economic matters; (d) escalation of hostility, sometimes sparked by a peacekeeper's unprofessional behaviour (such as displaying weapons at a checkpoint) or by popular frustration; (e) de-escalation – ending hostilities, building a 'culture of confidence', negotiating assured ceasefire and conciliation; and (f) negotiation (including various respectful discourse strategies) and, importantly, confidence-building (using friendly, facilitative conversation, for instance) and negotiation (Harleman, 1998).

Always, 'the approach for solving the conflict should be of a de-escalating nature' (Harleman, 1998: 107).

Psychological 'ambiguities' manifest in the interaction of events, norms and social identities must be addressed (Britt, 1998; Franke, 2003). Known psychological principles related to conflict resolution should be incorporated within peacekeeping operations (Woodhouse, 1998). For a further review of participation in, and support of, UN peacekeeping operations, see Bobrow and Boyer (1997).

Psychological areas   Britt and Adler's (2003b; see especially, 2003a) collection spans diverse areas of psychology: social, organizational, health, clinical and cross-cultural. Each area is considered in terms of a relevant framework, practical problems and interventions that are viable not only for the antagonists but also for the peacekeepers' welfare and effectiveness. The volume's research (some chapters from which have already been cited above) covers many of the best-known instances of UN peacekeeping and provides details of a variety of psychological costs and benefits that accrue to peacekeepers, both during and after their stays of duty, and of implications for successful interventions.

Psychological research carried out during peacekeeping operations needs to incorporate general principles of evaluation research, such as those detailed by Cronbach (1982), and has some special considerations as well (Castro, 2003). Among general principles (probably applicable to research in the whole of peace psychology) is attention to sampling not only of units (participants or conflicts) but also of types of intervention, of measuring operations and of times and places. One should consider, formally or informally, the nature of possible 'control groups', adequate breadth of data so as to avoid missing unexpected but valuable findings, and clear (even if 'loose') specification of the kinds of treatments being sampled.

Some specific matters, as discussed by Castro, include early involvement of key personnel in the research (not least for help in identifying key issues), a set of demonstrably apt theoretical perspectives alongside an openness to general enquiry, and particular attention to factors that facilitate peacekeepers' performance and well-being, and a multi-method approach (at least including both questionnaires and interviews).

The most basic and arguably most important of the aforementioned Parsonsian functional areas typically has to do with 'meaning' and values – which help 'set the stage'. Britt (2003) has analysed how peacekeepers assign meaning to their service and how, in turn, the meaning predicts whether the typically stressful experience will be a positive one. Social identity should best emphasize a common identity and positive attitude rather than fomenting prejudice and discrimination on the part of the population or the peacekeepers. The peacekeeping organization's policies and procedures (related to values or ethos) should be tailored in part to the well-being of the peacekeepers in order to attenuate stressors such as boredom and (realistic) fears (Thomas and Castro, 2003; Thompson and Pasto, 2003). Such tailoring needs to take into account mission-specific properties, such as whether or not the peacekeeping has been more invited or imposed and, no doubt, whether a ceasefire is already in place (Weisaeth, 2003).

The remaining three functional areas (interpersonal, goal-orientation and resources) are embodied in the need not only to ensure adequate numbers of personnel but also to provide adequate training related to the specific tasks and necessary information (Wisher, 2003; see also Adler and Bartone, 1997, for a case example of Partnership for Peace training with Albanians). Attending task-oriented goal orientation may entail considering the motivations and commitments of the particular peacekeepers involved (Galantino, 2003).

Interpersonal matters include using cultural diversity among peace-keepers as a strength rather than a source of divisiveness (Elron, Halevy, Ben Ari and Shamir, 2003; Soeters and Bos-Bakx, 2003). Once cohe-siveness is achieved, it is important for this, too, to become a strength for achieving goals rather than a source for consensual inadequacy and stonewalling (Winslow, 1998; see also classic social psychological work such as found in Homans's *The human group*, 1950). Planning should allow for group developmental phases over the course of a mission, as when cohesion may gradually increase, peak and then decline (Bartone and Adler, 1999).

Typically (and ironically) peacekeepers often have a military back-ground – though even drawing on a volunteer army need not mean a group conforming to the stereotype of consisting of the uneducated and unemployable (Kirkland, 1996)! Various research projects deal with adapting soldiers to peacekeeping work. After the event, care in debrief-ing military personnel, including peacekeepers, can help prevent post-traumatic stress disorder (Z. Solomon, Neria and Witztum, 2000); front-line treatment generally needs to be fairly brief and immediate to the onset of symptoms, administered close to the traumatic incident, and concerned mainly with recent experiences and emotions rather than with personal histories. Post-combat intervention needs to include even asymptomatic soldiers but, for them, only to the extent of periodic monitoring for delayed onset of stress symptoms. See also, Greenberg,

Thomas, Iverson, Unwin, Hull and Wessely (2003); Litz, King, King and Orsillo (1997); Lundeberg et al. (1990).

For additional research relating to stress and peacekeeping, see Adler, Litz and Bartone (2003); Asmundson, Wright, McCreary and Pedlar (2003); Bartone, Adler and Vaitkus (1998); Fetherston (2002); Foreman and Eraenen (1999); D. P. Hall (1997); Hotopf et al. (2003); Lamerson and Kelloway (1996); Litz, Gray and Bolton (2003); Litz, Orsillo and Friedman (1997); Litz, Orsillo, Friedman, Ehlich and Batres (1997); Moldjord, Fossum and Holen (2003); Shigemura and Nomura (2002); Whitman (2001). For projects engaging community residents to prevent violence, see Bowen, Gwiasda and Brown (2004).

Bargaining and diplomacy

Reconciliation can sometimes be promoted by informal workshops where representatives of different sides in a conflict may meet in the presence of facilitators and away from the glare of media publicity or of formal diplomatic requirements (see the description of Kelman's work, towards the end of chapter 1, and works cited in Blumberg, Hare, Kent and Davies, in press, conflict resolution links). Sometimes, in the early stages of such meetings, direct conversation between antagonists is impossible, and go-betweens are required in order for communication to be potentially civil and productive. Facilitative one-on-one conversation is not, however, limited to going between extremely hostile parties.

In the TRANSCEND approach, delineated by Galtung and Tschudi (2001), a routine pre-negotiation phase entails trained facilitators talking informally and individually with conflict parties to stimulate a creative appreciation of the arrays of outcome options that may be available.

Perhaps obviously, a willingness to compromise makes nonviolent conflict resolution more likely. One of the reasons why democratic nations are typically more able to avoid war seems to be simply that they are more likely to make mutual concessions – a finding from a substantial dataset about militarized conflicts in the past two centuries (Mousseau, 1998). It is at least plausible, though context-dependent, that procedures eliciting negotiation flexibility from non-democratic states would likewise reduce the incidence of armed conflict.

Certainly where goals are at least partly superordinate (in relation to global climate change, for instance), an appropriate 'regime' or management scheme, that takes account of the culture and history of a broad spectrum of parties, may help lead to viable treaties (Lipschutz, 1991).

Most of the negotiation literature is concerned with 'distributive' procedures, in which one side's loss is another's gain, though mutually advantageous trade-offs might still be found because the relative gains for the parties may differ across issues. By contrast, it has become almost a truism to note the advantages of regarding conflicts as 'non-zero-sum', where creative solutions may enable everyone to win. Happily, some actual practical suggestions for fostering 'integrative' negotiations have been derived by D. W. Johnson and R. I. Johnson (2003), based on extensive (mainly school-based) empirical research. In part these draw on interdependence theory, with multiple variables, to generalize the findings as to the combinations of choices that may lead to viable outcomes.

For additional findings, comments and examples, see: Beriker and Druckman (1991); McCartney and Turner (2000); Zartman (2003). For a review of C. Gelphi's approach to bargaining in international crises, see Klotz (2004). For research on bargaining in more general contexts of peace psychology and conflict resolution, see chapter 9 (and see also, Hare, Blumberg, Davies and Kent, 1994, chapters 9 and 10).

Peacemaking

Although the line between them is fuzzy, peacekeeping implies procedures for maintaining (or – increasingly – achieving) a fragile ceasefire, say, whereas peacemaking suggests reaching a more durable peace. And peacebuilding, which is considered briefly in the section after this one, concerns a sustainable, just peace, that addresses institutionalized, as well as direct, violence. The present section emphasizes reconciliation at interstate and intercultural levels (as in the prevention of war). For discussion that focuses particularly on conflict resolution, also including concern for a more 'micro' level (such as between groups), see chapter 9. (For conflict resolution within groups, at http://learn.gold.ac.uk select psychology, then Small Groups for conflict resolution links.)

An at least nominal contribution to peacemaking comes from the 'official' recognition of its importance by various national and international psychological bodies (Harari, 1992). Cairns (2001) has documented the increasing interest and contribution that psychologists have been making to peacemaking, war prevention and indeed to related broader arenas.

There seems to be no bar in principle to peacemaking becoming part of the education and ethos of a society, perhaps using methods such as those taught by Johnson and Johnson (as discussed in chapter 9, under 'Conflict: starting, stopping and using constructively'). Moreover, conflict resolution can be taught in a way that increases academic achievement, perhaps by 'releasing' the 'tensions' associated with authoritarianism and reducing what Wilhelm Reich (1972) called 'muscular armouring' (cf. Aronson and Yates, 1983, for findings related to the 'jigsaw classroom' and Peters, 1985, for Jane Elliott's salutary classroom exercise).

Even without formal training citizens can – sometimes though not necessarily through collective action – make a substantial contribution to achieving peace and justice (Montiel, 1997; cf. Austin, 1996; see also, Hare and Blumberg, 1968, 1977).

Peacekeeping and peacemaking were both involved in an exemplar intervention for attempting to diagnose and transform a 'violent community' using a multilevel variety of programmes to foster (for example) appropriate, comprehensive effective community leadership (Twemlow and Sacco, 1996).

Peacemaking, at least in multicultural settings, does require an appreciation of differences in perspective and preferably a sharing of perspectives – in particular, with regard to using both typically individualistic Western procedures and collectivist non-Western ones (Pedersen, 2001). Pederson provides a matrix that helps identify the differences (and unexpected lack of differences!) in perspective and moreover provides a contribution for training people in gaining imperative cross-cultural understanding.

Part of peacemaking may entail augmenting a series of stages such as forgiveness, reconciliation and conflict resolution (Borris and Diehl, 1998; see also, Burlingame-Lee (2004) for a review of Long and Brecke's work on war and reconciliation). Another part may require rebuilding criminal justice systems; Vaccaro (1998) suggests that psychological factors play a crucial role in international bodies being able to assist in such rebuilding. For instance, in a situation where infrastructure and indigenous police may be non-existent or show disarray and bias, possibly violent settlement of disputes must be deterred and public trust typically needs to be built for re-established law enforcement, courts, prisons and indeed laws.

Individual differences in propensity for peacemaking in an untrained population do need to be recognized. In a survey of how male attenders at Finnish ice hockey games would respond to a fight erupting nearby, Russell and Mustonen (1998) found that the majority would watch, about a quarter would indeed try to stop the fight, some would leave, and some would encourage the fighters (5 per cent) or join in (2 per cent).

It is preferable, of course, if (all things being equal) conflict can be avoided in the first place. A non-militarized response to military threat may, on average, increase the likelihood of a successful outcome and actually lessen the probability of the threatened party being defeated and decrease the likelihood (and imminence) of future confrontations (Hensel and Diehl, 1994). Non-militarized responses were associated with other variables (such as low issue salience and power weakness), some of which would probably make future confrontation anyway less likely but some of which might make it (otherwise) more likely. In contrast with conventional wisdom, non-militarized responses to an aggressive confrontation make future militarized disputes between the two parties *less* likely than militarized responses do. (One cannot of course be certain that the same result would obtain if the nature of the response was to have been somehow experimentally randomized!) Also, they do not particularly adversely affect the likelihood of losing the immediate dispute though they are more likely to be associated with compromise than with an outright win.

Hensel and Diehl's findings are broadly parallel to the classic laboratory results in Deutsch and Krauss's (1960; Shomer, Davis and Kelley, 1966; see also, Blumberg, Hare, Kent and Davies, in press) Acme-Bolt trucking game in which (essentially) two players needing to take turns using a scarce resource within an electronic game had better outcomes if 'weapons' and their threatened use – such as the possibility of a participant blocking the other's access – were unavailable to either party (and, particularly, were not available to *both* parties). Other factors leading to more profitable solutions in procedures such as these include participants having a cooperative orientation towards each other, the size of conflict being seen to be small and communication channels being not only open but also facilitated by a neutral third party.

Peacebuilding

Peacebuilding can entail a broad (re)structuring of society, typically but not necessarily in the wake of conflict, so as to foster political, economic and social systems that minimize structural as well as direct violence – that is, deal with institutionalized racism, sexism and poverty, and foster justice and sustainable development. What such a goal 'looks like' may vary according to setting, but the process (unlike peacemaking) may – as Montiel (2001) explains – entail considerable tension and distress, though one would also expect it ultimately to 'release' tension and enhance openness and achievement, as implied above in the report of Johnson and Johnson's educational procedures for conflict resolution.

Building on a growing tradition for behavioural scientists to contribute positively to peacebuilding, Lykes (1999) has urged psychologists to be aware of the cultural contexts in which conflicts take place (partly by attending to symbolic and gendered discourse) in order to understand the perspectives of marginalized peoples. Bercovitch and Kadayifci (2002), too, urge attention to contextual and perceptual factors in order – they suggest – to use mediation as an essential part of peacebuilding.

For additional research on psychologists' contributions and potential contributions to peacebuilding, see: Gerstein and Moeschberges (2003) for a review of ways in which counsellors may construct cultures of peace; Oppenheimer (1995) on social constraints against war-like behaviour in order to institutionalize peace; and González-Vallejo and Sauveur (1998). See also: Fitzduff (2003) for a review of Ho-Won Jeong's edited collection on approaches to peacebuilding and R. Taylor (2004) for a review of Colin Knox and Padraic Quirk's *Peace building in Northern Ireland, Israel and South Africa: transition, transformation and reconciliation*.

Partly to preclude hopelessness, Wessells, Schwebel and Anderson (2001) derive four specific areas in which peace psychologists, from virtually all fields of psychology and neighbouring disciplines, can make practical (again, context-aware) contributions to peacebuilding. These four areas are *sensitization* – consciousness-raising in a wide variety of arenas; *consultation* – at all levels, from schools to the United Nations, but in partnerships that avoid cultural imperialism; *activism* – empowering people, for instance by means of peace education at a variety of ages and levels; and *public policy work* – advocacy for high ethical standards and monitoring injustice, be it in relation to the institutionalization of orphans or working towards the abolition of human rights abuses.

Summary and conclusion

Psychological contributions to understanding the nature of war are also helpful in working towards and maintaining peace. These include documenting the counter-productive aspects of aggression and of rigid decision-making.

Re-analysis of historical events and phenomena may help in dealing with contemporary ones. Examples include the curtailment of civil liberties during wars, the (helpful or specious) use of historical narrative to justify a preferred course of action, the retrospective psychodynamic analysis of heads of state and other policy-makers and investigations based on bringing together 'key players' after – sometimes decades after – an event such as the Cuban missile crisis.

Since the end of the Cold War UN peacekeeping has expanded both in frequency and scope, no longer being limited to being invited into international situations where a ceasefire is already in place. Thus peacekeepers may need diverse training in *establishing* as well as maintaining peace, and the psychological and physical welfare of the peacekeepers themselves requires mindful consideration.

Various innovative procedures for peacekeeping and peacemaking – directed towards creatively positive outcomes – include, for example, informal facilitated workshops between conflicting parties. Cultural differences in norms for social interaction in general, and peacemaking in general, must be taken on board. Non-militarized responses to an aggressive confrontation may make future militarized disputes between the two parties less likely than militarized responses would.

Psychologists may also particularly contribute to peacebuilding in establishing successful ways of addressing structural violence – associated, for instance, not only with relatively long-range post-war periods but also with lessening poverty and prejudice.

13　The Middle East, Russia and other specific areas

A. Paul Hare

In this chapter we review research country by country and by region on the assumption that persons who wish to help reduce conflict in any of these areas may wish to know about the approaches that have already been tried and variables related to conflict resolution that have already been identified. However, with so many variables and so many articles it is rare to find two reports of research on the same subject. It is clear that some of the authors who discuss topics such as the cognitive complexity of peacemaking, cultural identity, trauma and the usefulness of intergroup workshops assume that their research has wider applications. Indeed, references to some of the same material appear in other chapters in this volume and some material related to a particular country, for example on children in Northern Ireland, only appears in another chapter. Thus all of the references to a given country could only be discovered by consulting the index.

For too many years, three areas of the world have had on-going conflicts in which religious and ethnic differences have played a prominent part: the Middle East with a focus on Israel and its neighbours, Northern Ireland and South Africa. More recently actions in countries that were parts of the former Soviet Union have revealed that 'ethnic cleansing' did not disappear with the fall of Nazi Germany in the 1940s. A few of these countries appear in the list of countries at the end of the chapter. However, the focus of the research on Russia reviewed here is concerned mainly with the arms race between the US and the USSR during the Cold War. There are still lessens to be learned from psychological processes that were especially typical of the Cold War, but readers should bear in mind that the topics covered in this chapter relate as much to the distribution of existing research as they do to regions of particular contemporary global concern.

The chapter concludes with summaries or references to one or more examples of research in a longish alphabetical list of countries and areas that includes: Afghanistan, Angola, Argentina, Armenia, Asia, Australia, Bosnia-Herzegovina, Brazil, Cambodia, Central Europe,

China, Colombia, Croatia, Cuba, Cyprus, Czechoslovakia, Eastern Europe, El Salvador, England, Eritrea, Estonia, Eurasia, Europe, Germany, Greece, Guatemala, India, Japan, Korea, Kosovo, Latin America, Liberia, Macedonia, Pakistan, Philippines, Rwanda, Serbia, Somalia, South Asia, Southeast Asia, Spain, Sri Lanka, Uganda, United States, Vietnam and Yugoslavia.

Middle East

Middle East, general In a study of reciprocity, triangularity and cooperation in the Middle East, 1979–95, Goldstein, Pevehouse, Gerner and Telhami (2001) analysed international conflicts in the Middle East to assess the relevance of the literature on international reciprocity as a means to achieving stable cooperation. The authors sought to determine whether bilateral reciprocity or great-power influence (or both) promotes the emergence of international cooperation in regional conflicts. Machine-coded events data and vector auto-regression were used to conduct a time series analysis of twelve international dyads in the Middle East in the time periods 1979–90 and 1991–5. Bilateral reciprocity was found to be widespread in both time periods, characterizing nearly all dyads of sustained conflict and a majority of other dyads with various power and proximity characteristics. Results show that significant triangular responses to US actions occurred in only a few cases – Iraq with its neighbours and Israel with Palestine. Neither bilateral reciprocity nor triangular response was found to predict changes in long-term conflict and cooperation. Rather, the presence of one or both of these response patterns appeared to be a necessary, but not sufficient, condition for regional states to increase long-term cooperation.

In research on popular support for Lebanon's radical Shiite organization, Hizballah, Harik (1996) tested whether a hypothesis explaining popular support for Middle Eastern fundamentalist movements in general adequately describes the grassroots appeal of Hizballah. Survey data from 405 respondents in 1993 showed that Hizballah adherents were less likely than expected to be deeply religious, to have a low SES, and to have a strong political alienation. It is suggested that constraints imposed on Islamic goals by Lebanon's pluralist society and its powerful neighbour Syria have influenced the moderate trend of Hizballah. Harik concludes that Islamist success in carving a niche in a community still seeking self-identity and adequate national representation means that Islamists are unlikely to lose external backers' support should Middle East peace negotiations reduce Hizballah's resistance role.

For the analysis of crisis phases in the Middle East, Schrodt and Gerner (1997) use several statistical techniques which they suggest might be applied to provide an early warning of an impending crisis.

Simulations and models   On the Middle East peace process, Harel and Morgan (1994) describe a negotiation exercise set in the context of the Middle East conflict to facilitate an understanding about how power differentials impact negotiation. The exercise involves multi-party negotiation that can evolve into coalition negotiation. Individuals are divided into teams of Israelis, Syrians, Jordanians and Palestinians, and must negotiate to reach a peace agreement. After completing the exercise, individuals are debriefed about leadership style, group dynamics, power differentials and negotiations. Exercise variations and recommendations for facilitators are included.

Using a game-theoretic model, G. L. Sorokin (1994) studied the relationship between alliance formation and general deterrence in regional rivalries. In a game-theoretic model under complete information, an alliance is formed only when the potential ally would not intervene without one and would always intervene with one. General deterrence succeeds under complete information unless the potential attacker is stronger than the target and values the stakes highly, and the potential ally would never intervene. General deterrence under incomplete information sometimes fails because of the potential attacker's mistaken beliefs about the probability that the target would win or the potential ally would intervene. The model is illustrated by examining the conflict between Israel and its rivals, Egypt and Syria, taking into account the role of the US as Israel's potential ally.

Peacemaking and post settlement   On the Israeli peacemaking experience with Egypt, Bar-Siman-Tov (1995) uses Begin's decisions, as prime minister, concerning peace with Egypt from 1977 through 1982 as an example of the problems of value complexity in shifting from war to peace and modes of coping. For how religion can bring peace to the Middle East, see Caspary (2003).

Israel–Egypt   In a study of cognitive structure of peacemaking, Z. Maoz and Astorino (1992) examine the hypothesis that the structure of beliefs of political leaders is related to the degree of cooperation exhibited by their nation towards a traditional enemy. This relationship is examined by focusing on the association between cognitive complexity (measured by structural as opposed to content-based indices) and the proportion of cooperative behaviour exchanged between Israel and

Egypt over the period of 1970–8. Findings indicate that measures of cognitive complexity consistently and significantly affected the proportion of Egyptian cooperative behaviour vis-à-vis Israel in subsequent periods. Specifically, the higher the level of cognitive complexity in verbal expression, the higher the subsequent proportion of cooperative behaviour exhibited by Egypt towards Israel. This relationship was not replicated in the Israeli case.

Concerning arms transfers to Israel, Egypt and Syria, Mayer and Rotte (1999) discuss a 1995 article in the *Journal of Conflict Resolution* in which D. Kinsella and H. K. Tillema argued that, between 1948 and 1991, American arms transfers to Israel exercised a restraining influence on both Israel and its Arab rivals, whereas Soviet transfers to Egypt and Syria tended to destabilize the region. Mayer and Rotte re-examine Kinsella and Tillema's Poisson results by applying a more sophisticated statistical method to their dataset. Using a multiplicative Poisson model that allows for variation in the coefficients depending on a metrical reference variable, they show how the impact of superpower activity on Middle Eastern interventions has changed with the influx of weaponry. They confirm that US arms transfers decreased the likelihood of military intervention in the region, whereas Soviet supplies did not affect it. Contrary to Kinsella and Tillema, however, the authors show that the stabilizing effect of arms transfers clearly decreases with the total amount of armaments supplied to the region.

Lebanon   In a study of the willingness to forgive by Muslim and Christian Lebanese, Azar and Mullet (2002) examined: (a) the overall level of willingness to forgive expressed by Muslim and Christian Lebanese adults who lived through the Lebanese civil war, (b) the factorial structure of the responses given, (c) the way education, community and other characteristics were related to the factorial structure, and (d) the relationship of the Lebanese data with data previously gathered by E. Mullet et al. in France. A sample of 240 participants (aged 18–65 years) from six different communities, Shiite, Sunni, Druze, Catholic, Orthodox and Maronite, were asked to express their degree of agreement with 38 statements related to forgiveness in general or in specific circumstances. Overall, participants expressed significant disagreement with statements expressing the desire to seek revenge (the Forgiveness versus Revenge factor), and disagreement with statements indicating that the attitude of 'close others' was important (the Social and Personal Circumstances factor). They were generally neutral towards statements related to possible obstacles to forgiveness, clear malevolence, extreme severity of consequences, or lack of repentance by the offender (the

Obstacles factor). Mean responses were similar to the ones registered in France. (For research on peacebuilding by women in Lebanon, see Abu-Saba, 2003.)

Persian Gulf War   On American Congressional voting, Burgin (1994) explored the factors that US Congressional staff people perceived that members considered when deciding how to vote on the Persian Gulf issue. The nature and importance of three influences were analysed: the members' own views, the supportive constituency and the president. Members' staffs were asked to separately rate the impact of nine different factors on their bosses' votes on the legislation regarding US strategy in the Gulf. Analysis partially confirms the view that legislators' personal policy assessments are the most significant in foreign and defence policy votes. Supportive constituents powerfully affected members, particularly members who were not in the president's party, were relatively new to Congress, represented 'safe' districts, did not hold key institutional positions, nor faced election in 1992. Republican staffers thought their bosses perceived the president's influence as being as weighty as that of supportive constituents.

On the willingness of the US to rebuild Iraq and Kuwait, Skitka, McMurray and Burroughs (1991) investigated how people's attributions of responsibility for the Persian Gulf War and associated affective reactions influenced how much they believed the US should help rebuild Iraq and Kuwait once hostilities ceased. Data were collected at two different junctures of Operation Desert Storm from 93 college students within 48 hours after the start of the ground war and 57 college students the morning after the ceasefire. Students allocated the amount of the total time needed to rebuild Iraq and Kuwait that they thought was fair after being primed with either a pessimistic or optimistic economic forecast. Attribution of responsibility for the war was the best predictor of aid allocated to Iraq, followed by political ideology, and then scarcity. Scarcity was the best predictor of aid to Kuwait. (On reactions of Vietnam veterans to the Persian Gulf War that may reawaken traumatic memories, see Kobrick, 1993; on views from social and behavioural sciences, see Blumberg and French, 1994.)

Middle East, other   On the Iranian hostage rescue mission, McDermott (1992) uses prospect theory, a descriptive theory of decision-making under risk, to examine the failed rescue mission of the American hostages in Iran in April 1980. Her argument is that President Carter was in a domain of losses both internationally and domestically at the time of the crisis. In this context, loss aversion predisposed him to take military risks to secure the release of the hostages that he would not ordinarily have been willing to pursue.

For additional research see: on post-traumatic nightmares in Kuwait, Barrett and Behbehani (2003); on the importance of human needs during the Gulf War, Tang and Ibrahim (1998); on empathizing with Saddam Hussein, updated, White (1994).

Israeli–Palestinian conflict

Attitudes For an examination of the attitudes of Israeli political leaders about the intifada, Aronoff (2001) evaluated the opinions of Israeli prime ministers Y. Rabin, Y. Shamir, S. Peres and B. Netanyahu to determine the role that ideology, perceptions of time, and cognitive complexity play in explaining whether and to what extent political leaders change their attitudes and policy predispositions towards an international enemy in response to new information. Aronoff used interview data and communications committee meetings to analyse attitudes and policy preferences towards the Palestinian Liberation Organization (PLO). Although each of these prime ministers once supported hardline policies, Rabin and Peres of the Labor Party experienced a shift in attitude and policy, eventually negotiating agreement in which the PLO was recognized. The Likud Party's Shamir and Netanyahu vigorously opposed this change. This analysis evaluates the influence of ideology on image of the enemy, perception of the intifada, reaction to the intifada, and ability to negotiate agreement with the Palestinians for each of these prime ministers. It is determined that individual time horizons help to explain rates and mechanisms of attitudinal and policy change among those with similar ideological leanings and that the perceptions of time may influence an individual's potential for a re-evaluation of the image of the enemy.

Astorino-Courtois (1995) examined structural components of Arab and Israeli decision-makers' beliefs about foreign affairs and their effect on regional relations, using cognitive and behavioural data and a mathematical test model. Cognitive data were collected from texts of decision-makers' public speeches and statements. Data for measures of international behaviour were taken from the Conflict and Peace Data Bank. Analyses indicate cautious decision-making including a tendency towards restraint in uncertain decision situations. Results suggest that prior to the decision to initiate or provoke a war, Arab and Israeli leaders try to minimize perceived conflict escalations by moderating their behaviour.

For an analysis of the effects of Israeli policy shifts on Syrian decision-making regarding the resolution of their conflict, Astorino-Courtois and

Trusty (2000) used an analytic framework developed by Maoz to reconstruct the structure of the Syrian decision problems in light of the positions of the I. Rabin, S. Peres and B. Netanyahu governments. A. Mintz and N. Geva's poliheuristic decision model is applied to evaluate the relationship between the 'difficulty' of the decision task, the process and the outcome. Results indicate that the impact of the Netanyahu government's hard-line policy was to increase the difficulty of a Syrian strategy choice to resolve the conflict, the bargaining position of the Peres government had the same effect, and the Rabin government's moderately hard line allowed the greatest opportunity for agreement.

Concerning cultural identity and the demonization of the relevant other, Bar-On (2000) concludes that trauma in the Middle East is deeply associated with the struggle during the last hundred years between Arabs and Jews. He suggests that there is a subtle need of evolving cultures, that of having a visible enemy. Bar-On argues that heroic myths may organize societies and shape their worldview, even though at the same time they lead to perpetuation of hostilities, projection of hatred, major human losses and repeated traumatization. Such organizing myths are reluctantly abandoned when opportunities for peace arise. He suggests that the prospect of losing one's enemy has generated the current identity crises in Israeli society because it serves to shatter the previously rigid ethos born as a reaction to the Holocaust.

Bar-Tal (1999) examined the extent of the reflections of the Israeli–Arab conflict's ethos in school textbooks. One hundred and twenty-four textbooks on Hebrew language and literature, history, geography and civic studies, approved for use in the school system (elementary, junior-high and high schools in the secular and religious sectors) by the Ministry of Education in March 1994, were content analysed in Israel. The analysis examined the extent to which the textbooks presented societal beliefs reflecting ethos of conflict: societal beliefs of security, positive self-image, victimization, delegitimization of the opponent, unity and peace. The results show that societal beliefs of security received most emphasis followed by societal beliefs of positive self-image and Jewish victimization. The majority of books stereotype Arabs negatively.

Haddad (2002c) examined the attitudes of Lebanese Christians concerning peace with Israel. One thousand residents (aged 18–46+ years) of Lebanon completed surveys concerning issues, attitudes and expectations of likely results. Results show that the respondents accepted different forms of interaction with Israelis: most supported peace, were clearly opposed to the idea of confrontation, and called for a unilateral peace treaty with Israel. Most of the respondents viewed peace as a major reshuffling force capable of restoring their lost political role in the country.

On attitudes towards Palestinian resettlement, Haddad (2002a) conducted a study to assess the impact of social distance on attitudes towards Palestinian resettlement using comprehensive cross-cultural survey research. A survey was done with 688 male and 385 female Lebanese respondents in six subgroups (Maronites, Greek-Catholics, Greek-Orthodox, Shiite, Sunni, Druze). The results are clear and consistent for all Lebanese subgroups. Social distance is a significant predictor of attitudes towards resettlement for all six subgroups. Specifically, social distance is inversely and consistently associated with unfavourable attitudes towards the prospect of the permanent settlement of Palestinian refugees in Lebanon. These findings indicate, on one hand, that the majority of Sunnis and Druze respondents endorse communal ties with Palestinians and approve their permanent economic, social and political integration. However, social distance influences political attitudes towards Palestinian resettlement, namely in the case of Christian and Shiite groups. Hence, for most Lebanese the question is about their own political survival, not Palestinian resettlement. (For research on the negative relationship between a high investment in political Islam and approval of US foreign policy, see Haddad, 2002b.)

Landau, Beit-Hallahmi and Levy (1998) investigated the perception of personal well-being among different segments of Israeli society for various levels of national stress. The three measures utilized (health worries, happiness and coping) were derived from 203 surveys of national samples totalling 112,005 participants, conducted between June 1967 and August 1979. Gender, education, age, religiosity and ethnic origin were correlated with these indicators during periods of low, medium and high national stress. In general, lower levels of well-being were reported by women, the less educated, the older age groups, the religious and those of Eastern origin, as predicted. Contrary to expectation, health worries decreased during times of high national stress.

For an analysis of collective identity, Litvak-Hirsch, Bar-On and Chaitin (2003) examined the ways in which one's perception of the other contributes to processes involved in the construction of collective identity. They present analyses and comparisons of semi-structured interviews – using a dilemma concerning ownership of a house – that were undertaken with twenty Jewish and Palestinian university students, citizens of Israel, who participated in a one-year seminar that dealt with the Palestinian–Israeli conflict. Analyses of the entire sample showed that, during the year, all of the participants enhanced their self-awareness of the complexity of the conflict. Each group emphasized the processes that reflect the role of the conflict in the construction of its collective identity. The Palestinians appeared to be in the process of constructing their identity and the Jews in the process of deconstructing theirs while trying to cope with their need for security during the on-going conflict.

I. Maoz, Ward, Katz and Ross (2002) conducted several studies to investigate the tendency for political antagonists, in the Palestinian–Israeli context, to derogate each other's compromise proposals. In study one, 113 Israeli Jews evaluated an actual Israeli-authored peace plan less favourably when it was attributed to the Palestinians than when it was attributed to their own government. In study two, 72 Israeli Jews and 68 Israeli Arabs similarly devalued a Palestinian plan when it was ascribed to the 'other side'. Furthermore, both Arabs and Jewish 'hawks' (but not Jewish 'doves') perceived a proposal attributed to the doveish Israeli government as relatively bad for their own people and good for their adversaries.

To examine the relationship between political expectations and cultural perceptions, Mishal and Morag (2002) noted that in the various Arab–Israeli peace negotiations that had taken place since the late 1970s, each party entered the process, and continues to function within it, from the vantage point of different political expectations and cultural perceptions. These differences derive from the political features and social structures of the Arab parties and the Israeli side, which range from hierarchical to networked. Israel leans towards hierarchical order, whereas the Arab parties are more networked; these differences in the social and political environments influence the negotiating culture of each party. Hierarchical states develop goal-oriented negotiating cultures, whereas networked states have process-oriented negotiating cultures. The expectations that each side has of the other side to fulfil its part of the bargain are different as well; in hierarchical states such expectations are based on contracts, whereas in networked states such expectations are based on trust. They conclude that because it is unlikely that different cultural perceptions and the gap between the parties can be significantly bridged, it may be possible to cope with mutual problems if all parties were willing to accept a reality of perceptional pluralism.

Attitudes, other   On the influence of the intifada on the perception of the peace process, see a case study by Amir, Yitzhaki-Verner and Bar-On (1996); of Allon and Peres on the Palestinian issue, Ben Yehuda-Agid and Auerbach (1991); of Americans regarding information sources, al-Azzam and Zahir (1990); on societal belief formation,

Bar-Tal (1990, 1998); on siege mentality beliefs in Israel, Bar-Tal and Antebi (1992); on hope and fear regarding the peace process, Bar-Tal and Vertzberger (1997); on American students' reactions to news of the Hebron massacre, Gan, Hill, Pschernig and Zillmann (1996); on attributions and responses of Israeli children and youth to the Arab–Israeli conflict, Hoffman and Bizman (1996); on aspects of army–civilian encounters, I. Maoz (2001); on the 'double marginality' of Palestinian self-categorization, Suleiman (2002); on personality integrative complexity and attitudes, Tibon (2000); on attitudes of Croatian, Israeli and Palestinian children towards war, Jagodic (2000). See also: Bargal (2004); Laor, Wolmer and Cohen (2004); I. Maoz (2003); I. Maoz, Bar-On, Bekerman and Jaber-Massarwa (2004); Okasha (2003); Orr, Sagy and Bar-On (2003); Rouhana (2004).

Trauma   Bar-On (1999) describes the culture of the dying and the culture of the living as two polarities between which Israeli society has been trying to find its way during the last 100 years. He concentrates on the trauma associated with the Palestinian–Israeli conflict when detailing the cultural background of Israeli society. The impact of the peace process in relation to the question of trauma and its relief is examined. Bar-On contends that the Israeli concept of mental health has changed radically during the last 50 years. During the early years, it was based on informal institutions and strong ideologically oriented collective cohesion and combined with a strong demand for denial and suppression of private, emotional needs which were considered to be weakness, and lately, it has moved to the extreme opposite.

For an analysis of the characteristics of calls to Israeli hotlines during the Gulf War, Gilat, Lobel and Gil (1998) present results of a survey of 3,215 calls received at seven telephone emergency service centres (TES) in Israel during the Gulf War, when citizens of Israel experienced severe stress resulting from SCUD missile attacks. Whereas former surveys have shown that characteristics of calls to TES in Israel are generally not affected by external stressogenic events, a remarkable change was recorded in both the quantity and quality of calls received in TES centres in Israel during the Gulf War. The relative frequencies of problem categories presented by callers during the Gulf War revealed a significant increase in 'environmental pressures', a category that reflected the stressful situation of the war, as opposed to intra- or interpersonal problems typical of peacetime calls. A comparison between this group of 'war calls' and a control group of 'non-war calls' revealed that the two groups represented populations of callers differing in socio-demographic characteristics, expectations, and benefits from the calls.

The authors suggest that TES is a source of psychological first-aid in a community crisis situation. (As regards support groups for parents of soldiers in Israel, see Kacen and Sofer 1997.)

Psychological aspects and emotions   Bizman and Hoffman (1993) examined Israeli Jews' (37 male and 59 female university students) causal attribution for the Arab–Israeli conflict, expectations and feelings regarding its course, and preferred strategies of response. Questionnaire data reveal that expectations regarding continuation or escalation of conflict were related to the stability dimension. Increased shame and guilt, reduced pride as Israelis, and anger towards Arabs were associated with assigning the causes of the conflict to Israel. Relative preference for negotiation and concession rather than non-resolution were linked with attributions to uncontrollable internal causes or to controllable unstable ones. Discussion focused on the role of attributional analysis as a heuristic in understanding and predicting individuals' expectations, emotions and policy preferences regarding international conflict.

In a study of stress and burnout related to intifada, Pines (1994) investigated levels of stress and burnout related to the Palestinian intifada among five groups of Israelis: 32 left-wingers, 35 right-wingers, 32 Orthodox Jews, 30 high-ranking officers, and 30 Arabs. The interviewees, who were 16–74 years old, completed a questionnaire presented in personal interviews. Findings suggest that people are most stressed by problems related to spheres of life. However, people do not burn out if they find existential significance in what they do, even if the situation is stressful. Significant differences were found in levels of burnout in the following rank order (with the most burnout listed first): left, Arabs, right, officers and Orthodox Jews. Differences in burnout are explained by the differences in existential significance that the intifada holds for each. The interpretation is supported by different interviews and a burnout workshop conducted with representatives of fourteen peace organizations in Israel.

Rosenbaum and Ronen (1997) investigated the ability of 11–12-year-olds and their parents to infer each other's anxiety level under the threat of missile attacks during the 1991 Gulf War in Israel. An information exchange model for appraising other people's emotions served as the basis for predicting agreement rates among family members. As predicted, children's ratings of parental anxiety were primarily associated with their own anxiety (projected information), whereas parents' ratings of their spouses' and their children's anxiety were primarily predicted from spouses' self-reported anxiety (target-emitted information) and spouses' evaluations of the children's anxiety (shared information), respectively. Mother–father concordance on ratings of each other's and children's anxiety was significantly higher than parent–child agreement on parental and child anxiety. Agreement on parental anxiety among the three sources was partially a function of physical closeness among informants. Results suggest that, at least within the nuclear family, under an external threat inferences about each other's anxiety level are partly based on social exchange of emotionally relevant information.

Psychological aspects, other   On fear overriding hope in Israeli society, see Bar-Tal (2001); on unconscious aspects, Falk (1992); on grief and rage, Gabriel (1992); on the paradox of political relationships, a folie à deux, Lachkar (1994); on reaction of Israeli youth to assassination of Rabin, Raviv, Sadeh, Raviv and Silberstein (1998); on psychological changes in Japanese forces training for the Golan Heights, Kodama, Nomura and Ogasdwara (2000).

Oslo peace agreements   As an example of managing equivocality and relational paradox, Donohue (1998) notes that during the Oslo peace negotiations between the PLO and the Israelis, including the intermediaries, the parties constructed their relational parameters slowly to move them away from a position of isolationist peace to a position of unconditional peace in which they would be able to forge an agreement.

Oslo, other   On peacebuilding by educators, Abu-Nimer (2000); a comment on Abu-Nimer's article, Dane (2000); on the option of a two-state solution, Kelman (1999a); on when settlement and resolution are in conflict for business ventures, Mazen (1998).

Peace initiative   On cooperation on substance abuse as an example of a 'bottom-up' initiative, Isralowitz, Sussman, Afifi and Rawson (2001) describe the working exchange between Israelis, Palestinians and international experts who engaged in a process to promote communications, cooperation and coordination of efforts directed towards peace as well as the prevention and treatment of drug abuse in the region. From 1997 to 1999, a programme of training workshops and courses, drug prevention and treatment skills development and collaborative research was conducted on the basis of mutual respect and cooperation among Palestinians and Israelis. By tapping into the issue of substance abuse and by focusing on its professional and academic dimensions, this initiative engaged representative delegations of the police force, academia, treatment centres and various government ministries. While events of this period underscored the dependence of 'bottom-up' peace initiatives on the prevailing political situation, the experience revealed the vital role of NGO frameworks in providing a safety net for promoting and sustaining relations as well as addressing an issue of common concern. This case study shows that addiction professionals, both clinicians and researchers, can be instrumental in conflict resolution as well as the prevention and treatment of drug abuse. For research on conflict resolution in Israel using toleration, avoidance, self-help, bipartisan negotiation and third-party settlement, see Landau (1997).

Intergroup workshops   Kelman (1998) describes an action research programme devoted to the development of interactive problem-solving – an unofficial third-party approach to resolution of international and intercommunal conflicts, and its application to the Israeli–Palestinian conflict is described. The article summarizes the social-psychological assumptions underlying the approach, referring to (1) the point in the societal and intersocietal process of international conflict at which the individual is the appropriate unit of analysis; (2) the inter-societal character of international conflict and its resolution; (3) conflict as an interactive process with an escalatory, self-perpetuating dynamic; (4) the need to use a wide range of influence processes in international conflict relationships; and (5) conflict as a dynamic phenomenon, marked by the occurrence and possibility of change. Next, the intervention methodology is described, focusing on the problem-solving workshops with politically influential Israelis and Palestinians that the author and his colleagues have been organizing. Recent developments in the work are then presented, including a continuing workshop that met from 1990–3, and then a current joint working group on the final-status political issues in the Israeli–Palestinian negotiations. See also, on promoting joint thinking, Rouhana and Kelman (1994).

Regarding intergroup interaction, I. Maoz (2002) notes that in the past few decades, planned intergroup contact interventions have played an important role in attempts at conflict management and peacebuilding. Based on previous research and observations, the author focuses this research on the question, is there really any contact going on between the groups in conflict? The goal of this study was to construct and apply a measure assessing the extent of intergroup interaction in such interventions. The data were collected through observations of planned encounters between Jews and Arabs that were conducted in Israel in 1999–2000. The findings show variability in the extent of intergroup interaction in the investigated programmes. While the majority of these encounters (about 65 per cent) were characterized by a high extent of intergroup interaction, about 20 per cent of them contained a medium level of interaction and around 15 per cent a low level one. The findings further indicate that programmes targeted at high school students and adults were characterized by higher levels of intergroup interaction while programmes targeted at preschool to 4th grade children and especially programmes targeted at 5th–9th graders included a lower extent of such interaction.

For an analysis of culture, dialogue and perception change, Mollov and Lavie (2001) examined the effects of an intercultural dialogue as a means of peacebuilding on a people-to-people level, with a focus on the Israeli–Palestinian conflict. As respondents, 90 Israeli and 89 Palestinian university students completed questionnaires concerning general impressions of the characteristics of the other side; 33 participants contributing to an Israeli–Palestine dialogue were also assessed. Results show that the religiously based dialogue has the potential to move mutual perceptions to more favourable positions based on the similarities between Islam and Judaism. Such dialogue also clarified to both sides the identification each side has with the same land. It is concluded that the employed peacebuilding method can be useful in the Israeli–Palestinian context and in other acute interethnic conflict venues.

Intergroup workshops, other On a Lewinian approach, see Bargal and Bar (1992); on Jewish-Arab school for peace, Feuerverger (1998).

Policy On Soviet policy towards the Arab–Israeli conflict, see Breslauer (1991).

Culture On Arab communication patterns, see Feghali (1997).

Anti-war groups On objecting Israeli soldiers and Peace Now activists, Linn (1995) interviewed two groups of objecting Israeli reserve soldiers who chose to resolve their dilemmas with the morally controversial war in Lebanon (1982–5) in line with two different morally preferred actions. The first group (Refusers) consisted of 36 soldiers who had refused to serve in Lebanon and received brief sentences in military prison. The second group consisted of 24 Peace Now activists. Both groups completed the Test of Moral Development (Form B). Results indicate that for the Refusers, the right to refuse seemed to emerge directly from the unjust situation in which they found themselves. The Peace Now activists viewed refusal as a dangerous luxury. With respect to a claim for personal moral consistency, Peace Now activists adopted a conventional mode of action: that of group protest civilians. Refusers seemed to be unique in their ability to maintain moral consistency in their action. With respect to a claim for moral integrity, both groups viewed their actions as moral.

Israeli–Palestinian conflict, other   On televised debates, see Bores (2003); on stress and response in Israeli and Palestinian families, see Lavee, Ben-David and Azaiza (1997).

Russia

Arms control   Tudge, Chivian, Robinson, Andreyenkov and Popov (1990–1) surveyed adolescents (aged 10–29 years) in the US (n = 2,695) and USSR (n = 2,781) in 1986 and 1988 to examine the relationship between worry about nuclear war and optimism about the future. Sampling spanned a period in which relations between the two countries had improved. The 1986 participants from both countries indicated that they were very worried about nuclear war (54 per cent for US participants, 93 per cent for USSR ones). In 1988, worry was still high (46 per cent for the US, 88 per cent for the USSR). USSR participants expressed a greater degree of worry about all problem items surveyed except not being able to find a satisfying job (in 1986 and 1988) and getting cancer (only in 1988).

For additional research see: on learning in Soviet strategic policy, Blacker (1991); on perceptions of Western college students about the arms race, Thompson (1991); on interactive learning and arms control, Weber (1991).

Foreign policy   In an edited collection of articles entitled *Learning in US and Soviet foreign policy*, Breslauer and Tetlock (1991) provide descriptions of the part played by learning in international relations. For references to chapters in the book, see: on learning in US policy, Dallin (1991); on attempted learning during the Brezhnev era, Griffiths (1991); on learning, Brezhnev, Gorbachev and 'Reagan doctrine', Hopf (1991); on learning, and Nixon–Kissinger, Larson (1991); on learning about nuclear non-proliferation, Lavoy (1991); on learning about the US policy of arms control, Levine (1991); on use of the term 'learning' in US–Soviet foreign policies, Tetlock (1991); on Soviet policy towards China, Whiting (1991).

Regarding the transition of US–Soviet relations, George (1991) discusses the limited relevance of structural-realist theory, emphasizing the necessity to make use of an alternative theoretical approach that focuses on the impact of domestic structure and politics on a state's foreign policy. Three variables (the security dilemma, ideology and geopolitical aspects) provide a link between international relations theory and political psychology in a discussion of the transition in US–USSR relations between 1985 and 1990. In addition to drawing general lessons from the abortive detente of the 1970s, both superpowers began the task of adapting to important new developments in their internal and external environment. The transition in Soviet–American relations credits important elements of the leadership of both countries with the good sense to rethink the fundamental assumptions, goals and practices that disturbed relations for many years.

Zisk (1990) summarizes the emerging Soviet academic consensus about the need for joint, peaceful solutions to international environmental and security problems and discusses four common themes in the writings of Soviet academics. These themes involve fatalism, the importance of building trust between nations, the current inapplicability of Marxist-Leninist theory, and the value of perestroika. Subgroups of Soviet academics have taken various theoretical approaches to the problem of international conflict resolution. While debates over specific theoretical approaches and state policies regarding international conflict and cooperation continue among Soviet scholars, the old framework of class struggle has been replaced by a worldview that recognizes the importance of shared interests.

Koopman, Shiraev, McDermott, Jervis and Snyder (1998) examined the views of Russian and American elites involved in international relations and national security. In 1992, a survey (using parallel questions in Russian and English) among elites in Russia and the US to enquire about views concerning international relations and foreign policy was conducted. The results suggested that Russian and American elites' thinking was organized by a shared belief schema that could be labelled cooperative internationalism or support for detente, using concepts derived from previous investigations. Also, both Russian and American elites seemed to hold parallel belief structures that could be labelled militant internationalism or support for deterrence. Among the Russians, these two types of beliefs accounted for a significant degree of variance in perceptions of national and international security threats and attributions for liberalization of the Soviet Union towards East Europe. Among the Americans, however, perceptions of national and international security threats and attributions for liberalization of the Soviet Union were seldom related to these two types of beliefs. Koopman et al. conclude that this may help to account for the dramatic

differences found by country in perceived security threats and attributions for Soviet liberalization.

Foreign policy, other   On Reagan and foreign policy, see Shimko
(1992); on the Cuban missile crisis, Blight and Lang (1995); on Soviet
policy towards Western Europe since World War Two, J. Haslam (1991);
on policy relevant theory and the challenge of diagnosis: the end of the
Cold War as a case study, Herrmann (1994).

Chernobyl and the Armenian earthquake   On the psychosocial
aftermath, see Giel (1991).

Afghanistan   On Jimmy Carter and Soviet invasion, see Glad
and Whitmore (1991).

Ecology problems   On Soviet perceptions, see Barbara W. Hall
(1990).

Russia, other   On security, oil, and the Russo-Chechen conflicts, see Ashour (2004); on American and post-Soviet perspectives on
contemporary issues in psychology, Halpern and Voiskounsky (1997);
on the American Psychological Association's relations with Russian
psychologists, Nissim-Sabat (1996); on children of glasnost, Pearson
(1990); on perestroika, glasnost and international cooperation, Rakos
(1991); on 1980–90 changes in American attitudes towards the Soviet
Union, Richman (1991); on intergroup relations in the state of the
former Soviet Union, Hagendoorn, Linssen and Tumanov (2001); on
Soviet behaviour towards Arab clients, McInerney (1992); on common
security, R. R. Rogers (1991).

Specific areas

Northern Ireland   Cassidy and Trew (1998) observe that the
conflict in Northern Ireland is often described in terms of a clash of
identities, national and religious. This study aimed to determine the
relative importance of these identities using a multidimensional approach
to examine the identity structures of 216 students. Analyses revealed that
national and religious identities were accorded low salience and centrality
relative to other identities. The study also investigated relations between
a variety of identity dimensions derived from two identity traditions:
social identity theory and identity theory. The differing patterns of

relationships to emerge across groups and across identities suggest that the process of identification in Northern Ireland is a complex one.

For an exploration of the relationship between history and identity, Devine-Wright (2001) used a social psychological perspective to explore the role of historical commemoration in contexts of intergroup conflict. A theoretical position was developed that indicated socio-political and psychological functions of commemoration at the group and individual levels of analysis. It was also claimed that commemoration can serve to reduce group cohesion if the manner in which commemoration is conducted is perceived to clash with important shared values. One hundred and three respondents (aged 18–86 years) completed a postal survey focused upon the Orange parades in Northern Ireland. At the intergroup level of analysis, not surprisingly, Catholic respondents evaluated the commemorations more negatively than Protestant respondents did. At the intragroup level of analysis, Protestant respondents who had participated in the parades were more likely to evaluate the parades positively, to oppose change and to regard history as being a more important foundation of their sense of identity, in comparison to Protestants who chose not to participate in the parades. For a comment on the research, see Pick (2001).

On 'deserving' victims of political violence, Knox (2001) notes that the plight of the victims of political violence in Northern Ireland and the enduring suffering of their families recently has assumed much greater public prominence. Some see this new-found concern by government for victims as no more than a necessary part of the political and public relations management of the prisoners' early release programme within which victims were mere pawns in the wider unstoppable agenda for a peace deal. Preconceived notions of perpetrators and victims have been politically contested in ways which suggest there are those who are 'deserving' or 'undeserving' of victimhood status. This article considers one category of victim, those subject to paramilitary 'punishment' – beatings and shootings – and argues that they have become expendable and legitimate targets for violence in Northern Ireland. They are expendable in the sense that any attempt to deal with the problem in a serious way would have widespread political ramifications for parties currently in devolved government. They are legitimate in that victims' culpability derives from the communities within which they live and their 'punishment' is meted out by paramilitaries acting on the communities' behalf.

For an analysis of group identity and expectations for the future, Leach and Williams (1999) conducted a study to address shortcomings in the examination of group identity and actual intergroup conflict, with a specific focus on Northern Ireland. Much of the conflict in Northern Ireland is based on investments in one of three opposing political futures possible for the region: remaining part of Britain, joining Ireland, or becoming independent. Speculative scenarios describing each of these futures were randomly assigned to 71 Protestant and 71 Catholic undergraduates in Northern Ireland, and their expectations regarding material and civic improvement for their ingroup and peace and reconciliation between the groups were assessed. Two dimensions of religious identity, measured by the Identity and Public subscales of R. Luhtanen and J. Crocker's (1992) Collective Self-Esteem Scale (CSES), moderated the differences between groups, but only for their expectations of peace and reconciliation. The authors found that stronger expectations of improvement for the ingroup were related to higher scores on the Public subscale, regardless of religion or the political future presented. Therefore it was concluded that group identity had a complex, context-dependent relationship to intergroup conflict.

On policing, Hamilton (1995) reviews research on the key issues facing the police service in Northern Ireland. The relationship of the (then) Royal Ulster Constabulary (RUC) with the community and its paramilitary role to counter the threat posed by the Irish Republican Army are described. The RUC has historically been associated with the Protestant/Unionist community, and this has caused problems in its relationship with the Catholic community. Although attitudes towards the RUC are by no means homogeneous within the Catholic community, a significant proportion of Catholics continue to perceive the force as discriminatory and politically partisan. The RUC's legacy has left an undercurrent of hostility and distrust, particularly among working-class Catholics. The force's accountability, the procedures for investigating complaints against the force, the low percentage of Catholic recruitment, and issues surrounding community policing are also examined.

For a study of the use of the word 'alienation', Dunn and Morgan (1995) examine the social and political dynamics that resulted in the word being used by and about Protestants. The extent to which the current application of the word reflects, or has an impact on, community relations and the possibility of a peaceful and normal society is also explored. Forty people, including religious leaders, politicians and educationalists, were interviewed in 1993 before the ceasefires. All respondents were Protestant. An attempt was made to understand what they meant when they used the word 'alienation'. Results indicate the existence of real and complex feelings of unease and uncertainty among Protestants, justifying the use of the term. These feelings are explored and analysed with respect to a range of themes including politics, legislation, security, media, culture, identity and community development. Implications for economic and social policy are examined along with the dangers to the peace process.

Ferguson (2000) compares the level of just world beliefs held by Northern Irish Protestant and Catholic 16–18-year-olds (n = 181), before and after the 1994 paramilitary ceasefires. Analysis of the data indicated that the Protestant sample held stronger just world beliefs than the Catholic sample, while the introduction of peace to the streets of Northern Ireland strengthened the level of beliefs in a just world held by both ethnopolitical groups. Religious discrimination was suggested as the cause of the weaker just world beliefs among the Catholic sample, while the increase in just world beliefs after the ceasefire was due to an increased hope for peace in Northern Ireland.

Northern Ireland, other On psychology's contribution to understanding conflict and promoting peace, see Cairns (1994), Cairns, Wilson, Gallagher and Trew (1995); on British and Irish memories of ethnic conflict, Cairns, Lewis, Mumcu and Waddell (1998); on the effects of conflict on young people, Gallagher (2004); on terrorism, culture and communal conflict, Grove and Carter (1999); on the impact of the Northern Ireland conflict on social identity, groupthink and integrative complexity in Great Britain, Hergovich and Olbrich (2003); on individual and situational factors related to terrorism, Heskin (1994); on ceasefires and increasing drug use, Higgins and McElrath (2000); on use of media by terrorists, Kingston (1995); on Gerry Adams and the peace process, Mastors (2000); on political socialization among young Loyalists, McAuley (2004); on families of politically motivated prisoners, McEvoy, O'Mahony, Horner and Lyner (1999); on therapeutic responses to community violence, Reilly, McDermott and Coulter (2004).

South Africa For a study of criminal violence replacing political violence, Barbarin, Richter, de Wet and Wachtel (1998) collected data from archival sources. Representative national surveys, and a prospective study of the effects of urbanization, are used to depict trends in violence and reactions of citizens during South Africa's transition to democracy. Violence has shifted in form from state-sponsored attacks on opponents of apartheid, to politically motivated interethnic conflict, and finally to community violence classified as familial and criminal. Archival data show clearly that politically motivated violence declined precipitously by the end of 1994. Although personal and property crimes have increased modestly and total violence has remained stable, the level of fear reported by citizens has not. Even though the direct experience of violence reported by individuals did not increase, the overwhelming majority of South Africans felt less safe in 1994 both inside and outside of their homes than at the height of political violence. The post-transformation peace is being lost to anxiety about criminal violence.

On building communities of peace, Kagee, Naidoo and Van Wyk (2003) note that while political conflicts in many countries have resulted in large-scale destruction and loss of life, South Africa has been successful in avoiding a violent conflict following the demise of apartheid. The Truth and Reconciliation Commission (TRC) has been seen as an important mechanism contributing to South Africa's successful management of its political challenges. Yet, the legacy of apartheid continues beyond the work of the TRC, and several social problems such as poverty, unemployment, crime and substance abuse continue to affect many South African communities. Psychology is uniquely poised to assist in addressing these social problems and in contributing to the development of a community of peace. Academic psychology departments have responded by implementing an undergraduate programme aimed at training professional counsellors to respond to community needs in post-apartheid South Africa.

The use of 'forums' is described by Robinson (1998). After the Mandela government took power in 1994 in South Africa, one of its highest priorities was providing power to the impoverished rural areas, and particularly the infrastructure-poor black 'townships'. In addition to a scarcity of resources, multiple stakeholders with very different agendas were integrally a part of the decision-making process. To this extent, what happened with the electricity industry is a metaphor for the multiple issues – social, economic and political – which had to be negotiated by the new society. The multiple stakeholders were brought together in a 'forum', a non-regulatory advisory body which was designed to specifically include all relevant interested parties in an open ('transparent') problem-solving process. This forum system was extensively used in the 18–24 months immediately before and after the 1994 elections to deal with a host of issues. The National Electricity Forum was one of the earliest and most successful of these forums. This case reviews the build-up to the 1994 elections, describes how the forum process worked, and outlines its structure.

On the definition of violence in South African newspapers, Seedat (1999) suggests that in the absence of a national health information system in South Africa, the control and management of violence tends to be guided by the media. A content analysis of 241 South African newspaper reports (published in 1987, 1990 and 1995) reveals how the media present a primary and secondary construction of violence. The primary construction, based on the few articles that provide demographic information, portrays violence as a criminal-cum-political and public phenomenon that mainly involves young African men. In this primary construction the key instruments of violence are guns, sharp objects, hands, fists and explosives. The secondary construction, based on the omission of details, places the accent on the weapons of violence rather than on the victims and perpetrators. Violence is defined as a ubiquitous, faceless, meaningless, unpredictable and incomprehensible behavioural act. Such skewed constructions may spawn spectacular prevention initiatives that have limited impact. The need for public health workers to engage the media critically and work for the creation of a comprehensive health information system is emphasized.

Concerning grief work in Mozambique and South Africa, Errante (1999) examines the manner in which socialization patterns learned in times of protracted and violent conflict in South Africa and Mozambique may influence, as well as be influenced by, the quality of peace work. It addresses the legacy of these socialization patterns for sustaining peace work, how community healing resources redirected these patterns during early phases of reconciliation in both countries, and how the strain of on-going peace compromises the community resources that made these early efforts possible. Peace requires that reconciling groups surrender aspects of the social, symbolic and material world that sustained them during periods of conflict, and this can provoke feelings of loss and grief. An important dimension of peace, therefore, is grief work: reconciling groups must discharge these feelings of loss, while securing the symbolic and material resources with which they can build post-conflict 'reconciled identities'.

Truth and Reconciliation Commission   On perceptions of psychological healing, see de la Rey and Owens (1998); on remorse, forgiveness and rehumanization, Gobodo-Madikizela (2002); a review of the book: *The South African Truth Commission: the politics of reconciliation,* Shea (2002); on national unity at the expense of economic and social reparation, van der Walt, Franchi and Stevens (2003).

South Africa, other   On televised debates, see Bores (2003); on discourses of black South Africans, Duncan (2003); on post-apartheid race, ethnicity and intercultural relations, Franchi (2003a, 2003b; Franchi and Swart, 2003); on who pays for peace, Hamber (2001); on Nelson Mandela as partisan and peacemaker, Lieberfeld

(2003); on psychology, conflict and peace, Louw and Van Hoorn (1997); on violence against women, Padayachee and Singh (1998); on 'race' in psychology's discourse, Stevens (2003); on reciprocity in dyadic foreign policy behaviour, Van Wyk and Radloff (1993).

Countries with few references (listed alphabetically)

Afghanistan   On women under the Taliban, see Fish and Popal (2003).

Angola   On psychological interventions and post-war reconstruction, see Wessells and Monteiro (2001).

Argentina   On treatment of mass trauma due to socio-political events, see Edelman, Kersner, Kordon and Lagos (2003).

Armenia   On a country's history of challenges, Karakashian (1998) gives the example of a small nation of 3.5 million people, selected to conceptualize thriving in reference to the individual, the nuclear and extended family, the community, the state, the geopolitics of the land, the diaspora and the cultural traditions. Armenia is selected not only because it is unique in the amount of adversity it has endured, but also because, as a very small nation, it has survived the challenges of centuries whereas other comparable civilizations have not. Karakashian analyses the cultural and geohistorical characteristics of Armenia, the development and role of a diaspora in the preservation of identity, and the contribution of parenting in the development of resilience and thriving. She concludes that the strength of the family and child-rearing practices contributes to thriving of the individual and society. In addition, cultural factors, such as the arts, literature, sports, institutions, the church, intercultural networks and the need to make up for the damages of genocide, earthquakes and other adversities, contribute to the strength of the people. She proposes that these characteristics of one society, albeit a small one, are suggestive of the universal human characteristics that contribute to thriving.

Asia   Montiel (2003) presents a contextualized psychology of peace in Asia that considers features of direct and structural violence in the region. In Asia, direct violence takes the form of intrastate intermediate-sized armed conflicts. Structural violence, on the other hand, is associated with foreign invasions and authoritarian regimes, chronic poverty and cultural heterogeneity of non-migrant groups marked by asymmetric power relations. Because of the nature of social conflict in Asia, Montiel suggests that peace psychologists working in this region should focus on active nonviolent political transformation, healing protracted-war traumas, beliefs supporting economic democratization, social voice and identity, culture-sensitive political peacemaking and psychopolitical aspects of federalizing to address a territorial conflict.

A foreword to a special issue of *Peace and Conflict: Journal of Peace Psychology* on Asian peace psychology is provided by Wagner (2003). See also: on the contribution of Asian peace psychology, Leung (2003).

Australia   Wessells and Bretherton (2000) discuss the psychological dimensions of reconciliation with indigenous peoples in Australia, and develop a tripartite framework for conceptualizing reconciliation as a process of systems change that involves coming to terms with the past, building peace and nonviolent conflict resolution, and establishing social justice. They suggest that work on reconciliation needs to be multicultural, and that to impose Western views and methods may inflict damage and continue the history of oppression. By working in partnership with local communities, psychologists are seen as helping to create culturally relevant approaches that integrate local resources with Western views and tools.

Bosnia-Herzegovina   On the role of artistic processes in peace-building, see Zelizer (2003).

Brazil   On uneasy peace, the intertribal relations in Brazil's Upper Xingu, see Gregor (1990); on assessing Brazil's culture of peace, Milani and Branco (2004).

Cambodia   On planning and change, Hill (2000) questions the appropriateness of highly structured strategic planning approaches in situations of complexity and change, using the Cambodian–German Health Project as a case study. The Cambodian–German Health Project was initiated in October 1995 as a bilateral health aid project between the German government and the government of the Kingdom of Cambodia, but was disrupted by military action that occurred in 1997. Following the military action, the project was initially suspended, then substantially redrafted within a new framework of assistance, and eventually re-established after an interval of eight months. Based on participant observation and organizational analysis in the Cambodian public health sector, Hill examines the rhetoric of values, objectives and strategies outlined in the original project documents and their assumptions and implications, and the responses to the changing political situation. He demonstrates the limitations of these planning processes in complex situations of high uncertainty, with little reliable information and a rapidly changing environment. He recommends changes that shift the focus away from planning towards informed strategic management that enables more rapid response to emerging risks and opportunities.

Central Europe   On psychological notes, Scheye (1991) describes the impact of the post-World War Two division of Eastern Europe into a region dominated by Soviet communism on individual and collective psychic structures. Interviews conducted in Central Europe in the summer and autumn of 1990 suggest that many Central European citizens experienced pre-1989 Soviet communist hegemony in terms of a true/private versus a false/public self split. The Central European self was split along three distinct and separate dimensions: (1) national–international; (2) civil society–government; and (3) intrapsychically. The divided self prompted people to create inner retreats to protect and expose their true selves. As the external communist coercion disappeared, the intimate bonds between and among true selves dissolved, giving rise to a Central European identity crisis.

For lessons from ethnic conciliation in Eastern Europe, I. Shapiro (1999) describes an evaluation of an initiative to conciliate conflicts among and between minorities and majority group members at five sites in Bulgaria, the Czech Republic, Hungary and Slovakia. Case analysis of the Partners for Democratic Change's Local Ethnic Conciliation Programme examined social psychological factors in resolving ethnic minority–majority conflicts, adaptation of a Western conflict resolution model, strategic development of citizen-based initiatives, and the role of conflict resolution in social change and development of civil society. By self-defined standards, the projects seem successful and have achieved some narrowly defined goals, but the uniqueness of each project suggests a need to develop site-specific criteria. There was limited effectiveness in improving minority–majority group relations. Lessons discussed include bridging ethnic and civic identities, the importance of middle-range theory and application, balancing prescriptive and elicitive models of conflict resolution, conflict resolution as agent of social change, networking to establish roots in the community, and working with moderate groups.

China   On Sino-Japanese relations and national stereotypes, Y. Kashima et al. (2003) suggest that national stereotypes may provide a useful social psychological perspective in which to consider intergroup relations between national groups. They explored auto-stereotypes and hetero-stereotypes of China and Japan to shed light on one of the most critical intergroup relations in East Asia, namely Sino-Japan relations. Chinese and Japanese undergraduate students see themselves as more likeable and warmer than the other, though they both view Japan as more competent than China. They also examined hypotheses that current stereotypes may reflect shared perceptions of the past international conflicts, and may be influenced by the way people frame the international circumstance of their own country – namely, whether to regard it as linked to Asia or to the Pacific Rim. Moderate support was found for these ideas. Chinese who regarded past Sino-Japan conflicts as more important tended to have a more negative auto-stereotype, but Japanese who did so held a somewhat more positive auto-stereotype. Japanese students who linked Japan to the Pacific Rim more strongly held more positive stereotypes of themselves and Chinese, although there was no relation between this belief and stereotypes among Chinese students.

On cooperative and competitive conflict, Tjosvold, Leung and Johnson (2000; Tjosvold, Hui and Yu, 2003) apply M. Deutsch's theory of cooperation and competition, particularly in terms of understanding conditions and dynamics through which conflict becomes constructive, to the collectivist culture of China. Their studies show that the Chinese have been found to use open discussion productively, especially within a cooperative context, and to value relationship-oriented democratic leadership. Research in China is beginning to challenge and extend Deutsch's theory.

China, other   On Chinese business negotiating style, see T. Fang (1999); on constructive conflict in international business, Tjosvold, Hui and Law (2001); on the strategic basis of learning in US policy towards China, 1949–88, Garrett (1991).

Colombia   On peace cultures, see de Valderrama, Lopez and Gomez (2003).

Croatia   On homicides in war and peace, Pozgain, Mandic and Barkic (1998) conducted an interdisciplinary investigation of homicides in the Osijek area during the war (1991–4) and pre-war periods (1988–91). Similarities between the 35 pre-war and 102 wartime perpetrators are related to social-demographic characteristics. Nevertheless, significant differences are found in the homicidal method of selection of victims; almost one-half of the pre-war homicides were the results of marital conflict, a significantly larger proportion than during war. In the pre-war homicides, there were more victims that initiated the conflict, while in the war homicides, there were more victims who were passive within the conflict. Also during the war period, a significantly larger number of homicides were committed with firearms. The major contributing factors in homicide genesis were acute alcohol intoxication and personality disorder among perpetrators. Besides these factors, the war stressors and access to firearms were significant factors during the war homicides. The authors conclude that prevention efforts should be directed towards consequential measures and further investigation suggests that the emphasis must be put on victimological aspects of the homicide problem. See also: on Adam Curle healing wounds of war, Mitchels (2003).

Cuba   On the missile crisis, see Sergeev, Akimov, Lukov and Parshin (1990); on ontologies, problem presentation and the missile crisis, Sylvan and Thorson (1992).

Cyprus   On integrating conflict resolution training and consultation, see L. Diamond and Fisher (1995).

Czechoslovakia   On 'from revolution to reconstruction', Drapela (1992) discusses the positive outcomes of Czechoslovakia's 'velvet revolution' in 1989 and problems that the country has to cope with. Of particular concern are three areas: the legacy of communist rule, relations between Czechs and Slovaks and the ruined national economy. These problems have affected the psychological function of people. Episodes of anxiety and depression seem to be the most frequent complaints made by clients. It appears that most helping professionals in Czechoslovakia are reasserting their original mission, to assist people rather than manipulate them.

Eastern Europe   On militant nationalism, Pick (1997) discusses the causes of militant nationalism specific to the historical time and region. Specifically, four hypotheses are offered: (1) nationalism went under ground and in the former satellite nations, it emerged from something like a deep freeze reconstituted in its 1940s form because it was virtually outlawed under communism; (2) the stage was set for a new content to fit into the same mould, because communist ideology was paranoid and militant nationalism happened to be a beautiful fit; (3) the fall of communism brought about an identity crisis in many individuals, and a chauvinistic national identity filled the vacuum; and (4) a high incidence of victimization in the region's population was also conducive to making militant nationalism attractive. The hypotheses are supported by examples.

El Salvador On Ignacio Martin-Baro, a personal remembrance, see Kelman (1995b).

England On Churchill–Roosevelt bases-for-destroyers exchange, Gold and Raven (1992) use B. H. Raven's power/interaction model to analyse the strategies employed by Winston Churchill in 1940 to influence Franklin Roosevelt to exchange 50 US destroyers for the use of British bases. The influence strategy used the six bases of power, with the subtle use of referent power being of critical importance. Stage-setting devices, ameliorative strategies, motivations, extrinsic goals, effectiveness of the strategies used, and the attempts to resist them were also examined. Also noted is the effectiveness of complex tactics such as using indirect informational power, avoiding reactance, phrasing what might have been considered coercive power so that it appeared to be informational power with fear appeal, interpretative commitment, and the effective use of third parties to enhance influence.

On the operational code of Prime Minister Tony Blair, Schafer and Walker (2001) use operational code analysis to determine propensities for Prime Minister Blair's leadership in the foreign policy domain. The 'Verbs In Context System' of operational code content analysis is explained and employed to analyse Blair's speeches. They proceed to expand the operational code construct – a fairly static conceptualization used to build indexes of philosophical and instrumental beliefs and to create a continuum measuring cooperation and conflict behaviour. A more 'domain-specific' and dynamic operational code conceptualization is developed that allows resulting profiles to account for contextual changes in cognitive and affective attributes. They also compare Blair's diagnostic, choice and shift propensities towards democracies and dictatorships and use the results to investigate the 'democratic peace' phenomenon. Evidence is also presented that supports cultural explanations for peace between democracies, a more dynamic view of personality as it operates within political contexts, and the presence of institutional role variables associated with the office of prime minister.

On British decisions during the Munich and Polish crises, Walker and Watson (1994) address the impact of crisis management strategies, stress and groupthink conditions on the integrative complexity of British decision-makers in ten decision-making episodes during two

Anglo-German crises in 1938 and 1939. A systematic random sample of Prime Minister N. Chamberlain's statements during British cabinet deliberations in the intragovernmental arena and British messages to Germany in the intergovernmental arena during the acute phase of each crisis was scored for integrative complexity. ANOVA demonstrated a significant independent relationship between strategy and integrative complexity plus a significant interaction effect between strategy and arena on integrative complexity. There were significant differences in Chamberlain's integrative complexity between early and later episodes of the Polish conflict in the intragovernmental arena. No such differences were found with the Munich conflict.

Eritrea   On war trauma among young people, see Farwell (2003/2004).

Estonia   On group process in the resolution of ethnonational conflicts, see Apprey (2001).

Eurasia   On a review of van Tongeren, van de Veen and Verhoeven's collection describing extensive resources and information about conflict prevention, see Ehteshami (2003).

Europe   On learning in US policy, Thies (1991).

Germany   On Roosevelt and the 1938 Munich crisis, Farnham (1992) compares prospect theory with rational choice theory in explaining President Roosevelt's decision-making during the Munich crisis in September 1938. Roosevelt's decision-making manifested a number of phenomena associated with prospect theory, including a change in the decision frame and corresponding preference reversal, risk acceptance to avoid loss, and the operation of certainty effects. An analysis of Roosevelt's decision-making behaviour during the crisis shows that prospect theory does in fact explain it more satisfactorily than does the theory of rational choice. In addition, the analysis suggests that affect may sometimes play a role in causing decision frames to change.

On structures of national identity in East and West Germany, Westle (1992) analyses representative, longitudinal surveys in 1990 and 1991 comparing East and West Germany after their unification. No change was found in the West Germans' affective support for political groups and activities when compared to international information. There was no extreme form of nationalism. East Germans identified largely with non-political Germany. Conflicts were found between the former East

German political party and the united Germany. Affective support was absent. While West Germans gave diversified support to their democratic form of government, East Germans relied only on their formal political evaluations. Westle suggested that support for legitimizing political processes would depend largely on the economic and political output or performance in East Germany.

For additional research on the status of psychological peace research, see Boehnke (1992); on psychosocial aspects of German unification, Maaz (1992); on media coverage of conflict between the US and Libya in 1986, Staab and Wright (1991).

Greece   On identities and psychodynamics of Greek–Turkish relations, Volkan and Itzkowitz (2000) examine the evolution of the modern Turkish and Greek identities and the psychological forces at work, both consciously and unconsciously, in the conflictual relationship between these two groups. They examine history through a psychoanalytic lens. They describe how historians and psychoanalysts may collaborate in illustrating how and why identity issues of large groups emerge as a silent, but important, factor in international relationships.

Volkan and Itzkowitz trace the intermittent border disputes between Turkey and Greece to unelaborated losses surrounding the rise and fall of the Ottoman Empire. Generations of Greeks and Turks, they claim, have incorporated mental representations of past glories and past humiliations – the Greek loss of Constantinople to the Turks in 1453 and the Turkish loss of the Ottoman Empire – into their collective national identities. Collective narcissistic injuries, never properly mourned, become transformed into feelings of victimization. These transgenerationally transmitted 'chosen traumas' continue to nourish violent outbreaks in Turkish–Greek relations. They are tied to their respective national identities.

Guatemala   On a K'iche' Mayan narrative of remembrance and forgetting, Foxen (2000) analyses collective and individual memory processes following a situation of war and terror in Guatemala. Nearly two decades after the most brutal period of a 36-year civil war, the notions of memory and truth are seen as critical socio-political issues; institutional memory projects have taken an important place in the peace process and in Mayanist political struggles. For many Mayan Indians, however, there is no unified narrative of social memory. The post-war memory work of many Mayan Indians vacillates between discourses and strategies used to make sense out of a chaotic past and an unstable present. By examining the story of a transnational K'iche' Mayan man,

Foxen problematizes the notion of social memory and truth as used conventionally in institutional political discourse. Scientific (psychiatric) literature on trauma and violence is seen as framing memory within Western assumptions regarding individualism, morality and narrative coherence. It is argued that, for Mayans whose memory work falls outside the boundaries of such institutions and discourses, the ability to balance a variety of worldviews and explanations for past brutality becomes a crucial coping mechanism in the fragmented post-war era. For additional research on developmental transformation of racially oppressed Mayans, see Quintana and Segura-Herrera (2003).

India   On discriminatory policy and the outbreak of ethnopolitical violence, see Lounsbery and Pearson (2003).

Japan   On patriotism, nationalism and internationalism, Karasawa (2002) examined national attitudes among Japanese citizens. A National Identity Scale was developed and administered to a non-student sample (n = 385; aged 19–81 years) and an undergraduate sample (n = 586) in a metropolitan area of Japan. The results revealed aspects that are common (i.e. etic) to different nationalities and those that are indigenous (i.e. emic) to Japanese people. Factor analyses identified etic factors of patriotism (i.e. love of the homeland), nationalism (belief in superiority over other nations), and internationalism (preference for international cooperation and unity). Attachment to the ingroup and ethnocentrism were thus shown to be separate dimensions. Distinct from these factors, commitment to national heritage emerged as an emic component of Japanese national identity. The discriminant validity of these factors was demonstrated in differential relationships with other variables, such as ideological beliefs and amount of knowledge. Commitment to national heritage was associated with conservatism, whereas internationalism was related to liberal ideology, a high level of media exposure and knowledge of international affairs.

For a study of psychological effect of the Nagasaki atomic bombing on survivors, Ohta et al. (2000) conducted a mental health survey using a 30-item General Health Questionnaire (GHQ-30) and an interview survey of an atomic bombing experience with survivors of the Nagasaki atomic bombing in 1997. At home visit interviews, complete answers to the GHQ-30 were obtained from 3,756 subjects (aged 51–99 years). Overall psychological distress measured on the basis of the GHQ-30 was greater in the atomic bombing survivors than in the controls. As for the contents of psychological distress, those concerning emotion such as anxiety and depression were milder in survivors than in the controls, but those related to social activities such as apathy, disturbance of human relations, and loss of enjoyment of living were more severe. Furthermore, recurring and distressing recollection of the experience of the atomic bombing, suspicion over the relationship between the bombing and an unhealthy physical condition, and the experience of witnessing death or severe injury of close relatives due to the atomic bombing were significantly related to the degree of psychological distress of the survivors.

Honda et al. (2002) studied the mental health conditions among atomic bomb survivors in Nagasaki. A mental health survey was conducted using a twelve-item version of the General Health Questionnaire (GHQ-12) and a mail survey on atomic bomb exposure conditions and lifestyle using a self-administered questionnaire. A total of 3,526 atomic bomb survivors (aged 50–80+ years) in Nagasaki responded and a high GHQ-12 score, as defined when the responses to four or more items were positive, was observed in 296 (8.4 per cent) of the sample. They found that the risk of a high GHQ-12 score will decrease 0.98-fold with every one-year increase in age, and will increase 1.45-fold and 1.70-fold in those who lost family members due to the bombing and those who had acute symptoms, respectively, compared with those who did not. It was evident that the atomic bomb exposure has affected survivors' mental health and that the care of their mental health is important (see also, Sawada, Chaitin and Bar-On, 2004).

Japan, other   On the Yasukuni shrine, see Breen (2004); on scapegoating blacks, Hughes (2003); on the second generation of atomic bomb survivors, Tatara (1998); on the lantern floating ritual, Warner (2001).

Korea   On attitudes and identity of South and North Koreans, Kim and Oh (2001) conducted two studies investigating the explicit and implicit attitudes towards, and identification with, South and North Korea by a sample of South Koreans (aged 18–34 years) and North Koreans (aged 19–50 years) who voluntarily defected to the South. North Korean defectors showed (a) more positive evaluations of South Korea on explicit self-report measures, but more favourable evaluations of the North on an implicit measure, and (b) on average, North–South neutral identity on an explicit measure, but stronger self-association with the North on an implicit measure. In contrast, South Koreans indicated consistently positive attitudes towards, and identification with, the South on both explicit and implicit measures.

Kim (2003) conducted a follow-up study of the research by Kim and Oh in 2001, who reported the existence of implicit (non-conscious) prejudicial attitudes towards South and North Korea by South Koreans and by North Koreans who voluntarily defected to South Korea, although the two groups showed no difference in explicit (conscious) forms of prejudice. This study tested the explicit and implicit attitudes of South Koreans initially reported in 1998, by assessing the attitudes shortly after the North and South Korea Summit held in June 2000, as well as two years later in 2002. A substantial reduction in South Koreans' explicit negative attitudes against North Korea was found shortly after the summit, but the reduction waned two years later, relative to the initial data reported in 1998. In contrast, little change was observed in implicit pro-South attitudes across the three different times.

Kosovo   On lessons for the documentation of war crimes: Alison Smith (2000), based upon experiences of the International Crisis Group's Humanitarian Law Documentation Project in Western Kosovo, advances a series of recommendations for effective intervention by aid workers in areas where considerable trauma has been inflicted on civilians. In particular, she argues that in documenting war crimes, the primary responsibility of the interviewer is to the well-being of the witness. This includes not only emergency survival needs such as adequate shelter, food and clothing; it also means taking care of their mental health needs. This should be done by training interviewers in recognizing symptoms of mental disorders and providing immediate assistance for those who need it as well as ensuring that there are facilities available in the longer term to address the inevitable consequences of mass violence.

In order to provide this type of assistance, the mental health needs of humanitarian workers themselves must also be addressed. There must be adequate facilities staffed by experienced people to help both local and international workers deal with the type of work they are doing. In both of these situations, the persons providing training and treatment must themselves be trained in post-conflict situations and issues arising as a result of mass trauma. For additional research on psychological aspects of the crisis, see White (2000).

Latin America   On explaining the long peace, see Centeno (2001); on metaphors for regional peace, Rohrer (1991).

Liberia   On African peacekeeping and Sierra Leone, see Olonisakin (2003).

Macedonia   For a book about conflict resolution, see Ackerman (2002); on before and after trauma, Broughton (2003); on between a bad peace and a good war, Hislope (2003).

Pakistan   On profiling the politically violent, Khan and Smith (2003) demonstrate that empirical evidence relating individualism–collectivism (IC) to socio-political factors is still scarce. Their survey explores how factors generally purported to represent an Asian society (i.e. collectivism) relate to context-specific characteristics of political groups within that society (i.e. the endorsement of political violence). The city of Karachi in Pakistan has a long history of political, sectarian and criminal violence, economic inequality and complex associations between religion and politics. Where traditional occupational routes are blocked, violent activism may provide an alternative, politicized route to the attainment of life goals. This leads to the hypothesis that political violence has its roots in individualist self-construal and in individualist value orientations. There were 195 political activists surveyed from Muttahida Quami Movement (MQM), a violent secular party, and from Jamaat e Islami (JI), a nonviolent Islamist party. Results support the reasoning that individualist violence in the Karachi political context is related to the achievement of status and 'culture-change' within a discourse of resistance politics.

Philippines   On the social psychology of People Power II, Macapagal and Nario-Galace (2003) looked at the nonviolent process of the Philippines' People Power II, using first-person observations and newspaper accounts. This phenomenon is explained in terms of subjective experiences of the activists, organizational features of the political movement and collective behaviours involved in active nonviolence. During People Power II, participants felt angry, afraid, stressed and yet happy. Psychological antidotes to fear were Filipino cultural dispositions such as 'bahala na' (leave it to God), 'lakas ng loob' (inner strength), and one's Christian faith. On the cognitive level, People Power II participants believed that Philippine President Joseph Estrada was guilty of the charges filed against him, the judicial and political systems were no longer effective, and active nonviolence could make Estrada step down from office. Civil society groups utilized mass media and information technology to network, mobilize and conscientize the public-at-large. During People Power II, Filipino street protesters employed active nonviolent tactics such as communicating with a wider audience, representing their group, acting symbolically, pressuring the opponent, dramatizing and singing, sponsoring public assemblies, and withdrawing support from the politically powerful.

On Filipino children's understanding of war and peace, Oppenheimer and Kuipers (2003) report on ten-year-old Filipino children's understanding of peace, war and strategies to attain peace. In total, 56 children were presented with a semi-structured interview consisting of free associations to peace and questions pertaining to the definitions of peace and war and strategies to attain peace. The children were divided into three groups that were selected from a rural environment (n = 24), and from middle (n = 16) and low (n = 16) socio-economic backgrounds in the capital city of Manila. The categorized and coded responses indicated that within the Filipino sample, rural children offered less elaborate responses to the questions than urban children resulting in a generally lower frequency overall of response categories for the rural children. However, Filipino children do not fundamentally differ from their peers in other countries in their understanding of or reasoning about peace and war, but rather in thematic contents by which this understanding is expressed. The emphasis on materially related themes such as the reduction of poverty, the increase of employment rates, and good educational opportunities not only distinguished lower from middle-class participants but also illustrated differences in the environments in which Filipino children mature.

Rwanda   On the justice and healing system (called Inkiko-Gacaca), see Honeyman et al. (2004) and E. Staub (2004).

Serbia   On why Serbs fought, motives and misperceptions, see White (1996).

Somalia   On self-disclosure and post-traumatic stress disorder in peacekeepers, see Bolton, Glenn, Orsillo, Roemer and Litz (2003).

South Asia   For a review of Rita Manchanda's edited book on the role of gender in conflict areas, see Skjelsbaek (2003).

Southeast Asia   On violence against women, see Norsworthy (2003; Norsworthy and Khuankaew, 2004).

Spain   On indicators for a culture of peace, see Morales and Leal (2004).

Sri Lanka   On 'from war to peace', examples, plus Mozambique, see Nordstrom (1997); on political violence and ethnic conflict, John D. Rogers, Spencer and Uyangoda (1998).

Uganda   On counselling for peace, see Annan, Amuge and Angwaro (2003).

United States   See much of the research cited in other chapters.

Vietnam   On learning from Vietnam veterans: Lifton (1992); on language education and foreign relations, Wright (2002).

Yugoslavia   On the Dayton Peace Agreement, Beriker-Atiyas and Demirel-Pegg (2000) studied the nature of the negotiated outcomes of the eight issues of the Dayton Peace Agreement in terms of their integrative and distributive aspects. In cases where integrative elements were found, further analysis was conducted by concentrating on D. G. Pruitt's five types of integrative solutions: expanding the pie, cost cutting, non-specific compensation, logrolling and bridging. The results showed that real-world international negotiations can arrive at integrative agreements even when they involve redistribution of resources (in this case the redistribution of former Yugoslavia). Another conclusion was that an agreement can consist of several distributive outcomes and several integrative outcomes produced by different kinds of mechanisms. Similarly, in single issues more than one mechanism can be used simultaneously. Some distributive bargaining was needed in order to determine how much compensation was required. Finally, each integrative formula had some distributive aspects as well. For additional research, see: on war, trauma, genocide and Kosovo in news and classroom, Elovitz (1999); on culture and conflict, Hofstede's theory, Soeters (1996).

Summary and conclusion

A reader of this chapter will have noted that the forty-plus countries and regions listed are dispersed widely around the globe and that the over-eighty reports of research that are included in this review in some detail also cover a wide variety of topics, not counting the hundreds of references that only appear with a one-line indication of the content. In only a few instances do several studies deal with the same theme. Thus, given the lack of continuity in the material in the chapter, one should not expect much more than a list of findings in the summary. However, some general conclusions will be added at the end.

For the Middle East in general, having a 'great power' involved appeared to be a necessary but not sufficient condition for long-term cooperation. Supporters for the Hizballah in Lebanon were found to be more moderate than expected, and simulations and models provide information about possible coalition formation and the relationship between the completeness of information and deterrence.

Concerning the political beliefs of political leaders in Israel and Egypt in relation to the degree of cooperation between the two countries, the higher the proportion of cognitive complexity in the verbal expression of the leaders, the higher the proportion of cooperative behaviour exhibited by Egypt towards Israel, but not vice versa. For the region, including Syria, in the latter half of the twentieth century, arms transfers by the US decreased the likelihood of military intervention but USSR supplies did not affect it.

In Lebanon, after the civil war there was a willingness to forgive by both Muslim and Christian adults. During the war in the Persian Gulf, members of staffs of the American Congress reported that their bosses' personal policy assessments were the most significant determinants of foreign and defence policy votes. For US college students the attribution of responsibility for the Gulf War was the best predictor of aid for Iraq and scarcity predicted support for aid for Kuwait. US President Carter appeared to be averse to losses when he authorized the mission to free American hostages in Iran in 1980.

Several of the studies of the Israeli–Palestinian conflict have dealt with the political leadership. For some Israeli leaders individual time horizons help to explain rates and mechanisms of attitudinal and policy change. Both Arab and Israeli decision-makers try to minimize perceived conflict escalations by minimizing their behaviour.

14 Sustainable development

Herbert H. Blumberg

Addressing structural violence on a reasonably permanent basis entails striving towards 'sustainable development'. This catch-all phrase suggests the need for a flexible but reasonably stable system in a variety of spheres: environmental, economic, political and social. All of these include psychological processes partly because they require an awareness of 'sustainable principles' among the general public and an understanding of attitude formation, as well, among experts in the various fields. Arguably, this is one of the most important areas of peace psychology because (in a sense) it subsumes many of the other topics.

Research in this area (a) delineates specific (mainly environmental) problems or topics of concern – and (it is to be hoped) establishes criteria for prioritizing them, (b) covers specific areas (such as social welfare), (c) gives broadly applicable, practical suggestions based on psychological principles, and (d) considers underlying theoretical perspectives. Although these categories are largely treated separately in the present chapter, there is of course a fuzzy line among them. To take just one example, is over-discounting of the future (discussed briefly below) a problem or a principle?

Some especially clear, reasonably comprehensive reports of psychological aspects of sustainable development in environmental and other domains were presented in a special series of articles in the May 2000 issue of the *American Psychologist*; also, for example, the *Journal of Social Issues* devoted its Fall 2000 issue to 'promoting environmentalism'. Some of these articles are among those considered below. In a subsequent issue devoted to the theme 'peace psychology comes of age', Winter (2006) and Pilisuk and Zazzi (2006) document the association between (a) conflict and terrorism and (b) resource issues, ranging from unsound contemporary practices to scarcities left from colonial land distribution and degradation. More positively, efforts towards sustainable development are also broadly in the service of just and peaceful societies.

Specific problems

Oskamp (2000a, 2000b) suggests that the most serious long-term threats to the world stem primarily from human actions that are producing damaging, irreversible changes in life-supporting systems on earth. He provides a concise description of major environmental problems including: global warming and climate change due to the greenhouse effect; loss of much of the ozone layer; deforestation and species extinction; exhaustion of fisheries, agricultural land and water supplies; acid rain and toxic pollution of air and water supplies; human exposure to toxic chemicals; additive or synergistic effects; and, in particular, population growth (notwithstanding decreases in the *rate* of growth) and overconsumption.

To accomplish much-needed behavioural changes, he summarizes advice from Howard (2000), McKenzie-Mohr (2000), Stern (2000) and Winter (2000): (a) advocating voluntary simplicity, (b) effecting a variety of specific concrete actions, (c) providing clear behavioural norms, (d) focusing technological advances on pro-environmental goals, (e) promoting relevant organized group activity, and (f) stressing sustainable living patterns as a 'super-ordinate goal' – that is, one which transcends individual interests – for nations and peoples to share in.

Although nuclear weapons proliferation remains a serious 'environmental' threat, at least the United States nuclear weapons complex has apparently shifted its orientation from production to environmental clean-up, and from a closed system to a surprisingly open one (Reed, Lemak and Hesser, 1997). Nevertheless, using a systems-based paradigm of organization, Reed et al. conclude that systemic considerations are perhaps making the changes unnecessarily difficult.

Cognitive biases can represent a problem in their own right. Heuristic-based cognitive biases are known generally to lead to suboptimal behaviours and choices (Tversky and Kahneman, 1980); environmentally responsible behaviour is not exempt. One partly cognitive problem that cuts across a variety of environmental issues is people's individual and collective tendencies to over-discount the future. A simple (hypothetical) economic example might be one's (reasonable) preference to have, say, £600,000 (or dollars) now rather than £1,000,000 in ten years' time – even if taxes made it highly unlikely that one could ever recover the £400,000 difference. Framing environmental recklessness – for example, generating some nuclear waste materials that require 10,000-year isolation! – in terms of future discounting can help crystallize support for more rational alternatives (Ahearne, 2000).

Another heuristic-based bias has to do with 'availability' – that is, with how easy it is to visualize examples of a particular threat. Even when the probable risk associated with a given problem (be it terrorism, nuclear war or global warming) remains intact, the problem and remedial efforts may slip in and out of public awareness as a result of the presence (or absence) of events that make it too easy (or too difficult) to visualize the relevant hazards. Ungar (1992) describes how concern for global warming went in, and then out, of 'fashion' following a frightening drought during the summer of 1988. The quixotic nature of public prioritizing seems itself to represent a threat to – or sometimes an opportunity for – sustainable development.

Specific arenas

This section considers diverse facets of sustainability, such as human welfare, the ecology of families and cultural diversity. The list is hetero-geneous but labelled as 'arenas' and 'facets' because the present matters seem too important to be described as miscellany! They do at least cover the four functional areas (mentioned in chapters 3 and 12) of resources, goals, interpersonal matters and underlying meaning.

One seeming prerequisite for sustainable development is a 'caring society'. P. M. Oliner and Oliner's (1995) distillation of relevant guidelines – from a variety of social psychological and other disciplinary perspectives – helps provide the means for individuals to strengthen the caring quality of their private and public lives. Some main relevant elements, corresponding to chapters in their collection, are: ways of pursuing 'care', interpersonal and intergroup bonding (corporate and societal entities meeting basic needs and providing a forum for monitor-ing), empathizing, learning caring norms, practising care and assuming personal responsibility, diversifying (accepting multicultural society), networking, resolving conflicts, 'making global connections' and 'crafting the future' (where a caring business, for instance, would exemplify all of the above properties).

Partly because breaches of sustainable principles (such as deforest-ation in poverty-stricken regions) tend to run in tandem with inadequate support for human welfare, facets of social welfare are very probably inextricably tied in with sustainable development. Theoretical as well as practical considerations in achieving and maintaining international social welfare are incorporated in an overview by Midgley (1997). Midgley and the contributors to his volume consider – among other matters – the adjustments needed in relation to the effects of inter-national globalization from several perspectives. These perspectives relate to social work and, especially, social programmes related to international development, which need to be adapted to serve the poor (e.g. by promoting productive employment), refugees and human well-being more generally. A combination of local involvement and international cooperation is needed (see, for example, Kelsey, 2003). Some facilitation, at least, of relevant social-welfare goals has been provided by the United Nations and the fairly universal governmental support of (or at least agreement with) its objectives (Rao, 1990).

Without a consistent, progressive policy at, at least, the national level, even well-mediated meetings designed to deal with disputes – e.g. between the timber industry and environmentalists in the Pacific Northwest – may fail (Daniels and Walker, 1995); disputants may, for instance, have critical differences with regard to any or all functional areas – e.g. as to what constitutes legitimate participation in such meetings, the extent of reliance on scientific 'facts', power imbalances and – implicitly – the values held by the parties concerned.

Martin (1991) considers the group dynamics that hinder, or sometimes support, technological change (which may itself favour, hinder or be neutral with regard to sustainable development). Some teachers may resent students learning mainly from Internet-based sources; workers may (not surprisingly) resent technologies perceived to threaten their jobs. Classical social psychological research (e.g. Coch and French, 1948) – and later, rigorous confirmatory research citing and supporting classical studies – supports the value of democratic organizational decision-making with regard, especially, to implementing changes. In research that goes beyond group dynamics (unless the technology is itself regarded as an additional group member?), Martin reviews the broad importance of considering human–machine interactions in a very wide variety of fields.

Ethnocentrism (see, for example, Brown's analysis – Brown, 1965: 477–546) is among the group-dynamic and personality phenomena that hinder consensus on achieving worldwide sustainable systems (Leach, 1997). By contrast, fostering the ability to empathize with, if not endorse, diverse viewpoints is palliative (cf. Conway, Suedfeld and Tetlock, 2001; Janis, 1982; Tetlock, 1988). Like transnational corporate affiliations in general (Fedor and Werther, 1996), international alliances for the environment must consider not only legal, financial and strategic goals (in functional areas that are arguably concerned with interpersonal norms, resources and goals/motivations) but also cultural compatibility (values).

Although war and aggressiveness are not biologically 'innate' in people, a readiness to form in-group attachments – which give rise to ethnocentrism and nationalism – may well have an evolutionary basis (M. B. Smith, 1992), as may well (also) an aptitude for learning cooperation in order to resolve common problems. Indeed some analysts posit that environmental change may foster broader (e.g. Europe-wide) social identity (Chase, 1996). Phenomena as diverse as refugee immigration and advanced communication technology may also contribute to (or hinder) international identity (Mays et al., 1996).

In a salutary consideration of expanding identities, though, Spink (1997) and Evan (1997) wonder why global identity is not *more* widespread than it is and why violations of human rights persist as widely as they do. (For a partly related psychodynamic analysis, see Ribas, 1993.)

There may be simultaneous processes favouring broader and narrower identities. Mijuskovic (1992) distinguishes between organic, holistic communities and atomistic societies which do value individual freedom and mechanical explanations but may foment a sense of loneliness. Atomization may, as it were, be concurrent with globalization. Basing his conclusions on structured interviews with managers from over 50 international ventures set up in Hungary, Meschi (1997) discusses the value of deliberately valuing cultural integration.

Paradoxically, a cultural ethos of unconditional cooperation and agreement may keep disagreements and conflicts hidden, thereby *constraining* the resolution of problems. That is the conclusion reached by Gaines and Whitehouse (1998), based on their study related to the international testing of anti-dementia drugs. In contrast to the negative effects of constraining debate, productive teams have been found frequently to disagree internally, critically analysing matters in a positive, assertive, task-oriented way (Hofner Saphiere, 1996; cf. description of optimal leadership profile near end of section on social psychology and personality in chapter 2; and see also, Donnellon, 1996).

It is not obvious that helping American business gain a foothold in Russia will necessarily contribute to worldwide sustainable development. Nonetheless Tongren, Hecht and Kovach's (1995) ten suggestions for American firms wishing to succeed in Russia – related to cultural value profiles and to links with specific practices (concerned with ethics, work norms, aspirations and incentives) – are themselves instructive as a possible exemplar for using integrative cultural practices to foster international cooperation. Such cooperation is not static but may be viewed as going through stages – consideration, negotiation, production-run and evaluation – within the lifespan of a project (McLarney and Rhyno, 1998).

Anyone interested in an exercise for helping to explore the idea that different societies understand the world differently could consult

Fantini's (1995) experiential exercise that (happily) covers resources, goals, interpersonal matters and, especially, worldviews.

Sustainable development must of course provide for stable but flexible institutions such as the family (or its equivalent). Hildebrand (1991) describes an 'ecological system framework' for studying families worldwide in terms of resources, population growth, food, housing, education and disparities based on sex, ethnicity or other factors. She delineates global governmental properties that favour peaceful, just and secure development for children. For a study of a game designed to elicit children's own environmental visions, see Kytta, Kaaja and Horelli (2004).

The stability and flexibility of occupational roles also come under the rubric of sustainable development – perhaps in particular including roles, such as counselling, that particularly help support others in social systems (C. C. Lee, 1997). C. C. Lee (1998) gives special consideration to worldwide action for tolerance and nation-building that would integrally help relieve the endemic suffering of women and children especially (see also, Leppanen, 2004).

Still more general considerations regarding human resource management are portrayed by Kim (1999), who considers issues such as multicultural management groups and international management of negotiations in general.

Practical suggestions (including some underlying principles)

International agreement with regard to key environmental issues is most likely to be reached following times of impasse and crisis, according to Zartman (1992); and relevant negotiations are most likely to be successful if they incorporate (a) defining the problems in resolvable ways and (b) using trade-offs to implement the defined resolutions.

On-going careful analysis is required as to preferred behaviours and the means of achieving them – by individual actions, by social norms and by legislation or other means. Descriptive norms should be consistent with prescriptive ones. To take a simple concrete example, signs warning people not to remove wood from the petrified forest (a prescriptive norm) were rendered less effective when they included a further sentence as to how many tons of wood people removed each year (a contrasting descriptive norm) (Cialdini, 2003). Likewise, in an experiment by Cialdini, passers-by were more likely to litter (breaking an implicit prescriptive norm) in an area that was already littered (descriptive norm). This finding, moreover, interacted with the *salience* of a littering norm: seeing a model litter in a clean area elicited particularly *low* levels of littering from participants and seeing a model litter in an already-littered area elicited particularly *high* levels of littering.

Other social psychological principles related to communication and attitude change – and to majority and minority influence – are also applicable to environmental views. To review some of these principles very briefly: classically, researchers have considered the source, medium and recipient of messages. Attitude change is enhanced if, for instance, the source is seen as expert and sincere, and if the medium (which is often mainly mass communication) also includes support from 'face-to-face' social interaction (Hovland, Janis and Kelley, 1953). Recent research on communications media has especially emphasized the advantages and drawbacks of different forms of computer-mediated communication as contrasted with (among other things) face-to-face interaction (see e.g. Blumberg, Hare, Kent and Davies: in press; and, for application to international collaboration, see e.g. Walther, 1997).

According to 'information-processing paradigms', effective attitude change requires that new information pass through a dozen or so 'hurdles'. McGuire (1985) presents these as requiring that the potential recipient of a message experience: exposure to the message (recipient's physical presence), attention, understanding, agreeing, coding so as to remember, retrieving at a relevant time and using the message content as a basis for changed behaviour.

Social influence (as studied classically by Sherif, Asch, Milgram and Moscovici) suggests that people are (generally) likely to be especially influenced by views held by a large (preferably unanimous) majority of others in a group – and that nevertheless a persistent, flexible minority may eventually exert disproportionately large influence (see, for example, Moscovici and Paicheler, 1983; Brehm, Kassin and Fein, 2005: chapter 7).

Several of the foregoing principles are exemplified in a laboratory study by Nonami (1996) in which pro-environmental influence was especially strong when a relevant message was put forward by a self-sacrificing minority that would actually suffer individual loss if the environmentally sound behaviour it was espousing were to be adopted.

McKenzie-Mohr's (2000) social engineering approach seems particularly apt for dealing with the practicalities of changing behaviour. He gives several empirical examples. Among them: having student bicyclists visit householders to confer, in person, about energy savings worked far better than simply sending information packets in the post;

lawn-watering gauges are more effective if people also receive hints on how to remind themselves to check them.

Successful educational programmes may be manifest in informal environmental workshops devoted in part to considering people's conflicting interests with regard to problems such as biodiversity and sustainable use of natural resources (Colvin, 1993). One is reminded of the informal quasi-political workshops related to the Middle East, Cyprus and elsewhere – in which dissenting parties meet informally, in the presence of facilitators at a fairly secluded site, to consider their underlying (as distinct from their 'public') goals and needs, in order to work towards nonviolent conflict resolution (see, for example, Kelman, 1992). An obvious advantage of workshops related to environmental issues is the typically greater presence of strong superordinate (common) goals related to human welfare and survival.

Education is particularly important for helping people to prioritize issues and to be clear as to the (different) changes needed in aid of different problems (Francis, Boyes, Qualter and Stanisstreet, 1993). Francis et al. found, for instance, that many students are environmentally aware but nonetheless confuse ozone layer depletion – a behavioural success story involving halting production of CFC gases – with the still-rampant greenhouse effect, to which CFCs have not been the most important contributor. Moreover, (a) calculating the environmental advantages of (for instance) even half-filled trains over full aircraft – not to mention (b) providing the means for quicker and cheaper train journeys! – requires considerable sophisticated expertise and publicity as regards relevant findings.

Multinational corporations are often blamed for impeding sustainable development but it would seem that they can also contribute to positive global change if they foster environmentally sound practices and (addressing structural violence) foster equal employment opportunities at all levels (Cooperrider and Dutton, 1999; see also, Roth, 1995). Indeed, corporate potential for positive contributions represents one of seven or so strands for multitrack diplomacy in general (L. Diamond and McDonald, 1996).

Kozminski's (1991) analysis of international integration of economic activity concludes that such integration is at least capable of fostering economic progress in both developed and 'third world' countries – and of reducing poverty. As a possible example consistent with this view, Michael Manley (former head of state in Jamaica) described mutual-help programmes, such as the direct marriage of Jamaica's natural alumina resources and Mexico's energy to produce energy – without the need for both to be exported to the United States as an intermediary

(International Broadcasting Trust, 1983). Nath (1990) agrees that virtually all nations are party to an economically interdependent world and suggests that the major challenge to meaningful global development is to find viable ways of fostering proper, open dialogue between developed and developing countries.

One can argue that sustainable development is promoted not only by (biological species) biodiversity but also by socio-cultural diversity within a world that is interdependent generally, not just in economic spheres – and that ethnic group members may be especially effective in promoting recognition of the value of such diversity (Penn and Kiesel, 1994).

Underlying principles (including some practical views)

As if to complement Oskamp's summary of environmental threats to human survival, noted at the outset of the section on specific problems, above, Nevin (1991) suggests that essentially the same threats to survival have a common contingency (reward) structure and can be addressed from a behavioural perspective whereby adaptive actions are rewarded (see also, Ishaq, 1991).

Using alternative perspectives that may nonetheless lead, at least in part, to similar conclusions, Walsh (1996) suggests a transpersonal approach to human and planetary survival. According to Walsh, mental health professionals may play a particularly useful part by stressing objective appraisal of solutions that incorporate contributions from a variety of contrasting perspectives at all system levels – for instance, behaviourist and psychodynamic, Western and Eastern, empirical and impressionistic.

Notwithstanding the ethnic conflicts that have proliferated since the end of the Cold War (see, for example, Miall, Ramsbotham and Woodhouse, 1999), a more inclusive human identity may be viewed not only as essential for survival but also feasible (Evan, 1997). Evan cites transnational organizations, development of an international bill of rights and the spread of the Internet as (generally) encouraging examples.

Non-governmental organizations have accumulated at least a modest track record for successfully promoting sustainability. The Earth Charter has been described as (an example of) a focus for supporting committed, sound environmental action based on ethical premises, and for fostering environmental security, peace and justice that are essential for sustainable development (Brenes and Winter, 2001).

Brenes and Winter's work is framed in terms of the importance of environmental security. More general security may also be regarded as supporting sustainable systems. Notably, the perception of security may be at least as important as empirical security. Although actual instances of terrorism have diminished in the period following 11 September 2001 (this is true for both state-sponsored and non-state-sponsored instances), much popular perception is on the increase, and the fear of terrorism (and activity carried out in the name of this concern) has no doubt contributed to ethnocentrism and instability (cf. Webel, 2004; see also, chapters 10, 15 and 16).

In an almost allegorical account, industrialized civilization may be compared with a psychotherapeutic client, as in Schmuck's (2003) review of Dobkowski and Wallimann (2002); a critical look at globalization principles, at scarcity and at conflict may suggest causes and treatment for 'pathologies'.

In an apparently prescient (and to some extent hindsightful) paper, Brody (1992) suggests that until humankind achieves 'a universal concept of justice [and] commonalities across political and cultural boundaries', ethnic, economic, social and quasi-religious conflicts will continue worldwide and incidentally create mass refugee migrations that exacerbate problems in target countries.

People's major values, as represented within Rokeach's Value Survey, do seem to be organized into 'clusters'. Concern to have a clean (safe and pollution-free) environment apparently is most closely related to a cluster that includes equality, world peace and beauty (Simmons, Binney and Dodd, 1992); in a random sample of adults in the early 1990s, a clean environment did at least tie (with self-respect!) for being fifth most important among 21 values – behind freedom, family security, health and world peace.

Straddling various disciplines, D. C. Lee (1992) posits a multidimensional, hierarchical ethical theory, whereby people's relationship with the environment and society can foster a broad spectrum of creativity, transcending contemporary political systems and environmental threats.

An arguably complementary analysis suggesting more of a push towards homogenization has been empirically grounded on simulations of communication and cultural change – as put forward in Greig's (2002) paper, 'The end of geography? . . .'

Gilbert (1997) provides a salutary reminder that homogenization may, as it were, crowd out environmentally crucial local knowledge. Using rural South Africa as an example, Gilbert suggests 'ways in which attention to the interface between local and exogenous knowledge may help to ensure greater equity, social justice, and sustainable transformation' (1997: 275). Reuveny and Maxwell (2001) describe a dynamic game-like paradigm to represent the interplay, in primitive societies, among conflict and other phenomena related to scarce renewable resources.

In a contrasting (but not conflicting!) stance – and notwithstanding apparent contemporary instances of profligacy – Princen (1997) suggests that a human readiness to learn restraint in the use of scarce resources has historical and evolutionary roots – a tendency that can be cultivated to the world's advantage.

Summary and conclusion

Threats to a long-term sustainable environment, many of them originating in human behaviour, represent a form of structural violence. One important goal of peace psychology is to address such threats. Contributions include, for instance, application of known principles of persuasion and attitude change and also awareness of biased cognitive processes. An example of the latter would be attempts to remedy the effects of biased perception manifest, for instance, in over-discounting the future (over-emphasizing short-term benefits) and focusing overly on problems that are easier to visualize.

Appropriate action seems to benefit from a caring society and one that is concerned about social welfare, defined broadly. A combination of local involvement and international cooperation is needed. As with successful minority influence in general, progress towards sustainability may require marrying a clear, persistent vision of necessary goals with flexible culture-sensitive approaches towards achieving them.

A variety of practical suggestions (including some underlying principles) are available. These relate to social influence, information-processing and other psychological processes, including a behavioural perspective whereby adaptive actions (including recognition of a more inclusive human identity) are rewarded.

Websites related to sustainable development

http://iisdl.iisd.ca/
www.ec.gc.ca/eco/
www.toolsofchange.com/
www.uni-bonn.de/ihdp/
www.cbsm.com
www.globalactionplan.org.uk/
www.greenchoices.org
www.climatecrisis.net

Part V

Terrorism

15   Terrorist threats

Anna Costin

This chapter outlines and discusses both established and more recent psychological theories and explanations for the causes of terrorism. Since the terrorist attacks on the United States on 11 September 2001, a wealth of research on the causes and nature of terrorism has been published. Therefore a high level of selectivity in citation of work has been applied in order to make this chapter appropriately concise. Traditional theories of behaviour from academic psychology – social, cognitive and psychodynamic – can be applied to this phenomenon, but this chapter focuses in the main on those that have been applied directly to terrorism. As W. Reich (1990) states, we cannot understand the psychology of terrorism without understanding the socio-political conditions, religious beliefs and basic psychological mechanisms that allow humans to undertake acts contravening the morals that usually inhibit them. Reich (1990) argues that terrorism cannot be understood exclusively in psychological terms; it is necessary to take an interdisciplinary approach. The theoretical and practical importance of studying this field speaks for itself. At the present time, and with the advent of weapons of mass destruction and modern technology, international terrorism is threatening global security on a scale not seen before.

A lot of research on terrorism is focused on the Middle East and on Islam in particular, not because this part of the world and this religion are intrinsically linked to terrorism but because terrorism coming from this region and in the name of Islam has been very prominent in recent years. The focus of this chapter is on terrorism in general – not limited to one region or type although many given examples relate to Islam, for the reason stated above. Suicide and non-suicide terrorism have been interwoven in the structure of the chapter; the latter has been treated as a particular variety of the same behaviour, as opposed to an entirely different phenomenon.

This chapter addresses the psychology of terrorism by looking to different models of behaviour for explanations and to the role of psychopathology and religion. Because of the nature of terrorism, the methodology for studying it does not always allow comprehensive analysis and research in the way in which other forms of behaviour can be studied. Therefore, for many of the theories offered there is little empirical evidence to either support or refute them. They can only be evaluated in light of more general knowledge about the world, society, violence, conflict and basic psychology. As a result, evaluation of the arguments is not always possible and this chapter has a descriptive focus in parts. The issues in methodology are discussed in more detail later on. This chapter concludes by offering suggestions of how psychology can contribute to reducing terrorism.

Defining terrorism

What is terrorism? All those who have tried to define it have deliberated this question at length. One major problem is that very few groups or individuals label themselves as terrorist. It is a label afforded to them by their enemy. The age-old adage of 'one man's terrorist is another man's freedom fighter' is central in understanding this definition difficulty. It is not definitively clear how terrorism is different from crime in general, or war, if it is different at all. The UK government has defined terrorism as 'the use or threat, for the purpose of advancing a political, religious or ideological course of action, of serious violence against any person or property' (Townshend, 2002: 3). However, the prescribed offences attributed to terrorism are usually already criminal offences. So, terrorism can be defined as political crime, but how is this different from both civil and international war? War and terrorism are not dissimilar. However, with terrorism there is usually the lack of combat between sides, both of which are armed. Targets, usually civilian, may be attacked indiscriminately, with no opportunity for self-defence. Townshend (2002) states that terrorism defies the international law of war – the law that distinguishes combatants from non-combatants, legitimate from illegitimate targets.

Terrorism is often defined as violence designed to yield desired results by instilling fear in people (Bassiouni, 1981). Intimidation of the public is a key element, distinguishing terrorism from other forms of violence. Victims are incidental to the terrorists' goals. A widespread sense of personal vulnerability is felt by the public, because ordinary civilians are targeted (Bandura, 1986).

Merari (1990) argues that with suicidal terrorism it is important to distinguish between those who are ready to die and those seeking to die; those who wanted to die and those who were deceived, coerced and persuaded into suicide terrorism (by those who sent them on the mission). There is variability of the situational context of the suicidal act. It is hard to know the number of genuine suicide attacks as opposed to attacks in which perpetrators were used as expendable pawns by their organizations.

In regards to studying the psychology of terrorism, it is important to remember that it is not a psychological label, but a political term (Silke, 2003b). In summary, terrorism can be defined as the use of violence for political/ideological ends, against the unarmed by the armed.

Issues in methodology

Research on terrorism – which began in the 1970s – faces persistent problems in defining the concept, data collection, establishing integrative theory and avoiding attributing terrorism to personality disorders and irrationality (Crenshaw, 2000). Crenshaw argues that psychological explanations of terrorism must involve different levels of analysis. The individual must be linked to the group and to society. Research in this field is limited, incomplete and not always of good quality. Up until now, psychological findings on terrorism have not been well disseminated outside of academia – this is one reason why terrorism is often seen as being perpetrated by insane people. As Silke (2003a) states, terrorism is not a simple phenomenon with simple solutions, but attempts to gain an objective understanding of it have been extremely deficient, and this deficiency has prolonged many conflicts.

Horgan (2003) contends that the grievances of most terrorist organizations may be imaginary, historical or self-serving. This poses a huge stumbling block if the concept of addressing grievances is seen as a way of countering terrorism. He argues that viewing terrorism as a process can help to prioritize the questions we need to ask and can focus policy decisions and resource allocation.

Brannan, Esler, Strindberg and Anders (2001) propose talking to terrorists and using social identity theory – used in a cultural difference context – as a methodology. Factors about recruitment are hard to come by given the covert nature of terrorism (Whittaker, 2002). W. Reich (1990) has outlined the limits and opportunities of psychological enquiry. Some of the essential points are:

1. Over-generalization – terrorism is too varied for psychological principles to be applied to explain all types/examples. Terrorist groups do not share the same characteristics, nor do individual terrorists.

2. Reductionism – it is unjustifiable to attribute all/much terrorist behaviour to a single cause, e.g. mental illness, neurochemistry, personality type, religion.
3. Inaccessibility to direct research on terrorists – many terrorists believe attempting to explain their motivations in psychological terms reduces the validity of their actions. Furthermore, research on suicide bombers is obviously extremely difficult, although there is a technique developed by Isometsa and Lonnqvist (1998) called psychological autopsy, whereby a suicide victim's life is analysed by looking at any clinical history they may have and through talking to friends and relatives.

Psychopathology and terrorism

There has been much speculation – both amongst researchers and society at large – for many years concerning the mental health of terrorists. Many studies have tried to find a link between psychopathology and terrorism. It is in some ways more reassuring to think of terrorists as suffering from some form of psychiatric illness that makes them different from the rest of us, than to think of them as normal fellow human beings. This can be explained by attribution theory – we tend to see our own behaviour as externally driven – a normal response to our environment, other people's as internally driven – stemming from their own personality and drives, especially when that behaviour is very different from our own.

Silke (1998) reviewed evidence of studies that have tried to apply a psychopathology label to terrorists. He found that evidence in support of the pathology model is weak. However, he argues that there is an emerging trend in the findings, which asserts that terrorists have the traits of personality disorders but do not meet the criteria for a clinical diagnosis. He argues that this has tainted them with an aura of mental illness without offering a method of testing this hypothesis. However, there are some examples that strongly imply a level of fanaticism and coldness not found in normal people, but this is rare. Silke (2001a) concludes that the overwhelming majority of terrorists – including those who commit suicidal acts – are normal and that researchers who conclude that they are not normal tend to be those who have had very little contact with them. Furthermore, Crenshaw (1981) argues that the only outstanding common characteristic of terrorists is their normality.

Colvard (2002) argues that terrorist groups are comprised of ordinary people in extraordinary groups. She argues that psychologists should focus on group processes rather than individual psychopathology. Violence can belong to a rational strategy, used to attain goals for a moral cause (Crenshaw, 1990). This is discussed in more detail later. Della Porta (1992) states that radical thinking is made easier by membership of a group, where one can search for an identity. This is comparable with membership of gangs and cults. People often join gangs for social relationships rather than because of political grievance. This is corroborated by the fact that very few members of aggrieved groups become terrorists (Silke, 2001a). Silke (2001a) argues that whilst terrorists may be normal, terrorism is not. This is a very important point – it is possible for normal people to act/react in extreme and abnormal ways due to a variety of factors.

H. Gordon (2002) argues that although suicide is classed as abnormal behaviour in psychiatry (DSM-IV) (American Psychiatric Association, 1994) and that research has found that the majority of those who kill themselves are suffering from a mental disorder at the time, the perpetrators of, for example, 11 September 2001 attacks would regard these as acts of martyrdom, not suicide. Furthermore, it cannot be ascertained whether all of the hijackers were aware that they were on a suicide mission because suicide notes were found from only six out of nineteen hijackers (Jenkins, 2001).

On the other hand, H. Gordon (2002) addresses whether the lack of studies in psychiatry on martyrdom reflects the fact that suicide bombing is not linked to psychopathology, or whether it is an oversight in psychiatry. He argues that even though suicide terrorism can be explained in socio-political terms, and thus there need not be a psychiatric label applied to it, psychiatric terminology may not yet have enough depth to include the behaviour and emotions of people whose levels of hate, low self-esteem and alienation are enough to lead to mass death, including their own.

J. M. Post (2000) argues for the viability of post-traumatic stress disorder (PTSD) as an explanation for acts of terrorism. He cites the case of a terrorist tried for hijacking an Egyptian airliner, who pleaded not guilty by reason of insanity, on the basis of PTSD. Post was called as an expert psychiatric witness to explain to the jury how the defendant had been socialized to violence in the Palestinian refugee camps, where he was recruited into terrorism in order to regain his people's land. Such a situation is worsened by the intergenerational transmission of hatred. Post claimed the defendant was suffering from PTSD as a result of his pro-terrorist upbringing and socialization to violence. It is important to acknowledge that Post is not arguing for all terrorists to be viewed as suffering from PTSD and that each case should be considered individually.

A different view, proposed by Pomerantz (2001), is that terrorism is the by-product of a group mental disorder. It is an extreme form of destructive cult behaviour – leaders suffering from personality disorders convince vulnerable individuals to adhere to their 'rational' belief system. Pomerantz argues that terrorism is rarely the result of legitimate political and religious grievances. There is not much consensus with this viewpoint, amongst the majority of researchers in this field. So if the majority of terrorists are not suffering from a psychiatric condition, what does drive their acts of catastrophic destruction? We must now look at other approaches.

A terrorist personality

As stated above, a pattern of certain traits of personality disorders and types has been found in many terrorists studied. This section looks at whether there is a terrorist personality type. J. M. Post (1990) states that research has failed to find a universal personality type for terrorism. However, memoirs, records and interviews indicate that individuals with particular personality traits are disproportionately drawn to terrorism. These traits are: being action oriented, aggressive and excitement seeking. Prominent psychological mechanisms found are: externalization and splitting – these are also found in narcissistic and borderline personalities. Post argues that these traits significantly contribute to the uniformity of terrorist psychology. Splitting is an important concept within this context. This is a characteristic of individuals whose personality development is affected by a particular type of damage that occurred in childhood. This leads to the development of the injured self whereby the good parts of the self are split into 'me' and the bad parts are split into 'not me'. These bad parts are projected on to others. Such people need an outside enemy to blame. They find the absolute terrorist rhetoric of 'them and us' very appealing. In 1982 the German Ministry of the Interior sponsored research into the background of 250 West German terrorists. The researchers found developmental histories characterized by such narcissistic wounds and a reliance on splitting and externalizing (Bollinger, 1982). J. M. Post (1990) states that it is, however, unwise to generalize this finding to other terrorist groups. However, future research should compare terrorists to a control group of normal people, to discover how common splitting and externalization are in a normal, non-terrorist population. Post argues that terrorists may have a fragmented psychological identity and come from the margins of society. By joining a fundamentalist/nationalist group they can consolidate their psychosocial identity at a time of societal instability. For many, being a member of a terrorist group may be the first time they feel they truly belong. J. M. Post (1990) argues that terrorists commit violent acts because of psychological forces that draw them to act in violent ways. They develop a special logic that becomes the justification for their violent acts. Their logic consists of 'us versus them' and 'they' must be destroyed.

Studies of the personalities of suicide terrorists are practically impossible. The most consistent characteristic appears to be a broken family background. Israeli (1997) found that a disproportionately high number of suicide terrorists are from broken homes and are of low socio-economic status. This could facilitate an intention to become a martyr in order to prove one's worth. H. Gordon (2002) argues that findings are based more on journalistic than scientific inquiry. The terrorist is usually a young male aged 19–25, from a devout Muslim family, unmarried and not the main wage earner of his family. Many lived in refugee camps in Gaza and had a father or brother killed in the intifada. They had a strong sense of hopelessness, were too poor to study, unable to find work, and had a strong sense of Palestinian identity. The 11 September hijackers were generally older than their Palestinian counterparts and of higher educational attainment. Gordon argues that the profile of the suicide bomber is susceptible to change according to evolving circumstances. So, although evidence is inconclusive, it would appear that common early life experience might contribute to a personality type found in many terrorists.

Religion and terrorism

The link between religion and terrorism is not new – it goes back more than 2000 years. However, for most of the twentieth century terrorist groups have been motivated by non-religious issues. We are now witnessing a return of religious terrorism. The aims of religious terrorists go further than the socio-political changes sought by non-religious terrorists (Hoffman, 1998). Whereas secular terrorists attempt to appeal to the people they claim to represent, some religious terrorists use infinite levels of violence – anyone who is not a member of their religion can be regarded as a target. A highly topical example of this would be the al-Qaeda network, responsible for the 11 September attacks on the United States as well as other high-profile terrorist incidents in recent years. They may see violence as an end in itself – not as a means to an end. These groups are unpredictable – traditional policies of counter-terrorism are not effective. New approaches are needed (Hoffman, 1998).

Steven (2002) argues that many factors influence the decision to join a terrorist group – religion mostly provides justification and encouragement as well as widening recruitment appeal to potential members. Steven argues that there is no 'one size fits all' theory – it depends on the situation, the case study and is often a combination of different factors. But, by looking at the common motivating factors, it is clear that recruits are not just devoutly or fanatically religious. Steven compiled a list of factors motivating entry, which include: ideology, religion, politics, provocation, protection, fascination with weapons, youth rebellion, substitute family, friends, status and identity.

Suicide bombings have come to be associated, in the media, with Islam but the last ten years has witnessed Christian, Hindu and Islamic suicide bombing. The Hindu groups have been responsible for more attacks than all the Islamic groups combined (Silke, 2001b) up until the Iraqi insurgency that started in 2003. Sri Lanka's Liberation Tigers of Tamil Eelam, popularly known as the Tamil Tigers, are prolific perpetrators of suicide attacks. Merari (1990) concluded that culture and religion are relatively unimportant in this phenomenon – people wish to do it for personal reasons and the terrorist group just offers the means and the excuse.

All the major religions – Christianity, Islam, Judaism – condemn suicide. Suicide bombing could be the result of misguided religious fervour (Merari, 1990). It is not common in Muslim countries (Racy, 1970). This illegality is overridden by martyrdom. Clerical authorities may interpret religious texts in a way that justifies violence. Hizbullah (a Lebanese shi'ite militant group) justified suicide bombing as being honourable to die for God, in retaliation against oppression (H. Gordon, 2002). Merari (1990) states that by the end of 1986 it was clear that the majority of suicide car bombings in Lebanon were perpetrated by secular, non-shi'ite groups – not Islamist groups, as originally thought. In an unpublished study quoted in a British newspaper (E. Silver, 2001) a leading Palestinian psychiatrist in Gaza, Dr Eyad El-Sarraj, argued that religion was an important but not sufficient factor in martyrdom. He argued that other factors were the need to identify with a symbol of power and a desire for revenge and that (Palestinian) suicide bombers see their fathers as unable to protect them from oppression; thus they see an alternative in dying for God's cause. H. Gordon (2002) argues that although religious factors are not the only motivations of suicide bombers, the return of fundamentalism at the present time renders religion a world threat, when used as a force for evil.

Psychological approaches

The next sections of this chapter look at the different approaches to psychology for understanding terrorist behaviour.

The psychoanalytic approach

P. W. Johnson and Feldman (1992) argue that behaviourists have failed to develop a consensus for explaining membership in terrorist groups. They argue that psychoanalytic self-psychology can provide a useful framework for this. The terrorist group serves different functions for its members – all of which promote self-cohesion and strengthen identity. They argue that this implies a degree of narcissism in the group's members. Membership of such a group is beneficial to narcissistically vulnerable personalities. Lachkar (2002) also sees suicide bombers from a psychoanalytic perspective. She argues that primitive defences – like shame, unresolved Oedipal issues and omnipotent denial – are ways of communicating expressions of interlocking dynamics. Lachkar argues that Islamic terrorists are motivated by identification with the absence of a father, a syndrome which she argues is compatible with collective borderline personality disorder. The arguments in both of these publications (P. W. Johnson and Feldman, 1992; Lachkar, 2002) are in line with J. M. Post's (1990) argument regarding narcissistic/borderline traits.

Moss (2003) argues that terrorism is a result of dis-identification, which is the precondition for pitilessness and limitless activities directed against the objects of our hatred. He argues that psychoanalytic theory can help us to identify with objects and decrease our capacities for terrorizing.

Demause (2002) proposes that the origins of terrorism lie in the abusive family background of the terrorists. He argues that they are raised in a misogynist, fundamentalist system in which girls are often treated as being polluted. As a result of this they have a negative maternal style and inflict their own miseries upon their children. Thus from childhood, Islamic terrorists have been taught to destroy the part of themselves, and – by projection – others, that desires personal pleasure and liberty. Through a discussion of the fantasy analysis of terrorists' word choice, in which terms relating to sexual attack are constantly used, the author suggests the best preventative measure against terrorism is to develop better child-rearing methods.

Bohleber (2002) identified the ideological/religious factor as an essential component in terrorist motivation. It is argued that this is the operative force behind the combination of narcissistic ideal condition and terrorist mass-murder. The author draws parallels between Islamic fundamentalism and ethnocentric German nationalism after World War Two; they have the same ubiquitous, unconscious fantasies: care fantasies and sibling rivalry, purity and the idea of the other, visions of unity and fantasies of fusion.

Juergensmeyer (2001) has suggested that terrorism in the Middle East may be due to sexual frustration of the perpetrators. This lack of sexual release is due to high unemployment; terrorism is the equivalent of an orgasmic catharsis – a way of releasing sexual tension. This hypothesis appears to be untestable – like much in the psychoanalytic approach – but as Juergensmeyer (2001) points out, the reason for the suicide bomber is being promised seventy virgins in paradise, as an incentive, needs to be explained. This need not be seen as a sign of sexual frustration though – seventy virgins are probably appealing to most heterosexual men, regardless of their current sexual satisfaction. A similar stance is taken by Baruch (2003), who contends that the traumatic separation of the sexes in Islamic societies is a major cause of fundamentalism and leads to the search for political violence. Suicide bombing is an outcome of detesting one's sexual impulses. She argues that psychoanalysis is best able to address the irrational parts of terrorism and that it needs to give more attention to the Islamic world, as its principles are so far only accepted in the West.

Wirth (2003) argues that Freud's hypothesis regarding Thanatos, the death instinct, must not be viewed as a mono-causal interpretation of destructive behaviour. Although the human destructive instinct is ever present, the extent to which an individual acts upon that instinct depends on many other factors including: malign narcissism, delusions of grandeur, feelings of powerlessness, traumatizations, fanaticism, fundamentalism and paranoid worldviews. The author posits that the events of 11 September 2001 resulted from a collective trauma.

Normal behaviour in extremely aversive conditions

The next sections of this chapter look at why and how normal people become terrorists. Before looking at the next approaches, it is important to acknowledge the extremely aversive social conditions that a lot of – but certainly not all – terrorists have had to endure in their lives, prior to and after becoming a terrorist. For example, in Palestine, many young Muslim Arabs have been severely disadvantaged through the oppressive policies of the Israeli government. They turn to terrorism to try and improve the life of their community, because they cannot see any alternative to this extreme anti-social behaviour. Furthermore their use of violence is not condemned by their political leaders, thus giving them institutional support. Dollard, Doob, Miller, Mowrer and Sears's (1939) frustration–aggression hypothesis can be applied to such a situation, as can relative deprivation theory. Violence becomes the given method of initiating pro-social change, along with an intergenerational transmission of hatred and violence; it becomes a vicious circle for the disaffected youth. Bandura's (1973) social learning theory related to violence can be applied to this situation too. In Northern Ireland, young Catholic men have endured similar circumstances and suffer a similar fate. Given the context of their behaviour, it does not appear as abnormal or evil as it may do at first sight. However, the majority of people from disaffected communities do not become terrorists, so although terrorists may be psychologically normal, terrorism as a behaviour is abnormal (Silke, 2003b). The next two sections look at the cognitive and social psychological factors that underpin this behaviour – for both legitimately aggrieved individuals and the anarchic-ideologue terrorists whose motives and grievances are more questionable. Regarding the psychology of terrorism, the cognitive and social approaches are interrelated.

The cognitive approach

Crenshaw (1990) argues that one way of looking at terrorist behaviour is to see it as a result of wilful choice – the efficiency of violence is measured against alternative strategies. Such an approach is part of rational choice theory. Crenshaw (1990) concludes that strategic choice is just one factor that can account for terrorism; rational choice theory is not all-encompassing. Bandura (1986) argues that believing in the efficiency of terrorism is one way in which moral inhibitions against mass destruction are disengaged. His argument is outlined below.

On the premise that the majority of terrorists are not mentally ill, do not have personality disorders nor are religious fanatics, how do essentially normal people come to act in such abnormal and abhorrent ways? Bandura (1986) outlines the mechanisms of moral disengagement that allow normal individuals to commit acts of terrorism. He argues that self-sanction plays a central role in the regulation of inhumane conduct. People refrain from behaving in ways that go against their morals – such behaviour leads to self-condemnation, thus a negative affective state. But morals are not fixed and self-sanctioning mechanisms only operate if activated. There are many different ways in which these moral standards can be disengaged (Bandura, 1986). Selective activation/disengagement of moral standards allows different types of behaviour by the same individual. Psychosocial mechanisms of disengagement are outlined below. Bandura points out that these mechanisms operate in everyday life as well as in extreme circumstances like political violence. It is easy to get individuals to murder reviled political figures/officials but the murder of innocent people in cold blood requires much stronger psychological disengagement mechanisms. Intensive psychological training is needed.

1. *Moral justification.* Immoral acts can be made moral through cognitive reconstruction. This is most strikingly seen in military conduct. Violence is more justifiable when nonviolent alternatives are seen as being redundant and the suffering inflicted by the enemy outweighs that inflicted by terrorist actions. Cognitive restructuring can be used to promote self-serving/destructive purposes, but also militant action designed to improve negative social conditions.

2. *Euphemistic labelling.* By using language to confer a respectable status upon reprehensible acts, people are relieved of personal responsibility for their detrimental actions. This has been proved in laboratory studies of aggression – when aggression is sanctioned, people more readily use it (Diener, Dineen, Endresen, Beaman and Fraser, 1975). An example of euphemistic labelling is the term used for civilians killed by terrorism: 'collateral damage' (Gambino, 1973).

3. *Advantageous comparison.* Self-condemned actions can be justified by contrasting them with inhumanities. If one's own conduct is compared as trivial in relation to some other act, the more readily it is self-justified. Thus, suicide terrorists become martyrs. Bandura states, 'After destructive means become invested with high moral purpose, functionaries work hard to become proficient at them and take pride in their destructive accomplishments' (Bandura, 1986: 172).

4. *Displacement of responsibility.* With displaced responsibility, people see their actions as stemming from the orders of an authority, not their own will. Thus they are free from self-prohibiting reactions. This displacement also reduces concern regarding the welfare of victims (Tilker, 1970). Shi'ite clerics have produced moral justifications for acts which violate Islamic law. This persuades them of the morality of terrorism and also maintains the integrity of the group to other Islamic nations. The religious code does not allow suicide or terrorizing innocent people. Clerics justify such acts by arguing that oppressive circumstances cause people to resort to extreme measures and that dying in a suicide bombing for a moral cause is akin to dying in a military battle.

5. *Diffusion of responsibility.* When actions are devised and carried out by a group, no one individual feels responsible (Bandura, Underwood and Fromson, 1975; Zimbardo, 1969).

6. *Disregard for consequences.* Individuals readily remember information relating to the benefits of the harmful behaviour; they do not easily recall its harmful effects. The misrepresentation may include active attempts to discredit the consequent harm. Self-censure need not be activated when consequences of one's actions are ignored, distorted and disbelieved. When the aggressor cannot see the harm he has inflicted, he is more likely to be distressed. Most organizations have chains of command in which superiors formulate plans, intermediaries transmit to executors and executors carry them out. Thus the superior never has to see the consequences of his harmful plan first hand.

7. *Dehumanization.* Self-inhibitory mechanisms against destructive behaviour can be disengaged by divesting the intended victims of human qualities. It is easier to brutalize people when they are seen as beasts. In some situations, such as the Stanford prison experiment, the acquisition of power leads to people behaving in dehumanizing ways (Haney, Banks and Zimbardo, 1973). Many studies have found this to be true.

8. *Attribution of blame.* Attributing blame to the group's antagonists enables terrorists to self-exonerate their own actions. Terrorists can claim their acts were motivated by self-protection/desperation, when power-holders ignore their legitimate grievances. 'The fact that attribution of blame can give rise to devaluation and moral justification illustrates how the various disengagement mechanisms are often interrelated and work together in weakening internal control' (Bandura, 1986: 185).

9. *Gradualization.* Terrorist behaviour evolves through extensive, gradual training. It does not emerge overnight. Through Beck's paradigm of distortions, Beck (2002) promotes the cognitive approach to understanding violence as the best model for analysing terrorist behaviour. This approach to hot violence (violence stemming from anger) is based on two premises; firstly, it does not make a difference if an individual is operating alone or in a group. Secondly, the perpetrator has strong negative biases towards the victim, and violence is thus justified. Beck has based his analysis on many of Bandura's (1986) mechanisms of disengagement.

Beck (2002) argues that terrorists are not deranged individuals; they are people who believe that killing their enemy is justified. They are guided by an ideology of hate. The perpetrators of the 11 September

2001 attacks on the United States saw the US as a hostile superpower, its politics and culture a threat to Islam. The collective self-image of the terrorist group is strengthened as the image of the enemy is strengthened in their minds; they see themselves as righteous and courageous. Muslim extremists see such terrorist acts as Satan versus Allah. Beck (2002) argues that their ideology is so strong that it suspends the traditional moral inhibitions to killing. Terrorists attack the image of the enemy that they have projected onto innocent civilians.

Beck argues that although terrorists are not deranged, they do have cognitive distortions, like others who use violence. These distortions can be within the individual or the whole group. Such distortions include:

1. Over-generalization – the presumed wrongdoings of the enemy spread to the whole population
2. Dichotomous thinking – people are seen as totally bad or totally good
3. Tunnel vision – their thoughts and behaviour become exclusively focused on destroying the enemy; they do not consider the human lives they are taking.

Beck (2002) argues that the leaders of these groups have their own geopolitical goals; terrorism is just an extreme continuation of politics. For the perpetrators of terrorist acts, it is important that they regard destruction of the enemy as more important than their own life – particularly in the case of suicide terrorism, as seen in the 11 September attacks and on a regular basis in Israel.

Beck (2002) goes on to argue that among the factors that drive people to violence are coercion, corruption and actual damage. The respective responses to these are rebellion, purification and revenge, guided by a clear sense of oppression. Beck argues that domestic terrorists in the US – such as Timothy McVeigh who bombed the Federal Building in Oklahoma City in 1995 – are motivated by rebellious feelings. They tend to be right-wing individualists who feel that they are being oppressed by the government through certain laws and taxes. Anti-American groups in Islamic states express revulsion at the corruption by the US. They advocate purification of this corruption. Beck (2002) has used the term 'prisoners of hate' to describe how the distorted cognitions of terrorists imprison their minds. Violence in the Middle East – by both Muslim and Jewish groups – is often carried out in the name of God. This claim of acting for a higher purpose removes the responsibility from the perpetrator(s), and thus is one way of bypassing natural inhibitions against killing. Beck (2002) also acknowledges a behavioural component – this is through repeated conditioning to destroy the targets, until it becomes like a reflex. This was part of the training of American soldiers in

Vietnam and may explain why some of them slew villagers; their inhibition against killing was gone. (For a discussion of how terrorist behaviour can be understood in terms of relational frame theory, see Dixon, Dymond, Rehfeldt, Roche and Zlomke, 2003.)

The social approach

J. M. Post (1987) argues that a common conclusion in studies on the psychology of terrorism is that terrorists are marginally alienated individuals who need to join a group of people with similar views. This gives specific strength to the potency of group dynamics in mediating terrorist behaviour. Terrorists almost always come from a disaffected group in society. The move to becoming a terrorist is usually due to a catalyst event, e.g. extreme violence by the police or security forces (Silke, 2001b). Potential suicide bombers have usually had at least one relative or friend killed by the 'enemy' (Kushner, 1996). They are not coerced into suicide acts by their group; they tend to join with this aim in mind. Leaders of groups are often instructed by their superiors to turn away people who join in order to be suicide bombers. However, if they persist in expressing this wish they are often chosen (Kushner, 1996).

Under influences of group dynamics, violence becomes easy to accept by those who may never have chosen it alone (Bion, 1961, also cited in J. M. Post, 1990). This is seen in gangs and cults across different cultures. As Bion (1961) demonstrated, individual behaviour is strongly influenced by group dynamics. This dynamic differs between nationalist-separatists and anarchic-ideologues. The former often maintain relationships with family and community, the latter often burn all bridges, making a complete break to join underground groups. There is pressure to conform within the group in order to be accepted. Galanter, Rabkin and Deutsch (1979) found that the greater the contentment of new members, the greater the chances of them committing anti-social acts.

Based on 'groupthink' (Janis, 1972), Semel and Minix (1979) found that groups opted for riskier behaviour than that chosen by individuals. This momentum has important implications for mass-casualty terrorism, e.g. use of nuclear weapons, through risk-increasing group dynamics of terrorism. Group cohesiveness and a strong leader are essential (Whittaker, 2002). However, Merari (1990) argues that there is no evidence to support the idea that influence of a strong leader is itself enough to lead a non-suicidal person to commit terrorist suicide. But, such influence may be an ancillary factor – channelling an existing suicidal tendency into a certain modus operandi. This view is in line with drive theories of aggression (Baron and Richardson, 1994). Adolescents are the majority of recruits – adolescence is a time when self-image and esteem are weak, thus they are vulnerable to pressures from others and from political/religious indoctrination (Whittaker, 2002).

Steven (2002) documented that the recruitment processes of some terror groups such as the GIA (Groupe Islamique Armée) in Algeria involve alleviating the negative social conditions under which their potential recruits are forced to live. In Algeria there is 50 per cent unemployment, limited food and medicine and a government seen as benefiting from the oil industry. The GIA recruited through mosques, handing out much-needed food and medicine. In return for receiving scarce basic prerequisites, who wouldn't join in with organized violence directed at those perceived responsible for causing the deprivation?

Only the most committed members undertake the most important assignments, which are often overseas, to ensure that they won't be swayed by the 'enemy' lifestyle (Steven, 2002). Long-term indoctrination camps act as the catalyst between joining an organization and extremism and suicide bombing. The end result is rational individuals who end up with a mindset that leads to their conducting extreme acts, including suicide bombing.

Terrorists learn from the experience of other groups, often through the media (Crenshaw, 1990). Crenshaw argues that the types of groups likely to use terrorism are those that do not have the support of the majority, those who originate in authoritarian states and those who are impatient for action.

Silke (2001b) points to four social determinants of suicide attacks: there is a cultural precedent for self-sacrifice in conflict; the conflict is long-running; there are many casualties already on both sides; and the perpetrators do not think they are close to victory. The Sri Lankan Tamil Tigers have constantly used suicide attacks because they have always met with success – thus have been rewarded for this behaviour. Most groups will not remain committed to such attacks as they are very expensive in terms of membership. H. Gordon (2002) argues that suicide bombing, although an individual act, is one that occurs in a collective context, subject to being sanctioned by sections of the community/ terrorist group.

However, not all terrorism takes place in a group context. For example, there are the cases of lone terrorism such as the Unabomber and Timothy McVeigh in the United States, and the Nail Bomber in England, all of whom acted in defence of ideological causes, rather than nationalist-separatist ones. We can thus see that social psychological factors play a powerful role in the causes and conduct of terrorist behaviour.

Psychology's contribution to the reduction of terrorism and conflict resolution

Beck (2002) argues that the humanistic code needs to be enforced as an alternative to the characteristics of, for example, nationalism and militant religiosity. He argues that altruism is the antidote to narcissism. For the world to effectively work, group narcissistic goals must yield to humanistic ones. This has been achieved to some extent by the EU and the UN.

The Centre for Conflict Resolution has been established in Northern Ireland to moderate the troubles in the province. Their programme for reconciliation includes:

1. Psychoeducational sessions for mediators.
2. Group sessions for former opponents.
3. The training of cognitive therapists to participate in this work.

The University of Pennsylvania, among other institutions, has commenced a new specialty in this field. In addition, in spring 2005 the US Department of Homeland Security funded the Center for the Study and Reduction of Terrorism (START) opened at the University of Maryland with a $12 million grant. This is a positive move by the most powerful country in the world, in recruiting psychology to the war on terror.

McCauley (1991) argues that retaliating with military power can be more dangerous to a government than to their targeted terrorist group. Twenty-five years of such retaliation have not reduced the threat to Israel from Palestinian groups. The most effective measure may be to do nothing more than would be done if the violence were a criminal act without political association. Colvard (2002) argues that violence by either governments or terrorists can be damaging – weakening their moral status and reducing public support.

Nevin (2003) looked at whether retaliation reduces or increases terrorism. By looking at different terrorist attacks and the government responses to those attacks, he concluded that there was no reliable evidence that retaliation either increased or decreased the average intensity of terrorist attacks. He argues that governments should therefore seek alternative approaches to reduce terrorist activity.

Silke (2001a) argues that while most terrorist groups do not wish to sacrifice their operatives, those that do can operate more lethally. Governments must identify those that are more likely to do so. He has compiled an action plan for dealing with terrorism from a psychological viewpoint, which may be summarized as follows:

1. Recognize that terrorists are normal.
2. Causes of terrorism need to be focused on – why do these normal people become terrorists? Nobody wakes up one day and decides to plant bombs that afternoon – it is part of a process.
3. Address the genuine grievances of disaffected groups.
4. Ensure security forces are restrained in their use of force when dealing with these groups – Hoffman (1998) argues that military responses do not act as deterrents.
5. Develop effective policies based on good understanding. Allowing the belief that all terrorists are crazy/evil, to persist closes other avenues for peace. Silke (2001a) suggests that a reputable public body is needed to guarantee that consistent and objective understanding of terrorism is available.
6. Establish a national or European centre for the understanding of terrorism. There is a desperate shortage of researchers in this field. However, there is already one such centre in the United States. Silke concludes, 'psychology offers real insight into the understanding of terrorism' (Silke, 2001a: 581). It can reduce ignorance, misconceptions and prejudice.

J. M. Post (1987) argues that policies should be made to fit specific terrorist groups. The smaller and more autonomous the group, the more counter-productive is external force. Such inherently unstable groups may self-destruct if left alone. The most effective anti-terrorism policy is one that prevents potential recruits becoming terrorists. It is important to facilitate exit pathways for terrorists, reduce support for the group and reduce the appeal of terrorism for disaffected youth. J. M. Post (1987) argues that reactive retaliation may strengthen the ideology of the terrorist and that it is essential to identify the locus of control of the terrorist group in order to assess the effects of counter-terrorist policies. Post's suggestions are based on his clinical interviews with terrorists and from generalizing gang/cult behaviour to terrorist behaviour.

Steven (2002) also argues that exit factors (exit from the terrorist group) need to be reinforced, harmless alternatives to joining terror groups need to be found and more effective counter-terrorism policies need to be put in place. The factors which he identifies as motivating exit include: negative reactions, lost faith in cause and desire for a normal life. Factors deterring exit include: positive aspects of group membership, having nowhere to go and loss of protection. The problem is compounded by time; the longer a member remains, the greater the group becomes their universe. Group members have a shared, collective experience. Not being able to tell others outside the group about your life can lead to serious problems in forming relationships. Employability is often diminished because of lack of references and experience. Furthermore, how can you go from being a freedom fighter to a shop worker? Most people join when in their youth. Steven (2002) explains that a terrorist may not necessarily be able to leave, even if they want to (Steven, 2002). Deterring factors can be too strong to overcome.

Bandura's (1986) suggestion for terrorism resolution is that civilized conduct requires social systems that uphold compassionate behaviour and renounce cruelty, as well as humane personal codes.

Sidman (2003) discusses terrorism as behaviour and argues that science-based solutions must offer a set of technical operations that cannot be carried out by rote, in addition to a theoretical foundation. The author argues that behavioural engineering must always be fine-tuned to fit particular actions in the contexts in which they occur. The identification of reinforcing consequences will suggest a method of reducing further terrorist attacks, by eliminating the outcomes of terrorism. Sidman contends that an empirical principle of applied behavioural analysis is that undesirable behaviour can often be eliminated non-coercively by identifying its reinforcement and then providing that same reinforcement for desirable behaviour.

Reid (2003) posits that the control of terrorist behaviour and related damage lies in eliminating or weakening the terrorist himself and controlling or eliminating the routes of terrorist attack. It also lies in decreasing terrorist funding. He contends that it does not lie in meeting terrorists' demands by paying them or promising political change or by being fearful or angering the perpetrators. Furthermore, he argues that strategies of mollification virtually always lead to more actual or threats of violence by reinforcing terrorist behaviour and strengthening their reputation and position.

Levant (2002) states that the nature of terrorism is fundamentally psychological. Therefore, psychology as a scientific discipline can contribute to defeating this global threat. Social, criminal, peace, religion, multicultural and military psychology are amongst the areas that can contribute to this. Levant argues that one way in which we can both reduce the incentives for terrorism and lessen its impact is to enhance the resilience of society to such acts. If we react with less fear, we reduce its effect.

However, there are limits to the contribution that psychology can make. Crenshaw (1990) argues that, often, expertise on terrorism is only activated during crisis management – when demand for it peaks.

Furthermore, as long as terror groups receive funding – from both governments, political movements and interested sponsors – and as long as there continues to be international arms dealing, oppressive, authoritarian governments, poverty, deprivation, greed and corruption, there will continue to be terrorism.

Additional studies

For an eclectic paradigm of psychological factors associated with political terrorism, see J. I. Ross (1996). For additional relevant information see: Allen (2004); Argyrides and Downey (2004); Bacon (2004) (a review of Chris E. Stout, *Psychology of terrorism: coping with the continuing threat*, an abridgement of Stout, 2002); Baum and Dougall (2002); Boscarino, Figley and Adams (2003, 2004); Bourne, Healy and Beer (2003); Budson et al. (2004); Bunn and Braun (2003); Cabaniss, Forand and Roose (2004); Coryn, Beale and Myers (2004); Davis (2003); Elieli (2004); Ellens (2004a, 2004b); Everly (2003); Ford (2004); Fremont (2004); Gigerenzer (2004); Gittelman (2003/2004); A. Gordon (2004); Grieger, Fullerton and Ursano (2004); Heldring (2004); Henderson-King, Henderson-King, Bolea, Koches and Kauffman (2004); Hindley (2004); Hoffman (1999); Hough (2004); Kaiser, Vick and Major (2004); Kaplan, Bradley and Ruscher (2004); Kernberg (2003); S. Levin, Henry, Pratto and Sidanius (2003); M. A. Levy, Haglund et al. (2004); Maerli, Schaper and Barnaby (2003); Malin and Fowers (2004); McCormick (2003); Merskin (2004); Miliora (2004); A. M. Miller and Heldring (2004); Moghadam (2003); Moghaddam and Maarsella (2004); Newman (2004); Orme-Johnson, Dillbeck and Alexander (2003); Pandiani and Banks (2002); Pastor (2004); Pedahzur, Perliger and Weinberg (2003); Piven (2004); Powell and Self (2004); Pyszczynski, Solomon and Greenberg (2003); Richmond (2003); James R. Rogers and Soyka (2004); Salib (2003b); Scharoun and Dziegielewski (2004); Schbley (2003); Schouten, Callahan and Bryant (2004); Sciancalepore and Motta (2004); Selth (2004); R. C. Silver (2004); R. Stein (2003); Bradley D. Stein et al. (2004); Steinhausler (2003); Sternberg (2003); Stewart (2004); Suedfeld (2004); Terrorism and Disaster (2004) (a review of *Terrorism and disaster: individual and community mental health interventions*, edited by Robert Ursano, Carol Fullerton and Ann Norwood); Torabi and Seo (2004); Twemlow (2004); Weinstein (2004); Wilson (2000); Wurmser (2004); Yedidia and Itzhaky (2004); Zaitseva and Hand (2003).

Summary and conclusion

There are many methodological problems in studying the psychology of terrorism. The majority of research has found that the vast majority of terrorists are normal. Many do, however, display a common pattern of psychodynamics. Religion does appear to play a part in some terrorist acts, although it is often relatively unimportant, and due to misinterpretation of texts. Moral disengagement has been proposed as a way that allows people in both the individual and group context to commit acts of abhorrent violence and destruction. Furthermore, individuals who resort to terrorism may have cognitive distortions that trap them in an ideology of hate and revenge. Group dynamics can go a long way in mediating terrorism. Most terrorism takes place within a collective context and through various processes that can influence thoughts and behaviour related to violence. Psychology can play a significant part in reducing terrorism. The suggestions it offers include making terrorism a less attractive option for those who may potentially resort to it, facilitating exit pathways for existing terrorists, addressing the grievances of genuinely disaffected groups and for governments to be restrained in their retaliation. Recognizing that terrorists are essentially normal is an important step. However, terrorism is not just a psychological phenomenon, thus cannot be understood exclusively in these terms. As Whittaker (2002) states, the causes of terrorism lie within the individual, the group and the nature of the larger society in which it develops. There is a desperate shortage of research in this field and future studies need to use direct research where possible, to look at each form of terrorism individually, study the rewards of the terrorist lifestyle, look at recruitment and exit factors and the consequences of counter-terrorist policy in more detail.

'It is an example and product of human interaction gone awry and is worth studying and understanding in the human terms that befit it: as conflict, struggle, passion, drama, myth, history, reality and not least psychology' (W. Reich, 1990: 279).

16   Victims of terrorism

Anna Costin

When discussing the victims of terrorism, it is essential to bear in mind the important distinction between single acts of terrorism, and on-going campaigns. It can be difficult to define terrorist attacks in situations of protracted political violence – such as that in Northern Ireland, Israel–Palestine and Sri Lanka. Protracted political violence tends to be characterized by highly variable degrees of violence. Acts of terrorism within that conflict tend to become part of daily life, abhorred by society at large, but not unexpected.

Isolated acts of terrorism – which can be linked to on-going conflict, such as the IRA's campaign on the British mainland in the 1980s and 1990s – tend to be high-impact incidents with high casualties. Browne (2003) writes that psychological reactions to on-going terrorism are not unlike reactions to war. Summerfield (1996) states that many modern conflicts are a combination of both warfare and terrorism. Exposure to acute trauma is followed by distress symptoms and a period of adjustment then a return to normality. That is not to say that isolated attacks have better outcomes. Such exposure can lead to high levels of post-traumatic stress symptoms, whereas on-going terrorism can lead to adaptive coping.

Disaster studies classify victims into direct (physically present or in close proximity to an event), secondary (family members and close friends of victims and professionals who assist them such as emergency personnel) and indirect (individuals in a community affected by the secondary effects).

A lot of research on the psychological effects of terrorism has been undertaken following the World Trade Center attacks on 11 September 2001. There is also much literature relating to the Oklahoma City bombing in 1995. These incidents devastated the United States, a country that was seen as immune from terrorism and provided much research fodder for the American psychological and medical communities. A vast amount of research has also been carried out in Northern Ireland during the course of the protracted conflict commonly referred to as the 'Troubles'. While such research can be seen to be specific to those incidents and conflicts, a lot of evidence can be generalized to other situations of terrorism.

This chapter outlines the research that has been conducted specifically on the effects of terrorism. Many studies have looked at traumatic occurrences in general and have applied those findings to the consequences of terrorism. Whilst these studies can validly be applied to terrorism they are not included in this discussion.

The effects of terrorism upon children have been included in the general discussion within this chapter. For specific effects of protracted political conflict upon children, refer to chapter 6. There is a dearth of research on the effects of acute, isolated terrorism on children. As in relation to adults, the majority of evidence to date draws on the literature on warfare, general child trauma and loss and separation and this is applied to cases of terrorism. For a discussion of the research on child victims of terrorism, see Browne (2003).

Acute exposure and mental health

The majority of studies that have looked at the consequences of terrorist attacks upon psychological well-being have focused on post-traumatic stress disorder (PTSD). However, the literature does show that responses can involve a range of symptoms including extreme stress, substance misuse and mood disorders. Epidemiological studies have found that the majority of people exposed to terrorist incidents do not go on to develop mental health problems, using DSM or ICD criteria, although most would suffer psychological distress in the immediate aftermath.

Exposure rates to traumatic events such as terrorism exceed rates of psychopathology. Therefore there exists a differential response pattern in victims. Psychological distress – and in extreme cases even PTSD – can be expected as a normal reaction to a highly traumatic event, such as a terrorist attack. However, more psychopathological conditions, such as chronic PTSD, can develop in some individuals. Galea et al. (2002) investigated trends in probable PTSD prevalence in the general population of New York City in the first six months following the World Trade Center attacks. They found that the current prevalence of probable PTSD related to the 11 September attacks in Manhattan declined from 7.5 per cent one month after the attacks to 0.6 per cent six months after the attacks. They observed that although the prevalence of PTSD symptoms was consistently higher among people who were more directly affected by the attacks, a significant number of people who were not directly affected also met criteria for probable PTSD. These data suggest a rapid resolution of the majority of the probable PTSD symptoms in the general population of New York City in the first six months following the attacks.

Chen, Chung, Chen, Fang and Chen (2003) examined the psychological impact of the 11 September disaster on the neighbourhood around the World Trade Center. Assessments were made of 555 residents from the Chinatown community. Prevalent anxiety was found in general community residents and additional depression in those who lost relatives or friends. The mental health of this community improved five months later, but more than half of residents continued to show at least one symptom of emotional distress, with those who had lost a relative reporting higher distress. Those in their forties and fifties appeared to have relatively higher emotional distress than both younger and older groups. It is important to note that this study assessed emotional well-being and found emotional distress, not psychopathology.

Sprang (2003) describes the individual vulnerability factors that increase the risk of PTSD post-terrorism. The factors include: lower IQ and levels of education, lower socio-economic status, being female, being from an ethnic minority, familial transmission of PTSD, family history of psychopathology, past psychiatric disturbance and poor coping skills. Tucker, Pfefferbaum, Nixon and Dickson (2000) determined which variables predicted the development of post-traumatic stress disorder symptoms in adults seeking mental health assistance six months after the 1995 Oklahoma City bombing, perpetrated by the lone, domestic terrorist Timothy McVeigh. Variables most highly associated with PTSD symptoms included having been injured in the incident, feeling anxious or afraid (peri-traumatic responses), and responding that counselling helped. Event characteristics of the attack are also implicated in subsequent psychopathology such as the death rate and the degree of human culpability (Rubonis and Bickman, 1991).

Jehel, Paterniti, Brunet, Duchet and Guelfi (2003) identified the factors that predict the occurrence and severity of PTSD after a terrorist attack. They evaluated 32 victims of a bomb attack in a Paris subway in 1996; 39 per cent of participants met PTSD criteria at a six months' follow-up, 25 per cent still had PTSD at 32 months. Women showed more PTSD at 32 months than did men. Employment status, physical injuries and psychotropic drug use before the attack were independent predictors of severity of PTSD at 32 months.

In a study designed to explore the differential effects of exposure to terrorism following the Oklahoma City bombing, Sprang (1999) found that proximity to the event increased the likelihood of subsequent psychopathology, through problems with regulation of self and trust in the world. Sprang posits that longer-term distress might depend upon individual interpretations of the event, and the extent to which the individual felt personally affected and victimized by the uncontrollable event.

Coping strategies were also studied. Sprang (1999) found that individuals with an avoidance-oriented coping strategy, who were directly affected by the incident, reported the highest level of victimization and perception of future threat, compared to those with a task-oriented or emotion-oriented coping strategy. Benight, Freyaldenhoven, Hughes, Ruiz and Zoschke (2000) found that coping self-efficacy judgements predicted psychological distress following the Oklahoma City bombing. Duchet, Jehel and Guelfi (2000) found that risk factors for developing PTSD following a terrorist attack in the Paris transportation system in 1996 were the presence of acute stress signs, and the type of subjective experience of the event. The absence of physical wounds appears to be linked to difficulty in recognizing psychological trauma. The authors state that a supplementary risk factor is the presence of avoidance emotion-focused coping strategies.

Gidron, Gal and Zahavi (1999) studied the use of three coping strategies in Israeli bus commuters: emotion-focused coping, problem-focused coping, and denial, and their relationship to anxiety from terrorism. Problem-focused coping was positively correlated with anxiety from terrorism; commuting frequency was negatively correlated. The authors conclude that combining minimal problem-focused preventative acts with distraction and reduced perceived vulnerability may be of benefit.

Cognitive-emotional effects

Sacco, Galletto and Blanzieri (2003) investigated the effects of the World Trade Center terrorist attacks on decision-making. Using prospect theory as a theoretical framework, and with a sample of Italian students, the authors tested how individual decision-making processes were affected. The results showed the emergence of two tendencies: a strong, long-term lasting search for security when the outcome of a decision is perceived as a gain, and a medium-term risk-avoiding behaviour in the loss domain. These tendencies were found to be absent during normal historic periods.

Qin et al. (2003) examined emotional reactions to and subsequent memory of the World Trade Center terrorist attacks in individuals with a history of PTSD. They found that individuals with PTSD reported being more negatively affected by the attacks, at the ten-month follow-up, but not initially. They also found that PTSD participants had a tendency to inflate the emotional aspects of their memory over time. Also for this group, age was negatively correlated with event memory, suggesting accelerated memory decline with age associated with PTSD.

Dumont, Yzerbyt, Wigboldus and Gordijn (2003) investigated whether social categorization affected emotional reactions, behavioural tendencies and actual behaviours, following the World Trade Center attacks. They found that when participants' attention was focused on an identity that included American victims into a common ingroup, they reported more fear and stronger fear-related behavioural tendencies than when victims were categorized as outgroup members.

Mehl and Pennebaker (2003) used electronically activated recorder (EAR) methodology to track the social lives of eleven people in the days following the World Trade Center attacks. They found that participants gradually shifted from group conversations to dyadic interactions. Exploratory analysis revealed that an increase in dyadic interactions was marginally related to better psychological adjustment at follow-up.

Lerner, Gonzalez, Small and Fischhoff (2003) predicted, on the basis of appraisal-tendency theory, opposite effects for anger and fear on risk judgements and policy preferences following 9/11. In a nationally representative sample of 973 Americans, fear increased risk estimates and plans for precautionary measures; anger had the opposite effect. Females had more pessimistic risk estimates than did males, emotion differences explaining 60–80 per cent of the gender difference. Emotions also predicted diverging public policy preferences.

Krauss et al. (2003) assessed the effect of the World Trade Center attacks on impoverished HIV-affected families in New York's Lower East Side. Parents felt they had dealt with the initial effects of the incident well, but had concerns about their ability to cope with continued threat. This challenge was compounded by the fact that they saw the number and quality of safe places from which to view and interpret events decrease, and their opportunities to establish reserves that would help them cope diminish.

In a study of US college students in the weeks following the World Trade Center attacks, Frederickson, Tugade, Waugh and Larkin (2003) found that, consistent with Fredrickson's 1998 and 2001 broaden-and-build theory, positive emotions in the aftermath of crises buffer resilient people against depression and fuel thriving.

Pyszczynski, Solomon and Greenberg (2003) explored the emotions that arose in individuals after the World Trade Center attacks, using terror management theory, an existential psychological model that explains why humans react the way they do to the threat of death and how this reaction influences their post-threat cognition and emotion. The authors' model is applicable to all instances of terrorism.

Effects on suicidal behaviour

Salib (2003a) assessed the effect of the World Trade Center attacks on the rate of suicide and homicide in England and Wales. Results found that the number of suicides reported in the month of September 2001 was significantly lower than other months in 2001 and any September of the previous 22 years in England and Wales. There was no evidence of a similar effect on homicide. The author concludes that the tragic events of the World Trade Center attacks appear to have had a brief but significant inverse effect on suicide. The results support Durkheim's theory that periods of external threat create group integration within society and lower the suicide rate through the impact on social cohesion. Sharkey (1997) found similar evidence for parasuicides.

On-going terrorism

Muldoon (2003) writes that social polarization is a profound effect of protracted political violence, such as the 'Troubles' in Northern Ireland and the occupation in Palestine. Various studies have found that this contributes to a vicious cycle of violence through the hardening of political attitudes. Punamaki and Suleiman (1990) found that political hardship led to increased active coping and political activity; likewise, Muldoon and Wilson (2001) found a relationship between experience of political violence and adherence to traditional ideologies in adolescents in Northern Ireland. It is therefore hard to make a clear distinction between victim and perpetrator of terrorism in these situations. Such commitment can be classed as a protective factor.

From a psychodynamic perspective, Lotto (2003) suggests that the attacks of 11 September provided the stimulus to release and focus the always present but usually latent urges to decrease our anxieties by striking out and punishing those we hold responsible – responding to narcissistic injury with narcissistic rage. He argues that the danger is that we succumb to the regressive pull of primitive splitting, to become super-patriots. Inevitably, the innocent become victims and the vicious cycle of injury and retribution goes on through protracted violence.

Cairns (1994) and Daly (1999) contend that studies looking at mental health problems in the community are generally stronger than those looking at the rate of psychiatric admissions. This is because the latter are vulnerable to social biases. In a community survey in Northern Ireland, Barker et al. (1988) found that 22 per cent of the sample exceeded the cut-off point for psychopathology. Other studies have found similar evidence. Joseph, Cairns and McCollam (1993) found that young people appear to display few psychological symptoms as a result of the troubles in Northern Ireland. Similar evidence has been reported by Donnelly (1995). Therefore the effects of on-going political violence appear to be limited – for both adults and children alike. Browne (2003) cautions that the situation in Northern Ireland is not comparable to situations of protracted conflict in a lot of other countries, where there is poverty and disease.

A similar figure for psychological distress was reported in relation to an acute, isolated incident; Hoven, Mandell and Duarte (2003) found that in the wake of 9/11, in New York City, major psychiatric disorders, including PTSD, separation anxiety, depression and agoraphobia, could be found in 25 per cent of the city's children. It is of course normal to expect a range of distress symptoms after such an incident, the majority of which will subside over a relatively short period.

Ronen, Rahav and Appel (2003) found that, in line with previous research, prolonged exposure to terrorism results in habituation. With reference to a terrorist attack in Tel Aviv, they studied two groups of Israeli Jewish adolescents who had similar proportions of both emotional and geographical proximity to the event: (a) local Tel Aviv adolescents, for whom the attack constituted a single, isolated acute stress, and (b) adolescents from a border settlement, for whom this attack constituted one in a continuous series of exposures to terrorist attacks.

As expected, following the terrorist attack, the acute stress group reported a higher increase in fears than the continuous stress group. Regarding emotional proximity to the event, adolescents who personally knew a victim or were physically close to the terrorist attack – in both groups – reported more fears and symptoms than those who did not know a victim. Geographical proximity did not affect the continuous stress group whereas it did affect the acute stress group. Significant differences emerged between the groups in trait anxiety, symptoms and increases in fear. Participants with high trait anxiety reported a higher level of state anxiety, more symptoms, and a higher increase in fears. Contrary to expectations, analyses revealed no significant gender differences.

Klingman (1992) found that self-reported levels of stress decreased in Israeli students between the first and fourth week of the Gulf

War. McIvor (1981) found similar evidence for international students studying in Northern Ireland.

Denial and distancing are another strategy used to cope with on-going violence. Empirical evidence for this comes from a study of perceptions of violence in Northern Ireland: individuals who inaccurately perceived their high-violence town to have little or no violence had better mental health (Cairns and Wilson, 1984). Similar evidence was found in Israel by Rofe and Lewin (1982). Somerfield and McCrae (2000) summarize the available research as suggesting that the most psychologically resilient choose the most suitable coping strategy to deal with the incident encountered.

Victims of terrorism and the media

Perl (1997) cites three new trends in terrorism, linked to the media: increasingly violent attacks, anonymous acts and attacks on journalists.

Pfefferbaum (2003) states that due to the fact that media coverage is so fundamental to the process, it may be impossible to separate the impact of the media from the impact of the actual event. Coverage of terrorism tends to be concentrated and captures acute distress; it is a conduit for the terrorists' aims. Indirect victims are the principal targets of terrorism. They are reached largely through the media and they often see little difference between themselves and direct victims. Direct victims can be exploited by aggressive media coverage that can retraumatize them through secondary exposure.

Terr et al. (1999) suggest a spectrum classification for indirect exposure to trauma. This includes distant trauma, reaction to an event not directly observable, vicarious trauma and reaction to a highly threatening event that was not directly observable but was nationally threatening. The media serve as a channel in these forms of indirect trauma.

A relationship between television exposure and post-traumatic stress reactions in indirect victims has been reported in certain studies (Schuster et al., 2001; Pfefferbaum, Gurwitch et al., 2000; Pfefferbaum et al., 1999; Pfefferbaum et al., 2001). Pfefferbaum et al. (2000) studied the effects of the Oklahoma bombing on children who lost friends and acquaintances in the attack. Those who lost a friend watched significantly more bombing-related television coverage than those without losses and they had significantly more post-traumatic stress symptoms than those who lost an acquaintance. The authors argue that parents and those working with children should be aware of the impact of loss even when it involves non-family members. Schuster et al. (2001) found an association between the number of hours of television news following the World Trade Center attacks and the number of reported stress symptoms in children.

Slone (2000) found that exposure to media coverage of terrorism in Israel induced anxiety effects in subjects. Slone argues that the results support the powerful effect of the mass media in contributing to the psychological sequelae of terrorism. Keinan, Sadeh and Rosen (2003) examined the attitudes and reactions of individuals towards media coverage of terrorist acts in Israel. The results suggested that although a considerable proportion of individuals preferred detailed coverage of attacks, when coverage included horrific details, the readiness for receiving such information declined. The results indicate that exposure to detailed coverage was associated with the development of symptoms similar to PTSD. Individual differences in attitudes and reactions towards media coverage were found as a function of participants' political orientation and information-seeking style and gender. Wayment and Cordova (2003) suggest that individuals who were exposed to the 11 September attacks through the media, but suffered no personal bereavement, may have experienced a collective loss.

However, Pfefferbaum (2003) contends that this does not indicate a causal relationship; media images of terrorism may lead to heightened arousal in some people, but those people may be drawn to media coverage to maintain that heightened arousal. Furthermore, Everly and Mitchell (2001) state that credible and adequate information may decrease the chaos felt following a terrorist incident.

Interventions

General post-trauma interventions are usually applied to helping the victims of terrorism; the following studies have examined how such interventions relate to outcomes following terrorism specifically.

Sprang (1999) states that following terrorist incidents, many individuals do not seek professional help for psychological distress, believing that they do not need it, or they turn to family, friends or religion for informal support.

Using the 2002 Bali bombing as a case in question, Tehrani (2002) states that following a disaster the mind creates a trauma memory in which sensory impressions are indelibly recorded. She argues that help and support provided in the days and weeks after a disaster are essential to psychological recovery. When the initial threat of death has passed, a sense of elation at having cheated death can form; this can lead to death guilt – survivors feeling guilty that they survived when others did not. Tehrani states that the first step in supporting victims of a disaster, is to re-establish feelings of personal safety and security. By establishing a sense of control through contacting relatives and friends and officially marking the event it will be easier for survivors to make the transition from shock to recovery. Support offered should not add to feelings of being out of control. Andersson, Bunketorp and Allebeck (1997) found that social support has consistently been found to be a powerful indicator of recovery from trauma reactions. Early psychological interventions may interfere with the survivors' own coping processes (Shalev, 2000). Talking to friends and relatives is a natural process that helps survivors to understand and accept the trauma that they have been through (S. Rose and Tehrani, 2002). B. Stein (1997) emphasizes the role of community prevention and intervention programmes in dealing with the effects of terrorism; particularly the role of school psychologists for helping children and teachers foster inner strength and resources to deal with the crisis.

Psychological debriefing is one way that survivors of terrorism can talk about their experience in a safe and structured way. The survivor can receive information on normal reactions to such an event (Friedman, 2000). There is a growing body of research that shows that when debriefing is used as part of a total care package it is effective in reducing post-trauma symptoms (Dyregrov, 1998). If post-trauma responses continue for more than a few weeks, it may be necessary to consider trauma therapy: namely, cognitive-behavioural, psychodynamic or eye movement desensitization and reprogramming (EMDR). Tehrani (2002) also argues that the possibility of terrorism can be more damaging than the real thing, following from the loss of the belief in the world as a safe place. She argues that this is why terrorism is such an effective tool.

Burlingame and Layne (2001) contend that group-based interventions for survivors of terrorist attacks are a promising technique for delivering effective post-trauma intervention to a wide variety of populations. Fivush, Edwards and Mennuti-Washburn (2003) studied the effects of expressive narrative writing, particularly the use of cognitive processing and emotion words, for alleviating post-World Trade Center stress. Individuals who used more cognitive processing and emotion words in their narratives subsequently recalled being less shocked and upset upon hearing the news of the attacks.

Marshall and Suh (2003) state that following the World Trade Center attacks, trauma symptomology was found in hundreds of thousands of people – most of whom were not relatives of the deceased or escapees. They suggest that evidence-based treatments such as prolonged exposure therapy have proven successful in treating 9/11-related PTSD. The authors state that the clinician must be sensitive to cultural issues in clinical presentation and treatment expectations.

Frederick (1994) discusses psychophysiological measures, such as pulse rate and blood pressure, coupled with incident specific-therapy, that have been most effective in treating stress disorders provoked by terrorism or torture. Frederick argues that focusing upon disturbing stimuli in slow motion while in a relaxed state has been enormously successful in both diagnosis and treatment of severe cases of psychic trauma. This process is accompanied by psychotherapy in order to unravel and resolve past associative experiences and their negative residuals that may be related to the present distress. This process must always be enhanced and never compromised.

Additional studies

For additional relevant information see: Aber, Gershoff, Ware and Kotler (2004); Auger, Seymour and Roberts (2004); Bartholomew and Wessely (2002); Becker (2002); Coates and Schechter (2004); D. S. Diamond, Pastor and McIntosh (2004); L. Fang and Chen (2004); Feerick and Prinz (2003); Foresto (2004); Gershoff and Aber (2004); Gidron (2002); Gil-Rivas, Holman and Silver (2004); Gould, Munfakh, Kleinman, Lubell and Provenzano (2004); Hardaway (2004); Henry, Tolan and Gorman-Smith (2004); Hock, Hart, Kang and Lutz (2004); P. T. Joshi and Lewin (2004); Kleinman (2002); Kutz (2002); Kyle and Angelique (2002); Liverant, Hofmann and Litz (2004); L. Miller (2004); Njenga, Nicholls, Nyamai, Kigamwa and Davidson (2004); North and Pfefferbaum (2002); Pastor (2004); Phillips, Prince and Schiebelhut (2004); Plante and Canchola (2004); Reissman, Klomp, Kent and Pfefferbaum (2004); Tota (2004); Ursano, Fullerton and Norwood (2003); Wadsworth et al. (2004).

Summary and conclusion

A differential response pattern to terrorism is found among direct, secondary and indirect victims. Evidence generally shows that the majority of both adults and children are resilient to both acute and on-going attacks. Short-term psychological distress is common following an incident; certain factors make the development of psychopathology more likely. Habituation often occurs in individuals enduring protracted terrorism. The media is a powerful tool in both keeping the public informed and in exacerbating the atrocity itself. A range of coping skills are drawn upon to help deal with the experience; many individuals rely on their own coping skills rather than formal therapy following attacks. Various interventions have been proposed and applied for helping terrorism victims and as with all psychological therapy, different types are suited to different individuals and different situations. More research is needed in all of these areas in order to increase the knowledge base for professionals dealing with the consequences of terrorism.

References

Because of the comparatively large number of duplicate surnames, authors' full first names have been given wherever possible, if these appeared in the original work. In instances where only initials are provided here but another work displays the full name of evidently the same author, the instances with the initials are sequenced below as if the first name were spelled out. Journal issue numbers are given (in brackets) after volume number, if the pagination for a particular journal restarts at page 1 for each issue in a volume.

Aall, Pamela (2002) Guessing the rules: conflict resolution in the post-cold war era. *Peace and Conflict: Journal of Peace Psychology*, 8(3): 277–80.

Abelson, Robert P. (1995) *Statistics as principled argument*. Hillsdale, NJ, and Hove, UK: Lawrence Erlbaum.

Aber, J. Lawrence, Gershoff, Elizabeth T., Ware, Angelica and Kotler, Jennifer A. (2004) Estimating the effects of September 11th and other forms of violence on the mental health and social development of New York City's youth: a matter of context. *Applied Developmental Science*, 8: 111–29.

Abu-Nimer, Mohammed (2000) Peace building in postsettlement: challenges for Israeli and Palestinian peace educators. *Peace and Conflict: Journal of Peace Psychology*, 6: 1–21.

Abu-Saba, Mary Bentley (1999) Human needs and women peacebuilding in Lebanon. *Peace and Conflict: Journal of Peace Psychology*, 5: 37–51.

(2003) Peacebuilding by women in Lebanon. In S. Krippner and T. M. McIntyre (eds.), *The psychological impact of war trauma on civilians: an international perspective* (pp. 249–56). Westport, CT: Praeger Publishers/ Greenwood Publishing Group, Inc.

Ackerman, Alice (2002) Conflict prevention: Macedonia holds good will. *Peace and Conflict: Journal of Peace Psychology*, 8(3): 293–6.

(2003) The prevention of armed conflicts as an emerging norm in international management: the OSCE and the UN as norm leaders. *Peace and Conflict Studies*, 10(1): 1–14.

Adair, Wendi L. (2003) Integrative sequences and negotiation outcome in same- and mixed-culture negotiations. *International Journal of Conflict Management*, 14: 273–96.

Adams, David et al. (1990) The Seville statement on violence. *American Psychologist*, 45: 1167–8.

Adelswaerd, Viveka and Oeberg, Britt Marie (1998) The function of laughter and joking in negotiation activities. *Humor: International Journal of Humor Research*, 11: 411–29.

Adler, Amy B. and Bartone, Paul T. (1997) Military psychologists and the partnership for peace program in Albania. *Military Medicine*, 162: 492–4.

Adler, Amy B. and Britt, Thomas W. (2003) The psychology of the peacekeeper: common themes and future directions. In T. W. Britt and A. B. Adler (eds.), *The psychology of the peacekeeper: lessons from the field* (pp. 313–18). Westport, CT: Praeger Publishers/Greenwood Publishing Group.

Adler, Amy B., Litz, Brett T. and Bartone, Paul T. (2003) The nature of peacekeeping stressors. In T. W. Britt and A. B. Adler (eds.), *The psychology of the peacekeeper: lessons from the field* (pp. 149–67). Westport, CT: Praeger Publishers/Greenwood Publishing Group.

Adorno, Theodore W., Frenkel-Brunswik, Else, Levinson, Daniel J. and Sanford, R. Nevitt (1950) *The authoritarian personality*. New York: Harper.

Ahearne, John F. (2000) Intergenerational issues regarding nuclear power, nuclear waste, and nuclear weapons. *Risk Analysis*, 20: 763–70.

Aiello, Antonio (2001) Ulteriori evidenze su 'Pantanella Shish-Mahal', una simulazione giocata sul tema del conflitto inter-etnico, per la formazione alla multiculturalita ed alla pace [Further evidence on the use of 'Pantanella Shish-Mahal', a gaming simulation on the topic of interethnic conflict, for the creation of multiculturalism and peace]. *Rassegna di Psicologia*, 18 (3): 103–11.

Ajzen, I. (1988) *Attitudes, personality, and behaviour*. Buckingham, Buckinghamshire: Open University Press.

al-'Azzam, 'Abd al-Majid and Zahir, Ahmad (1990) US public opinion sources and the Israeli–Arab struggle: a field study on sample trends in American society. *Dirasat*, 17(3-A): 182–201.

Albeck, Joseph H., Adwan, Sami and Bar-On, Dan (2002) Dialogue groups: TRT's guidelines for working through intractable conflicts by personal storytelling. *Peace and Conflict: Journal of Peace Psychology*, 8: 301–22.

Alexander, Jill and McConnell, Stephen (1993) Children as peacemakers: promoting the development of cooperation and conflict resolution. In V. K. Kool (ed.), *Nonviolence: social and psychological issues* (pp. 107–28). Lanham, MD: University Press of America.

Allen, Jon G. (2004) September 11: trauma and human bonds. *Bulletin of the Menninger Clinic*, 68: 188–9.

Allport, Gordon W. (1954) *The nature of prejudice*. Reading, MA: Addison-Wesley.

Alonso, H. (1993) *Peace as a woman's issue: a history of the US movement for world peace and women's rights*. Syracuse, NY: Syracuse University Press.

Alvarez, Ann Rosegrant and Cabbil, Lila M. (2001) The MELD program: promoting personal change and social justice through a year-long multicultural group experience. *Social Work with Groups*, 24(1): 3–20.

American Psychiatric Association (1994) *DSM IV* (4th edn.). Washington, DC: Author.

Amir, Sharon, Yitzhaki-Verner, Tali and Bar-On, Dan (1996) 'The recruited identity': the influence of the intifada on the perception of the peace process from the standpoint of the individual. *Journal of Narrative and Life History*, 6: 193–223.

Amoo, Samuel G. and Zartman, I. William (1992) Mediation by regional organizations: the Organization of African Unity (OAU) in Chad. In J. Bercovitch and J. Z. Rubin (eds.), *Mediation in international relations: multiple approaches to conflict management* (pp. 131–48). New York: St. Martin's Press, Inc.

Anderson, Anne and Christie, Daniel J. (2001) Some contributions of psychology to policies promoting cultures of peace. *Peace and Conflict: Journal of Peace Psychology*, 7: 173–85.

Anderson, Norman II. (1968) Likeableness ratings of 555 personality-trait words. *Journal of Personality and Social Psychology*, 9: 272–9.

Anderson, Royce (2004) A definition of peace. *Peace and Conflict: Journal of Peace Psychology*, 10: 101–16.

Andersson, A. L., Bunketorp, O. and Allebeck, P. (1997) High rates of psychosocial complications after road traffic injuries. *Injury*, 28: 539–43.

Annan, Jeannie R., Amuge, Anne Paulyn and Angwaro, Sr, Teddy (2003) Counseling for peace in the midst of war: counselors from Northern Uganda share their views. *International Journal for the Advancement of Counselling*, 25: 235–45.

Antrim, Lance N. and Sebenius, James K. (1992) Formal individual mediation and the negotiators' dilemma: Tommy Koh at the Law of the Sea Conference. In J. Bercovitch and J. Z. Rubin (eds.), *Mediation in international relations: multiple approaches to conflict management* (pp. 97–130). New York: St. Martin's Press, Inc.

Apfel, Roberta J. and Simon, Bennett (2000) Mitigating discontents with children in war: an ongoing psychoanalytic inquiry. In A. C. G. M. Robben and M. M. Suarez-Orozco (eds.), *Cultures under siege: collective violence and trauma* (pp. 102–30). New York: Cambridge University Press.

Apprey, Maurice (2001) Group process in the resolution of ethnonational conflicts: the case of Estonia. *Group Analysis*, 34: 99–113.

Aquino, Karl (1998) The effects of ethical climate and the availability of alternatives on the use of deception during negotiation. *International Journal of Conflict Management*, 9: 195–217.

Arbatov, Alexei G. (1991) Arms control and arms reduction: view II. In V. A. Kremenyuk (ed.), *International negotiation: analysis, approaches, issues* (pp. 288–301). San Francisco: Jossey-Bass Inc. Publishers.

Argyrides, Marios and Downey, Jerrold L. (2004) September 11: immediate and long term effects on measures of aggression, prejudice, and person perception. *North American Journal of Psychology*, 6: 175–88.

Arias, Ricardo, Soifer, Raquel and Wainer, Alberto (1990) Disavowal of the danger of nuclear war: effect of cultural factors on mental attitudes. *International Review of Psycho-Analysis*, 17: 89–95.

Aron, A. (1988) Refugees without sanctuary: Salvadorans in the United States. In A. Aron (ed.), *Flight, exile and return: mental health and the refugee* (pp. 23–53). San Francisco: Committee for Health Rights in Central America.

Aronoff, Yael S. (2001) When and why do hard-liners become soft? An examination of Israeli prime ministers Shamir, Rabin, Peres, and Netanyahu. In

O. Feldman and L. O. Valenty (eds.), *Profiling political leaders: cross-cultural studies of personality and behavior* (pp. 185–201). Westport, CT: Praeger Publishers/Greenwood Publishing Group.

Arons, Sandrine (2003) Self-therapy through personal writing: a study of Holocaust victims' diaries and memoirs. In T. M. McIntyre and S. Krippner (eds.), *The psychological impact of war trauma on civilians: an international perspective* (pp. 123–33). Westport, CT: Praeger Publishers/Greenwood Publishing Group.

Aronson, Elliot and Yates, Suzanne (1983) Cooperation in the classroom: the impact of the jigsaw method on inter-ethnic relations, classroom performance, and self-esteem. In H. H. Blumberg, A. P. Hare, M. F. Davies and V. Kent (eds.), *Small groups and social interaction* (Vol. 1, pp. 119–30). Chichester and New York: John Wiley & Sons.

Ashford, Mary-Wynne and Huet-Vaughn, Yolanda (1997) The impact of war on women. In B. S. Levy and V. W. Sidel (eds.), *War and public health* (pp. 186–96). New York: Oxford University Press.

Ashour, Omar (2004) Security, oil, and internal politics: the causes of the Russo-Chechen conflicts. *Studies in Conflict and Terrorism*, 27: 127–43.

Asmundson, Gordon J. G., Wright, Kristi D., McCreary, Donald and Pedlar, David (2003) Post-traumatic stress disorder symptoms in United Nations peacekeepers: an examination of factor structure in peacekeepers with and without chronic pain. *Cognitive Behaviour Therapy*, 32: 26–37.

Astorino-Courtois, Allison (1995) The cognitive structure of decision making and the course of Arab–Israeli relations, 1970–1978. *Journal of Conflict Resolution*, 39: 419–38.

Astorino-Courtois, Allison and Trusty, Brittani (2000) Degrees of difficulty: the effect of Israeli policy shifts on Syrian peace decisions. *Journal of Conflict Resolution*, 44: 359–77.

Auger, Richard W., Seymour, John W. and Roberts, Walter B. Jr. (2004) Responding to terror: the impact of September 11 on K-12 schools and schools' responses. *Professional School Counseling*, 7: 222–30.

Augsburger, David W. (1992) *Conflict mediation across cultures: pathways and patterns*. Louisville, KY: Westminster/John Knox Press.

Aupperle, Kenneth E. and Karimalis, Grigorios N. (2001) Using metaphors to facilitate cooperation and resolve conflict: examining the case of Disneyland Paris. *Journal of Change Management*, 2: 23–32.

Austin, Timothy (1996) A rejoinder: in regards to critiques of my research on Filipino self-help and peacemaking in the Mindanao hinterland. *Human Organization*, 55: 248–9.

Avery, Patricia G., Johnson, David W., Johnson, Roger T. and Mitchell, James M. (1999) Teaching an understanding of war and peace through structured academic controversies. In A. Raviv, L. Oppenheimer and D. Bar-Tal (eds.), *How children understand war and peace: a call for international peace education* (pp. 260–80). San Francisco: Jossey-Bass/Pfeiffer.

Award for Distinguished Contribution in Psychology in the Public Interest: Susan T. Fiske (1992) Award for Distinguished Contribution in Psychology in the Public Interest: Susan T. Fiske. *American Psychologist*, 47: 498–501.

Axelrod, Lawrence J. and Newton, James W. (1991) Preventing nuclear war: beliefs and attitudes as predictors of disarmist and deterrentist behavior. *Journal of Applied Social Psychology*, 21: 29–40.

Azar, Fabiola and Mullet, Etienne (2002) Willingness to forgive: a study of Muslim and Christian Lebanese. *Peace and Conflict: Journal of Peace Psychology*, 8: 17–30.

Bacon, Victoria L. (2004) The quest to understand terrorism. *Psyc CRITIQUES*, 49(Supplement 9), [np].

Badekale, Adeola Joy (1994) Gender, development and peace. *IFE Psychologia: An International Journal*, 2(2): 57–66.

Baker, Carol and Ross, William H. (1992) Mediation control techniques: a test of Kolb's 'orchestrators' vs. 'dealmakers' model. *International Journal of Conflict Management*, 3: 319–41.

Baker, William D. and Oneal, John R. (2001) Patriotism or opinion leadership? The nature and origins of the 'rally round the flag' effect. *Journal of Conflict Resolution*, 45: 661–87.

Balabanis, George (1998) Antecedents of cooperation, conflict and relationship longevity in an international trade intermediary's supply chain. *Journal of Global Marketing*, 12(2): 25–46.

Bandura, A. (1973) *Aggression: a social learning analysis*. Upper Saddle River, NJ: Prentice Hall.

(1986) Mechanisms of moral disengagement. In W. Reich (ed.), *Origins of terrorism: psychologies, ideologies, theologies, states of mind* (pp. 161–92). Cambridge: Cambridge University Press.

Bandura, A., Underwood, B. and Fromson, M. E. (1975) Disinhibition of aggression through diffusion of responsibility and dehumanisation of victims. *Journal of Research in Personality*, 9: 253–69 (also cited in Bandura, 1986).

Bar-On, Dan (1999) Israeli society between the culture of death and the culture of life. In K. Nader, N. Dubrow and B. H. Stamm (eds.), *Honoring differences: cultural issues in the treatment of trauma and loss* (pp. 211–33). Philadelphia, PA: Brunner/Mazel.

(2000) Cultural identity and demonization of the relevant other: lessons from the Palestinian–Israeli conflict. In A. Y. Shalev, R. Yehuda and A. C. McFarlane (eds.), *International handbook of human response to trauma* (pp. 115–25). Dordrecht, Netherlands: Kluwer Academic Publishers.

(2002) Conciliation through storytelling: beyond victimhood. In G. Salomon and B. Nevo (eds.), *Peace education: the concept, principles, and practices around the world* (pp. 109–16). Mahwah, NJ: Lawrence Erlbaum Associates.

(2003) How light pierces darkness. *Peace and Conflict: Journal of Peace Psychology*, 9: 383–6.

Bar-On, Dan, Eland, Jeanette, Kleber, Rolf J., Krell, Robert, Moore, Yael, Sagi, Abraham, Soriano, Erin, Suedfeld, Peter, van der Velden, Peter G. and van Ijzendoorn, Marinus H. (1998) Multigenerational perspectives on coping with the Holocaust experience: an attachment perspective for understanding the developmental sequelae of trauma across generations. *International Journal of Behavioral Development*, 22: 315–38.

Bar-Siman-Tov, Yaacov (1995) Value-complexity in shifting from war to peace: the Israeli peace-making experience with Egypt. *Political Psychology*, 16: 545–65.

Bar-Tal, Daniel (1990) Israeli–Palestinian conflict: a cognitive analysis. *International Journal of Intercultural Relations*, 14: 7–29.

(1993) American convictions about conflictive USA–USSR relations: a case of group beliefs. In S. Worchel and J. A. Simpson (eds.), *Conflict between people and groups: causes, processes, and resolutions* (pp. 193–213). Chicago: Nelson-Hall, Inc.

(1997) Formation and change of ethnic and national stereotypes: an integrative model. *International Journal of Intercultural Relations*, 21: 491–523.

(1998) Societal beliefs in times of intractable conflict: the Israeli case. *International Journal of Conflict Management*, 9: 22–50.

(1999) Reflections of the intractable Israeli–Arab conflict in Israeli school textbooks. *Megamot*, 39: 445–91.

(2000) From intractable conflict through conflict resolution to reconciliation: psychological analysis. *Political Psychology*, 21: 351–65.

(2001) Why does fear override hope in societies engulfed by intractable conflict, as it does in the Israeli society? *Political Psychology*, 22: 601–27.

Bar-Tal, Daniel and Antebi, Dikla (1992) Siege mentality in Israel. *International Journal of Intercultural Relations*, 16: 251–75.

Bar-Tal, Daniel and Jacobson, Dan (1998) A psychological perspective on security. *Applied Psychology: An International Review*, 47: 59–71.

Bar-Tal, Daniel and Vertzberger, Yaacov Y. I. (1997) Between hope and fear: a dialogue on the peace process in the Middle East and the polarized Israeli society. *Political Psychology*, 18: 667–700.

Barath, Arpad (2003) Cultural art therapy in the treatment of war trauma in children and youth: projects in the former Yugoslavia. In T. M. McIntyre and S. Krippner (eds.), *The psychological impact of war trauma on civilians: an international perspective* (pp. 155–70). Westport, CT: Praeger Publishers/Greenwood Publishing Group.

Barbarin, Oscar A., Richter, Linda, de Wet, Thea and Wachtel, Amy (1998) Ironic trends in the transition to peace: criminal violence supplants political violence in terrorizing South African Blacks. *Peace and Conflict: Journal of Peace Psychology*, 4: 283–305.

Barber, James D. (1990) The promise of political psychology. *Political Psychology*, 11: 173–83.

Bargal, David (2004) Structure and process in reconciliation-transformation workshops: encounters between Israeli and Palestinian youth. *Small Group Research*, 35: 596–616.

Bargal, David and Bar, Haviva (1992) A Lewinian approach to intergroup workshops for Arab–Palestinian and Jewish youth. *Journal of Social Issues*, 48(2): 139–54.

Barker, M., McClean, S. I., McKenna, P. G., Reid, N. G., Strain, J. J., Thompson, K. A., Williamson, A. P. and Wright, M. E. (1988) *Diet, lifestyle and health in Northern Ireland*. Coleraine, Northern Ireland: University of Ulster.

Barnes, Bruce E. (2002) Building conflict resolution infrastructure in the Central and South Pacific: indigenous populations and their conflicts with governments. *Conflict Resolution Quarterly*, 19: 345–61.

Baron, R. A. and Byrne, D. (2006) *Social psychology* (11th edn.). Boston: Allyn and Bacon.

Baron, R. A. and Richardson, D. R. (1994) *Human aggression*. New York: Plenum.

Barrett, Deirdre and Behbehani, Jaffar (2003) Post-traumatic nightmares in Kuwait following the Iraqi invasion. In T. M. McIntyre and S. Krippner (eds.), *The psychological impact of war trauma on civilians: an international perspective* (pp. 135–41). Westport, CT: Praeger Publishers/Greenwood Publishing Group.

Barron, Frank and Bradley, Pamela (1990) The clash of social philosophies and personalities in the nuclear arms control debate: a healthful dialectic? *Creativity Research Journal*, 3: 237–46.

Bartholomew, R. E. and Wessely, S. (2002) Protean nature of mass sociogenic illness: from possessed nuns to chemical and biological terrorism fears. *British Journal of Psychiatry*, 180: 300–6.

Bartone, Paul T. and Adler, Amy B. (1999) Cohesion over time in a peacekeeping medical task force. *Military Psychology*, 11: 85–107.

Bartone, Paul T., Adler, Amy B. and Vaitkus, Mark A. (1998) Dimensions in psychological stress in peacekeeping operations. *Military Medicine*, 163: 587–93.

Bartos, Otomar J. and Wehr, Paul Ernest (2002) *Using conflict theory*. Cambridge: Cambridge University Press.

Baruch, E. H. (2003) Psychoanalysis and terrorism: the need for a global 'talking cure'. *Psychoanalytic Psychology*, 20: 698–700.

Bassiouni, M. C. (1981) Terrorism, law enforcement and the mass media. *Journal of Criminal Law and Criminology*, 72: 1–51 (also cited in Reich, 1990).

Bastian, Maike and Bastian, Till (1990). Widerstand im Widerstand: Ersatzhandlungen und ueberwertige Ideen in Buergerrechtsbewegungen, diskutiert am Beispiel des 'Volkszaehlungsboykotts' 1987 [Resistance in the resistance movement: substitute actions and overrated ideas in civil-rights movements: the 1987 'census boycott']. *Gruppendynamik*, 21: 277–86.

Bastien, Betty, Kremer, Jurgen W., Kuokkanen, Rauna and Vickers, Patricia (2003) Healing the impact of colonization, genocide, and racism on indigenous populations. In T. M. McIntyre and S. Krippner (eds.), *The psychological impact of war trauma on civilians: an international perspective* (pp. 25–37). Westport, CT: Praeger Publishers/Greenwood Publishing Group.

Battegay, Raymond (2000) Individual responsibility versus archaic group dynamics in national and international politics. *Archives of Psychiatry and Psychotherapy*, 2(4): 5–15.

Baum, A. and Dougall, A. L. (2002) Terrorism and behavioural medicine. *Current Opinion in Psychiatry*, 15: 617–21.

Bazerman, Charles (2001) Nuclear information: one rhetorical moment in the construction of the information age. *Written Communication*, 18: 259–95.

Beck, A. T. (2002) Prisoners of hate. *Behaviour Research & Therapy*, 40: 209–16.

Becker, Steven M. (2002) Responding to the psychosocial effects of toxic disaster: policy initiatives, constraints, and challenges. In J. M. Havenaar, J. Cwikel and E. J. Bromet (eds.), *Toxic turmoil: psychological and societal consequences of ecological disasters* (pp. 199–216). New York: Kluwer Academic.

Beer, Francis A. (2001) *Meanings of war & peace*. College Station, TX: Texas A & M University Press.

Beersma, Bianca, Harinck, Fieke and Gerts, Maria J. J. (2003) Bound in honor: how honor values and insults affect the experience and management of conflicts. *International Journal of Conflict Management*, 14: 75–94.

Bekerman, Zvi (2002) Can education contribute to coexistence and reconciliation? Religious and national ceremonies in bilingual Palestinian–Jewish schools in Israel. *Peace and Conflict: Journal of Peace Psychology*, 8(3): 259–76.

Belay, Getinet (1997) Ethics in international interaction: perspectives on diplomacy and negotiation. In F. L. Casmir (ed.), *Ethics in intercultural and international communication* (pp. 227–65). Mahwah, NJ: Lawrence Erlbaum Associates, Inc., Publishers.

Bellany, Ian (1995) The offensive–defensive distinction, the international arms trade, and Richardson and Dewey. *Peace and Conflict: Journal of Peace Psychology*, 1: 37–48.

Ben Yehuda-Agid, Hemda and Auerbach, Yehudit (1991) Attitudes to an existence conflict: Allon and Peres on the Palestinian issue, 1967–1987. *Journal of Conflict Resolution*, 35: 519–46.

Benight, C. C., Freyaldenhoven, R. W., Hughes, J., Ruiz, J. M. and Zoschke, T. A. (2000) Coping self-efficacy and psychological distress following the Oklahoma City bombing. *Journal of Applied Social Psychology*, 30: 1331–44.

Bennett, D. Scott (1997) Measuring rivalry termination, 1816–1992. *Journal of Conflict Resolution*, 41: 227–54.

Bennett, D. Scott and Stam, Allan C. (2000) Research design and estimator choices in the analysis of interstate dyads: when decisions matter. *Journal of Conflict Resolution*, 44: 653–85.

Bercovitch, Jacob (1991) International mediation and dispute settlement: evaluating the conditions for successful mediation. *Negotiation Journal*, 7: 17–30.

(1992a) Mediators and mediation strategies in international relations. *Negotiation Journal*, 8: 99–112.

(1992b) The structure and diversity of mediation in international relations. In J. Bercovitch and J. Z. Rubin (eds.), *Mediation in international relations: multiple approaches to conflict management* (pp. 1–29). New York: St. Martin's Press, Inc.

(1996) Understanding mediation's role in preventive diplomacy. *Negotiation Journal*, 12: 241–58.

Bercovitch, Jacob and Houston, Allison (2000) Why do they do it like this? An analysis of the factors influencing mediation behavior in international conflicts. *Journal of Conflict Resolution*, 44: 170–202.

Bercovitch, Jacob and Kadayifci, Ayse (2002) Exploring the relevance and contribution of mediation to peace-building. *Peace and Conflict Studies*, 9(2): 21–40.

Bercovitch, Jacob and Rubin, Jeffrey Z. (eds.) (1992) *Mediation in international relations: multiple approaches to conflict management*. Basingstoke: Macmillan in association with the Society for the Psychological Study of Social Issues.

Beriker, Nimet and Druckman, Daniel (1991) Models of responsiveness: the Lausanne Peace Negotiations (1922–1923). *Journal of Social Psychology*, 131: 297–300.

Beriker-Atiyas, Nimet and Demirel-Pegg, Tijen (2000) An analysis of integrative outcomes in the Dayton peace negotiations. *International Journal of Conflict Management*, 11: 358–77.

Betancourt, Hector (1990) An attributional approach to intergroup and international conflict. In S. Graham and V. S. Folkes (eds.), *Attribution theory: applications to achievement, mental health, and interpersonal conflict* (pp. 205–20). Hillsdale, NJ: Lawrence Erlbaum Associates, Inc.

Bettencourt, B. Ann (1996) The intragroup dynamics of maintaining a successful grassroots organization: a case study. *Journal of Social Issues*, 52(1): 169–86.

Betz, Brian (1991) Response to strategy and communication in an arms race-disarmament dilemma. *Journal of Conflict Resolution*, 35: 678–90.

Bickmore, Kathy (1999) Elementary curriculum about conflict resolution: can children handle global politics? *Theory and Research in Social Education*, 27: 45–69.

Bigoness, William J. and DuBose, Philip B. (1992) Effects of arbitration condition and risk-taking propensity upon bargaining behavior. *International Journal of Conflict Management*, 3: 133–50.

Bion, W. (1961) *Experiences in groups*. London: Tavistock.

Bizman, Aharon and Hoffman, Michael (1993) Expectations, emotions, and preferred responses regarding the Arab–Israeli conflict: an attributional analysis. *Journal of Conflict Resolution*, 37: 139–59.

Blacker, Coit D. (1991) Learning in the nuclear age: Soviet strategic arms control policy, 1969–1989. In G. W. Breslauer and P. E. Tetlock (eds.), *Learning in US and Soviet foreign policy* (pp. 429–68). Boulder, CO: Westview Press.

Blake, Cecil (1998) The role of peace communication in conflict resolution in Africa. *Journal of Black Studies*, 28: 309–18.

Blight, J. G. (1992) Nuclear crisis psychologies: still 'crazy' (and still irrelevant) after all these years. In P. Suedfeld and P. E. Tetlock (eds.), *Psychology and social policy* (pp. 83–93). New York: Hemisphere Publishing Corp.

Blight, James G. and Lang, Janet M. (1995) Burden of nuclear responsibility: reflections on the critical oral history of the Cuban missile crisis. *Peace and Conflict: Journal of Peace Psychology*, 1: 225–64.

Bluehouse, Philmer and Zion, James W. (1993) Hozhooji naat'aanii: the Navajo justice and harmony ceremony. *Mediation Quarterly*, 10: 327–37.

Blumberg, Herbert H. (1977) Introduction. In A. P. Hare and H. H. Blumberg (eds.), *Liberation without violence: a third party approach*, London: Rex Collings.

(1993) Peace psychology: overview and taxonomy. In V. K. Kool (ed.), *Nonviolence: social and psychological issues* (pp. 167–82). Lanham, MD: University Press of America.

(1997) On taking too much: a point accumulation procedure for comparing mutual agreements with controlled individual initiatives. *Small Group Research*, 28: 171–93.

(1998) Peace psychology after the Cold War: a selective review. *Genetic, Social, and General Psychology Monographs*, 124: 5–37.

(2001) The common ground of natural language and social interaction in personality description. *Journal of Research in Personality*, 35: 289–312.

(2005, June) Peace psychology before and after September 2001. Presented at the Ninth International Symposium on the Contributions of Psychology to Peace, under the auspices of the International Union of Psychological Science, Portland, OR, USA.

Blumberg, Herbert H. and French, Christopher C. (eds.) (1992) *Peace: abstracts of the psychological and behavioral literature, 1967 to 1990*. Washington, DC: American Psychological Association.

(1994) *The Persian Gulf War: views from the social and behavioral sciences*. Lanham, MD: University Press of America.

Blumberg, Herbert H., Hare, A. Paul, Kent, M. Valerie and Davies, Martin F. (In press) *Small group research: basic issues*. Oxford: Peter Lang.

Boardman, Susan K. and Horowitz, Sandra V. (1994) Constructive conflict management and social problems: an introduction. *Journal of Social Issues*, 50(1): 1–12.

Bobrow, Davis B. and Boyer, Mark A. (1997) Maintaining system stability: contributions to peacekeeping operations. *Journal of Conflict Resolution*, 41: 723–48.

Bodine, Richard J. and Crawford, Donna K. (1998) *Handbook of conflict resolution education: a guide to building quality programs in schools*. San Francisco: Jossey-Bass.

Boehm, Christopher (2003) Global conflict resolution: an anthropological diagnosis of problems with world governance. In R. W. Bloom and N. K. Dess (eds.), *Evolutionary psychology and violence: a primer for policymakers and public policy advocates* (pp. 203–37). Westport, CT: Praeger Publishers/ Greenwood Publishing Group.

Boehnke, Klaus (1992) The status of psychological peace research in East and West Germany in a time of change. *Political Psychology*, 13: 133–44.

Boehnke, Klaus and Schwartz, Shalom H. (1997) Fear of war: relations to values, gender, and mental health in Germany and Israel. *Peace and Conflict: Journal of Peace Psychology*, 3: 149–66.

Boettcher, William A. (1995) Context, methods, numbers, and words: Prospect theory in international relations. *Journal of Conflict Resolution*, 39: 561–83.

Bogumil, David Daniel. (2001) Attribution and reciprocity in international relations: the attribution reciprocity model. *North American Journal of Psychology*, 3: 463–80.

Bohleber, W. (2002) Collective phantasms, destructiveness, terrorism. *Psyche-Zeitschrift fur Psychoanalyses und Ihre Anwendungen*, 56: 699–720.

Bollinger, D. (1982) *Language: the loaded weapon*. London: Longman.

Bolton, Elisa E., Glenn, D. Michael, Orsillo, Susan, Roemer, Lizabeth and Litz, Brett T. (2003) The relationship between self-disclosure and symptoms of posttraumatic stress disorder in peacekeepers deployed to Somalia. *Journal of Traumatic Stress*, 16: 203–10.

Bolton, Paul (2003) Assessing depression among survivors of the Rwanda genocide. In T. M. McIntyre and S. Krippner (eds.), *The psychological impact of war trauma on civilians: an international perspective* (pp. 67–77). Westport CT: Praeger Publishers/Greenwood Publishing Group.

Bonham, G. Matthew (1993) Cognitive mapping as a technique for supporting international negotiation. *Theory and Decision*, 34: 255–73.

Boniecki, Kurt A. and Britt, Thomas W. (2003) Prejudice and the peacekeeper. In T. W. Britt and A. B. Adler (eds.), *The psychology of the peacekeeper: lessons from the field* (pp. 53–70). Westport, CT: Praeger Publishers/Greenwood Publishing Group.

Bonta, Bruce D. (1997) Cooperation and competition in peaceful societies. *Psychological Bulletin*, 121: 299–320.

Boothby, N. (1986) Children and war. *Cultural Survival Quarterly*, 10(4): 28–30.
  (1988) Unaccompanied children from a psychological perspective. In E. Ressler, N. Boothby and D. Steinbock (eds.), *Unaccompanied children* (pp. 133–80). New York: Oxford University Press.
  (1996) Mobilising communities to meet the psychological needs of children in war and refugee crisis. In R. Apfel and B. Simon (eds.), *Minefields in their hearts* (pp. 149–64). New Haven, CT: Yale University Press.

Bores, Johannes (Jannie) (2003) Public affairs television and third party roles: the Nightline debates in South Africa (1985) and Israel (1988). *Peace and Conflict Studies*, 10(2): 1–19.

Borris, Eileen and Diehl, Paul F. (1998) Forgiveness, reconciliation, and the contribution of international peacekeeping. In H. J. Langholtz (ed.), *The psychology of peacekeeping* (pp. 207–22). Westport, CT: Praeger Publishers/ Greenwood Publishing Group, Inc.

Boscarino, Joseph A., Figley, Charles R. and Adams, Richard E. (2003) Fear of terrorism in New York after the September 11 terrorist attacks: implications for emergency mental health and preparedness. *International Journal of Emergency Mental Health*, 5: 199–209.
  (2004) Compassion fatigue following the September 11 terrorist attacks: a study of secondary trauma among New York City social workers. *International Journal of Emergency Mental Health*, 6: 57–66.

Boudreau, Thomas (2003) Intergroup conflict reduction through identity affirmation: overcoming the image of the ethnic or enemy 'other'. *Peace and Conflict Studies*, 10(1): 87–107.

Bourne, Lyle E. Jr., Healy, Alice F. and Beer, Francis A. (2003) Military conflict and terrorism: general psychology informs international relations. *Review of General Psychology*, 7: 189–202.

Bourne, Lyle E. Jr., Sinclair, Grant P., Healy, Alice F. and Beer, Francis A. (1996) Peace and gender: differential reactions to international treaty violations. *Peace and Conflict: Journal of Peace Psychology*, 2: 143–9.

Bowen, Linda K., Gwiasda, Victoria and Brown, M. Mitchell (2004) Engaging community residents to prevent violence. *Journal of Interpersonal Violence*, 19: 356–67.

Bowlby, J. (1982) *Attachment, separation and loss. Vol. 1: Attachment*. New York: Basic Books.

(1988) *A secure base*. New York: Basic Books.

Bowling, Daniel and Hoffman, David (2000) Bringing peace into the room: the personal qualities of the mediator and their impact on the mediation. *Negotiation Journal*, 16: 5–28.

Boyden, Jo (2003) The moral development of child soldiers: what do adults have to fear? *Peace and Conflict: Journal of Peace Psychology*, 9: 343–62.

Boyer, Mark A. (1999) Coalitions, motives, and payoffs: a classroom simulation of mixed-motive negotiations. *Social Science Computer Review*, 17: 305–12.

Boyer, Paul (1996) Hiroshima: the first response. In C. B. Strozier and M. Flynn (eds.), *Genocide, war, and human survival* (pp. 21–30). Lanham, MD: Rowman & Littlefield.

Bracher, Mark (1998) Valuing differences in order to make a difference: psychoanalytic theory and the practice of violence prevention. *Journal for the Psychoanalysis of Culture and Society*, 3: 1–23.

Bradshaw, Samuel L., Ohlde, Carroll D. and Horne, James B. (1991) The love of war: Vietnam and the traumatized veteran. *Bulletin of the Menninger Clinic*, 55: 96–103.

Brams, Steven J. and Taylor, Alan D. (1996) *Fair division: from cake-cutting to dispute resolution*. Cambridge: Cambridge University Press.

(1999) *The win-win solution: guaranteeing fair shares to everybody*. New York: W. W. Norton and Co, Inc.

Brannan, D. W., Esler, P. F., Strindberg, N. and Anders, T. (2001) Talking to terrorists: towards an independent analytical framework for the study of violent substate activism. *Studies in Conflict and Terrorism*, 24: 3–24.

Breen, John (2004) The dead and the living in the land of peace: a sociology of the Yasukuni shrine. *Mortality*, 9: 76–93.

Brehm, Sharon, Kassin, Saul and Fein, Steven (2005) *Social psychology* (6th edn.). Boston: Houghton Mifflin.

Brenes, Abelardo and Wessells, Michael (2001) Psychological contributions to building cultures of peace. *Peace and Conflict: Journal of Peace Psychology*, 7: 99–107.

Brenes, Abelardo and Winter, Deborah Du Nann (2001) Earthly dimensions of peace: the Earth Charter. *Peace and Conflict: Journal of Peace Psychology*, 7: 157–71.

Breslauer, George W. (1991) Learning in Soviet policy towards the Arab–Israeli conflict. In G. W. Breslauer and P. E. Tetlock (eds.), *Learning in US and Soviet foreign policy* (pp. 551–85). Boulder, CO: Westview Press.

Breslauer, George W. and Tetlock, Philip E. (eds.) (1991) *Learning in US and Soviet foreign policy*. Boulder, CO: Westview Press.

Brett, Jeanne M. (2000) Culture and negotiation. *International Journal of Psychology*, 35(2): 97–104.

(2001) *Negotiating globally: how to negotiate deals, resolve disputes, and make decisions across cultural boundaries.* San Francisco: Jossey-Bass/Pfeiffer.

Brett, Joan F., Pinkley, Robin L. and Jackofsky, Ellen F. (1996) Alternatives to having a BATNA in dyadic negotiation: the influence of goals, self-efficacy, and alternatives on negotiated outcomes. *International Journal of Conflict Management*, 7: 121–38.

Brewer, Marilynn B. (1996) When contact is not enough: social identity and intergroup cooperation. *International Journal of Intercultural Relations*, 20: 291–303.

Brewer, Paul R. and Steenbergen, Marco R. (2002) All against all: how beliefs about human nature shape foreign policy opinions. *Political Psychology*, 23: 39–58.

Britt, Thomas W. (1998) Psychological ambiguities in peacekeeping. In H. J. Langholtz (ed.), *The psychology of peacekeeping* (pp. 111–28). Westport, CT: Praeger Publishers/Greenwood Publishing Group, Inc.

(2003) Can participation in peacekeeping missions be beneficial? The importance of meaning as a function of attitudes and identity. In T. W. Britt and A. B. Adler (eds.), *The psychology of the peacekeeper: lessons from the field* (pp. 71–88). Westport, CT: Praeger Publishers/Greenwood Publishing Group.

Britt, Thomas W. and Adler, Amy B. (2003a) The psychology of the peacekeeper: an introductory framework. In T. W. Britt and A. B. Adler (eds.), *The psychology of the peacekeeper: lessons from the field* (pp. 3–10). Westport, CT: Praeger Publishers/Greenwood Publishing Group.

(eds.) (2003b) *The psychology of the peacekeeper: lessons from the field.* Westport, CT: Praeger Publishers/Greenwood Publishing Group.

Brock, S. E. (2002) Identifying psychological trauma victims. In S. E. Brock, P. J. Lazarus and S. R. Jimerson (eds.), *Best practices in school crisis prevention and intervention* (pp. 367–83). Bethesda, MD: National Association of School Psychologists.

Brock-Utne, Birgit (1985) *Educating for peace.* Tarrytown, NY: Pergamon.

(1990) The raising of a peaceful boy. *Educational and Psychological Interactions*, 105: 73–82.

(1994) Listen to women for a change. In R. Elias and J. Turpin (eds.), *Rethinking peace* (pp. 205–9). Boulder, CO: Lynne Rienner.

Brody, Eugene B. (1992) Global services to humanity. In J. H. Masserman and J. H. McGuire (eds.), *Social psychiatry and world accords* (pp. 16–29). New York, NY: Gardner Press, Inc. (from *PsycINFO*, 1993, Abstract No. 93-085007-003; 1993-97415-003).

Bronfenbrenner, Urie (1961) The mirror-image in Soviet–American relations: a social psychologist's report. *Journal of Social Issues*, 17(3): 45–56.

Brooks, Susan M., Conn, Sarah A., Ellis, Priscilla, Mack, Sally A., Murphy, Bianca Cody and Surrey, Janet (1992) Women and peacemaking: the importance of relationships. In S. Staub and P. Green (eds.), *Psychology and social responsibility: facing global challenges* (pp. 271–89). New York: New York University Press.

Broughton, Sally (2003) Before and after trauma: the difference between prevention and reconciliation activities in Macedonia. In S. Krippner and

T. M. McIntyre (eds.), *The psychological impact of war trauma on civilians: an international perspective* (pp. 231–8). Westport, CT: Praeger Publishers/ Greenwood Publishing Group, Inc.

Brown, Roger (1965) *Social psychology*. New York and London: Free Press (Collier-Macmillan).

Brown, Scott W., Boyer, Mark A., Mayall, Hayley J., Johnson, Paula R., Meng, Lin, Butler, Michael J., Weir, Kimberley, Florea, Natalie, Hernandez, Magnolia and Reig, Sally (2003) The GlobalEd Project: gender differences in a problem-based learning environment of international negotiations. *Instructional Science*, 31: 255–76.

Browne, D. (2003) Examining the impact of terrorism on children. In A. Silke (ed.), *Terrorists, victims and society: psychological perspectives on terrorism and its consequences*. Chichester: Wiley.

Brubaker, David and Verdonk, Tara (1999) Conflict transformation training in another culture: a case study from Angola. *Mediation Quarterly*, 16: 303–19.

Bruck, Peter (1993) Dealing with reality: the news media and the promotion of peace. In C. Roach (ed.), *Communication and culture in war and peace* (pp. 71–96). Newbury Park, CA: Sage Publications, Inc.

Brunet, Ariane and Rousseau, Stephanie (1996) *Acknowledging violations, struggling against impunity: women's rights as human rights*. Montreal, Canada: International Centre for Human Rights and Democratic Development, ICHRDD.

Bruton, Garry D. and Samiee, Saeed (1998) Anatomy of a failed high technology strategic alliance. *Organizational Dynamics*, 27: 51–63.

Budson, Andrew E., Simons, Jon S., Sullivan, Alison L., Beier, Jonathan S., Solomon, Paul R., Scinto, Leonard F., Daffner, Kirk R. and Schacter, Daniel L. (2004) Memory and emotions for the September 11, 2001, terrorist attacks in patients with Alzheimer's disease, patients with mild cognitive impairment, and healthy older adults. *Neuropsychology*, 18: 315–27.

Bunch, C. (1987) *Passionate politics: feminist theory in action*. New York: St. Martin's Press.

Bunn, George and Braun, Chaim (2003) Terrorism potential for research reactors compared with power reactors: nuclear weapons, 'dirty bombs', and truck bombs. *American Behavioral Scientist*, 46: 714–26.

Burgess, Heidi and Burgess, Guy (1996) Constructive confrontation: a transformative approach to intractable conflicts. *Mediation Quarterly*, 13: 305–22.

Burgin, Eileen (1994) Influences shaping members' decision making: Congressional voting on the Persian Gulf War. *Political Behavior*, 16: 319–42.

Burlingame, G. M. and Layne, C. M. (2001) Group-based interventions for trauma survivors: introduction to the special issue. *Group Dynamics: Theory, Research, and Practice*, 5: 243–5.

Burlingame-Lee, Laura (2004) Forgiveness, emotion, and evolution in making peace. *Peace and Conflict: Journal of Peace Psychology*, 10: 181–3.

Burton, John W. (1969) *Conflict & communication: the use of controlled communication in international relations*. New York: Free Press.

(1979) *Deviance, terrorism & war: the process of solving unsolved social and political problems*. Oxford: Martin Robertson.

(1994) Conflict styles and outcomes in a negotiation with fully-integrative potential. *International Journal of Conflict Management*, 5: 309–25.

Butler, Judith (2003) Violence, mourning, politics. *Studies in Gender and Sexuality*, 4: 9–37.

Butler, Michael J. (2003) US military intervention in crisis, 1945–1994: an empirical inquiry of just war theory. *Journal of Conflict Resolution*, 47: 226–48.

Butovskaya, Marina L. (2001) Reconciliation after conflicts: ethological analysis of post-conflict interactions in Kalmyk children. In J. M. Ramirez and D. S. Richardson (eds.), *Cross-cultural approaches to research on aggression and reconciliation* (pp. 167–90). Huntington, NY: Nova Science Publishers.

Butovskaya, Marina, Verbeek, Peter, Ljungberg, Thomas and Lunardini, Antonella (2000) A multicultural view of peacemaking among young children. In F. Aureli and F. B. M. de Waal (eds.), *Natural conflict resolution* (pp. 243–58). Berkeley, CA: University of California Press.

Byles, Joanna Montgomery (2003) Psychoanalysis and war: the superego and projective identification. *Journal for the Psychoanalysis of Culture and Society*, 8: 208–13.

Cabaniss, Deborah L., Forand, Nicholas and Roose, Steven P. (2004) Conducting analyses after September 11: implications for psychoanalytic technique. *Journal of the American Psychoanalytic Association*, 52: 717–34.

Cai, Deborah A., Wilson, Steven R. and Drake, Laura E. (2000) Culture in the context of intercultural negotiation: individualism-collectivism and paths to integrative agreements. *Human Communication Research*, 26: 591–617.

Cairns, E. (1994) Understanding conflict and promoting peace in Ireland: psychology's contribution. *The Irish Journal of Psychology*, 15: 480–93.

(1996) *Children and political violence*. Oxford: Blackwell.

Cairns, Ed (2001) War and peace. *Psychologist*, 14: 292–3.

Cairns, Ed and Lewis, Christopher Alan (2003) Empowering peace. *Psychologist*, 16: 142–3.

Cairns, Ed, Lewis, Christopher Alan, Mumcu, Ozlem and Waddell, Neil (1998) Memories of recent ethnic conflict and their relationship to social identity. *Peace and Conflict: Journal of Peace Psychology*, 4: 13–22.

Cairns, Ed and Wilson, R. (1984) The impact of violence on mild psychiatric morbidity in Northern Ireland. *British Journal of Psychiatry*, 145: 631–5.

Cairns, Ed, Wilson, Ronnie, Gallagher, Tony and Trew, Karen (1995) Psychology's contribution to understanding conflict in Northern Ireland. *Peace and Conflict: Journal of Peace Psychology*, 1: 131–48.

Calder, Nigel (1979) *Nuclear nightmares: an investigation into possible wars*. Harmondsworth: Penguin.

Campanella, Miriam L. (1993) The cognitive mapping approach to the globalization of world politics. In E. Laszlo and I. Masulli (eds.), *The evolution of cognitive maps: new paradigms for the twenty-first century* (pp. 237–54). Amsterdam: Gordon and Breach.

Caprioli, M. (2000) Gendered conflict. *Journal of Peace Research*, 37: 57–68.

Caprioli, Mary and Boyer, Mark A. (2001) Gender, violence, and international crisis. *Journal of Conflict Resolution*, 45: 503–18.

Carment, David and Rowlands, Dane (1998) Three's company: evaluating third-party intervention in intrastate conflict. *Journal of Conflict Resolution*, 42: 572–99.

Carnevale, Peter J. and Choi, Dong Won (2000) Culture in the mediation of international disputes. *International Journal of Psychology*, 35(2): 105–10.

Carter, April, Clark, Howard and Randle, Michael (compilers) (2006) *People power and protest since 1945: a bibliography of nonviolent action*. London: Housmans.

Casmir, Fred L. (ed.) (1997) *Ethics in intercultural and international communication*. Mahwah, NJ: Lawrence Erlbaum Associates.

Caspary, William R. (2003) Holy war, holy peace: how religion can bring peace to the Middle East. *Political Psychology*, 24(2): 415–17.

Cassidy, Clare and Trew, Karen (1998) Identities in Northern Ireland: a multi-dimensional approach. *Journal of Social Issues*, 54: 725–40.

Castano, Emanuele, Sacchi, Simona and Gries, Peter Hays (2003) The perception of the other in international relations: evidence for the polarizing effect of entitativity. *Political Psychology*, 24: 449–68.

Castro, Carl Andrew (2003) Considerations when conducting psychological research during peacekeeping missions: the scientist and the commander. In T. W. Britt and A. B. Adler (eds.), *The psychology of the peacekeeper: lessons from the field* (pp. 11–27). Westport, CT: Praeger Publishers/Greenwood Publishing Group.

Cederman, Lars Eril and Rao, Mohan Penubarti (2001) Exploring the dynamics of the democratic peace. *Journal of Conflict Resolution*, 45: 818–33.

Centeno, Miguel Angel (2001) Explaining the long peace: war in Latin America. In D. Chirot and M. E. P. Seligman (eds.), *Ethnopolitical warfare: causes, consequences, and possible solutions* (pp. 179–202). Washington, DC: American Psychological Association.

Chafetz, Glenn, Abramson, Hillel and Grillot, Suzette (1996) Role theory and foreign policy: Belarussian and Ukrainian compliance with the nuclear nonproliferation regime. *Political Psychology*, 17: 727–57.

Chapin, Wesley D. (1998) The balance of power game. *Simulation and Gaming*, 29: 105–12.

Charny, Israel W. (ed.) (1994) *The widening circle of genocide*. New Brunswick, NJ: Transaction Publishers.

Chase, Jonathan (1996) A safe European home? Global environmental change and European national identities. In G. M. Breakwell and E. Lyons (eds.), *Changing European identities: social psychological analyses of social change* (pp. 209–25). Oxford: Butterworth-Heinemann.

Chataway, Cynthia J. (1998) Track II diplomacy: from a Track I perspective. *Negotiation Journal*, 14: 269–87.

Cheldelin, Sandra, Greenberg, Melanie, Honeyman, Christopher and Volpe, Maria R. (2002) An experiment in 'practice to theory' in conflict resolution. *Negotiation Journal*, 18: 301–3.

Chen, H., Chung, H., Chen, T., Fang, L. and Chen, J. P. (2003) The emotional distress in a community after the terrorist attack on the World Trade Center. *Community Mental Health Journal*, 39: 157–65.

Chimienti, Giovanni and Abu Nasr, Julinda (1992–3) Children's reactions to war-related stress: II. The influence of gender, age, and the mother's reaction. *International Journal of Mental Health*, 21(4): 72–86.

Chiozza, Giacomo and Choi, Ajin (2003) Political leaders and the management of territorial disputes, 1950–1990. *Journal of Conflict Resolution*, 47: 251–78.

Chiozza, Giacomo and Goemans, H. E. (2003) Peace through insecurity: tenure and international conflict. *Journal of Conflict Resolution*, 47: 443–67.

Chirot, Daniel and Seligman, Martin E. P. (2001) *Ethnopolitical warfare: causes, consequences, and possible solutions*. Washington, DC: American Psychological Association.

Christie, Daniel J. (1997) Reducing direct and structural violence: the human needs theory. *Peace and Conflict: Journal of Peace Psychology*, 3: 315–32.

(2003) Opposing ideologies on the immutability of human behavior and social systems. *Peace and Conflict: Journal of Peace Psychology*, 9: 333–7.

(2004) Whose peace education? Psychology and geohistorical contexts of peace education. *Contemporary Psychology: APA Annual Review of Books*, 49: 456–8.

(2006) Post-Cold War peace psychology: more differentiated, contextualized, and systemic. Special issue, *Journal of Social Issues*, 62(1).

Christie, Daniel J. and Hanley, C. Patricia (1994) Some psychological effects of nuclear war education on adolescents during Cold War II. *Political Psychology*, 15: 177–99.

Christie, Daniel J., Wagner, Richard V. and Winter, Deborah DuNann (eds.) (2001) *Peace, conflict, and violence: peace psychology for the 21st century*. Upper Saddle River, NJ: Prentice Hall.

Cialdini, R. B. (2003) Crafting normative messages to protect the environment. *Current Directions in Psychological Science*, 12: 105–9.

Cioffi-Revilla, Claudio (1999) Origins and age of deterrence: comparative research on old world and new world systems. *Cross Cultural Research: The Journal of Comparative Social Science*, 33: 239–64.

Clark, David H. (2001) Trading butter for guns: domestic imperatives for foreign policy substitution. *Journal of Conflict Resolution*, 45: 636–60.

Clarke, Bruce B. (1993) Conflict termination: a rational model. *Studies in Conflict and Terrorism*, 16: 25–50.

Clayton, Claudia J., Ballif Spanvill, Bonnie and Hunsaker, Melanie D. (2001) Preventing violence and teaching peace: a review of promising and effective antiviolence, conflict-resolution, and peace programs for elementary school children. *Applied and Preventive Psychology*, 10: 1–35.

Coalition to End the Use of Child Soldiers (2000) Americas report. Retrieved 28 July 2000, from http://www.childsoldiers.org/americas

Coates, Susan and Schechter, Daniel (2004) Preschoolers' traumatic stress post-9/11: relational and developmental perspectives. *Psychiatric Clinics of North America*, 27: 473–89.

Cobb, Sara B. (1991) Resolucion de conflictos: una nueva perspectiva [Conflict resolution: a new perspective]. *Acta Psiquiatrica y Psicologica de America Latina*, 37: 31–6.

Coch, Lester and French, John R. P. (1948) Overcoming resistance to change. *Human Relations*, 1: 512–32.

Cohn, Carol (1987) Slick'ems, glick'ems, Christmas trees, and cookie cutters: nuclear language and how we learned to pat the bomb. *Bulletin of the Atomic Scientists*, 43(5): 17–24. [A slightly longer version of this paper was published also in 1987 as 'Sex and death in the rational world of defense in intellectuals', *Signs*, 12: 687–718.]

Cohn, Carol and Enloe, Cynthia (2003) A conversation with Cynthia Enloe: feminists look at masculinity and the men who wage war. *Signs*, 28: 1187–1207.

Cohrs, J. Christopher and Moschner, Barbara (2002) Antiwar knowledge and generalized political attitudes as determinants of attitude towards the Kosovo war. *Peace and Conflict: Journal of Peace Psychology*, 8: 139–55.

Colaresi, Michael (2001) Shocks to the system: great power rivalry and the leadership long cycle. *Journal of Conflict Resolution*, 45: 569–93.

Colaresi, Michael P. and Thompson, William R. (2002) Hot spots or hot hands? Serial crisis behavior, escalating risks, and rivalry. *Journal of Politics*, 64: 1175–98.

Coleman, Peter T. (1997) Redefining ripeness: a social-psychological perspective. *Peace and Conflict: Journal of Peace Psychology*, 3: 81–103.

(2000) Fostering ripeness in seemingly intractable conflict: an experimental study. *International Journal of Conflict Management*, 11: 300–17.

(2003) Characteristics of protracted, intractable conflict: towards the development of a metaframework-I. *Peace and Conflict: Journal of Peace Psychology*, 9(1): 1–37.

Coleman, Peter T. and Deutsch, Morton (2001) Introducing cooperation and conflict resolution into schools: a systems approach. In D. J. Christie, R. V. Wagner and D. D. Winter (eds.), *Peace, conflict, and violence: peace psychology for the 21st century* (pp. 223–39). Upper Saddle River, NJ: Prentice Hall.

Collyer, Charles E. (2003) A nonkilling paradigm for political scientists, psychologists, and others. *Peace and Conflict: Journal of Peace Psychology*, 9: 371–2.

Columbus, Peter J. (1993) Attitudes about reality and college students' opinions about nuclear war. *Psychological Reports*, 73: 249–50.

Colvard, K. (2002) The psychology of terrorists. *British Medical Journal*, 324: 359.

Colvin, Jean G. (1993) Workshops in the forest: a model international environmental exchange program in Ecuador. *Journal of Environmental Education*, 24(3): 23–5.

Comas-Diaz, Lillian and Jansen, Mary A. (1995) Global conflict and violence against women. *Peace and Conflict: Journal of Peace Psychology*, 1: 315–31.

Conlon, Donald E. and Ross, William H. (1992) Influence of movement towards agreement and third party intervention on negotiator fairness judgments. *International Journal of Conflict Management*, 3: 207–21.

Conway, L. G. III, Suedfeld, P. and Tetlock, P. E. (2001) Integrative complexity and political decisions that lead to war or peace. In R. V. Wagner, D. J. Christie and D. Winter (eds.), *Peace, conflict, and violence: peace psychology for the 21st century* (pp. 66–75). Upper Saddle River, NJ: Prentice Hall.

Cooper, James M. (1999) State of the nation: therapeutic jurisprudence and the evolution of the right of self-determination in international law. *Behavioral Sciences and the Law*, 17: 607–43.

Cooperrider, David L. and Dutton, Jane E. (eds.) (1999) *Organizational dimensions of global change: no limits to cooperation.* Thousand Oaks, CA: Sage Publications.

Coryn, Chris L., Beale, James M. and Myers, Krista M. (2004) Response to September 11: anxiety, patriotism, and prejudice in the aftermath of terror. *Current Research in Social Psychology*, 9(12).

Covell, Katherine, Rose-Krasnor, Linda and Fletcher, Kitty (1994) Age differences in understanding peace, war, and conflict resolution. *International Journal of Behavioral Development*, 17: 717–37.

Coy, Patrick G. (1993) Protective accompaniment: how Peace Brigades International secures political space and human rights nonviolently. In V. K. Kool (ed.), *Social and psychological issues* (pp. 235–45). Lanham, MD: University Press of America.

Crary, Daniel R. (1992) Community benefits from mediation: a test of the 'peace virus' hypothesis. *Mediation Quarterly*, 9: 241–52.

Crenshaw, M. (1981) The causes of terrorism. *Comparative Politics*, 13: 379–99.
  (1990) The logic of terrorism: terrorist behaviour as a product of strategic choice. In W. Reich (ed.), *Origins of terrorism: psychologies, ideologies, theologies, states of mind* (pp. 7–24). Cambridge: Cambridge University Press.
  (2000) The psychology of terrorism: an agenda for the 21st century. *Political Psychology*, 21: 405–20.

Crocker, Chester A., Hampson, Fen Osler and Aall, Pamela R. (2003) Ready for prime time: the when, who, and why of international mediation. *Negotiation Journal*, 19: 151–67.

Cronbach, Lee J. (1982) *Designing evaluations of educational and social programs.* San Francisco: Jossey-Bass Inc., Publishers.

Cross, John G. (1991) Economic perspective. In V. A. Kremenyuk (ed.), *International negotiation: analysis, approaches, issues* (pp. 164–79). San Francisco: Jossey-Bass Inc., Publishers.

Custance, Deborah M. (2002) Has the killer ape been slain by natural diplomacy? *Peace and Conflict: Journal of Peace Psychology*, 8: 361–3.

Dalai Lama, Dass, Ram, Welwood, John, Fox, Warwick, Devall, Bill, Sessions, George, Elgin, Duane, Grof, Stanislav, Grof, Christina and Russell, Peter (1993) Minding our world: service and sustainability. In R. Walsh and F. Vaughan (eds.), *Paths beyond ego: the transpersonal vision* (pp. 232–53). Los Angeles, CA: Perigee Books/Jeremy P. Tarcher, Inc.

Dallin, Alexander (1991) Learning in US policy towards the Soviet Union in the 1980s. In G. W. Breslauer and P. E. Tetlock (eds.), *Learning in US and Soviet foreign policy* (pp. 400–26). Boulder, CO: Westview Press.

Daly, O. E. (1999) Northern Ireland: the victims. *British Journal of Psychiatry*, 175: 201–4.

D'Andrea, Micheal and Daniels, Judy (1996) Promoting peace in our schools: developmental, preventive, and multicultural considerations. *School Counselor*, 44: 55–64.

Dane, Leila F. (ed.) (1992) *Examining the merits of conflict resolution as an academic discipline: its applications to everyday real life situations in the Middle East*. McLean, VA: Institute for Victims of Trauma.
— (2000) Mentioning the unmentionable: a commentary on Abu-Nimer's article. *Peace and Conflict: Journal of Peace Psychology*, 6: 23–6.

Danieli, Yael (ed.) (2002) *Sharing the front line and the back hills: international protectors and providers: peacekeepers, humanitarian aid workers and the media in the midst of crisis*. Amityville, NY: Baywood Publishing Co.

Daniels, Steven E. and Walker, Gregg B. (1995) Managing local environmental conflict amidst national controversy. *International Journal of Conflict Management*, 6: 290–311.

Davidson, John A. and Newman, Margaret (1990) Australian perceptions of the nuclear arms race: a conflict of interests or a misunderstanding? *Australian Psychologist*, 25: 15–24.

Davidson, John A. and Versluys, Michelle (1999) Effects of brief training in cooperation and problem solving on success in conflict resolution. *Peace and Conflict: Journal of Peace Psychology*, 5: 137–48.

Davis, Walter A. (2003) Death's dream kingdom: the American psyche after 9–11. *Journal for the Psychoanalysis of Culture and Society*, 8: 127–32.

Dawes, A. (1997) Cultural imperialism in the treatment of children following political violence and war: a Southern African perspective. Paper presented at the Fifth International Symposium on the Contributions of Psychology to Peace. Melbourne, Australia.

Dawes, Andrew (1990) The effects of political violence on children: a consideration of South African and related studies. *International Journal of Psychology*, 25: 13–31.

Dawes, Andy (2001) Psychologies for liberation: views from elsewhere. In D. J. Christie, R. V. Wagner and D. D. Winter (eds.), *Peace, conflict, and violence: peace psychology for the 21st century* (pp. 295–306). Upper Saddle River, NJ: Prentice Hall.

Deaux, Kay, Dane, Francis C. and Wrightsman, Lawrence S. (1993) *Social psychology in the '90s* (6th edn.). Monterey, CA: Brooks/Cole.

de Cerreno, Allison L. C. and Keynan, Alexander (eds.) (1998) *Scientific cooperation, state conflict: the roles of scientists in mitigating international discord*. New York: New York Academy of Sciences (Annals of the New York Academy of Sciences, Vol. 866).

de Dreu, Carsten K. W., Emans, Ben J. M. and van de Vliert, Evert (1992) The influence of own cognitive and other's communicated gain or loss frame on negotiation behavior. *International Journal of Conflict Management*, 3: 115–32.

DeKay, Michael L., Small, Mitchell J., Fischbeck, Paul S., Farrow, R. Scott, Cullen, Alison, Kadane, Joseph B., Lave, Lester B., Morgan, M. Granger and Takemura, Kazuhisa (2002) Risk-based decision analysis in support of precautionary policies. *Journal of Risk Research*, 5: 391–417.

de la Rey, Cheryl (2001) Reconciliation in divided societies. In D. J. Christie, R. V. Wagner and D. D. Winter (eds.), *Peace, conflict, and violence: peace psychology for the 21st century* (pp. 251–61). Upper Saddle River, NJ: Prentice Hall.

de la Rey, Cheryl and Owens, Ingrid (1998) Perceptions of psychosocial healing and the Truth and Reconciliation Commission in South Africa. *Peace and Conflict: Journal of Peace Psychology*, 4: 257–70.

Della Porta, Donatella (1992) Life histories analysis of social movement activists. In M. Diani and R. Eyerman (eds.), *Studying collective action* (pp. 168–93). London: Sage.

Demause, Lloyd (1992) America's search for a fighting leader. *Journal of Psychohistory*, 20: 121–34.

Demause, L. (2002) The childhood origins of terrorism. *Journal of Psychohistory*, 29: 340–8.

De Rivera, Joseph (2003) Aggression, violence, evil, and peace. In T. Millon and M. J. Lerner (eds.), *Handbook of psychology: personality and social psychology* (Vol. 5, pp. 569–98). New York: John Wiley.

(2004a) Assessing cultures of peace. *Peace and Conflict: Journal of Peace Psychology*, 10: 95–100.

(2004b) A template for assessing cultures of peace. *Peace and Conflict: Journal of Peace Psychology*, 10: 125–46.

Der Karabetian, Aghop (1992) World-mindedness and the nuclear threat: a multinational study. *Journal of Social Behavior and Personality*, 7: 293–308.

Derlega, Valerian J., Cukur, Cem Safak, Kuang, Jenny C. and Forsyth, Donelson R. (2002) Interdependent construal of self and the endorsement of conflict resolution strategies in interpersonal, intergroup and international disputes. *Journal of Cross-Cultural Psychology*, 33: 610–25.

de Souza, Luciana Karine (2003) E possivel uma psicologia para a paz? Apresentando a Peace Psychology ['Is a peace psychology possible? Presenting peace psychology']. *PSICO*, 34: 39–56.

de Soysa, Indra, Oneal, John R. and Park, Yong Hee (1997) Testing power-transition theory using alternative measures of national capabilities. *Journal of Conflict Resolution*, 41: 509–28.

Deutsch, Morton (1986) The malignant (spiral) process of hostile interaction. In R. K. White (ed.), *Psychology and the prevention of nuclear war* (pp. 131–54). New York: New York University Press.

(1993) Educating for a peaceful world. *American Psychologist*, 48: 510–17.

(1994) Constructive conflict management for the world today. *International Journal of Conflict Management*, 5: 111–29.

(1995) William James: the first peace psychologist. *Peace and Conflict: Journal of Peace Psychology*, 1: 27–36.

(1999) Hope with optimism: a commentary on Brewster Smith's article. *Peace and Conflict: Journal of Peace Psychology*, 5: 17–21.

Deutsch, Morton and Coleman, Peter T. (eds.) (2000) *The handbook of conflict resolution: theory and practice*. San Francisco, CA: Jossey-Bass/Pfeiffer.

Deutsch, Morton and Krauss, R. M. (1960) The effect of threat upon interpersonal bargaining. *Journal of Abnormal and Social Psychology*, 61: 181–9.

de Valderrama, Blanca Patricia Ballesteros, Lopez, Wilson and Gomez, Monica Novoa (2003) El analisis del comportamiento en los temas sociales: una propuesta para una cultura de paz ['Behaviour analysis of social issues: a proposal for a peace culture']. *Revista Latinoamericana de Psicologia*, 35: 299–316.

Devine-Wright, Patrick (2001) History and identity in Northern Ireland: an exploratory investigation of the role of historical commemorations in contexts of intergroup conflict. *Peace and Conflict: Journal of Peace Psychology*, 7: 297–315.

De Vita, Glauco (2000) Inclusive approaches to effective communication and active participation in the multicultural classroom. *Active Learning in Higher Education*, 1: 168–80.

Diamond, Dickson S., Pastor, Larry H. and McIntosh, Roger G. (2004) Medical management of terrorism-related behavioral syndromes. *Psychiatric Annals*, 34: 690–5.

Diamond, Louise and Fisher, Ronald J. (1995) Integrating conflict resolution training and consultation: a Cyprus example. *Negotiation Journal*, 11: 287–301.

Diamond, Louise and McDonald, John W. (1996) *Multi-track diplomacy: a systems approach to peace*. West Hartford, CT: Kumarian Press.

Dickson-Gomez, Julia (2002) Growing up in guerrilla camps: the long-term impact of being a child soldier in El Salvador's civil war. *Ethos*, 30: 327–56.

Diener, E., Dineen, J., Endresen, K., Beaman, A. L. and Fraser, S. C. (1975) Effects of altered responsibility, cognitive set, and modelling on physical aggression. *Journal of Personality and Social Psychology*, 31: 143–56.

Dixon, M. R., Dymond, S., Rehfeldt, R. A., Roche, B. and Zlomke, K. R. (2003) Terrorism and relational frame theory. *Behaviour and Social Issues*, 12: 129–47.

Dobkowski, Michael N. and Wallimann, Isidor (eds.) (2002) *On the edge of scarcity: environment, resources, population, sustainability, and conflict*. Syracuse, NY: Syracuse University Press.

Dodds, Josiah and Lin, Chong de (1992) Chinese teenagers' concerns about the future: a cross-national comparison. *Adolescence*, 27: 481–6.

Dodge, C. (1991) National and societal implications of war on children. In C. Dodge and M. Raundalen (eds.), *Reaching children and war: Sudan, Uganda, and Mozambique* (pp. 7–20). Bergen, Norway: Sigma Verlag.

Dollard, J., Doob, L., Miller, N., Mowrer, O. H. and Sears, R. R. (1939) *Frustration and aggression*. New Haven, CT: Yale University Press.

Donnellon, Anne (1996) *Team talk: the power of language in team dynamics*. Boston, MA: Harvard University Business School Press.

Donnelly, M. (1995) Depression among adolescents in Northern Ireland. *Adolescence*, 30: 339–50.

Donohue, William A. (1998) Managing equivocality and relational paradox in the Oslo peace negotiations. *Journal of Language and Social Psychology*, 17: 72–96.

(2003) The promise of an interaction-based approach to negotiation. *International Journal of Conflict Management*, 14: 167–76.

Donohue, William A., Ramesh, Closepet and Borchgrevink, Carl (1991) Crisis bargaining: tracking relational paradox in hostage negotiation. *International Journal of Conflict Management*, 2: 257–74.

Donohue, William A. and Roberto, Anthony J. (1996) An empirical examination of three models of integrative and distributive bargaining. *International Journal of Conflict Management*, 7: 209–29.

Dorsch, E., Livingston, J. and Rankin, J. (1991) If patriarchy creates war, can feminism create peace? In A. Hunter (ed.), *Genes and gender. Vol. 6: On peace, war and gender, a challenge to genetic explanations* (pp. 138–50). New York: The Feminist Press.

Doty, Richard G., Winter, David G., Peterson, Bill E. and Kemmelmeier, Markus (1997) Authoritarianism and American students' attitudes about the Gulf War, 1990–1996. *Personality and Social Psychology Bulletin*, 23: 1133–43.

Dovidio, John F., Maruyama, Geoffrey and Alexander, Michele G. (1998) A social psychology of national and international group relations. *Journal of Social Issues*, 54: 831–46.

Downie, Bryan M. (1991) When negotiations fail: causes of breakdown and tactics for breaking the stalemate. *Negotiation Journal*, 7: 175–86.

Downie, Sue (2002) Peacekeepers and peace-builders under stress. In Y. Danieli (ed.), *Sharing the front line and the back hills: international protectors and providers: peacekeepers, humanitarian aid workers and the media in the midst of crisis* (pp. 9–30). Amityville, NY: Baywood Publishing Co.

Downs, George W. (1991) Arms races and war. In P. E. Tetlock, J. L. Husbands, R. Jervis, P. C. Stern and C. Tilly (eds.), *Behavior, society, and nuclear war* (Vol. 2, pp. 73–109). New York: Oxford University Press.

Drake, Laura E. (1995) Negotiation styles in intercultural communication. *International Journal of Conflict Management*, 6: 72–90.

(2001) The culture–negotiation link: integrative and distributive bargaining through an intercultural communication lens. *Human Communication Research*, 27: 317–49.

Drapela, Victor J. (1992) Czechoslovakia: from revolution to reconstruction. *International Journal for the Advancement of Counselling*, 15: 79–89.

Druckman, Daniel (1990) The social psychology of arms control and recipro-cation. *Political Psychology*, 11: 553–81.

(1993) The situational levers of negotiating flexibility. *Journal of Conflict Resolution*, 37: 236–76.

(1997) Dimensions of international negotiations: structures, processes and outcomes. *Group Decision and Negotiation*, 6: 395–420.

(2001) Nationalism and war: a social-psychological perspective. In D. J. Christie, R. V. Wagner and D. D. Winter (eds.), *Peace, conflict, and violence: peace psychology for the 21st century* (pp. 49–65). Upper Saddle River, NJ: Prentice Hall.

(2003) Puzzles in search of researchers: processes, identities, and situations. *International Journal of Conflict Management*, 14: 3–22.

(2004) Departures in negotiation: extensions and new directions. *Negotiation Journal*, 20: 185–204.

Druckman, Daniel and Druckman, James N. (1996) Visibility and negotiating flexibility. *Journal of Social Psychology*, 136: 117–20.

Druckman, Daniel and Hopmann, P. Terrence (1991) Content analysis. In V. A. Kremenyuk (ed.), *International negotiation: analysis, approaches, issues* (pp. 244–63). San Francisco: Jossey-Bass Inc, Publishers.

Druckman, Daniel, Martin, Jennifer, Nan, Susan Allen and Yagcioglu, Dimostenis (1999) Dimensions of international negotiation: a test of Ikle's typology. *Group Decision and Negotiation*, 8: 89–108.

Druckman, Daniel, Ramberg, Bennett and Harris, Richard (2002) Computer-assisted international negotiation: a tool for research and practice. *Group Decision and Negotiation*, 11: 231–56.

Duchet, C., Jehel, L. and Guelfi, J. D. (2000) About two victims exposed to a terrorist bombing in the Paris transportation system, Port Royal, 3 December 1996: psychotraumatic vulnerability and resistance to troubles. *Annales Medico-Psychologiques*, 158: 539–48.

Dudley-Grant, G. Rita, Bankart, C. Peter and Dockett, Kathleen (2003) On the path to peace and wholeness: conclusion to *Psychology and Buddhism*. In K. H. Dockett, G. R. Dudley-Grant and C. P. Bankart (eds.), *Psychology and Buddhism: from individual to global community* (pp. 277–86). New York: Kluwer Academic/Plenum Publishers.

Dugan, Maire A. (1991) The consortium on peace research, education, and development (COPRED), peace education, and the prevention of war. In D. Leviton (ed.), *Horrendous death and health: towards action* (pp. 179–85). New York: Hemisphere Publishing Corp.

Dumont, M., Yzerbyt, V., Wigboldus, D. and Gordijn, E. H. (2003) Social categorisation and fear reactions to the September 11th terrorist attacks. *Personality and Social Psychology Bulletin*, 29: 1509–20.

Duncan, Norman (2003) 'Race' talk: discourse on 'race' and racial difference. *International Journal of Intercultural Relations*, 27: 135–56.

Dunn, Seamus and Morgan, Valerie (1995) Protestant alienation in Northern Ireland. *Studies in Conflict and Terrorism*, 18: 175–85.

Dupont, Christophe and Faure, Guy Olivier (1991) The negotiation process. In V. A. Kremenyuk (ed.), *International negotiation: analysis, approaches, issues* (pp. 40–57). San Francisco: Jossey-Bass Inc, Publishers.

du Preez, Peter (1997) In search of genocide: a comparison of Rwanda and South Africa. *Peace and Conflict: Journal of Peace Psychology*, 3: 245–59.

Dyer, Wayne W. (2003) *There's a spiritual solution to every problem*. New York: Quill/HarperCollins Publishers.

Dyregrov, Atle (1998) Psychological debriefing: an effective method? *Traumatology*, 4(2), Article 1. Retrieved 16 August 2005 from http://www.fsu.edu/~trauma/art1v4i2.html

Edelman, Lucila, Kersner, Daniel, Kordon, Diana and Lagos, Dario (2003) Psychosocial effects and treatment of mass trauma due to socio-political events: the Argentine experience. In T. M. McIntyre and S. Krippner (eds.), *The psychological impact of war trauma on civilians: an international perspective* (pp. 143–53). Westport, CT: Praeger Publishers/Greenwood Publishing Group.

Edelstein, Ilana and Gibson, Kerry (2003) A psycho-analytic contribution to the concept of reconciliation. *Psycho-analytic Psychotherapy in South Africa*, 11(1): 17–22.

Ediger, Marlow (2003) War and peace in the curriculum. *Journal of Instructional Psychology*, 30: 288–93.

Edwards, Todd C. and Oskamp, Stuart (1992) Components of antinuclear war activism. *Basic and Applied Social Psychology*, 13: 217–30.

Efraime, B. (1999) Female child soldiers in Mozambique: psychotherapeutic assistance for war's most silenced victims. [Grant proposal submitted for funding.]

Ehteshami, Anoushiravan (2003) Conflict prevention in Eurasia. *Peace and Conflict: Journal of Peace Psychology*, 9: 377–8.

Ekblad, Solvig (2002) Ethnopolitical warfare, traumatic family stress, and the mental health of refugee children. In C. E. Stout (ed.), *The psychology of terrorism: clinical aspects and responses: Vol. 2. Psychological dimensions to war and peace* (pp. 27–48). Westport, CT: Praeger Publishers/Greenwood Publishing Group.

El-Bushra, Judy and Piza Lopez, Eugenia (1994) *Development in conflict: the gender dimension*. New York: Oxford University Press.

Elbedour, Salman (1998) Youth in crisis: the well-being of Middle Eastern youth and adolescents during war and peace. *Journal of Youth and Adolescence*, 27: 539–56.

Elbedour, Salman, ten Bensel, Robert and Maruyama, Geoffrey M. (1993) Children at risk: psychological coping with war and conflict in the Middle East. *International Journal of Mental Health*, 22(3): 33–52.

Elieli, Rina Bar-Lev (2004) Terrorism and war: unconscious dynamics of political violence. *British Journal of Psychotherapy*, 21: 146–51.

Ellens, J. Harold (2004a) Fundamentalism, orthodoxy, and violence. In J. H. Ellens (ed.), *The destructive power of religion: violence in Judaism, Christianity, and Islam: Vol. 4. Contemporary views on spirituality and violence* (pp. 119–42). Westport, CT: Praeger Publishers/Greenwood Publishing Group.

(2004b) Jihad in the Qur'an, then and now. In J. H. Ellens (ed.), *The destructive power of religion: violence in Judaism, Christianity, and Islam: Vol. 3. Models and cases of violence in religion* (pp. 39–52). Westport, CT: Praeger Publishers/Greenwood Publishing Group.

Ellis, Donald G. and Maoz, Ifat (2003) A communication and cultural codes approach to ethnonational conflict. *International Journal of Conflict Management*, 14: 255–72.

Elovitz, Paul H. (1999) War, trauma, genocide, and Kosovo in the news and classroom. *Journal of Psychohistory*, 27: 188–99.

Elron, Efrat, Halevy, Nir, Ben Ari, Eyal and Shamir, Boas (2003) Cooperation and coordination across cultures in the peacekeeping forces: individual and organizational integrating mechanisms. In T. W. Britt and A. B. Adler (eds.), *The psychology of the peacekeeper: lessons from the field* (pp. 261–82). Westport, CT: Praeger Publishers/Greenwood Publishing Group.

Ember, Melvin and Ember, Carol R. (1994) Prescriptions for peace: policy implications of cross-cultural research on war and interpersonal violence. *Cross-Cultural Research: The Journal of Comparative Social Science*, 28: 343–50.

Emmett, Judith D., Monsour, Florence, Lundeberg, Mary, Russo, Thomas, Secrist, K., Lindquist, N., Moriarity, S. and Uhren, P. (1996) Open classroom meetings: promoting peaceful schools. *Elementary School Guidance and Counseling*, 31: 3–10.

Emminghaus, Wolf B., Kimmel, Paul R. and Stewart, Edward C. (1997) Primal violence: illuminating culture's dark side. *Peace and Conflict: Journal of Peace Psychology*, 3: 167–92.

Engelmann, Wilfried (1994) Conditions for disarmament: a game theoretical model. *Group Decision and Negotiation*, 3: 321–32.

English, Tony (2001) Tension analysis in international organizations: a tool for breaking down communication barriers. *International Journal of Organizational Analysis*, 9(1): 58–83.

Errante, Antoinette (1999) Peace work as grief work in Mozambique and South Africa: postconflict communities as context for child and youth socialization. *Peace and Conflict: Journal of Peace Psychology*, 5: 261–79.

Escalona, Sibylle K. (1982) Growing up with the threat of nuclear war: some indirect effects on personality development. *American Journal of Orthopsychiatry*, 52: 600–7.

Esses, Victoria M., Jackson, Lynne M. and Armstrong, Tamara L. (1998) Intergroup competition and attitudes towards immigrants and immigration: an instrumental model of group conflict. *Journal of Social Issues*, 54: 699–724.

Etheredge, Lloyd S. (1992) On being more rational than the rationality assumption: dramatic requirements, nuclear deterrence, and the agenda for learning. In E. Singer and V. Hudson (eds.), *Political psychology and foreign policy* (pp. 59–75). Boulder, CO: Westview Press.

Ettin, Mark F., Fidler, Jay W. and Cohen, Bertram D. (eds.) (1995) *Group process and political dynamics*. Madison, CT: International Universities Press.

Euwema, Martin C., Van de Vliert, Evert and Bakker, Arnold B. (2003) Substantive and relational effectiveness of organizational conflict behavior. *International Journal of Conflict Management*, 14: 119–39.

Evan, William M. (1997) Identification with the human species: a challenge for the twenty-first century. *Human Relations*, 50: 987–1003. [AN 1997-05738-005.]

Everly, G. S. (2003) Psychological counter-terrorism. *International Journal of Emergency Mental Health*, 5: 57–9.

Everly, G. S. and Mitchell, J. T. (2001) America under attack: the '10 Commandments' of responding to mass terrorist attacks. *International Journal of Emergency Mental Health*, 3: 133–5.

Falk, Avner (1992) Unconscious aspects of the Arab–Israeli conflict. In L. B. Boyer and R. M. Boyer (eds.), *The psychoanalytic study of society: Vol. 17. Essays in honor of George D. and Louise A. Spindler* (pp. 213–47). Hillsdale, NJ: Analytic Press, Inc.

Falla, Ricardo (1988) Struggle for survival in the mountains: hunger and other privations inflicted on internal refugees from the central highlands. In R. M. Carmack (ed.), *Harvest of violence: the Maya Indians and the Guatemalan crisis* (pp. 235–55). Norman, OK: University of Oklahoma Press.

Fang, Lin and Chen, Teddy (2004) Community outreach and education to deal with cultural resistance to mental health services. In N. B. Webb (ed.), *Mass trauma and violence: helping families and children cope* (pp. 234–55). New York: Guilford Press.

Fang, Tony (1999) *Chinese business negotiating style*. Thousand Oaks, CA: Sage Publications.

Fantini, Alvino E. (1995) ABA-ZAK: a world view exercise. *International Journal of Intercultural Relations*, 19: 297–302.

Farnham, Barbara (1992) Roosevelt and the Munich crisis: insights from prospect theory. *Political Psychology*, 13: 205–35.

Farwell, Nancy (2003/2004) In war's wake: contextualizing trauma experiences and psychosocial well-being among Eritrean youth. *International Journal of Mental Health*, 32(4): 20–50.

Faure, Guy Olivier (1993) Negotiation concepts across cultures: implementing nonverbal tools. *Negotiation Journal*, 9: 355–9.

  (1995) Conflict formulation: going beyond culture-bound views of conflict. In B. B. Bunker and J. Z. Rubin (eds.), *Conflict, cooperation, and justice: essays inspired by the work of Morton Deutsch* (pp. 39–57). San Francisco: Jossey-Bass Inc, Publishers.

  (1999) The cultural dimension of negotiation: the Chinese case. *Group Decision and Negotiation*, 8: 187–215.

Fearon, James D. (1994) Signaling versus the balance of power and interests: an empirical test of a crisis bargaining model. *Journal of Conflict Resolution*, 38: 236–69.

Fedor, Kenneth J. and Werther, William B. (1995) Making sense of cultural factors in international alliances. *Organizational Dynamics*, 23(4): 33–48.

Fedor, Kenneth J. and Werther, William B. Jr. (1996) The fourth dimension: creating culturally responsive international alliances. *Organizational Dynamics*, 25(2): 39–53.

Feeney, Melisah C. and Davidson, John A. (1996) Bridging the gap between the practical and the theoretical: an evaluation of a conflict resolution model. *Peace and Conflict: Journal of Peace Psychology*, 2: 255–69.

Feerick, M. M. and Prinz, R. J. (2003) Next steps in research on children exposed to community violence or war/terrorism. *Clinical Child and Family Psychology Review*, 6: 303–5.

Feghali, Ellen Kussman (1997) Arab cultural communication patterns. *International Journal of Intercultural Relations*, 21: 345–78.

Feldman, Ofer and Valenty, Linda O. (eds.) (2001) *Profiling political leaders: cross-cultural studies of personality and behavior*. Westport, CT: Praeger Publishers/Greenwood Publishing Group.

Felsman, J. K., Leong, F., Johnson, M. and Felsman, I. (1990) Estimates of psychological distress among Vietnamese refugees: adolescents, unaccompanied minors, and young adults. *Social Science and Medicine*, 31: 1251–6.

Ferguson, Neil (2000) The impact of sectarian justice and the paramilitary ceasefires on adolescent just world beliefs in Northern Ireland. *Irish Journal of Psychology*, 21: 70–7.

Ferguson, N. and Cairns, E. (1996) Political violence and moral maturity in Northern Ireland. *Political Psychology*, 17: 713–25.

Fernandez-Dols, Jose-Miguel, Hurtado-de-Mendoza, Alejandra and Jimenez-de-Lucas, Isabel (2004) Culture of peace: an alternative definition and its measurement. *Peace and Conflict: Journal of Peace Psychology*, 10: 117–24.

Feshbach, Seymour (1990) Psychology, human violence, and the search for peace: issues in science and social values. *Journal of Social Issues*, 46(1): 183–98.

(1999) The central role of identity: some comments on Brewster Smith's article. *Peace and Conflict: Journal of Peace Psychology*, 5: 23–5.

Fetherston, Betts (2002) Double bind: an essay on counseling training. *Counseling and Psychotherapy Research*, 2: 108–25.

Feuerverger, Grace (1998) Neve Shalom/Wahat Al-Salam: a Jewish–Arab school for peace. *Teachers College Record*, 99: 692–730.

Firer, Ruth (2002) The Gordian knot between peace education and war education. In G. Salomon and B. Nevo (eds.), *Peace education: the concept, principles, and practices around the world* (pp. 55–61). Mahwah, NJ: Lawrence Erlbaum Associates.

Fischhoff, Baruch (1991) Nuclear decisions: cognitive limits to the thinkable. In P. Tetlock, J. L. Husbands, R. Jervis, P. C. Stern and C. Tilly (eds.), *Behavior, society, and nuclear war* (Vol. 2, pp. 110–92). New York: Oxford University Press.

Fish, Adam and Popal, Rona (2003) The women of Afghanistan and the freedom of thought. In T. M. McIntyre and S. Krippner (eds.), *The psychological impact of war trauma on civilians: an international perspective* (pp. 19–24). Westport, CT: Praeger Publishers/Greenwood Publishing Group.

Fishbein, Harold D. and Dess, Nancy (2003) An evolutionary perspective on intercultural conflict: basic mechanism and implications for immigration policy. In R. W. Bloom and N. K. Dess (eds.), *Evolutionary psychology and violence: a primer for policymakers and public policy advocates* (pp. 157–202). Westport, CT: Praeger Publishers/Greenwood Publishing Group.

Fisher, Roger (1964) Fractionating conflict. In R. Fisher (ed.), *International conflict and behavioral science* (pp. 91–109). New York: Basic Books.

(1994) Deter, compel, or negotiate? *Negotiation Journal*, 10: 17–32.

Fisher, Ronald J. (1993) Developing the field of interactive conflict resolution: issues in training, funding, and institutionalization. *Political Psychology*, 14: 123–38.

(1998) Applying group processes to international conflict analysis and resolution. In R. S. Tindale, L. Heath, J. Edwards, E. J. Posavac, F. B. Bryant, J. Myers, Y. Suarez-Balcazar and Henderson-King, E. (eds.), *Theory and research on small groups* (pp. 107–26). New York: Plenum Press.

(2003) Toward a graduate curriculum in war trauma relief and ethnopolitical conflict resolution. In T. M. McIntyre and S. Krippner (eds.), *The psychological impact of war trauma on civilians: an international perspective* (pp. 217–30). Westport, CT: Praeger Publishers/Greenwood Publishing Group.

Fisher, S. (1996) Occupation of the womb: forced impregnation as genocide. *Duke Law Journal*, 46: 91–133.

Fiske, Susan T. (1992) People's reactions to nuclear war: implications for psychologists. In S. Staub and P. Green (eds.), *Psychology and social responsibility: facing global challenges* (pp. 305–26). New York: New York University Press.

Fitzduff, Mari (2003) Peacebuilding needs? *Peace and Conflict: Journal of Peace Psychology*, 9: 379–81.

Fivush, R., Edwards, V. J. and Mennuti-Washburn, J. (2003) Narratives of 9/11: relations among personal involvement, narrative content and memory of the emotional impact over time. *Applied Cognitive Psychology*, 17: 1099–1111.

Flannery, Daniel J., Vazsonyi, Alexander T. and Liau, Albert (2003) Initial behavior outcomes for the Peace Builders universal school-based violence prevention program. *Developmental Psychology*, 39: 292–308.

Flynn, James, Peters, Ellen, Mertz, C. K. and Slovic, Paul (1998) Risk, media, and stigma at Rocky Flats. *Risk Analysis*, 18: 715–27.

Fogarty, Brian E. (2000) *War, peace, and the social order*. Boulder, CO: Westview Press.

Ford, Carol A. (2004) Living in a time of terrorism: what about older adolescents and young adults? *Families, Systems, and Health*, 22: 52–3.

Fordham, Benjamin O. (2004) A very sharp sword: the influence of military capabilities on American decisions to use force. *Journal of Conflict Resolution*, 48: 632–56.

Foreman, Clay and Eraenen, Liisa (1999) Trauma of world policing: peacekeeping duties. In J. M. Violanti and D. Paton (eds.), *Police trauma: psychological aftermath of civilian combat* (pp. 189–200). Springfield, IL: Charles C. Thomas.

Foresto, Lisa A. (2004) Adolescent responses to the 9/11/01 terrorist attacks? *NYS Psychologist*, 16(3): 38–41.

Fortgang, Ron S. (2000) Taking stock: an analysis of negotiation pedagogy across four professional fields. *Negotiation Journal*, 16: 325–38.

Fox Cardamone, Lee, Hinkle, Steve and Hogue, Mary (2000) The correlates of antinuclear activism: attitudes, subjective norms, and efficacy. *Journal of Applied Social Psychology*, 30: 484–98.

Foxen, Patricia (2000) Cacophony of voices: a K'iche' Mayan narrative of remembrance and forgetting. *Transcultural Psychiatry*, 37: 355–81.

Franchi, Vije (2003a) Across or beyond the racialized divide? Current perspectives on 'race', racism and 'intercultural' relations in 'post-apartheid' South Africa. *International Journal of Intercultural Relations*, 27: 125–33.

(2003b) The racialization of affirmative action in organizational discourses: a case study of symbolic racism in post-apartheid South Africa. *International Journal of Intercultural Relations*, 27: 157–87.

Franchi, Vije and Swart, Tanya M. (2003) From apartheid to affirmative action: the use of 'racial' markers in past, present, and future articulations of identity among South African students. *International Journal of Intercultural Relations*, 27: 209–36.

Francis, Claire, Boyes, Edward, Qualter, Anne and Stanisstreet, Martin (1993) Ideas of elementary students about reducing the 'greenhouse effect'. *Science Education*, 77: 375–92.

Franke, Volker C. (2003) The social identity of peacekeeping. In T. W. Britt and A. B. Adler (eds.), *The psychology of the peacekeeper: lessons from the field* (pp. 31–51). Westport, CT: Praeger Publishers/Greenwood Publishing Group.

Frederick, Calvin J. (1994) The psychology of terrorism and torture in war and peace: diagnosis and treatment of victims. In R. P. Liberman and J. Yager (eds.), *Stress in psychiatric disorders* (pp. 140–59). New York: Springer Publishing Co, Inc.

Frederick, Howard (1993) Communication, peace, and international law. In C. Roach (ed.), *Communication and culture in war and peace* (pp. 216–51). Newbury Park, CA: Sage Publications, Inc.

Fredrickson, B. L., Tugade, M. M., Waugh, C. E. and Larkin, G. R. (2003) What good are positive emotions in crises? A prospective study of resilience and emotions following the terrorist attacks on the United States on September 11th, 2001. *Journal of Personality and Social Psychology*, 84: 365–76.

Freeman, Joan (1991) Adolescent attitudes to nuclear war. *International Journal of Adolescence and Youth*, 2: 237–44.

Freire, Paulo (1972) *Pedagogy of the oppressed*. Harmondsworth, Middlesex: Penguin.

Freire, Paulo, Freire, Ana Maria Araújo and Macedo, Donaldo P. (2000) *The Paulo Freire reader*. New York: Continuum.

Fremont, Wanda P. (2004) Childhood reactions to terrorism-induced trauma: a review of the past 10 years. *Journal of the American Academy of Child and Adolescent Psychiatry*, 43: 381–92.

French, Perrin (1991a) The psychology of survival-directed action, part I: the national pathway to survival. In D. Leviton (ed.), *Horrendous death and health: toward action* (pp. 51–71). New York: Hemisphere Publishing Corp.

(1991b) The psychology of survival-directed action, part II: the citizens' pathway to survival. In D. Leviton (ed.), *Horrendous death and health: toward action* (pp. 73–161). New York: Hemisphere Publishing Corp.

Freud, Sigmund (1922) *Beyond the pleasure principle*. London: The International Psycho-analytical Press.

Freymond, Jean F. (1991) Historical approach. In V. A. Kremenyuk (ed.), *International negotiation: analysis, approaches, issues* (pp. 121–34). San Francisco: Jossey-Bass Inc, Publishers.

Friedman, M. J. (2000) *Post traumatic stress disorder: the latest assessment of treatment strategies*. Kansas City, MO: Compact Clinicals.

Friedman, Raymond A. (1992) The culture of mediation: private understandings in the context of public conflict. In D. M. Kolb and J. M. Bartunek (eds.), *Hidden conflict in organizations: uncovering behind-the-scenes disputes* (pp. 143–64). Newbury Park, CA: Sage Publications, Inc.

Friedman, Raymond (2002) New perspectives on teaching about conflict: simulations, cases, and exercises. *International Journal of Conflict Management*, 13: 318–19.

Fry, Douglas P. (1992) 'Respect for the rights of others is peace': learning aggression versus nonaggression among the Zapotec. *American Anthropologist*, 94: 621–39.

(2005) *The human potential for peace: an anthropological challenge to assumptions about war and violence*. Oxford: Oxford University Press.

Fry, Douglas P. and Bjoerkqvist, Kaj (eds.) (1997) *Cultural variation in conflict resolution: alternatives to violence*. Mahwah, NJ: Lawrence Erlbaum Associates.

Fuhr, Reinhard and Gremmler-Fuhr, Martina (2003) Reactivity – an integral Gestalt approach to fights and strife and a more peaceful world. *Gestalt Review*, 7: 147–70.

Fukushima, Osamu and Ohbuchi, Ken-ichi (1996) Antecedents and effects of multiple goals in conflict resolution. *International Journal of Conflict Management*, 7: 191–208.

Funes, Maria J. (1998) Social responses to political violence in the Basque country: peace movements and their audience. *Journal of Conflict Resolution*, 42: 493–510.

Gabriel, Ayala H. (1992) Grief and rage: collective emotions in the politics of peace and the politics of gender in Israel. *Culture, Medicine and Psychiatry*, 16: 311–35.

Gaerling, Tommy, Kristensen, Henrik, Backenroth-Ohsako, Gunnel, Ekehammar, Bo and Wessells, Michael G. (2000) Diplomacy and psychology: psychological contributions to international negotiations, conflict prevention, and world peace. *International Journal of Psychology*, 35(2): 81–6.

Gaertner, Samuel L., Dovidio, John F. and Bachman, Betty A. (1996) Revisiting the contact hypothesis: the induction of a common ingroup identity. *International Journal of Intercultural Relations*, 20: 271–90.

Gaines, Atwood D. and Whitehouse, Peter J. (1998) Harmony and consensus: cultural aspects of organization in international science. *Alzheimer Disease and Associated Disorders*, 12: 295–301.

Galanter, M., Rabkin, R. and Deutsch, A. (1979) The Moonies: a psychological study of conversion and membership in a contemporary religious sect. *American Journal of Psychiatry*, 136: 165–70.

Galantino, Maria Grazia (2003) Work motivation and the peacekeeper. In T. W. Britt and A. B. Adler (eds.), *The psychology of the peacekeeper: lessons from the field* (pp. 111–25). Westport, CT: Praeger Publishers/Greenwood Publishing Group.

Galea, S., Vlahov, D., Resnick, H., Ahern, J., Susser, E., Gold, J., Bucuvalas, M. and Kilpatrick, D. (2003) Trends of probable post-traumatic stress disorder in New York City after the September 11 terrorist attacks. *American Journal of Epidemiology*, 158: 514–24.

Gallagher, Tony (2004) After the war comes peace? An examination of the impact of the Northern Ireland conflict on young people. *Journal of Social Issues*, 60: 629–42.

Gallois, Cindy (2003) Reconciliation through communication in intercultural encounters: potential or peril? *Journal of Communication*, 53: 5–15.

Galtung, Johan (1997) Conflict life cycles in Occident and Orient. In D. P. Fry and K. Bjoerkqvist (eds.), *Cultural variation in conflict resolution: alternatives to violence* (pp. 41–9). Mahwah, NJ: Lawrence Erlbaum Associates, Inc.

(2004) *Transcend and transform: an introduction to conflict work*. London: Pluto Press.

Galtung, Johan and Tschudi, Finn (2001) Crafting peace: on the psychology of the TRANSCEND approach. In D. J. Christie, R. V. Wagner and D. D. Winter (eds.), *Peace, conflict, and violence: peace psychology for the 21st century* (pp. 210–22). Upper Saddle River, NJ: Prentice Hall.

Gambino, R. (1973, November/December) Watergate lingo: a language on non-responsibility. *Freedom at Issue*, 22: 7–9, 15–17.

Gan, Su-lin, Hill, John R., Pschernig, Elke and Zillmann, Dolf (1996) The Hebron massacre, selective reports of Jewish reactions, and perceptions of volatility in Israel. *Journal of Broadcasting and Electronic Media*, 40: 122–31.

Gandhi, Arun (2004) Nonviolence as a comprehensive philosophy. *Peace and Conflict: Journal of Peace Psychology*, 10: 87–90.

Garbarino, James (1995) The American war zone: what children can tell us about living with violence. *Journal of Developmental and Behavioral Pediatrics*, 16(6): 431–5.

Garbarino, J. and Bedard, C. (1996) Spiritual challenges to children facing violent trauma. *Childhood: A Global Journal of Child Research*, 3: 457–78.

Garrett, Banning N. (1991) The strategic basis of learning in US policy towards China, 1949–1988. In G. W. Breslauer and P. E. Tetlock (eds.), *Learning in US and Soviet foreign policy* (pp. 208–63). Boulder, CO: Westview Press.

Garrod, A., Beal, C. R., Jaeger, W., Thomas, J., Davis, J., Leiser, N. and Hodzic, A. (2003) Culture, ethnic conflict and moral orientation in Bosnian children. *Journal of Moral Education*, 32: 131–50.

Gartner, Scott Sigmund, Segura, Gary M. and Wilkening, Michael (1997) All politics are local: local losses and individual attitudes towards the Vietnam war. *Journal of Conflict Resolution*, 41: 669–94.

Gartner, Scott Sigmund and Siverson, Randolph M. (1996) War expansion and war outcome. *Journal of Conflict Resolution*, 40: 4–15.

Gaubatz, Kurt T. (1991) Election cycles and war. *Journal of Conflict Resolution*, 35: 212–44.

Gelpi, Christopher (1997) Democratic diversions: governmental structure and the externalization of domestic conflict. *Journal of Conflict Resolution*, 41: 255–82.

Gelpi, Christopher and Grieco, Joseph M. (2001) Attracting trouble: democracy, leadership tenure, and the targeting of militarized challenges, 1918–1992. *Journal of Conflict Resolution*, 45: 794–817.

George, Alexander L. (1991) The transition of US–Soviet relations, 1985–1990: an interpretation from the perspective of international relations theory and political psychology. *Political Psychology*, 12: 469–86.

Gerber, Gwendolyn L. (2004) War and gender: how gender shapes the war system and vice versa. *Sex Roles*, 50: 141–2.

Gershoff, Elizabeth T. and Aber, J. Lawrence (2004) Assessing the impact of September 11th, 2001, on children, youth, and parents: methodological challenges to research on terrorism and other nonnormative events. *Applied Developmental Science*, 8: 106–10.

Gerstein, Lawrence H. and Moeschberger, Scott L. (2003) Building cultures of peace: an urgent task for counseling professionals. *Journal of Counseling and Development*, 81(1): 115–19.

Geva, Nehemia and Hanson, D. Christopher (1999) Cultural similarity, foreign policy actions, and regime perception: an experimental study of international cues and democratic peace. *Political Psychology*, 20: 803–27.

Geva, Nehemia, Mayhar, James and Skorick, J. Mark (2000) The cognitive calculus of foreign policy decision making: an experimental assessment. *Journal of Conflict Resolution*, 44: 447–71.

Ghosh, Dipankar (1993) Risk propensity and conflict behavior in dyadic negotiation: some evidence from the laboratory. *International Journal of Conflict Management*, 4: 223–47.

Gidron, Y. (2002) Post-traumatic stress disorder after terrorist attacks: a review. *Journal of Nervous and Mental Disease*, 190: 118–21.

Gidron, Y., Gal, R. and Zahavi, S. (1999) Bus commuters' coping strategies and anxiety from terrorism: an example of the Israeli experience. *Journal of Traumatic Stress*, 12: 185–92.

Giebels, Ellen, de Dreu, Carsten K. W. and van de Vliert, Evert (1998) The alternative negotiator as the invisible third at the table: the impact of potency information. *International Journal of Conflict Management*, 9: 5–21.

Giel, R. (1991) The psychosocial aftermath of two major disasters in the Soviet Union. *Journal of Traumatic Stress*, 4: 381–92.

Gigerenzer, Gerd (2004) Dread risk, September 11, and fatal traffic accidents. *Psychological Science*, 15: 286–7.

Gilat, Izhak, Lobel, Thalma E. and Gil, Tsvie (1998) Characteristics of calls to Israeli hotlines during the Gulf War. *American Journal of Community Psychology*, 26: 697–704.

Gilbert, Andrew (1997) Small voices against the wind: local knowledge and social transformation. *Peace and Conflict: Journal of Peace Psychology*, 3: 275–92.

Gillibert, Jean (1993) Culture d'extermination. [Culture of extermination.] *Revue Française de Psychanalyse*, 57: 1113–26.

Gil-Rivas, Virginia, Holman, E. Alison and Silver, Roxane Cohen (2004) Adolescent vulnerability following the September 11th terrorist attacks: a study of parents and their children. *Applied Developmental Science*, 8: 130–42.

Gittelman, Martin (2003/2004) Disaster and psychosocial rehabilitation: the New York City experience. *International Journal of Mental Health*, 32(4): 70–6.

Glad, Betty (1990a) Dilemmas of deterrence: rational and nonrational perspectives. In B. Glad (ed.), *Psychological dimensions of war* (pp. 277–94). Newbury Park, CA: Sage Publications, Inc.

(1990b) Limited war and learning: the American experience. In B. Glad (ed.), *Psychological dimensions of war* (pp. 264–73). Newbury Park, CA: Sage Publications, Inc.

(ed.) (1990c) *Psychological dimensions of war*. Newbury Park, CA: Sage Publications.

Glad, Betty and Whitmore, Brian (1991) Jimmy Carter and the Soviet invasion of Afghanistan: a psychological perspective. In J. Offerman-Zuckerberg (ed.), *Politics and psychology: contemporary psychodynamic perspectives* (pp. 117–42). New York: Plenum Press.

Glazier, Jocelyn Anne (2003) Developing cultural fluency: Arab and Jewish students engaging in one another's company. *Harvard Educational Review*, 73: 141–63.

Gleditsch, Nils Petter and Hegre, Havard (1997) Peace and democracy: three levels of analysis. *Journal of Conflict Resolution*, 41: 283–310.

Gobodo-Madikizela, Pumla (2002) Remorse, forgiveness, and rehumanization: stories from South Africa. *Journal of Humanistic Psychology*, 42(1): 7–32.

Goffman, Erving (1955) On face-work: an analysis of ritual elements in social interaction. *Psychiatry: Journal of Interpersonal Relations*, 18: 213–31.

Gold, Gregg J. and Raven, Bertram H. (1992) Interpersonal influence strategies in the Churchill–Roosevelt bases-for-destroyers exchange. *Journal of Social Behavior and Personality*, 7: 245–72.

Goldin, Stephen, Levin, Lilian, Persson, Lars Ake and Haeggloef, Bruno (2003) Child war trauma: a comparison of clinician, parent and child assessments. *Nordic Journal of Psychiatry*, 57: 173–83.

Goldman, Alan (1994) The centrality of 'ningensei' to Japanese negotiating and interpersonal relationships: implications for US–Japanese communication. *International Journal of Intercultural Relations*, 18: 29–54.

Goldstein, Joshua S., Pevehouse, Jon C., Gerner, Deborah J. and Telhami, Shibley (2001) Reciprocity, triangularity, and cooperation in the Middle East, 1979–97. *Journal of Conflict Resolution*, 45: 594–620.

Gomes, Mary E. (1992) The rewards and stresses of social change: a qualitative study of peace activists. *Journal of Humanistic Psychology*, 32: 138–46.

Gomes de Matos, Francisco (2000) Harmonizing and humanizing political discourse: the contribution of peace linguists. *Peace and Conflict: Journal of Peace Psychology*, 6: 339–44.

Gonzalez Posse, Valeria M. (1998) Postconflict peacebuilding and making efforts count: reconstruction, elections, and beyond. In H. J. Langholtz (ed.), *The psychology of peacekeeping* (pp. 195–206). Westport, CT: Praeger Publishers/Greenwood Publishing Group, Inc.

Gonzalez-Vallejo, Claudia and Sauveur, Giselda Barroso (1998) Peace through economic and social development. In H. J. Langholtz (ed.), *The psychology of peacekeeping* (pp. 17–30). Westport, CT: Praeger Publishers/Greenwood Publishing Group, Inc.

Goodman, Lisl Marburg and Hoff, Lee Ann (1990) *Omnicide: the nuclear dilemma*. New York: Praeger Publishers.

Gordon, Avishag (2004) The effect of database and website inconstancy on the terrorism field's delineation. *Studies in Conflict and Terrorism*, 27: 79–88.

Gordon, Carol and Arian, Asher (2001) Threat and decision making. *Journal of Conflict Resolution*, 45: 196–215.

Gordon, H. (2002) The 'suicide' bomber: is it a psychiatric phenomenon? *Psychiatric Bulletin*, 26: 285–7.

Goren, Harel and Bornstein, Gary (2000) The effects of intragroup communication on intergroup cooperation in the repeated Intergroup Prisoner's Dilemma (IPD) game. *Journal of Conflict Resolution*, 44: 700–19.

Gould, Madelyn S., Munfakh, Jimmie Lou Harris, Kleinman, Marjorie, Lubell, Keri and Provenzano, Danielle (2004) Impact of the September 11th terrorist attacks on teenagers' mental health. *Applied Developmental Science*, 8: 158–69.

Grace, John S. and Harris, Richard J. (1990) Conflict resolution styles and their relation to conflict type, individual differences, and formative influences. *Bulletin of the Psychonomic Society*, 28: 144–6.

Graessner, Sepp, Gurris, Norbert and Pross, Christian (eds.) [Translated by Jeremiah Michael Riemer] (2001) *At the side of torture survivors: treating a terrible assault on human dignity.* Baltimore, MD: Johns Hopkins University Press.

Graves, Glenn (2003) Post-traumatic stress syndrome and related disorders among civilian victims of sexual trauma and exploitation in Southeast Asia. In T. M. McIntyre and S. Krippner (eds.), *The psychological impact of war trauma on civilians: an international perspective* (pp. 203–13). Westport, CT: Praeger Publishers/Greenwood Publishing Group.

Grawitz, Madeleine (1990) La psychologie politique aux Etats-Unis. [Political psychology in the United States.] *Psychologie Française*, 35: 89–103.

Greenberg, N., Thomas, S. L., Iversen, A., Unwin, C., Hull, L. and Wessely, S. (2003) Do military peacekeepers want to talk about their experiences? Perceived psychological support of UK military peacekeepers on return from deployment. *Journal of Mental Health UK*, 12: 565–73.

Greenhalgh, Leonard and Kramer, Roderick M. (1990) Strategic choice in conflicts: the importance of relationships. In R. L. Kahn and M. N. Zald (eds.), *Organizations and nation-states: new perspectives on conflict and cooperation* (pp. 181–220). San Francisco: Jossey-Bass Inc, Publishers.

Greenstein, Fred I. (1994) Taking account of individuals in international political psychology: Eisenhower, Kennedy and Indochina. *Political Psychology*, 15: 61–74.

Gregor, Thomas A. (1990) Uneasy peace: intertribal relations in Brazil's Upper Xingu. In J. Haas (ed.), *The anthropology of war* (pp. 105–24). Cambridge: Cambridge University Press.

Greig, J. Michael (2001) Moments of opportunity: recognizing conditions of ripeness for international mediation between enduring rivals. *Journal of Conflict Resolution*, 45: 691–718.

(2002) The end of geography? Globalization, communications, and culture in the international system. *Journal of Conflict Resolution*, 46: 225–43.

Grieger, Thomas A., Fullerton, Carol S. and Ursano, Robert J. (2004) Posttraumatic stress disorder, depression, and perceived safety 13 months after September 11. *Psychiatric Services*, 55: 1061–3.

Griesinger, Tripp and Anderman, Eric M. (1997) Motivation to learn about current events. *Peace and Conflict: Journal of Peace Psychology*, 3: 193–212.

Griffiths, Ann L. (2002) Observations on Americans and war. *Peace and Conflict: Journal of Peace Psychology*, 8: 373–5.

Griffiths, Franklyn (1991) Attempted learning: Soviet policy toward the United States in the Brezhnev era. In G. W. Breslauer and P. E. Tetlock (eds.), *Learning in US and Soviet Foreign Policy* (pp. 630–83). Boulder, CO: Westview Press.

Grimshaw, Allen D. (1992) Research on the discourse of international negotiations: a path to understanding international conflict processes? *Sociological Forum*, 7: 87–119.

Grosh, James W., Duffy, Karen G. and Olczak, Paul V. (1995) Role of ethnic and gender differences in mediated conflicts. *International Journal of Conflict Management*, 6: 48–71.

Grove, Andrea K. and Carter, Neal A. (1999) Not all blarney is cast in stone: international cultural conflict in Northern Ireland. *Political Psychology*, 20: 725–65.

Grussendorf, Jeannie, McAlister, Alfred, Sandstroem, Patrick, Udd, Lina and Morrison, Theodore C. (2002) Resisting moral disengagement in support for war: use of the 'peace test' scale among student groups in 21 nations. *Peace and Conflict: Journal of Peace Psychology*, 8: 73–84.

Guerra, N. G., Huesmann, L. R. and Spindler, A. (2003) Community violence exposure, social cognition, and aggression among urban elementary school children. *Child Development*, 74: 1561–76.

Gurr, Ted Robert (2000) *People versus states: minorities at risk in the new century.* Washington, DC: United States Institute of Peace Press.

Haddad, Simon (2002a) The determinants of Lebanese attitudes towards Palestinian resettlement: an analysis of survey data. *Peace and Conflict Studies*, 9(2): 95–119.

— (2002b) Islam and US foreign policy towards the Middle East: an analysis of survey data. *Peace and Conflict: Journal of Peace Psychology*, 8: 323–41.

— (2002c) Lebanese Christians' attitudes towards Israel and the peace process. *Studies in Conflict and Terrorism*, 25: 403–20.

Haegglund, Solveig (1999) Peer relationships and children's understanding of peace and war: a sociocultural perspective. In A. Raviv, L. Oppenheimer and D. Bar-Tal (eds.), *How children understand war and peace: a call for international peace education* (pp. 190–207). San Francisco, CA: Jossey-Bass/Pfeiffer.

Hagendoorn, Louk, Linssen, Hub and Tumanov, Sergei (2001) *Intergroup relations in states of the former Soviet Union: the perception of Russians.* Philadelphia: Psychology Press.

Hakvoort, Ilse (1996) Children's conceptions of peace and war: a longitudinal study. *Peace and Conflict: Journal of Peace Psychology*, 2: 1–15.

Hakvoort, Ilse and Haegglund, Solveig (2001) Concepts of peace and war as described by Dutch and Swedish girls and boys. *Peace and Conflict: Journal of Peace Psychology*, 7: 29–44.

Hakvoort, Ilse and Oppenheimer, Louis (1998) Understanding peace and war: a review of developmental psychology research. *Developmental Review*, 18: 353–89.

— (1999) I know what you are thinking: the role-taking ability and understanding of peace and war. In A. Raviv, L. Oppenheimer and D. Bar-Tal (eds.), *How children understand war and peace: a call for international peace education* (pp. 59–77). San Francisco, CA: Jossey-Bass/Pfeiffer.

Hale, Claudia L., Bast, Cathy and Gordon, Betsy (1991) Communication within a dispute mediation: interactants' perceptions of the process. *International Journal of Conflict Management*, 2: 139–58.

Hall, Barbara W. (1990) Soviet perceptions of global ecological problems: an analysis of three patterns. *Political Psychology*, 11: 653–80.

Hall, Bradford J. (1994) Understanding intercultural conflict through an analysis of kernel images and rhetorical visions. *International Journal of Conflict Management*, 5: 62–86.

(1997) Culture, ethics, and communication. In F. L. Casmir (ed.), *Ethics in intercultural and international communication* (pp. 11–41). Mahwah, NJ: Lawrence Erlbaum.

Hall, Donald P. Jr. (1997) Peacekeeping duty and PTSD. *American Journal of Psychiatry*, 154: 1482–3.

Halpern, Diane F. and Voiskounsky, Alexander E. (eds.) (1997) *States of mind: American and post-Soviet perspectives on contemporary issues in psychology.* New York: Oxford University Press.

Hamber, Brandon (2001) Who pays for peace? Implications of the negotiated settlement in a post-apartheid South Africa. In D. Chirot and M. E. P. Seligman (eds.), *Ethnopolitical warfare: causes, consequences, and possible solutions* (pp. 235–58). Washington, DC: American Psychological Association.

Hamilton, Andrew (1995) Policing Northern Ireland: current issues. *Studies in Conflict and Terrorism*, 18: 233–42.

Haney, C., Banks, C. and Zimbardo, P. G. (1973) Interpersonal dynamics in a simulated prison. *International Journal of Criminology and Penology*, 1: 69–97.

Harak, G. Simon (1992) After the Gulf War: a new paradigm for the peace movement. *Journal of Humanistic Psychology*, 32(4): 11–40.

Harari, Carmi (1992) Psychology and international peacemaking in the changing world scene. In U. P. Gielen, L. L. Adler and N. A. Milgram (eds.), *Psychology in international perspective: 50 years of the International Council of Psychologists* (pp. 30–41). Amsterdam: Swets & Zeitlinger.

Hardaway, Thomas (2004) Treatment of psychological trauma in children of military families. In N. B. Webb (ed.), *Mass trauma and violence: helping families and children cope* (pp. 259–82). New York: Guilford Press.

Hare, A. Paul (1983) A functional interpretation of interaction. In H. H. Blumberg, A. P. Hare, M. F. Davies and V. Kent, *Small groups and social interaction* (Vol. 2, pp. 429–47). Chichester, England: Wiley.

(1992) Informal mediation by private individuals. In J. Bercovitch and J. Z. Rubin (eds.), *Mediation in international relations: multiple approaches to conflict management* (pp. 52–63). New York: St. Martin's Press, Inc.

(1995) Attitudes related to race and ethnic conflict. In J. B. Gittler (ed.), *Racial and ethnic conflict: perspectives from the social sciences* (pp. 79–94). Greenwich: JAI Press.

Hare, A. Paul, Al Ashhab, B. and Kressel, G. M. (2003) *Psychological Reports*, 93: 771–5.

Hare, A. Paul and Blumberg, Herbert H. (eds.) (1968) *Nonviolent direct action: American cases, social-psychological analyses.* Washington, DC: Corpus Books.

(eds.) (1977) *Liberation without violence: a third-party approach.* London: Rex Collings.

(1988) *Dramaturgical analysis of social interaction.* New York and London: Praeger.

Hare, A. Paul, Blumberg, Herbert H., Davies, Martin F. and Kent, M. Valerie (1994) *Small group research: a handbook.* Norwood, NJ: Ablex.

(1996) *Small groups: an introduction.* Westport, CT: Praeger.

Harel, Gedaliahu H. and Morgan, Sandra (1994) SHALOM/SALAAM: a simulation of the Middle East peace negotiations. *Simulation and Gaming*, 25: 285–92.

Harik, Judith Palmer (1996) Between Islam and the system: sources and implications of popular support for Lebanon's Hizballah. *Journal of Conflict Resolution*, 40: 41–67.

Harleman, Christian (1998) Psychological aspects of peacekeeping on the ground. In H. J. Langholtz (ed.), *The psychology of peacekeeping* (pp. 101–10). Westport, CT: Praeger Publishers/Greenwood Publishing Group, Inc.

Harris, Ian M. (2003) Peace education at the end of a bloody century. *Educational Studies: A Journal of the American Educational Studies Association*, 34: 336–51.

Harris, Ian M. and Morrison, Mary Lee (2003) *Peace education* (2nd edn.). Jefferson, NC: McFarland.

Haslam, Jonathan (1991) Soviet policy towards Western Europe since World War II. In G. W. Breslauer and P. E. Tetlock (eds.), *Learning in US and Soviet foreign policy* (pp. 469–503). Boulder, CO: Westview Press.

Haslam, S. Alexander, Turner, John C., Oakes, Penelope, McGarty, Craig and Hayes, B. K. (1992) Context-dependent variation in social stereotyping: I. The effects of intergroup relations as mediated by social change and frame of reference. *European Journal of Social Psychology*, 22: 3–20.

Hassan, Judith (1998) Counselling with Holocaust survivors. In C. Feltham (ed.), *Witness and vision of the therapists* (pp. 123–41). Thousand Oaks, CA: Sage Publications, Inc.

Hastings, Tom H. (2004) Culture of peace, politics of power. *Peace and Conflict: Journal of Peace Psychology*, 10: 175–9.

Hatfield, Elaine (1983) Equity theory and research: an overview. In H. H. Blumberg, A. P. Hare, V. Kent and M. F. Davies (eds.), *Small groups and social interaction* (Vol. 2, pp. 401–12). Chichester: John Wiley & Sons.

Hawkes, William G. and Stasson, Mark F. (1991) Theory-driven versus data-driven decisions about post-Cold-War international crises in the aftermath of the Persian Gulf War of 1990–1991. *Contemporary Social Psychology*, 15(4): 191–5.

Heldring, Margaret (2004) Talking to the public about terrorism: promoting health and resilience. *Families, Systems, and Health*, 22: 67–71.

Helm, Bob, Odom, Sue and Wright, Judith (1991) Publication patterns in the early years: dispute resolution in the Psychological Abstracts, 1980–1985. *Mediation Quarterly*, 9: 87–103.

Helms, Elissa (2003) Women as agents of ethnic reconciliation? Women's NGOs and international intervention in postwar Bosnia-Herzegovina. *Women's Studies International Forum*, 26: 15–33.

Helson, Harry (1964) *Adaptation-level theory: an experimental and systematic approach to behavior.* New York: Harper & Row.

Hendershot, Cyndy (1999) The Bomb and sexuality: creature from the black lagoon and revenge of the creature. *Literature and Psychology*, 45(4): 74–89.

Henderson, Errol A. (1997) Culture or contiguity: ethnic conflict, the similarity of states, and the onset of war, 1820–1989. *Journal of Conflict Resolution*, 41: 649–68.

Henderson-King, Donna, Henderson-King, Eaaron, Bolea, Bryan, Koches, Kurt and Kauffman, Amy (2004) Seeking understanding or sending bombs: beliefs as predictors of responses to terrorism. *Peace and Conflict: Journal of Peace Psychology*, 10: 67–84.

Henry, David B., Tolan, Patrick H. and Gorman-Smith, Deborah (2004) Have there been lasting effects associated with the September 11, 2001, terrorist attacks among inner-city parents and children? *Professional Psychology: Research and Practice*, 35: 542–7.

Hensel, Paul R. and Diehl, Paul F. (1994) It takes two to tango: nonmilitarized response in interstate disputes. *Journal of Conflict Resolution*, 38: 479–506.

Hergovich, Andreas and Olbrich, Andreas (2003) The impact of the Northern Ireland conflict on social identity, groupthink and integrative complexity in Great Britain. *Review of Psychology*, 10(2): 95–106.

Hernandez, Pilar and Romero, Amanda (2003) Adolescent girls in Colombia's guerrilla war: an exploration into gender and trauma dynamics. *Journal of Prevention and Intervention in the Community*, 26(1): 21–38.

Herr, Charles Fernandez and Lapidus, Leah Blumberg (1998) Nuclear weapons attitudes in relation to dogmatism, mental representation of parents, and image of a foreign enemy. *Peace and Conflict: Journal of Peace Psychology*, 4: 59–68.

Herrmann, Richard K. (1994) Policy-relevant theory and the challenge of diagnosis: the end of the Cold War as a case study. *Political Psychology*, 15: 111–42.

Herrmann, Richard K. and Shannon, Vaughn P. (2001) Defending international norms: the role of obligation, material interest, and perception in decision making. *International Organization*, 55: 621–54.

Heskin, Ken (1994) Terrorism in Ireland: the past and the future. *Irish Journal of Psychology*, 15: 469–79.

Hetsroni, Amir (1998) All we were saying was give peace a chance: the future of Israeli high school peace activists. *Peace and Conflict: Journal of Peace Psychology*, 4: 237–55.

Hewitt, J. Joseph (2003) Dyadic processes and international crises. *Journal of Conflict Resolution*, 47: 669–92.

Hewstone, Miles (2003) Intergroup contact: panacea for prejudice? *Psychologist*, 16: 352–5.

Hiebert, Dennis W. (2003) The insufficiency of integrity. *Pastoral Psychology*, 51: 293–307.

Higgins, Kathryn and McElrath, Karen (2000) The trouble with peace: the cease-fires and their impact on drug use among youth in Northern Ireland. *Youth and Society*, 32: 29–59.

Hildebrand, Verna (1991) Families: a global perspective. *Early Child Development and Care*, 67: 53–60.

Hilgers, Micha (1990) Depressive muster in der Westdeutschen Friedens- und Oekologiebewegung. [Depressive patterns in the West German peace and ecology movement] *Gruppendynamik*, 21: 269–76.

Hill, Peter S. (2000) Planning and change: a Cambodian public health case study. *Social Science and Medicine*, 51: 1711–22.

Hinde, Robert A. (1993) Aggression and war: individuals, groups, and states. In P. E. Tetlock, J. L. Husbands, R. Jervis, P. C. Stern and C. Tilly (eds.), *Behavior, society, and international conflict* (Vol. 3, pp. 8–70). New York: Oxford University Press.

Hindley, Nick (2004) Shocking violence II. Violent disaster, war, and terrorism affecting our youth. *Journal of Forensic Psychiatry and Psychology*, 15: 567–8.

Hinkle, Steve, Fox-Cardamone, Lee, Haseleu, Julia A., Brown, Rupert and Irwin, Lois-M. (1996) Grassroots political action as an intergroup phenomenon. *Journal of Social Issues*, 52(1): 39–51.

Hirshberg, Matthew S. (1993a) Consistency and change in American perceptions of China. *Political Behavior*, 15: 247–63.

(1993b) The self-perpetuating national self-image: cognitive biases in perceptions of international interventions. *Political Psychology*, 14: 77–98.

Hislope, Robert (2003) Between a bad peace and a good war: insights and lessons from the almost-war in Macedonia. *Ethnic and Racial Studies*, 26(1): 129–51.

Hjaerpe, Jan (1997) Historiography and Islamic vocabulary in war and peace: a memento for conflict resolution in the Muslim world. In D. P. Fry and K. Bjoerkqvist (eds.), *Cultural variation in conflict resolution: alternatives to violence* (pp. 115–22). Mahwah, NJ: Lawrence Erlbaum Associates, Inc.

Hock, Ellen, Hart, Margaret, Kang, Min Ju and Lutz, Wilma J. (2004) Predicting children's reactions to terrorist attacks: the importance of self-reports and preexisting characteristics. *American Journal of Orthopsychiatry*, 74: 253–62.

Hoffman, B. (1998) Religious extremism. In M. E. Sharpe (ed.), *The international encyclopedia of terrorism*. Chicago: Fitzroy Dearborn.

(1999) The mind of the terrorist: perspectives from social psychology. *Psychiatric Annals*, 29: 337–40.

Hoffman, Michael A. and Bizman, Aharon (1996) Attributions and responses to the Arab–Israeli conflict: a developmental analysis. *Child Development*, 67: 117–28.

Hofner Saphiere, Dianne M. (1996) Productive behaviors of global business teams. *International Journal of Intercultural Relations*, 20: 227–59.

Hogenraad, Robert (2003) The words that predict the outbreak of wars. *Empirical Studies of the Arts*, 21: 5–20.

Homans, George C. (1950) *The human group*. New York: Harcourt, Brace & World.

Honda, Sumihisa, Shibata, Yoshisada, Mine, Mariko, Imamura, Yoshihiro, Tagawa, Masuko, Nakane, Yoshibumi and Tomonaga, Masao (2002) Mental health conditions among atomic bomb survivors in Nagasaki. *Psychiatry and Clinical Neurosciences*, 56: 575–83.

Hones, Donald F. (1999) Making peace: a narrative study of a bilingual liaison, a school and a community. *Teachers College Record*, 101: 106–34.

Hones, Donald F. and Cha, Cher Shou (1999) *Educating new Americans: immigrant lives and learning*. Mahwah, NJ: Lawrence Erlbaum Associates.

Honeyman, Catherine, Hudani, Shakirah, Tiruneh, Alfa, Hierta, Justina, Chirayath, Leila, Iliff, Andrew and Meierhenrich, Jens (2004) Establishing collective norms: potentials for participatory justice in Rwanda. *Peace and Conflict: Journal of Peace Psychology*, 10: 1–24.

Honeyman, Christopher (2001) The wrong mental image of settlement. *Negotiation Journal*, 17: 7–15.

Hoobler, Gregory (2003) Management of issues and relationships during international conflict management: or how (not?) to end a war. *International Journal of Conflict Management*, 14: 297–317.

Hopf, Ted (1991) Peripheral visions: Brezhnev and Gorbachev meet the 'Reagan doctrine'. In G. W. Breslauer and P. E. Tetlock (eds.), *Learning in US and Soviet foreign policy* (pp. 586–629). Boulder, CO: Westview Press.

Hopmann, P. Terrence and Druckman, Daniel (1991) Arms control and arms reduction: view I. In V. A. Kremenyuk (ed.), *International negotiation: analysis, approaches, issues* (pp. 269–87). San Francisco: Jossey-Bass Inc, Publishers.

Horgan, Goretti and Rodgers, Paula (2000) Young people's participation in a new Northern Ireland society. *Youth and Society*, 32: 107–37.

Horgan, J. (2003, June) The social and psychological characteristics of terrorism and terrorists. Paper presented to the Root Causes of Terrorism Conference, Norwegian Institute of International Affairs (NUPI), Oslo.

Horvath, Peter (1996) Nuclear weapons concerns, agency beliefs, and social responsibility values in disarmament activism. *Peace and Conflict: Journal of Peace Psychology*, 2: 17–35.

Hoshmand, Lisa Tsoi and Kass, Jared (2003) Conceptual and action frameworks for peace. *International Journal for the Advancement of Counselling*, 25: 205–13.

Hotopf, Matthew, David, A. S., Hull, L., Ismail, K., Palmer, I., Unwin, C. and Wessely, S. (2003) The health effects of peace-keeping in the UK armed forces: Bosnia 1992–1996. Predictors of psychological symptoms. *Psychological Medicine*, 33(1): 155–62.

Hough, George (2004) Does psychoanalysis have anything to offer an understanding of terrorism? *Journal of the American Psychoanalytic Association*, 52: 813–28.

Houlihan, Margaret M. (2002) Warning: reading this book may challenge you to cross a divide. *Peace and Conflict: Journal of Peace Psychology*, 8: 377–9.

Hoven, C. W., Mandell, D. J. and Duarte, C. S. (2003) Mental health of New York City school children after 9/11: an epidemiological investigation. In S. W. Coates and J. L. Rosenthal (eds.), *September 11: Trauma and human bonds* (pp. 51–74). Hillsdale, NJ: Analytic Press.

Hovland, Carl I, Janis, Irving L. and Kelley, Harold H. (1953) *Communication and persuasion*. New Haven, CT: Yale University Press.

Howard, George S. (2000) Adapting human lifestyles for the 21st century. *American Psychologist*, 55: 509–15.

Howe, Tasha R. (2004) Lessons learned from political violence and genocide in teaching a psychology of peace: an interview with Linda Woolf. *Teaching of Psychology*, 31: 149.

Hubbard, Amy S. (1997) Face-to-face at arm's length: conflict norms and extra-group relations in grassroots dialogue groups. *Human Organization*, 56: 265–74.

Hughes, Sherick A. (2003) The convenient scapegoating of blacks in postwar Japan: shaping the black experience abroad. *Journal of Black Studies*, 33: 335–53.

Human Rights Watch/Children's Rights Project (1996) *Children in combat*. New York: Human Rights Watch.

Hunt, Scott A. and Benford, Robert D. (1994) Identity talk in the peace and justice movement. *Journal of Contemporary Ethnography*, 22: 488–517.

Hurlburt, Kris (2002) Precious lives honored to serve. In Y. Danieli (ed.), *Sharing the front line and the back hills: international protectors and providers: peacekeepers, humanitarian aid workers and the media in the midst of crisis* (pp. 161–9). Amityville, NY: Baywood Publishing Co.

Hurwitz, Jon and Peffley, Mark (1999) International attitudes. In J. P. Robinson, P. R. Shaver and L. S. Wrightsman (eds.), *Measures of political attitudes* (pp. 533–90). San Diego, CA: Academic Press.

Iida, Keisuke (1993) When and how do domestic constraints matter? Two-level games with uncertainty. *Journal of Conflict Resolution*, 37: 403–26.

Illich, Ivan D. (1973) *Deschooling society*. Harmondsworth, Middlesex: Penguin.

International Broadcasting Trust/Channel 4 (1983) *Utopia limited*. London: Author [Videocassettes].

Ireland, Michael J. and Gartner, Scott Sigmund (2001) Time to fight: government type and conflict initiation in parliamentary systems. *Journal of Conflict Resolution*, 45: 547–68.

Ishaq, Waris (ed.) (1991) *Human behavior in today's world*. New York: Praeger Publishers.

Isometsa, E. T. and Lonnqvist, J. K. (1998) Suicide attempts preceding completed suicide. *British Journal of Psychiatry*, 173: 531–3.

Israeli, Raphael (1997) Islamikaze and their significance. *Terrorism and Political Violence*, 9(3): 96–121.

Isralowitz, Richard, Sussman, Gary, Afifi, Mohamed and Rawson, Richard (2001) Substance abuse policy and peace in the Middle East: a Palestinian and Israeli partnership. *Addiction*, 96: 973–80.

Ito, Hideaki (1998) Examining the protestor of French nuclear testing. *Japanese Journal of Social Psychology*, 13: 170–82.

Jackson, James S., Brown, Kendrick T. and Kirby, Daria C. (1998) International perspectives on prejudice and racism. In J. L. Eberhardt and S. T. Fiske (eds.), *Confronting racism: the problem and the response* (pp. 101–35). Thousand Oaks, CA: Sage Publications, Inc.

Jagodic, Gordana Kuterovac (2000) Is war a good or a bad thing? The attitudes of Croatian, Israeli, and Palestinian children towards war. *International Journal of Psychology*, 35: 241–57.

James, William (1910) *The moral equivalent of war*. Boston: The Atlantic Monthly Press [pamphlet].

—— (1995) The moral equivalent of war. *Peace and Conflict: Journal of Peace Psychology*, 1: 17–26.

Jandt, Fred Edmund and Pedersen, Paul B. (eds.) (1996) *Constructive conflict management: Asia-Pacific cases*. Thousand Oaks, CA: Sage Publications.

Janis, Irving L. (1972) *Victims of groupthink*. Boston: Houghton-Mifflin.

(1982) *Groupthink: psychological studies of policy decisions and fiascoes*. Boston: Houghton Mifflin.

(1986) Problems of international crisis management in the nuclear age. *Journal of Social Issues*, 42(2): 201–20.

(1989) *Crucial decisions: leadership in policymaking and crisis management*. New York: Free Press.

(1996) Groupthink. In J. Billsberry (ed.), *The effective manager: perspectives and illustrations* (pp. 166–78). Milton Keynes, England: Open University Press; London: Sage Publications, Inc.

Janis, Irving L. and Mann, L. (1977) *Decision making: a psychological analysis of conflict, choice, and commitment*. New York: Free Press.

Janis, Irving L. and Mann, Leon (1992) Cognitive complexity in international decision making. In P. Suedfeld and P. E. Tetlock (eds.), *Psychology and social policy* (pp. 33–49). New York: Hemisphere Publishing Corp.

Janssen, Onne and van de Vliert, Evert (1996) Concern for the other's goals: key to (de)-escalation of conflict. *International Journal of Conflict Management*, 7: 99–120.

Jarvenpaa, Sirkka L. and Leidner, Dorothy E. (1999) Communication and trust in global virtual teams. *Organization Science*, 10: 791–815.

Jayaratne, Toby Epstein, Flanagan, Constance and Anderman, Eric (1996) Predicting college student attitudes towards the Persian Gulf War: the role of gender and television exposure. *Peace and Conflict: Journal of Peace Psychology*, 2: 151–71.

Jehel, L., Paterniti, S., Brunet, A., Duchet, C. and Guelfi, J. D. (2003) Prediction of the occurrence and intensity of post-traumatic stress disorder in victims 32 months after bomb attack. *European Psychiatry*, 18: 172–6.

Jenkins, B. M. (2001) The organisation men: anatomy of a terrorist attack. In J. F. Hoge and G. Rose (eds.), *How did this happen?* (pp. 1–14). Oxford: Public Affairs Ltd.

Jensen, Jorgen Pauli (1996) War-affected societies and war-affected children: what are the long-term consequences? *Childhood: A Global Journal of Child Research*, 3: 415–21.

Jerome, Laurence and Lewis, Christopher (1996) Nuclear anxiety revisited. *Journal of the American Academy of Child and Adolescent Psychiatry*, 35: 1108–9.

Jervis, Robert (1992) Political implications of loss aversion. *Political Psychology*, 13: 187–204.

(1994) Leadership, post-Cold War politics, and psychology. *Political Psychology*, 15: 769–77.

Johnson, Celia E. and Templeton, Rosalyn Anstine (1999) Promoting peace in a place called school. *Learning Environments Research*, 2: 65–77.

Johnson, David W. and Johnson, Roger T. (1995) Teaching students to be peacemakers: results of five years of research. *Peace and Conflict: Journal of Peace Psychology*, 1: 417–38.

(2000) Civil political discourse in a democracy: the contribution of psychology. *Peace and Conflict: Journal of Peace Psychology*, 6: 291–317.

(2003) Field testing integrative negotiations. *Peace and Conflict: Journal of Peace Psychology*, 9(1): 39–68.

Johnson, David W., Johnson, Roger T. and Tjosvold, Dean (2000) Constructive controversy: the value of intellectual opposition. In M. Deutsch and P. T. Coleman (eds.), *The handbook of conflict resolution: theory and practice* (pp. 65–85). San Francisco: Jossey-Bass/Pfeiffer.

Johnson, Melissa J. and Newcomb, Michael D. (1992) Gender, war, and peace: rethinking what we know. *Journal of Humanistic Psychology*, 32(4): 108–37.

Johnson, P. W. and Feldman, T. B. (1992) Personality types and terrorism. *Forensic Reports*, 5: 293–303.

Johnson, Paul E. (1999) Simulation modeling in political science. *American Behavioral Scientist*, 42: 1509–30.

Jonah, James O. C. (1992) The United Nations and international conflict: the military talks at Kilometre Marker-101. In J. Bercovitch and J. Z. Rubin (eds.), *Mediation in international relations: multiple approaches to conflict management* (pp. 176–205). New York: St. Martin's Press, Inc.

Jones, Edward E. (1990) *Interpersonal perception*. New York: Freeman.

Jones, Lynne (2002) Adolescent understandings of political violence and psychological well-being: a qualitative study from Bosnia Herzegovina. *Social Science and Medicine*, 55: 1351–71.

Jones, Tricia S. and Bodtker, Andrea (1998) A dialectical analysis of a social justice process: international collaboration in South Africa. *Journal of Applied Communication Research*, 26: 357–73.

Jones, Tricia S. and Remland, Martin S. (1993) Nonverbal communication and conflict escalation: an attribution-based model. *International Journal of Conflict Management*, 4: 119–37.

Joseph, S., Cairns, E. and McCollam, P. (1993) Political violence, coping and depressive symptomology in Northern Irish children. *Personality and Individual Differences*, 15: 471–3.

Joshi, Aparna, Labianca, Giuseppe and Caligiuri, Paula M. (2002) Getting along long distance: understanding conflict in a multinational team through network analysis. *Journal of World Business*, 37: 277–84.

Joshi, Paramjit T. and Lewin, Shulamit M. (2004) Disaster, terrorism: addressing the effects of traumatic events on children and their families is critical to long-term recovery and resilience. *Psychiatric Annals*, 34: 710–16.

Joshi, P. T. and O'Donnell, D. A. (2003) Consequences of child exposure to war and terrorism. *Clinical Child and Family Psychology Review*, 6: 275–92.

Jucovy, Milton E. (1992) Psychoanalytic contributions to Holocaust studies. *International Journal of Psycho-Analysis*, 73: 267–82.

Juergensmeyer, M. (2001) *Terror in the mind of God: the global rise of religious violence*. London: University of California Press.

Juhasz, Anne M. and Palmer, Laura L. (1991) Adolescent perspectives of ways of thinking and believing that promote peace. *Adolescence*, 26: 849–55.

Kacen, Lea and Sofer, Gita (1997) Support groups of 'shock absorbers' in periods of transition: a case study of groups for parents of soldiers in Israel. *International Social Work*, 40: 277–88.

Kagee, Ashraf, Naidoo, Anthony V. and Van Wyk, Sherine (2003) Building communities of peace: the South African experience. *International Journal for the Advancement of Counselling*, 25: 225–33.

Kahn, Robert L. and Kramer, Roderick M. (1990) Untying the knot: de-escalatory processes in international conflict. In R. L. Kahn and M. N. Zald (eds.), *Organizations and nation-states: new perspectives on conflict and cooperation* (pp. 139–80). San Francisco, CA: Jossey-Bass Inc, Publishers.

Kahn, Robert L. and Zald, Mayer N. (eds.) (1990) *Organizations and nation-states: new perspectives on conflict and cooperation*. San Francisco, CA: Jossey-Bass.

Kahneman, Daniel and Tversky, Amos (1979) Prospect theory: an analysis of decision under risk. *Econometrica*, 47: 263–91.

(1990) Prospect theory: an analysis of decision under risk. In P. K. Moser (ed.), *Rationality in action: contemporary approaches* (pp. 140–70). New York: Cambridge University Press.

Kaiser, Cheryl R., Vick, S. Brooke and Major, Brenda (2004) A prospective investigation of the relationship between just-world beliefs and the desire for revenge after September 11, 2001. *Psychological Science*, 15: 503–6.

Kalmanowitz, Debra and Lloyd, Bobby (eds.) (2005) *Art therapy and political violence: with art, without illusion*. Hove, East Sussex: Brunner-Routledge.

Kapitan, Lynn (1997) Making or breaking: art therapy in the shifting tides of a violent culture. *Art Therapy*, 14: 255–60.

Kaplan, Seth A., Bradley, Jill C. and Ruscher, Janet B. (2004) The inhibitory role of cynical disposition in the provision and receipt of social support: the case of the September 11th terrorist attacks. *Personality and Individual Differences*, 37: 1221–32.

Kaplowitz, Noel (1990) National self-images, perception of enemies, and conflict strategies: psychopolitical dimensions of international relations. *Political Psychology*, 11: 39–82.

Kapur, Basant and Chong, Kim Chong (2002) *Altruistic reveries: perspectives from the humanities and social sciences*. Boston, MA: Kluwer.

Karakashian, Meline (1998) Armenia: a country's history of challenges. *Journal of Social Issues*, 54: 381–92.

Karasawa, Minoru (2002) Patriotism, nationalism, and internationalism among Japanese citizens: an etic-emic approach. *Political Psychology*, 23: 645–66.

Kashima, Yoshihisa, Kashima, Emiko S., Gelfand, Michele, Goto, Sharon, Takata, Toshitake, Takemura, Kazuhisa and Zhang, Zhiyong (2003) War and peace in East Asia: Sino-Japanese relations and national stereotypes. *Peace and Conflict: Journal of Peace Psychology*, 9: 259–76.

Kaslow, Florence W. (1990) Treating Holocaust survivors. *Contemporary Family Therapy: An International Journal*, 12: 393–405.

Katz, Arthur M. (1990) The effects of nuclear war on human society. In B. Glad (ed.), *Psychological dimensions of war* (pp. 328–55). Newbury Park, CA: Sage Publications, Inc.

Kavka, Gregory S. (1991) Nuclear hostages. In R. G. Frey and C. W. Morris (eds.), *Violence, terrorism, and justice* (pp. 276–95). New York: Cambridge University Press.

Keashly, Loraleigh (1994) The influence of intervenor role on criteria for dispute intervention: parents and friends as intervenors. *International Journal of Conflict Management*, 5: 22–33.

Keating, Mark E., Pruitt, Dean G., Eberle, Rachael A. and Mikolic, Joseph M. (1994) Strategic choice in everyday disputes. *International Journal of Conflict Management*, 5: 143–57.

Keinan, G., Sadeh, A. and Rosen, S. (2003) Attitudes and reactions to media coverage of terrorist acts. *Journal of Community Psychology*, 31: 149–65.

Kelley, Harold H. and Michela, J. L. (1980) Attribution theory and research. *Annual Review of Psychology*, 31: 457–501.

Kelley, Michelle L. (1994) The effects of military-induced separation on family factors and child behavior. *American Journal of Orthopsychiatry*, 64: 103–11.

Kelman, Herbert C. (1991) A behavioral science perspective on the study of war and peace. In R. Jessor (ed.), *Perspectives on behavioral science: the Colorado lectures* (pp. 245–75). Boulder, CO: Westview Press.

(1992) Informal mediation by the scholar/practitioner. In J. Bercovitch and J. Z. Rubin (eds.), *Mediation in international relations: multiple approaches to conflict management* (pp. 64–96). New York: St Martin's Press.

(1995a) Decision making and public discourse in the Gulf War: an assessment of underlying psychological and moral assumptions. *Peace and Conflict: Journal of Peace Psychology*, 1: 117–30.

(1995b) Ignacio Martin-Baro: a personal remembrance of a martyred peace psychologist. *Peace and Conflict: Journal of Peace Psychology*, 1: 11–15.

(1997) Group processes in the resolution of international conflicts: experiences from the Israeli–Palestinian case. *American Psychologist*, 52: 212–20.

(1998) Social-psychological contributions to peacemaking and peacebuilding in the Middle East. *Applied Psychology: An International Review*, 47: 5–28.

(1999a) Building a sustainable peace: the limits of pragmatism in the Israeli–Palestinian negotiations. *Peace and Conflict: Journal of Peace Psychology*, 5: 101–15.

(1999b) Interactive problem solving as a metaphor for international conflict resolution: lessons for the policy process. *Peace and Conflict: Journal of Peace Psychology*, 5: 201–18.

(2001) The role of national identity in conflict resolution: experiences from Israeli–Palestinian problem-solving workshops. In R. D. Ashmore, L. Jussim and D. Wilder (eds.), *Social identity, intergroup conflict, and conflict reduction* (pp. 187–212). London: Oxford University Press.

Kelsey, Elin (2003) Constructing the public: implications of the discourse of international environmental agreements on conceptions of education and public participation. *Environmental Education Research*, 9: 403–27.

Keltner, Dacher and Robinson, Robert J. (1993) Imagined ideological differences in conflict escalation and resolution. *International Journal of Conflict Management*, 4: 249–62.

Kemmelmeier, Markus and Winter, David G. (2000) Putting threat into perspective: experimental studies on perceptual distortion in international conflict. *Personality and Social Psychology Bulletin*, 26: 795–809.

Kemp, G (2000, July) True nature of aggression in warfare. Paper presented at the meeting of the International Society for Research on Aggression, Valencia, Spain. [For an abstract see *Aggressive Behaviour*, 27(3).]

Kemp, Graham (2001) Definitions of international aggression: lessons for cross-cultural research. In J. M. Ramirez and D. S. Richardson (eds.), *Cross-cultural approaches to research on aggression and reconciliation* (pp. 51–8). Huntington, NY: Nova Science Publishers.

Kemp, Katherine E. and Smith, William P. (1994) Information exchange, toughness, and integrative bargaining: the roles of explicit cues and perspective-taking. *International Journal of Conflict Management*, 5: 5–21.

Kendall, Kathleen E. (1990) Application of communication research to political contexts. In D. O'Hair and G. L. Kreps (eds.), *Applied communication theory and research* (pp. 225–43). Hillsdale, NJ: Lawrence Erlbaum Associates, Inc.

Kendrick, Richard (2000) Swimming against the tide: peace movement recruitment in an abeyance environment. In P. G. Coy and L. M. Woehrle (eds.), *Social conflicts and collective identities* (pp. 189–204). Lanham, MD: Rowman & Littlefield Publishers.

Kent, Valerie (1983) Prosocial behaviour and small group processes. In H. H. Blumberg, A. P. Hare, V. Kent and M. F. Davies (eds.), *Small groups and social interaction* (Vol. 1, pp. 227–41). Chichester: John Wiley & Sons.

Kernberg, O. F. (2003) Sanctioned social violence: a psychoanalytic view: Part II. *International Journal of Psychoanalysis*, 84: 953–68.

Kersten, Gregory and Noronha, Sunil (1999) Negotiation via the world wide web: a cross-cultural study of decision making. *Group Decision and Negotiation*, 8: 251–79.

Khan, Nichola and Smith, Peter B. (2003) Profiling the politically violent in Pakistan: self-construals and values. *Peace and Conflict: Journal of Peace Psychology*, 9: 277–95.

Kidwell, Brian and Langholtz, Harvey J. (1998) Personnel selection, preparation, and training for UN peacekeeping missions. In H. J. Langholtz (ed.), *The psychology of peacekeeping* (pp. 89–100). Westport, CT: Praeger Publishers/Greenwood Publishing Group, Inc.

Kierulff, Stephen (1991) Belief in 'Armageddon theology' and willingness to risk nuclear war. *Journal for the Scientific Study of Religion*, 30: 81–93.

Kilgour, D. Marc, Hipel, Keith W. and Fang, Liping (1994) Negotiation support using the graph model for conflict resolution. *Group Decision and Negotiation*, 3: 29–46.

Kim, Do Yeong (2003) After the South and North Korea summit: malleability of explicit and implicit national attitudes of South Koreans. *Peace and Conflict: Journal of Peace Psychology*, 9: 159–70.

Kim, Do Yeong and Oh, Hye Jung (2001) Psychosocial aspects of Korean reunification: explicit and implicit national attitudes and identity of South Koreans and North Korean defectors. *Peace and Conflict: Journal of Peace Psychology*, 7: 265–88.

Kim, Pan Suk (1999) Globalization of human resource management: a cross-cultural perspective for the public sector. *Public Personnel Management*, 28: 227–43.

Kimmel, Paul R. (1994) Cultural perspectives on international negotiations. *Journal of Social Issues*, 50(1): 179–96.

(1995) Sustainability and cultural understanding: peace psychology as public interest science. *Peace and Conflict: Journal of Peace Psychology*, 1: 101–16.

(1998) Cultural and ethnic issues of conflict and peacekeeping. In H. J. Langholtz (ed.), *The psychology of peacekeeping* (pp. 57–71). Westport, CT: Praeger Publishers/Greenwood Publishing Group, Inc.

Kingsbury, Sherman (1995) Incremental change and transformation in persons and systems. In F. Massarik (ed.), *Advances in organization development* (Vol. 3, pp. 119–26). Norwood, NJ: Ablex Publishing Corp.

Kingston, Shane (1995) Terrorism, the media, and the Northern Ireland conflict. *Studies in Conflict and Terrorism*, 18: 203–31.

Kinsella, David and Russett, Bruce (2002) Conflict emergence and escalation in interactive international dyads. *Journal of Politics*, 64: 1045–68.

Kinzie, J. D., Sack, W., Angell, R., Manson, S., Clarke, G. and Ben, R. (1989) A three-year follow-up of Cambodian young people traumatised as children. *Journal of the American Academy of Child and Adolescent Psychiatry*, 28: 501–4.

Kinzie, J. D., Sack, W., Angell, R., Manson, S. and Rath, B. (1986) The psychiatric effects of massive trauma on Cambodian children: I. The children. *Journal of the American Academy of Child and Adolescent Psychiatry*, 25: 370–6.

Kirkland, Faris R. (1996) Can soldiers keep peace? A study of the recent history of the psychological dimensions of the US army. *Journal of Psychohistory*, 23: 427–37.

Klandermans, Bert (1991) New social movements and resource mobilization: the European and the American approach revisited. *Politics and the Individual*, 1(2): 89–111.

(1993) A theoretical framework for comparisons of social movement participation. *Sociological Forum*, 8: 383–402.

Kleiboer, Marieke (1996) Understanding success and failure of international mediation. *Journal of Conflict Resolution*, 40: 360–89.

Kleidman, Robert (1994) Volunteer activism and professionalism in social movement organizations. *Social Problems*, 41: 257–76.

Kleinman, S. B. (2002) Helping managers assist employees facing threats of terrorism. *Psychiatric Services*, 53: 1340–1.

Klineberg, Otto (1991) The contributions of psychology to international understanding: problems and possibilities. In R. W. Rieber (ed.), *The psychology of war and peace: the image of the enemy* (pp. 71–83). New York: Plenum Press.

Klingman, A. (1992) Stress reactions of Israeli youth during the Gulf War: a quantitative study. *Professional Psychology: Research and Practice*, 23: 521–7.

Klingman, Avigdor (2000) Children's affective reactions and coping under threat of uprooting: the case of the Golan Heights. *School Psychology International*, 21: 377–92.

Klingman, Avigdor, Goldstein, Zehava and Lerner, Pesia (1991) Adolescents' response to nuclear threat: before and after the Chernobyl accident. *Journal of Youth and Adolescence*, 20: 519–30.

Kloep, Marion (1991) Prejudice and peace: is the Swedish youth neutral in its attitudes? *Scandinavian Journal of Psychology*, 32: 31–7.

Klotz, Audie (2004) The power of legitimacy: assessing the role of norms in crisis bargaining. *Political Psychology*, 25: 142–5.

Knox, Colin (2001) The 'deserving' victims of political violence: 'punishment' attacks in Northern Ireland. *Criminal Justice: International Journal of Policy and Practice*, 1: 181–99.

Kobrick, Felice R. (1993) Reaction of Vietnam veterans to the Persian Gulf War. *Health and Social Work*, 18: 165–71.

Kodama, Yoshio, Nomura, Soichiro and Ogasawara, Tsuneyuki (2000) Psychological changes of Japan self-defense forces personnel during selection and training for the peacekeeping mission in the Golan Heights. *Military Medicine*, 165: 653–5.

Koenigs, R. J. (1996) Leadership can be taught. In S. E. Hare and A. P. Hare (eds.), *SYMLOG field theory: organizational consultation, value differences, personality and social perception* (pp. 73–83). Westport, CT: Praeger.

Kohr, Heinz Ulrich (1991) Psychological correlates of threat perception in West Germany, 1978 and 1981. In R. W. Rieber (ed.), *The psychology of war and peace: the image of the enemy* (pp. 251–62). New York: Plenum Press.

Kohr, Heinz Ulrich and Raeder, Hans Georg (1991) Generational learning and paradigms of military threat in West Germany. In R. W. Rieber (ed.), *The psychology of war and peace: the image of the enemy* (pp. 263–79). New York: Plenum Press.

Kool, Vinod K. (ed.) (1993) *Nonviolence: social and psychological issues*. Lanham, MD: University Press of America.

Koopman, Cheryl, McDermott, Rose, Jervis, Robert, Snyder, Jack and Dioso, J. (1995) Stability and change in American elite beliefs about international relations. *Peace and Conflict: Journal of Peace Psychology*, 1: 365–82.

Koopman, Cheryl, Shiraev, Eric, McDermott, Rose, Jervis, Robert and Snyder, Jack (1998) Beliefs about international security and change in 1992 among Russian and American national security elites. *Peace and Conflict: Journal of Peace Psychology*, 4: 35–57.

Korol, Mindy, Green, Bonnie L. and Gleser, Goldine C. (1999) Children's responses to a nuclear waste disaster: PTSD symptoms and outcome prediction. *Journal of the American Academy of Child and Adolescent Psychiatry*, 38: 368–75.

Korzenny, F. and Ting-Toomey, S. (eds.) (1990) *Communicating for peace: diplomacy and negotiation*. Newbury Park, CA: Sage. [*International and Intercultural Communication Annual, 14.*]

Kowalewski, David (1994) Teaching war: does it pacify students? *Journal of Instructional Psychology*, 21: 227–33.

Kowalski, Robin M. and Wolfe, Randall (1994) Collective identity orientation, patriotism, and reactions to national outcomes. *Personality and Social Psychology Bulletin*, 20: 533–40.

Kozan, M. Kamil (1997) Culture and conflict management: a theoretical framework. *International Journal of Conflict Management*, 8: 338–60.

Kozminski, Andrew K. (1991) Organizational and global management: a new road to social progress? *Psychology: A Journal of Human Behavior*, 28 (2): 48–56.

Kraft, Robert Nathaniel (2002) *Memory perceived: recalling the Holocaust.* Westport, CT: Praeger Publishers/Greenwood Publishing Group.

Kramer, Bernard M. and Moyer, Robert S. (1991) *Nuclear psychology bibliography.* Ann Arbor, MI: The Society for the Psychological Study of Social Issues.

Kramer, Roderick M., Meyerson, Debra and Davis, Gerald (1990a) Deterrence and the management of international conflict: cognitive aspects of deterrent decisions. In M. A. Rahim (ed.), *Theory and research in conflict management* (pp. 188–208). New York: Praeger Publishers.

(1990b) How much is enough? Psychological components of 'guns versus butter' decisions in a security dilemma. *Journal of Personality and Social Psychology*, 58: 984–93.

Krampen, Guenter, Jirasko, Marco, Martini, Massimo and Rihs-Middel, Margret (1990) Semantische Merkmale vier vielverwendeter politischer Begriffe in fuenf Nationalitaetsstichproben. [Semantic characteristics of four frequently used political concepts among five national samples.] *Zeitschrift für Experimentelle und Angewandte Psychologie*, 37: 459–85.

Kraus, Sarit and Wilkenfeld, Jonathan (1993) A strategic negotiations model with applications to an international crisis. *IEEE Transactions on Systems, Man, and Cybernetics*, 23: 313–23.

Krauss, B. J., Franchi, D., O'Day, J., Pride, J., Lozada, L., Aledort, N. and Bates, D. (2003) Two shadows of the twin towers: missing safe spaces and foreclosed opportunities. *Families in Society: The Journal of Contemporary Human Services*, 84: 523–9.

Kremenyuk, Victor A. (1991a) The emerging system of international negotiation. In V. A. Kremenyuk (ed.), *International negotiation: analysis, approaches, issues* (pp. 22–39). San Francisco: Jossey-Bass Inc, Publishers.

(ed.) (1991b) *International negotiation: analysis, approaches, issues.* San Francisco, CA: Jossey-Bass.

Kressel, Neil J. (ed.) (1993) *Political psychology: classic and contemporary readings.* New York: Paragon House.

(2003) The worldly psychologists. *Peace and Conflict*, 9: 373–6.

Krippner, Stanley and McIntyre, Teresa M. (eds.) (2003) *The psychological impact of war trauma on civilians: an international perspective.* Westport, CT: Praeger Publishers/Greenwood Publishing Group.

Kristiansen, Connie M. and Matheson, Kimberly (1990) Value conflict, value justification, and attitudes towards nuclear weapons. *Journal of Social Psychology*, 130: 665–75.

Kroth, Jerry (1992) *Omens and oracles: collective psychology in the nuclear age.* New York: Praeger Publishers.

Kugler, Jacek and Feng, Yi (1999) Explaining and modeling democratic transitions. *Journal of Conflict Resolution*, 43: 139–46.

Kumar, Rajesh (1999) A script theoretical analysis of international negotiating behavior. In R. J. Bies, R. J. Lewicki and B. H. Sheppard (eds.), *Research on negotiation in organizations* (Vol. 7, pp. 285–311). Stamford, CT: JAI Press (Elsevier).

Kuoch, Theanvy, Miller, Richard A. and Scully, Mary F. (1992) Healing the wounds of the Mahantdori. *Women and Therapy*, 13: 191–207.

Kushner, H. (1996) Suicide bombers: business as usual. *Studies in Conflict and Terrorism*, 19: 329–38.

Kutz, I. (2002) An intervention model for treating acute stress reaction following a terrorist attack or other catastrophes involving large number of casualties. *Journal of Psychosomatic Research*, 52: 361.

Kyle, K. and Angelique, H. (2002) Tragedy and catharsis in the wake of the 9/11 attacks. *Journal of Community and Applied Social Psychology*, 12: 369–74.

Kytta, Marketta, Kaaja, Mirkka and Horelli, Lisa (2004) An Internet-based design game as a mediator of children's environmental visions. *Environment and Behavior*, 36: 127–51.

Lachkar, Joan (1993) Parallels between marital and political conflict. *Journal of Psychohistory*, 20: 275–87.

(1994) Paradox of peace: folie à deux in marital and political relationships. *Journal of Psychohistory*, 22: 199–211.

Lachkar, J. (2002) The psychological make-up of a suicide bomber. *Journal of Psychohistory*, 29: 349–67.

Lacy, Dean and Niou, Emerson M. S. (2004) A theory of economic sanctions and issue linkage: the roles of preferences, information, and threats. *Journal of Politics*, 66: 25–42.

La Farge, Phyllis (1992) Teaching social responsibility in the schools. In S. Staub and P. Green (eds.), *Psychology and social responsibility: facing global challenges* (pp. 345–65). New York: New York University Press.

Lagadec, Patrick (2002) Crisis management in France: trends, shifts and perspectives. *Journal of Contingencies and Crisis Management*, 10(4): 159–72.

Lai, Brian and Reiter, Dan (2000) Democracy, political similarity and international alliances, 1816–1992. *Journal of Conflict Resolution*, 44: 203–27.

Lamerson, C. D. and Kelloway, E. K. (1996) Towards a model of peacekeeping stress: traumatic and contextual influences. *Canadian Psychology*, 37: 195–204.

Lampen, John (ed.) (2002) The toughest nut to crack: nonviolent alternatives to political violence. *Peace and Conflict: Journal of Peace Psychology*, 8(3): 285–7.

Landau, Simha F. (1997) Conflict resolution in a highly stressful society: the case of Israel. In D. P. Fry and K. Bjoerkqvist (eds.), *Cultural variation in conflict resolution: alternatives to violence* (pp. 123–36). Mahwah, NJ: Lawrence Erlbaum Associates, Inc.

Landau, Simha F., Beit-Hallahmi, Benjamin and Levy, Shilomit (1998) The personal and the political: Israelis' perception of well-being in times of war and peace. *Social Indicators Research*, 44: 329–65.

Langer, Ellen J., Bashner, Richard S. and Chanowitz, Benzion (1985) Decreasing prejudice by increasing discrimination. *Journal of Personality and Social Psychology*, 49: 113–20.

Langholtz, Harvey J. (1998a) The evolving psychology of peacekeeping. In H. J. Langholtz (ed.), *The psychology of peacekeeping* (pp. 3–15). Westport, CT: Praeger Publishers/Greenwood Publishing Group, Inc.

(ed.) (1998b) *The psychology of peacekeeping*. Westport, CT: Praeger Publishers/Greenwood Publishing Group.

(1998c) The psychology of peacekeeping: genesis, ethos, and application. *Peace and Conflict: Journal of Peace Psychology*, 4: 217–36.

Langholtz, Harvey J. and Leentjes, Peter (2001) UN peacekeeping: confronting the psychological environment of war in the twenty-first century. In D. J. Christie, R. V. Wagner and D. D. Winter (eds.), *Peace, conflict, and violence: peace psychology for the 21st century* (pp. 173–82). Upper Saddle River, NJ: Prentice Hall.

Langley, Winston E. (1997) Children and world peace: a modest proposal. *Journal of Psychohistory*, 24: 234–41.

Langlois, Catherine C. and Langlois, Jean Pierre P. (1999) Behavioral issues of rationality in international interaction: a game theoretic analysis. *Journal of Conflict Resolution*, 43: 626–45.

Lanir, Zvi (1991) Educating for democratic behavior in an intercultural context. *International Journal of Intercultural Relations*, 15: 327–43.

Laor, Nathaniel, Wolmer, Leo and Cohen, Donald J. (2004) Attitudes towards Arabs of Israeli children exposed to missile attacks: the role of personality functions. *Israel Journal of Psychiatry and Related Sciences*, 41: 23–32.

Lapsley, Daniel K. and Narváez, Darcia (2004) *Moral development, self, and identity*. Mahwah, NJ: Lawrence Erlbaum Associates.

Larsen, Knud S., Csepeli, Goyrgy, Dann, Hanns Dietrich, Giles, Howard, Ommundsen, Reidar, Elder, Robert and Long, Ed (1992) Attitudes towards nuclear disarmament: international comparisons of university students and activists. In S. Iwawaki, Y. Kashima and K. Leung (eds.), *Innovations in cross-cultural psychology* (pp. 164–72). Amsterdam, Netherlands: Swets & Zeitlinger.

Larson, Deborah Welch (1991) Learning in US–Soviet relations: the Nixon–Kissinger structure of peace. In G. W. Breslauer and P. E. Tetlock (eds.), *Learning in US and Soviet foreign policy* (pp. 350–99). Boulder, CO: Westview Press.

(1997) Trust and missed opportunities in international relations. *Political Psychology*, 18: 701–34.

Lau, Richard R. and Levy, Jack S. (1998) Contributions of behavioural decision theory to research in political science. *Applied Psychology: An International Review*, 47: 29–44.

Lavee, Yoav, Ben-David, Amith and Azaiza, Faisal (1997) Israeli and Palestinian families in the peace process: sources of stress and response patterns. *Family Process*, 36: 247–63.

Lavoy, Peter R. (1991) Learning and the evolution of cooperation in US and Soviet nuclear nonproliferation activities. In G. W. Breslauer and P. E. Tetlock (eds.), *Learning in US and Soviet foreign policy* (pp. 735–83). Boulder, CO: Westview Press.

Leach, Colin Wayne and Williams, Wendy R. (1999) Group identity and conflicting expectations of the future in Northern Ireland. *Political Psychology*, 20: 875–96.

Leach, Mark M. (1997) Training global psychologists: an introduction. *International Journal of Intercultural Relations*, 161–74.

Leatherman, Janie (2002) Turning minds to peace. *Peace and Conflict: Journal of Peace Psychology*, 8: 383–5.

Leavitt, Lewis A. and Fox, Nathan A. (eds.) (1993) *The psychological effects of war and violence on children*. Hillsdale, NJ: Lawrence Erlbaum Associates.

LeBaron, Michelle (2003) *Bridging cultural conflicts: a new approach for a changing world*. San Francisco, CA: Jossey-Bass.

Lebow, Richard Ned (1995) Psychological dimensions of post-Cold War foreign policy. In S. A. Renshon (ed.), *The Clinton presidency: campaigning, governing, and the psychology of leadership* (pp. 235–45). Boulder, CO: Westview Press.

Lee, Courtland C. (1997) The global future of professional counseling: collaboration for international social change. *International Journal of Intercultural Relations*, 21: 279–85.

 (1998) Professional counseling in a global context: collaboration for international social action. In C. C. Lee and G. R. Walz (eds.), *Social action: a mandate for counselors* (pp. 293–304). Alexandria, VA: American Counseling Association.

Lee, Donald C. (1992) *Toward a sound world order: a multidimensional, hierarchical ethical theory*. Westport, CT: Greenwood Press/Greenwood Publishing Group.

Leeds, Brett Ashley and Davis, David R. (1997) Domestic political vulnerability and international disputes. *Journal of Conflict Resolution*, 41: 814–34.

Leeds, Brett Ashley, Long, Andrew G. and Mitchell, Sara McLaughlin (2000) Reevaluating alliance reliability: specific threats, specific promises. *Journal of Conflict Resolution*, 44: 686–99.

Leftoff, Sondra (2003) Navajo peacemaking: a non-adversarial approach to justice. *NYS Psychologist*, 15(3): 19–22.

Leng, Russell J. (1993a) Influence techniques among nations. In P. E. Tetlock, J. L. Husbands, R. Jervis, P. C. Stern and C. Tilly (eds.), *Behavior, society, and international conflict* (Vol. 3, pp. 71–125). New York: Oxford University Press.

 (1993b) Reciprocating influence strategies in interstate crisis bargaining. *Journal of Conflict Resolution*, 37: 3–41.

Leppanen, Katarina (2004) At peace with earth – connecting ecological destruction and patriarchal civilisation. *Journal of Gender Studies*, 13: 37–47.

Lerner, J. S., Gonzalez, R. M., Small, D. A. and Fischhoff, B. (2003) Effects of fear and anger on perceived risks of terrorism: a national field experiment. *Psychological Science*, 14: 144–50.

Lerner, Melvin J. (1991) The belief in a just world and the 'heroic motive': searching for 'constants' in the psychology of religious ideology. *International Journal for the Psychology of Religion*, 1: 27–32.

LeShan, Lawrence (2002) *The psychology of war: comprehending its mystique and its madness*. New York: Helios Press.

Leung, Kwok (2003) Asian peace psychology: what can it offer? *Peace and Conflict: Journal of Peace Psychology*, 9: 297–302.

Leung, Kwok and Wu, Pei Guan (1990) Dispute processing: a cross-cultural analysis. In R. W. Brislin (ed.), *Applied cross-cultural psychology* (pp. 209–31). Newbury Park, CA: Sage Publications, Inc.

Lev-Wiesel, Rachel (2002) A model for promoting community cohesion in response to conflict. *Journal for Specialists in Group Work*, 27: 32–42.

Levant, R. F. (2002) Psychology responds to terrorism. *Professional Psychology: Research and Practice*, 33: 507–9.

Levin, Brian (2002) Precarious balance between civil liberties and national security: a historical perspective. *Humboldt Journal of Social Relations*, 27(2): 18–34.

Levin, S., Henry, P. J., Pratto, F. J. and Sidanius, J. (2003) Social dominance and social identity in Lebanon: implications for support of violence against the west. *Group Processes and Intergroup Relations*, 6: 353–68.

Levine, Robert A. (1991) The evolution of US policy towards arms control. In G. W. Breslauer and P. E. Tetlock (eds.), *Learning in US and Soviet foreign policy* (pp. 135–57). Boulder, CO: Westview Press.

Levinger, George (1998) Toward a greater focus on war's alternatives. *Peace and Conflict: Journal of Peace Psychology*, 4: 137–41.

Levinger, George and Rubin, Jeffrey Z. (1994) Bridges and barriers to a more general theory of conflict. *Negotiation Journal*, 10: 201–15.

Leviton, Daniel (ed.) (1991) *Horrendous death and health: towards action.* New York: Hemisphere Publishing Corp.

Levy, B. and Sidel, V. (eds) (1997) *War and public health.* New York: Oxford University Press.

Levy, Jack S. (1992) Prospect theory and international relations: theoretical applications and analytical problems. *Political Psychology*, 13: 283–310.

Levy, Mary Ann, Haglund, Pamela, Plaut, Linda, Emde, Robert, Stewart, Marguerite, Shaw, Ronnie, Ilvonen, Carol, Buirski, Cathy Krown, Singe, Mel, Hea, Rebecca and Edwards, William (2004) Healing after Columbine: reflections of psychoanalytic responders to community trauma. *Journal of the American Psychoanalytic Association*, 52: 759–81.

Levy, Sheldon G. (1995) Attitudes towards the conflict of war. *Peace and Conflict: Journal of Peace Psychology*, 1: 179–97.

(1999) Psychological reactions to incidents of political mass killing. *Peace and Conflict: Journal of Peace Psychology*, 5: 53–67.

Leyden-Rubenstein, Lori (2001) Peace on earth begins with inner peace. *Annals of the American Psychotherapy Association*, 4(6): 24.

Lieberfeld, Daniel (2003) Nelson Mandela: partisan and peacemaker. *Negotiation Journal*, 19: 229–50.

Lifton, Robert Jay (1992) *Home from the war: learning from Vietnam veterans.* Boston: Beacon Press.

(1993) From Hiroshima to the Nazi doctors: the evolution of psychoformative approaches to understanding traumatic stress syndromes. In J. P. Wilson and B. Raphael (eds.), *International handbook of traumatic stress syndromes* (pp. 11–23). New York: Plenum Press.

Lim, Rodney G. (1997) Overconfidence in negotiation revisited. *International Journal of Conflict Management*, 8: 52–79.

Lim, Rodney G. and Carnevale, Peter J. (1995) Influencing mediator behavior through bargainer framing. *International Journal of Conflict Management*, 6: 349–68.

Lindner, Evelin Gerda (2002) Healing the cycles of humiliation: how to attend to the emotional aspects of 'unsolvable' conflicts and the use of 'humiliation entrepreneurship'. *Peace and Conflict: Journal of Peace Psychology*, 8: 125–38.

Linn, Ruth (1995) The claim for moral maturity, consistency, and integrity among objecting Israeli soldiers. *Journal of Applied Social Psychology*, 25: 399–417.

(2001) Conscience at war: on the relationship between moral psychology and moral resistance. *Peace and Conflict: Journal of Peace Psychology*, 7: 337–55.

Lipschutz, Ronnie D. (1991) Bargaining among nations: culture, history, and perceptions in regime formation. *Evaluation Review*, 15: 46–74.

(1993) 'Bargaining among nations: culture, history, and perceptions in regime formation': Erratum. *Evaluation Review*, 17: 663.

Lipton, Judith Eve (1991) Nuclear war: horrendous death, death, and more death. In D. Leviton (ed.), *Horrendous death and health: towards action* (pp. 25–36). New York: Hemisphere Publishing Corp.

Lira, Elizabeth (2001) Violence, fear, and impunity: reflections on subjective and political obstacles for peace. *Peace and Conflict: Journal of Peace Psychology*, 7: 109–18.

Littlefield, Lyn, Love, Anthony, Peck, Connie and Wertheim, Eleanor H. (1993) A model for resolving conflict: some theoretical, empirical and practical implications. *Australian Psychologist*, 28: 80–5.

Litvak-Hirsch, Tal, Bar-On, Dan and Chaitin, Julia (2003) Whose house is this? Dilemmas of identity construction in the Israeli–Palestinian context. *Peace and Conflict: Journal of Peace Psychology*, 9: 127–48.

Litz, Brett T., Gray, Matt J. and Bolton, Elisa E. (2003) Posttraumatic stress disorder following peacekeeping operations. In T. W. Britt and A. B. Adler (eds.), *The psychology of the peacekeeper: lessons from the field* (pp. 243–58). Westport, CT: Praeger Publishers/Greenwood Publishing Group.

Litz, Brett T., King, Lynda A., King, Daniel W. and Orsillo, Susan M. (1997) Warriors as peacekeepers: features of the Somalia experience and PTSD. *Journal of Consulting and Clinical Psychology*, 65: 1001–10.

Litz, Brett T., Orsillo, Susan M. and Friedman, Matthew (1997) 'Posttraumatic stress disorder associated with peacekeeping duty in Somalia for US military personnel': reply. *American Journal of Psychiatry*, 154: 1483.

Litz, Brett T., Orsillo, Susan M., Friedman, Matthew, Ehlich, Peter and Batres, A. (1997) 'Posttraumatic stress disorder associated with peacekeeping duty in Somalia for US military personnel': correction. *American Journal of Psychiatry*, 154: 722.

Liverant, Gabrielle I., Hofmann, Stefan G. and Litz, Brett T. (2004) Coping and anxiety in college students after the September 11-super(th) terrorist attacks. *Anxiety, Stress and Coping: An International Journal*, 17: 127–39.

Llanos, Raimundo Abello, Amar, Jose, Botto, Armando, Carrillo, Rita, Castro, Yuliana, Linares, Eduardo and Racedo, Heydie (2001) Efectos de la violencia politica sobre las emociones de ira, miedo y ansiedad en ninos Colombianos de 11 y 12 anos. [Effects of political violence on emotions of wrath, fear, and anxiety in Colombian children aged 11 and 12 years.] *Avances en Psicologia Clinica Latinoamericana*, 19: 67–82.

Lohmann, Susanne (1997) Linkage politics. *Journal of Conflict Resolution*, 41: 38–67.

Long, William J. and Brecke, Peter (2003) *War and reconciliation: reason and emotion in conflict resolution*. Cambridge, MA: MIT Press.

Lootsma, F. A., Sluijs, J. M. and Wang, S. Y. (1994) Pairwise comparison of concessions in negotiation processes. *Group Decision and Negotiation*, 3: 121–31.

Lotto, D. (2003) Fascism resurgent. *Journal of Psychohistory*, 30: 296–305.

Lounsbery, Marie Olson and Pearson, Frederic S. (2003) Policy-making and connections to violence: a case study of India. *Peace and Conflict Studies*, 10: 20–45.

Louw, Johann and van Hoorn, Willem (1997) Psychology, conflict, and peace in South Africa: historical notes. *Peace and Conflict: Journal of Peace Psychology*, 3: 233–43.

Lowenstein, Ludwig F. (1990) Realistic versus less realistic peace activism. *New Jersey Journal of Professional Counseling*, 53(1): 2–6.

Lumsden, Malvern and Wolfe, Rebecca (1996) Evolution of the problem-solving workshop: an introduction to social-psychological approaches to conflict resolution. *Peace and Conflict: Journal of Peace Psychology*, 2: 37–67.

Lundeberg, Jan-Erik et al. (1990) Peace-keeping forces. In J.-E. Lundeberg, U. Otto, et al. (eds.), *Wartime medical services: Second International Conference; Stockholm, Sweden, 25–29 June 1990: Proceedings* (pp. 310–61). Stockholm: Foersvarets Forskningsanstalt (Foa).

Lustig, S. L., Kia-Keating, M., Knight, W. G., Geltman, P., Ellis, H., Kinzie, J. D., Keane, T. and Saxe, G. N. (2004) Review of child and adolescent refugee mental health. *Journal of the American Academy of Child and Adolescent Psychiatry*, 43: 24–36.

Luther, Catherine A. (2002) National identities, structure, and press images of nations: the case of Japan and the United States. *Mass Communication and Society*, 5: 57–85.

Lykes, M. Brinton (1999) Doing psychology at the periphery: constructing just alternatives to war and peace. *Peace and Conflict: Journal of Peace Psychology*, 5: 27–36.

Maaz, Hans Joachim (1992) Psychosocial aspects in the German unification process. *International Journal for the Advancement of Counselling*, 15: 91–101.

Macapagal, Maria Elizabeth J. and Nario Galace, Jasmin (2003) Social psychology of People Power II in the Philippines. *Peace and Conflict: Journal of Peace Psychology*, 9: 219–33.

Mack, John E. (1993) The passions of nationalism and beyond: identity and power in international relationships. In S. L. Ablon, D. Brown, E. J. Khantzian and J. E. Mack (eds.), *Human feelings: explorations in affect development and meaning* (pp. 333–53). Hillsdale, NJ: Analytic Press, Inc.

Macksoud, Mona S., Dyregov, Atle and Raundalen, Magne (1993) Traumatic war experiences and their effects on children. In J. P. Wilson and B. Raphael (eds.), *International handbook of traumatic stress syndromes* (pp. 625–33). New York: Plenum.

MacNair, Rachel (2003) *The psychology of peace: an introduction*. Westport, CT: Praeger.

Macnamara, Jim B. (2004) The crucial role of research in multicultural and cross-cultural communication. *Journal of Communication Management*, 8: 322–34.

Macy, Joanna Rogers (1983) *Despair and personal power in the nuclear age*. Philadelphia, PA: New Society Publishers.

Macy, Joanna (1992) Planetary perils and psychological responses: despair and empowerment work. In S. Staub and P. Green (eds.), *Psychology and social responsibility: facing global challenges* (pp. 30–58). New York and London: New York University Press.

Maerli, Morten Bremer, Schaper, Annette and Barnaby, Frank (2003) The characteristics of nuclear terrorist weapons. *American Behavioral Scientist*, 46: 727–44.

Majeski, Stephen J. and Fricks, Shane (1995) Conflict and cooperation in international relations. *Journal of Conflict Resolution*, 39: 622–45.

Malin, Adam M. and Fowers, Blaine J. (2004) Adolescents' reactions to the World Trade Center destruction: a study of political trauma in metropolitan New York. *Current Psychology: Developmental, Learning, Personality, Social*, 23: 77–85.

Mandell, Brian S. and Fisher, Ronald J. (1992) Training third-party consultants in international conflict resolution. *Negotiation Journal*, 8: 259–71.

Mann, Leon (1993) Protest movements as a source of social change. *Australian Psychologist*, 28: 69–73.

Mannix, Elizabeth A. (1993) The influence of power, distribution norms and task meeting structure on resource allocation in small group negotiation. *International Journal of Conflict Management*, 4: 5–23.

(1994) Will we meet again? Effects of power, distribution norms and scope of future interaction in small group negotiation. *International Journal of Conflict Management*, 5: 343–68.

Maoz, Ifat (2000) Multiple conflicts and competing agendas: a framework for conceptualizing structured encounters between groups in conflict – the case of a coexistence project of Jews and Palestinians in Israel. *Peace and Conflict: Journal of Peace Psychology*, 6: 135–56.

(2001) The violent asymmetrical encounter with the other in an army–civilian clash: the case of the intifada. *Peace and Conflict: Journal of Peace Psychology*, 7: 243–63.

(2002) Is there contact at all? Intergroup interaction in planned contact interventions between Jews and Arabs in Israel. *International Journal of Intercultural Relations*, 26: 185–97.

(2003) Peace-building with the hawks: attitude change of Jewish-Israeli hawks and doves following dialogue encounters with Palestinians. *International Journal of Intercultural Relations*, 27: 701–14.

Maoz, Ifat and Bar-On, Dan (2002) From working through the Holocaust to current ethnic conflicts: evaluating the TRT group workshop in Hamburg. *Group*, 26: 29–48.

Maoz, Ifat, Bar-On, Dan, Bekerman, Zvi and Jaber-Massarwa, Summer (2004) Learning about 'good enough' through 'bad enough': a story of a planned dialogue between Israeli Jews and Palestinians. *Human Relations*, 57: 1075–101.

Maoz, Ifat, Ward, Andrew, Katz, Michael and Ross, Lee (2002) Reactive devaluation of an 'Israeli' vs. 'Palestinian' peace proposal. *Journal of Conflict Resolution*, 46: 515–46.

Maoz, Zeev and Astorino, Allison (1992) The cognitive structure of peacemaking: Egypt and Israel, 1970–1978. *Political Psychology*, 13: 647–62.

Marburger, Daniel R. (1994) Research note: is exchangeable arbitrator behavior necessarily deliberate? *International Journal of Conflict Management*, 5: 181–91.

Marks, John and Fraenkel, Eran (1997) Working to prevent conflict in the new nation of Macedonia. *Negotiation Journal*, 13: 243–52.

Marshall, R. D. and Suh, E. J. (2003) Contextualising trauma: using evidence-based treatments in a multicultural community after 9/11. *Psychiatric Quarterly*, 74: 401–20.

Martin, Dominique (1991) Conflits et strategies suscites par l'innovation. [Conflicts and strategies triggered by technical change.] *Applied Psychology: An International Review*, 40: 365–79.

Martin-Baro, I. (1994) War and the psychological trauma of Salvadoran children. In A. Aron and S. Corne (eds.) [A. Wallace, trans.], *Writings for a liberation psychology* (pp. 122–35). Cambridge, MA: Harvard University Press.

Martini, Massimo and Krampen, Guenter (1990) Caratteristiche semantiche di concetti politici: una ricerca comparata. [Semantic properties of the political concepts: a comparative study.] *Ricerche di Psicologia*, 14(3): 101–27.

Masserman, Jules Hymen and Masserman, Christine H. McGuire (eds.) (1992) *Social psychiatry and world accords*. New York: Gardner Press.

Mastors, Elena (2000) Gerry Adams and the Northern Ireland peace process: a research note. *Political Psychology*, 21: 839–46.

Mattaini, Mark A. (2001) Constructing cultures of non-violence: the Peace Power! strategy. *Education and Treatment of Children*, 24: 430–47.

(2002) The science of nonviolence. *Behavior and Social Issues*, 11: 100–4.

Mattaini, Mark A. and Lowery, Christine T. (2000) Constructing cultures of nonviolence: the PEACE POWER! toolkit. In D. S. Sandhu and C. B. Aspy (eds.), *Violence in American schools: a practical guide for counselors* (pp. 123–38). Alexandria, VA: American Counseling Association.

Mauro, Jason Isaac (1997) Huck Finn and the post-nuclear age: lighting out for the new frontier. *Literature and Psychology*, 43(3): 24–40.

Mayer, Jochen and Rotte, Ralph (1999) Arms and aggression in the Middle East, 1948–1991: a reappraisal. *Journal of Conflict Resolution*, 43: 45–57.

Mays, Vickie M., Rubin, Jeffrey, Sabourin, Michel and Walker, Lenore (1996) Moving towards a global psychology: changing theories and practice to meet the needs of a changing world. *American Psychologist*, 51: 485–7.

Mayton, Daniel M. II (2001a) Gandhi as peacebuilder: the social psychology of *Satyagraha*. In D. J. Christie, R. V. Wagner and D. D. Winter (eds.), *Peace, conflict, and violence: peace psychology for the 21st century* (pp. 307–13). Upper Saddle River, NJ: Prentice Hall.

(2001b) Nonviolence within cultures of peace: a means and an end. *Peace and Conflict: Journal of Peace Psychology*, 7: 143–55.

Mayton, Daniel M. II, Diessner, Rhett and Granby, Cheryl D. (1996) Nonviolence and human values: empirical support for theoretical relations. *Peace and Conflict: Journal of Peace Psychology*, 2: 245–53.

Mayton, Daniel M. and Furnham, Adrian (1994) Value underpinnings of antinuclear political activism: a cross-national study. *Journal of Social Issues*, 50(4): 117–28.

Mayton, Daniel M. II, Peters, Danya J. and Owens, Rocky W. (1999) Values, militarism, and nonviolent predispositions. *Peace and Conflict: Journal of Peace Psychology*, 5: 69–77.

Mayton, Daniel M. and Sangster, Roberta L. (1992) Cross-cultural comparison of values and nuclear war attitudes. *Journal of Cross-Cultural Psychology*, 23: 340–52.

Mayton, Daniel M. II, Susnjic, Silvia, Palmer, B. James, Peters, Danya J., Gierth, Richard and Caswell, Rosalie N. (2002) The measurement of non-violence: a review. *Peace and Conflict: Journal of Peace Psychology*, 8: 343–54.

Mazen, Abdelmagid M. (1998) When settlement and resolution are in conflict: searching for a mideast peace dividend. *Negotiation Journal*, 14: 357–67.

Mazor, Aviva and Tal, Ido (1996) Intergenerational transmission: the individuation process and the capacity for intimacy of adult children of Holocaust survivors. *Contemporary Family Therapy: An International Journal*, 18: 95–113.

Mazurana, Dyan E. and McKay, Susan A. (1999) *Women and Peacebuilding*. Montreal, Canada: International Centre for Human Rights and Democratic Development.

Mazurana, Dyan E., McKay, Susan A., Carlson, Khristopher C. and Kasper, Janel C. (2002) Girls in fighting forces and groups: their recruitment, participation, demobilization, and reintegration. *Peace and Conflict: Journal of Peace Psychology*, 8: 97–123.

McAdam, Doug and Su, Yang (2002) The war at home: antiwar protests and Congressional voting, 1965–1973. *American Sociological Review*, 67: 696–721.

McAuley, James W. (2004) Peace and progress? Political and social change among young loyalists in Northern Ireland. *Journal of Social Issues*, 60: 541–62.

McCarthy, G. and Davies, S. (2003) Some implications of attachment theory for understanding psychological functioning in old age: an illustration from the long-term psychological effects of World War Two. *Clinical Psychology and Psychotherapy*, 10: 144–55.

McCartney, Tony and Turner, Colleen (2000) Reconciliation happens every day: conversations about working alliances between black and white Australia. *Australian Psychologist*, 35: 173–6.

McCauley, C. (1991) *Terrorism research and public policy*. London: Frank Cass. [Also cited in Colvard, 2002.]

McCormick, G. H. (2003) Terrorist decision making. *Annual Review of Political Science*, 6: 473–507.

McDermott, Rose (1992) Prospect theory in international relations: the Iranian hostage rescue mission. *Political Psychology*, 13: 237–63.

(1998) *Risk-taking in international politics: prospect theory in American foreign policy*. Ann Arbor, MI: University of Michigan Press.

McEvoy, Kieran, O'Mahony, David, Horner, Carol and Lyner, Olwen (1999) The home front: the families of politically motivated prisoners in Northern Ireland. *British Journal of Criminology*, 39: 175–97.

McFarland, Robert B. (2000) A psychohistory of Pearl Harbor and the atomic bomb. *Journal of Psychohistory*, 28: 191–202.

McGinnis, Michael D. (2000) Policy substitutability in complex humanitarian emergencies: a model of individual choice and international response. *Journal of Conflict Resolution*, 44: 62–89.

McGuire, William J. (1985) Attitudes and attitude change. In G. Lindzey and E. Aronson (eds.), *Handbook of social psychology* (3rd edn., Vol. 2, pp. 233–46). New York: Random House.

McInerney, Audrey (1992) Prospect theory and Soviet policy towards Syria, 1966–1967. *Political Psychology*, 13: 265–82.

McIntyre, Alice (2000) Constructing meaning about violence, school, and community: participatory action research with urban youth. *Urban Review*, 32: 123–54.

McIntyre, Teresa M. and Ventura, Margarida (2003) Children of war: psychosocial sequelae of war trauma in Angolan adolescents. In T. M. McIntyre and S. Krippner (eds.), *The psychological impact of war trauma on civilians: an international perspective* (pp. 39–53). Westport, CT: Praeger Publishers/ Greenwood Publishing Group.

McIvor, M. (1981) Northern Ireland: a preliminary look at environmental awareness. Paper presented to the Biennial Conference of the International Society of Behavioural Development, Toronto, Canada.

McKay, Susan (1995) Women's voices in peace psychology: a feminist agenda. *Peace and Conflict: Journal of Peace Psychology*, 1: 67–84.

(1996) Gendering peace psychology. *Peace and Conflict: Journal of Peace Psychology*, 2: 93–107.

(1998) The effects of armed conflict on girls and women. *Peace and Conflict: Journal of Peace Psychology*, 4: 381–92.

McKay, Susan and de la Rey, Cheryl (2001) Women's meanings of peacebuilding in post-apartheid South Africa. *Peace and Conflict: Journal of Peace Psychology*, 7: 227–42.

McKay, Susan and Mazurana, Dyan (2001) Gendering peacebuilding. In D. J. Christie, R. V. Wagner and D. D. Winter (eds.), *Peace, conflict, and violence: peace psychology for the 21st century* (pp. 341–9). Upper Saddle River, NJ: Prentice Hall.

McKenzie-Mohr, Doug (2000) Fostering sustainable behavior through community-based social marketing. *American Psychologist*, 55: 531–7.

McKenzie-Mohr, Doug and Dyal, James A. (1991) Perceptions of threat, tactical efficacy and competing threats as determinants of pro-disarmament behavior. *Journal of Social Behavior and Personality*, 6: 675–96.

McKenzie-Mohr, Doug, McLoughlin, John G. and Dyal, James A. (1992) Perceived threat and control as moderators of peace activism: implications for mobilizing the public in the pursuit of disarmament. *Journal of Community and Applied Social Psychology*, 2: 269–80.

McLarney, Cam and Rhyno, Shelley R. (1998) Beyond agency theory: the use of reciprocating relationships to predict international joint venture success. In T. A. Scandura and M. G. Serapio (eds.), *Research in international business and international relations: leadership and innovation in emerging markets* (Vol. 7, pp. 219–46). Stamford, CT: JAI Press, Inc.

McLernon, Frances and Cairns, Ed (1999) Children, peace, and war in Northern Ireland. In A. Raviv, L. Oppenheimer and D. Bar-Tal (eds.), *How children understand war and peace: a call for international peace education* (pp. 145–60). San Francisco, CA: Jossey-Bass/Pfeiffer.

(2001) Impact of political violence on images of war and peace in the drawings of primary school children. *Peace and Conflict: Journal of Peace Psychology*, 7: 45–57.

McLernon, Frances, Ferguson, Neil and Cairns, Ed (1997) Comparison of Northern Irish children's attitudes to war and peace before and after the paramilitary ceasefires. *International Journal of Behavioral Development*, 20: 715–30.

McManus, Martha M. (2004) Resilience and war trauma: peacekeepers' perspectives. Unpublished MPhil thesis, University of Bradford.

McWhirter, L. (1983) Northern Ireland: growing up with the troubles. In A. P. Goldstein and M. H. Segall (eds.), *Aggression in global perspective* (pp. 367–400). Elmsford, New York: Pergamon Press.

McWilliams, M. (1998) Violence against women in societies under stress. In R. E. Dobash and R. P. Dobash (eds.), *Rethinking violence against women* (pp. 111–40). Thousand Oaks, CA: Sage.

Mehl, M. R. and Pennebaker, J. W. (2003) The social dynamics of a cultural upheaval: social interactions surrounding September 11, 2001. *Psychological Science*, 14: 579–85.

Melville, M. and Lykes, B. (1992) Guatemalan Indian children and the sociocultural effects of government sponsored terrorism. *Social Science and Medicine*, 34: 533–49.

Mendelsohn, Michaela and Straker, Gill (1998) Child soldiers: psychosocial implications of the Graca Machel/UN study. *Peace and Conflict: Journal of Peace Psychology*, 4: 399–413.

Merari, A. (1990) The readiness to kill and die: suicidal terrorism in the Middle East. In W. Reich (ed.), *Origins of terrorism: psychologies, ideologies, theologies, states of mind* (pp. 192–207). Cambridge: Cambridge University Press.

Merry, Sally Engle (1995) Resistance and the cultural power of law. *Law and Society Review*, 29: 11–26.

Merskin, Debra (2004) The construction of Arabs as enemies: post-September 11 discourse of George W. Bush. *Mass Communication and Society*, 7: 157–75.

Meschi, Pierre Xavier (1997) Longevity and cultural differences of international joint ventures: towards time-based cultural management. *Human Relations*, 50: 211–28.

Mesquida, Christian G. and Wiener, Neil I. (1996) Human collective aggression: a behavioral ecology perspective. *Ethology and Sociobiology*, 17: 247–62.

Metzger, Janet G., Springston, Jeffrey K., Weber, Douglas and Larsen, Paul D. (1991) The Wisconsin treaty rights debate: narratives of conflict and change in a mid-level moral community. *International Journal of Intercultural Relations*, 15: 191–207.

Meyer, Mary K. (1998) Negotiating international norms: the Inter-American Commission of Women and the Convention on Violence against Women. *Aggressive Behavior*, 24: 135–46.

Miall, Hugh (2002) Shaping a vision: the task of peace studies. *Peace and Conflict: Journal of Peace Psychology*, 8: 387–8.

Miall, Hugh, Ramsbotham, Oliver and Woodhouse, Tom (1999) *Contemporary conflict resolution: the prevention, management and transformation of deadly conflicts*. Cambridge: Polity Press/Blackwell.

Mickley, G. Andrew and Bogo, Victor (1991) Radiological factors and their effects on military performance. In R. Gal and A. D. Mangelsdorff (eds.), *Handbook of military psychology* (pp. 365–85). Chichester: John Wiley & Sons.

Midgley, James (1997) *Social welfare in global context*. Thousand Oaks, CA: Sage Publications.

Mijuskovic, Ben (1992) Organic communities, atomistic societies, and loneliness. *Journal of Sociology and Social Welfare*, 19(2): 147–64.

Mikula, Gerold and Wenzel, Michael (2000) Justice and social conflict. *International Journal of Psychology*, 35(2): 126–35.

Milani, Feizi M. and Branco, Angela Uchoa (2004) Assessing Brazil's culture of peace. *Peace and Conflict: Journal of Peace Psychology*, 10: 161–74.

Milburn, Thomas W. (1998) Psychology, negotiation, and peace. *Applied and Preventive Psychology*, 7: 109–19.

Milburn, Tom and Isaac, Paul (1995) Prospect theory: implications for international mediation. *Peace and Conflict: Journal of Peace Psychology*, 1: 333–42.

Miliora, Maria T. (2004) The psychology and ideology of an Islamic terrorist leader: Usama bin Laden. *International Journal of Applied Psychoanalytic Studies*, 1: 121–39.

Miller, Arlene Michaels and Heldring, Margaret (2004) Mental health and primary care in a time of terrorism: psychological impact of terrorist attacks. *Families, Systems, and Health*, 22: 7–30.

Miller, K. (1994) Growing up in exile: mental health and meaning making among indigenous Guatemalan refugee children in Chiapas, Mexico. Unpublished doctoral dissertation, University of Michigan, Ann Arbor.

Miller, Kenneth E. (1998) Research and intervention with internally displaced and refugee children. *Peace and Conflict: Journal of Peace Psychology*, 4: 365–79.

Miller, Laurence (2004) Psychotherapeutic interventions for survivors of terrorism. *American Journal of Psychotherapy*, 58: 1–16.

Mintu-Wimsatt, Alma and Gassenheimer, Jule B. (2000) The moderating effects of cultural context in buyer–seller negotiation. *Journal of Personal Selling and Sales Management*, 20: 1–9.

Mintz, Alex and Geva, Nehemia (1993) Why don't democracies fight each other? An experimental study. *Journal of Conflict Resolution*, 37: 484–503.

Mishal, Shaul and Morag, Nadav (2002) Political expectations and cultural perceptions in the Arab–Israeli peace negotiations. *Political Psychology*, 23: 325–53.

Mitchell, Christopher (1999) Negotiation as problem solving: challenging the dominant metaphor. *Peace and Conflict: Journal of Peace Psychology*, 5: 219–24.

(2002) Beyond resolution: what does conflict transformation actually transform? *Peace and Conflict Studies*, 9(1): 1–23.

Mitchell, Sara McLaughlin, Gates, Scott and Hegre, Havard (1999) Evolution in democracy-war dynamics. *Journal of Conflict Resolution*, 43: 771–92.

Mitchels, Barbara (2003) Healing the wounds of war and more: an integrative approach to peace – the work of Adam Curle and others with Mir i dobro in Zupanja, Croatia. *British Journal of Guidance and Counselling*, 31: 403–16.

Miyahara, Akira, Kim, Min Sun, Shin, Ho Chang and Yoon, Kak (1998) Conflict resolution styles among 'collectivist' cultures: a comparison between Japanese and Koreans. *International Journal of Intercultural Relations*, 22: 505–25.

Moerk, Ernst L. (1995) Acquisition and transmission of pacifist mentalities in Sweden. *Peace and Conflict: Journal of Peace Psychology*, 1: 291–307.

(1997) Socialism and pacifism: historical relations, value homologies, and implications of recent political developments, or the return of history. *Peace and Conflict: Journal of Peace Psychology*, 3: 59–79.

(2002) Scripting war-entry to make it appear unavoidable. *Peace and Conflict: Journal of Peace Psychology*, 8(3): 229–48.

Moeschberger, Scott L. and Ordonez, Alicia (2003) Working towards building cultures of peace: a primer for students and new professionals. *International Journal for the Advancement of Counselling*, 25: 317–23.

Moghadam, A. (2003) Palestinian suicide terrorism in the second intifada: motivations and organisational aspects. *Studies in Conflict and Terrorism*, 26: 65–92.

Moghaddam, Fathali M. and Marsella, Anthony J. (eds.) (2004) *Understanding terrorism: psychosocial roots, consequences, and interventions*. Washington, DC: American Psychological Association.

Molander, Earl A. (1991) Bridge building from the grass roots: organization and management of citizen diplomacy programs. In D. Leviton (ed.), *Horrendous death and health: towards action* (pp. 227–44). New York: Hemisphere Publishing Corp.

Moldjord, Christian, Fossum, Lars Kristian and Holen, Are (2003) Coping with peacekeeping stress. In T. W. Britt and A. B. Adler (eds.), *The psychology of the peacekeeper: lessons from the field* (pp. 169–84). Westport, CT: Praeger Publishers/Greenwood Publishing Group.

Mollov, Ben and Lavie, Chaim (2001) Culture, dialogue, and perception change in the Israeli–Palestinian conflict. *International Journal of Conflict Management*, 12: 69–87.

Molyneux, Maxine (2004) Common ground or mutual exclusion: women's movements and international relations. *Gender, Work and Organization*, 11: 709–11.

Monge, Peter and Matei, Sorin Adam (2004) The role of the global telecommunications network in bridging economic and political divides, 1989 to 1999. *Journal of Communication*, 54: 511–31.

Monroe, Kristen R. (ed.) (2002) *Political psychology*. Mahwah, NJ: Lawrence Erlbaum Associates.

Montiel, Cristina Jayme (1995) Social psychological dimensions of political conflict resolution in the Philippines. *Peace and Conflict: Journal of Peace Psychology*, 1: 149–59.

(1997) Citizen-based peacemaking in a protracted war: two Philippine cases. *Peace and Conflict: Journal of Peace Psychology*, 3: 115–34.

(2001) Toward a psychology of structural peacebuilding. In D. J. Christie, R. V. Wagner and D. D. Winter (eds.), *Peace, conflict, and violence: peace psychology for the 21st century* (pp. 282–94). Upper Saddle River, NJ: Prentice Hall.

(2003) Peace psychology in Asia. *Peace and Conflict: Journal of Peace Psychology*, 9: 195–218.

Moore, Michael and Tyson, G. A. (1990) Perceptions and misperceptions: the Middle East and South Africa. *Journal of Social Psychology*, 130: 299–308.

Moore, Will H. (1995) Action-reaction or rational expectations? Reciprocity and the domestic–international conflict nexus during the 'Rhodesia problem'. *Journal of Conflict Resolution*, 39: 129–67.

Mor, Naomi (1990) Holocaust messages from the past. *Contemporary Family Therapy: An International Journal*, 12: 371–9.

Morales, J. Francisco and Leal, Jose Antonio (2004) Indicators for a culture of peace in Spain. *Peace and Conflict: Journal of Peace Psychology*, 10: 147–60.

Mork, Gordon R. (2003) Fundamentals of genocide scholarship. *Peace and Conflict: Journal of Peace Psychology*, 9: 175–6.

Morrell, Robert (2002) A calm after the storm? Beyond schooling as violence. *Educational Review*, 54: 37–46.

Morris, Michael W., Leung, Kwok and Lyengar, Sheena S. (2004) Person perception in the heat of conflict: negative trait attributions affect procedural preferences and account for situational and cultural differences. *Asian Journal of Social Psychology*, 7(2): 127–47.

Morris, Vivian Gunn, Taylor, Satomi Izumi and Wilson, Jeanne T. (2000) Using children's stories to promote peace in classrooms. *Early Childhood Education Journal*, 28: 41–50.

Mosco, Vincent (1993) Communication and information technology for war and peace. In C. Roach (ed.), *Communication and culture in war and peace* (pp. 41–70). Newbury Park, CA: Sage Publications, Inc.

Moscovici, Serge and Paicheler, Geneviève (1983) Minority or majority influences: social change, compliance, and conversion. In H. H. Blumberg, A. P. Hare, V. Kent and M. F. Davies (eds.), *Small groups and social interaction* (Vol. 1, pp. 215–24). Chichester: John Wiley & Sons.

Moss, D. (2003) Does it matter what the terrorists meant? In D. Moss (ed.), *Hating in the first person plural: psychoanalytic essays on racism, homophobia, misogyny, and terror*. New York: Other Press.

Mousseau, Michael (1998) Democracy and compromise in militarized interstate conflicts, 1816–1992. *Journal of Conflict Resolution*, 42: 210–30.

Mowlana, Hamid (1996) *Global communication in transition: the end of diversity?* Thousand Oaks, CA: Sage Publications.

Mowle, Thomas S. (2003) Worldviews in foreign policy: realism, liberalism, and external conflict. *Political Psychology*, 24: 561–92.

Muldoon, O. (2003) The psychological impact of protracted campaigns of political violence on societies. In A. Silke (ed.), *Terrorists, victims and society: psychological perspectives on terrorism and its consequences* (pp. 161–74). Chichester: Wiley.

Muldoon, O. and Cairns, E. (1999) Children, young people and war: learning to cope. In E. Frydenburg (ed.), *Learning to cope* (pp. 322–37). Oxford: Oxford University Press.

Muldoon, Orla T. and Trew, Karen (2000) Children's experience and adjustment to political conflict in Northern Ireland. *Peace and Conflict: Journal of Peace Psychology*, 6: 157–76.

Muldoon, Orla T., Trew, Karen and Kilpatrick, Rosemary (2000) The legacy of the troubles on the young people's psychological and social development and their school life. *Youth and Society*, 32: 6–28.

Muldoon, O. and Wilson, K. (2001) Ideological commitment, experience of conflict and adjustment in Northern Irish adolescents. *Medicine, Conflict and Survival*, 17: 112–24.

Mullen, John D. and Roth, Byron M. (1991) *Decision-making: its logic and practice*. Savage, MD: Rowman & Littlefield/Rowman & Allanheld.

Müller-Brettel, Marianne (1993a) *Bibliography on peace research and peaceful international relations: the contributions of psychology, 1900–1991*. München, London, New York, Paris: K. G. Saur.

(1993b) War and peace in the life of children – perspectives from developmental psychology – a literature review. *Psychologie in Erziehung und Unterricht*, 40: 81–96.

Munier, Bertrand R. and Rulliere, Jean Louis (1993) Are game theoretic concepts suitable negotiation support tools? From Nash equilibrium refinements towards a cognitive concept of rationality. *Theory and Decision*, 34: 235–53.

Munier, Bertrand and Zaharia, Costin (2002) High stakes and acceptance behavior in ultimatum bargaining: a contribution from an international experiment. *Theory and Decision*, 53: 187–207.

Murphy, Bianca C. and Polyson, James A. (1991) Peace, war, and nuclear issues in the psychology classroom. *Teaching of Psychology*, 18: 153–7.

Murray, Shoon Kathleen and Meyers, Jason (1999) Do people need foreign enemies? American leaders' beliefs after the Soviet demise. *Journal of Conflict Resolution*, 43: 555–69.

Mussano, Silvia Dorina (2004) Lessons in creative conflict management. *Peace and Conflict: Journal of Peace Psychology*, 10: 85–6.

Mustakova-Possardt, Elena (2003) *Critical consciousness: a study of morality in global, historical context*. Westport, CT: Praeger Publishers/Greenwood Publishing Group.

Myers-Bowman, Karen S., Walker, Kathleen and Myers-Walls, Judith A. (2003) A cross-cultural examination of children's understanding of the enemy. *Psychological Reports*, 93: 779–90.

Nachtwey, Jodi and Tessler, Mark (2002) The political economy of attitudes towards peace among Palestinians and Israelis. *Journal of Conflict Resolution*, 46: 260–85.

Nadler, Arie (2002) Postresolution processes: instrumental and socioemotional routes to reconciliation. In G. Salomon and B. Nevo (eds.), *Peace education: the concept, principles, and practices around the world* (pp. 127–41). Mahwah, NJ: Lawrence Erlbaum Associates.

Nath, Raghu (1990) Partnership for development: toward a macro-approach in organization development. In F. Massarik (ed.), *Advances in organization development* (Vol. 1, pp. 147–64). Norwood, NJ: Ablex Publishing Corp.

Nation, Tim (2003) Creating a culture of peaceful school communities. *International Journal for the Advancement of Counselling*, 25: 309–15.

Natlandsmyr, Jan Halvor and Rognes, Jorn (1995) Culture, behavior, and negotiation outcomes: a comparative and cross-cultural study of Mexican and Norwegian negotiators. *International Journal of Conflict Management*, 6: 5–29.

Neill, Alexander Sutherland (1960) *Summerhill: a radical approach to child rearing.* New York: Hart Publishing.

Nelson, Alan T. (1992) Why nonviolent peacemaking is important now. *Journal of Humanistic Psychology*, 32(4): 157–60.

Nelson, Linden L. and Christie, Daniel J. (1995) Peace in the psychology curriculum: moving from assimilation to accommodation. *Peace and Conflict: Journal of Peace Psychology*, 1: 161–78.

Nelson, Linden L., Golding, Natasha L., Drews, David R. and Blazina, Mary K. (1995) Teaching and assessing problem solving for international conflict resolution. *Peace and Conflict: Journal of Peace Psychology*, 1: 399–415.

Nelson, Linden L. and Milburn, Thomas W. (1999) Relationships between problem-solving competencies and militaristic attitudes: implications for peace education. *Peace and Conflict: Journal of Peace Psychology*, 5: 149–68.

Nemiroff, Lisa S. and McKenzie-Mohr, Doug (1992) Determinants and distinguishing variables of pro-disarmament behavior and responsible environmental behavior. *Journal of Social Behavior and Personality*, 7: 1–24.

Nepstad, Sharon Erickson (2004) Religion, violence, and peacemaking. *Journal for the Scientific Study of Religion*, 43: 297–301.

Nesdale, Drew and Todd, Patricia (2000) Effect of contact on intercultural acceptance: a field study. *International Journal of Intercultural Relations*, 24: 341–60.

Nevin, John A. (1991) Behavior analysis and global survival. In W. Ishaq (ed.), *Human behavior in today's world* (pp. 39–49). New York: Praeger Publishers.

Nevin, J. A. (2003) Retaliating against terrorists. *Behavior and Social Issues*, 12: 109–28.

Nevin, John A. and Fuld, Kenneth (1993) On armament traps and how to get out of them: lessons from research on doves. *Behavior and Social Issues*, 3: 63–74.

Newman, Martin (2004) Helping children cope with disasters and terrorism. *Journal of Child Psychology and Psychiatry and Allied Disciplines*, 45: 172.

Niens, Ulrike and Cairns, Ed (2001) Intrastate violence. In D. J. Christie, R. V. Wagner and D. D. Winter (eds.), *Peace, conflict, and violence: peace psychology for the 21st century* (pp. 39–48). Upper Saddle River, NJ: Prentice Hall.

Nikolic-Ristanovic, Vesna (1999) Living without democracy and peace: violence against women in the former Yugoslavia. *Violence Against Women*, 5: 63–80.

Nikolopoulos, Andreas G. (1995) Planning the use of power: an episodic model. *International Journal of Conflict Management*, 6: 257–72.

Nissani, Moti (1992) *Lives in the balance: the Cold War and American politics, 1945–1991*. Carson City, NV: Hollowbrook Publishing.

Nissim-Sabat, Denis (1996) The American Psychological Association's initiatives in the former Soviet Republic of Russia: where do we go from here? In V. A. Koltsova, Y. N. Oleinik, A. R. Gilgen and C. K. Gilgen (eds.), *Post-Soviet perspectives on Russian psychology* (pp. 135–43). Westport, CT: Greenwood Press/Greenwood Publishing Group, Inc.

Njenga, Frank G., Nicholls, P. J., Nyamai, Caroline, Kigamwa, Pius and Davidson, Jonathan R. T. (2004) Post-traumatic stress after terrorist attack: psychological reactions following the US embassy bombing in Nairobi: naturalistic study. *British Journal of Psychiatry*, 185: 328–33.

Noble, Jason (1999) Cooperation, conflict and the evolution of communication. *Adaptive Behavior*, 7: 349–70.

Nonami, Hiroshi (1996) The self-sacrificing minority and saving victims of environmental problems as a social conflict situation. *Psychologia: An International Journal of Psychology in the Orient*, 39: 33–41.

Nordstrom, Carolyn (1997) The eye of the storm: from war to peace – examples from Sri Lanka and Mozambique. In D. P. Fry and K. Bjoerkqvist (eds.), *Cultural variation in conflict resolution: alternatives to violence* (pp. 91–103). Mahwah, NJ: Lawrence Erlbaum Associates, Inc.

(1998) Deadly myths of aggression. *Aggressive Behavior*, 24: 147–59.

Norsworthy, Kathryn L. (2003) Understanding violence against women in Southeast Asia: a group approach in social justice work. *International Journal for the Advancement of Counselling*, 25: 145–56.

Norsworthy, Kathryn L. and Khuankaew, Ouyporn (2004) Women of Burma speak out: workshops to deconstruct gender-based violence and build systems of peace and justice. *Journal for Specialists in Group Work*, 29: 259–83.

North, C. S. and Pfefferbaum, B. (2002) Research on the mental health effects of terrorism. *Journal of the American Medical Association*, 288: 633–6.

O'Connor, Kathleen M. (1997) Motives and cognitions in negotiation: a theoretical integration and an empirical test. *International Journal of Conflict Management*, 8: 114–31.

Oegema, Dirk and Klandermans, Bert (1994) Why social movement sympathizers don't participate: erosion and nonconversion of support. *American Sociological Review*, 59: 703–22.

Offerman-Zuckerberg, J. (1991) *Politics and psychology: contemporary psychodynamic perspectives*. New York: Plenum.

Ognjenovic, Vesna, Skorc, Bojana and Savic, Jovan (2003) Social sources of life: rehabilitation in the former Yugoslavia. In T. M. McIntyre and S. Krippner (eds.), *The psychological impact of war trauma on civilians: an international perspective* (pp. 171–8). Westport, CT: Praeger Publishers/Greenwood Publishing Group.

Ohbuchi, Ken-ichi and Suzuki, Mariko (2003) Three dimensions of conflict issues and their effects on resolution strategies in organizational settings. *International Journal of Conflict Management*, 14: 61–73.

Ohta, Yasuyuki, Mine, Mariko, Wakasugi, Masako, Yoshimine, Etsuko, Himuro, Yachiyo, Yoneda, Megumi, Yamaguchi, Sayuri, Mikita, Akemi and Morikawa, Tomoko (2000) Psychological effect of the Nagasaki atomic bombing on survivors after half a century. *Psychiatry and Clinical Neurosciences*, 54: 97–103.

Okasha, Ahmed (2003) Psychological impediments to the peace process in the Middle East. *Arab Journal of Psychiatry*, 14: 75–81.

Olekalns, Mara, Brett, Jeanne M. and Weingart, Laurie R. (2003) Phases, transitions and interruptions: modeling processes in multi-party negotiations. *International Journal of Conflict Management*, 14: 191–211.

Olekalns, Mara and Smith, Philip L. (2003) Social motives in negotiation: the relationships between dyad composition, negotiation processes and outcomes. *International Journal of Conflict Management*, 14: 233–54.

Oliner, Pearl M. and Oliner, Samuel P. (1995) *Toward a caring society: ideas into action*. Westport, CT: Praeger Publishers/Greenwood Publishing Group.

Oliner, Pearl M., Oliner, Samuel P., Baron, Lawrence, Blum, Lawrence A., Krebs, Dennis L. and Smolenska, M. Zuzanna (eds.) (1992) *Embracing the other: philosophical, psychological, and historical perspectives on altruism*. New York: New York University Press.

Oliner, Samuel P. (1991a) Altruism: antidote to human conflict. *Humboldt Journal of Social Relations*, 16(2): 1–37.

(1991b) Altruism: antidote to war and human antagonism. In J. Offerman-Zuckerberg (ed.) *Politics and psychology: contemporary psychodynamic perspectives* (pp. 277–301). New York: Plenum Press.

Olonisakin, 'Funmi (2003) African peacekeeping and the impact on African military personnel. In T. W. Britt and A. B. Adler (eds.), *The psychology of the peacekeeper: lessons from the field* (pp. 299–309). Westport, CT: Praeger Publishers/Greenwood Publishing Group.

Olson, Marie and Pearson, Frederic S. (2002) Civil war characteristics, mediators, and resolution. *Conflict Resolution Quarterly*, 19: 421–45.

Olszanska, Justyna, Olszanski, Robert and Wozniak, Jacek (1993) Do peaceful conflict management methods pose problems in post-totalitarian Poland? *Mediation Quarterly*, 10: 291–302.

Olweean, Steve S. (2003) When society is the victim: catastrophic trauma recovery. In T. M. McIntyre and S. Krippner (eds.), *The psychological impact of war trauma on civilians: an international perspective* (pp. 271–6). Westport, CT: Praeger Publishers/Greenwood Publishing Group.

Opotow, Susan (2003) Forging social identity and social conflict. *Peace and Conflict: Journal of Peace Psychology*, 9: 177–9.

Oppenheimer, Louis (1995) Peace, but what about social constraints? *Peace and Conflict: Journal of Peace Psychology*, 1: 383–97.

(1996) War as an institution, but what about peace? Developmental perspectives. *International Journal of Behavioral Development*, 19: 201–18.

Oppenheimer, Louis and Kuipers, Ilona (2003) Filipino children's understanding of peace, war, and strategies to attain peace. *Peace and Conflict: Journal of Peace Psychology*, 9: 235–57.

Orme-Johnson, David W., Alexander, Charles N. and Davies, John L. (1990) The effects of the Maharishi technology of the unified field: reply to a methodological critique. *Journal of Conflict Resolution*, 34: 756–68.

Orme-Johnson, David W., Dillbeck, Michael C. and Alexander, Charles N. (2003) Preventing terrorism and international conflict: effects of large assemblies of participants in the Transcendental Meditation and TM-Sidhi programs. *Journal of Offender Rehabilitation*, 36: 283–302.

Orr, Emda, Sagy, Shifra and Bar-On, Dan (2003) Social representations in use: Israeli-Jewish and Palestinian high school students' collective coping and defense. *Megamot*, 42: 412–36.

Osgood, Charles E. (1962) *An alternative to war or surrender.* Urbana, IL: University of Illinois Press.

Oskamp, Stuart (1991) *Attitudes and opinions* (2nd edn.). Englewood Cliffs, NJ: Prentice-Hall.

(2000a) Psychological contributions to achieving an ecologically sustainable future for humanity. *Journal of Social Issues*, 56: 373–90.

(2000b) A sustainable future for humanity? How can psychology help? *American Psychologist*, 55: 496–508.

Oskamp, Stuart, Bordin, Jeffrey and Edwards, Todd C. (1992) Background experiences and attitudes of peace activists. *Journal of Psychology*, 126: 49–61.

Ostrove, Joan M. (1999) A continuing commitment to social change: portraits of activism throughout adulthood. In M. Romero and A. J. Stewart (eds.), *Women's untold stories: breaking silence, talking back, voicing complexity* (pp. 212–26). Florence, KY: Taylor & Francis/Routledge.

Ottosen, Rune (1994) The media and the Gulf War reporting: advertising for the arms industry? In H. H. Blumberg and C. C. French (eds.), *Persian Gulf War: views from the social and behavioral sciences* (pp. 329–48). Lanham, MD: University Press of America.

Oyama, Susan (1997) Essentialism, women and war: protesting too much, protesting too little. In M. M. Gergen and S. N. Davis (eds.), *Toward a new psychology of gender* (pp. 521–32). New York: Routledge.

Padayachee, Anshu and Singh, Swaroop Rani (1998) Violence against women: a long history for South African Indian women, with special reference to Hinduism and Hindu law. *Social Science International*, 14(1–2): 1–10.

Pagani, Fabrizio (1998) The peace process at its culmination: the reconciliation elections. In H. J. Langholtz (ed.), *The psychology of peacekeeping* (pp. 223–38). Westport, CT: Praeger Publishers/Greenwood Publishing Group, Inc.

Pahre, Robert (1994) Multilateral cooperation in an iterated prisoner's dilemma. *Journal of Conflict Resolution*, 38: 326–52.

(1997) Endogenous domestic institutions in two-level games and parliamentary oversight of the European Union. *Journal of Conflict Resolution*, 41: 147–74.

Palmer, Glenn and David, J. Sky (1999) Multiple goals or deterrence: a test of two models in nuclear and non-nuclear alliances. *Journal of Conflict Resolution*, 43: 748–70.

Palmer, Ian (2003) Soldiers: a suitable case for treatment? *British Journal of Guidance and Counselling*, 31: 359–73.

Pandiani, J. A. and Banks, S. M. (2002) Terrorism and people with mental illness. *Psychiatric Services*, 53: 1475.

Papayoanou, Paul A. (1997) Intra-alliance bargaining and US Bosnia policy. *Journal of Conflict Resolution*, 41: 91–116.

Pappas, James D. (2003) Poisoned dissociative containers: dissociative defenses in female victims of war rape. In T. M. McIntyre and S. Krippner (eds.), *The psychological impact of war trauma on civilians: an international perspective* (pp. 277–83). Westport, CT: Praeger Publishers/Greenwood Publishing Group.

Parlee, M. B. (1991) Women, peace and the reproduction of gender. In A. E. Hunter (ed.), *Genes and gender VI: on peace, war and gender, a challenge to genetic explanations* (pp. 104–20). New York: The Feminist Press.

Pastor, Larry H. (2004) Countering the psychological consequences of suicide terrorism. *Psychiatric Annals*, 34: 701–7.

Patchen, Martin (1993) Reciprocity of coercion and cooperation between individuals and nations. In R. B. Felson and J. T. Tedeschi (eds.), *Aggression and violence: social interactionist perspectives* (pp. 119–44). Washington, DC: American Psychological Association.

Patchen, Martin and Bogumil, David D. (1997) Comparative reciprocity during the Cold War. *Peace and Conflict: Journal of Peace Psychology*, 3: 37–58.

Patrikis, Peter C. (2003) Language and minority rights: ethnicity, nationalism and the politics of language. *Modern Language Journal*, 87: 149–50.

Pauwels, Noel, van de Walle, Bartel, Hardeman, Frank and Soudan, Karel (2000) The implications of irreversibility in emergency response decisions. *Theory and Decision*, 49: 25–51.

Pearn, J. (2003) Children and war. *Journal of Paediatrics and Child Health*, 39: 166–72.

Pearson, Landon (1990) *Children of glasnost: growing up Soviet*. Seattle, WA: University of Washington Press.

Pearson, Virginia M. S. and Stephan, Walter G. (1998) Preferences for styles of negotiation: a comparison of Brazil and the US. *International Journal of Intercultural Relations*, 22: 67–83.

Pecjak, Vid (1993) Verbal associations with socio-political concepts in three historical periods. *Studia Psychologica*, 35: 284–7.

Peck, Connie (1990) Conflict management and the prevention of war. *Australian Psychologist*, 25: 3–14.

Pedahzur, A., Perliger, A. and Weinberg, L. (2003) Altruism and fatalism: the characteristics of Palestinian suicide terrorists. *Deviant Behaviour*, 24: 405–23.

Pedersen, Paul (1993) Mediating multicultural conflict by separating behaviors from expectations in a cultural grid. *International Journal of Intercultural Relations*, 17: 343–53.

(1994) 'Mediating multicultural conflict by separating behaviors from expectations in a cultural grid': erratum. *International Journal of Intercultural Relations*, 18: 157–8.

Pedersen, Paul B. (2001) The cultural context of peacekeeping. In D. J. Christie, R. V. Wagner and D. D. Winter (eds.), *Peace, conflict, and violence: peace psychology for the 21st century* (pp. 183–92). Upper Saddle River, NJ: Prentice Hall.

Peffley, Mark and Hurwitz, Jon (1993) Models of attitude constraint in foreign affairs. *Political Behavior*, 15: 61–90.

Peirce, Robert S., Pruitt, Dean G. and Czaja, Sally J. (1993) Complainant–respondent differences in procedural choice. *International Journal of Conflict Management*, 4: 199–222.

Pelled, Lisa Hope (1996) Relational demography and perceptions of group conflict and performance: a field investigation. *International Journal of Conflict Management*, 7: 230–46.

Penn, Michael L. and Kiesel, Lori (1994) Toward a global world community: the role of black psychologists. *Journal of Black Psychology*, 20: 398–417.

Perl, S. (1997) *Terrorism, the media and the government: perspectives, trends and options for policymakers*. CRS Issue Brief, 22 October. From www.fas.org/irp/crs/crs-terror.htm

Peters, William [Director] (1985) *A class divided*. New Haven, CT: Yale University Films. [Videocassette.]

Peterson, Bill E., Winter, David G. and Doty, Richard M. (1994) Laboratory tests of a motivational-perceptual model of conflict escalation. *Journal of Conflict Resolution*, 38: 719–48.

Peterson, Candida C., Lawrence, Jeanette A. and Dawes, Irene (1990) The relationship of gender, sex role, and law-and-order attitudes to nuclear opinions. *Sex Roles*, 22: 283–92.

Pettigrew, Thomas F. (2004) Intergroup relations and national and international relations. In M. Hewstone and M. B. Brewer (eds.), *Applied Social Psychology* (pp. 225–42). Malden, MA: Blackwell Publishers.

Pevehouse, Jon C. (2004) Interdependence theory and the measurement of international conflict. *Journal of Politics*, 66: 247–66.

Pfefferbaum, B. (2003) Victims of terrorism and the media. In A. Silke (ed.), *Terrorists, victims and society: psychological perspectives on terrorism and its consequences* (pp. 175–87). Chichester: Wiley.

Pfefferbaum, B., Gurwitch, R. H., McDonald, N. B., Leftwich, M. J. T., Sconzo, G. M., Messenbaugh, A. K. and Schultz, R. A. (2000) Post-traumatic stress among young children after the death of a friend or acquaintance in a terrorist bombing. *Psychiatric Services*, 51: 386–8.

Pfefferbaum, B., Nixon, S. J., Krug, R. S., Tivis, R. D., Moore, V. L., Brown, J. M., Pynoos, R. S., Foy, D. and Gurwitch, R. H. (1999) Clinical needs assessment of middle and high school students following the 1995 Oklahoma City bombing. *American Journal of Psychiatry*, 156: 1069–74.

Pfefferbaum, B., Nixon, S. J., Tivis, R. D., Doughty, D. E., Pynoos, R. S., Foy, D. W. and Gurwitch, R. H. (2001) Television exposure in children after a terrorist incident. *Psychiatry*, 64: 202–11.

Phatak, Arvind V. and Habib, Mohammed M. (1999) The dynamics of international business negotiations. In R. J. Lewicki, D. M. Saunders and J. W. Minton (eds.), *Negotiation: readings, exercises, and cases* (3rd edn., pp. 373–85). Boston, MA: Irwin/McGraw-Hill.

Phillips, Deborah, Prince, Shantay and Schiebelhut, Laura (2004) Elementary school children's responses 3 months after the September 11 terrorist attacks: a study in Washington, DC. *American Journal of Orthopsychiatry*, 74: 509–28.

Pick, Thomas M. (1997) Eastern European militant nationalism: some causes and measures to counteract it. *Peace and Conflict: Journal of Peace Psychology*, 3: 383–93.

(2001) Commentary on 'History and identity in Northern Ireland'. *Peace and Conflict: Journal of Peace Psychology*, 7: 317–20.

Pierce, John C., Lovrich, Nicholas P. and Dalton, Russell J. (2000) Contextual influences on environmental knowledge: public familiarity with technical terms in nuclear weapons production in Russia and the United States. *Environment and Behavior*, 32: 188–208.

Pilisuk, Marc (1998) The hidden structure of contemporary violence. *Peace and Conflict: Journal of Peace Psychology*, 4: 197–216.

(2000) Selective civility, apolitical politics, limited democracy, and mainstream psychology. *Peace and Conflict: Journal of Peace Psychology*, 6: 345–50.

Pilisuk, Marc and Zazzi, Joanne (2006) Toward a psychosocial theory of military and economic violence in the era of globalization. *Journal of Social Issues*, 62: 41–62.

Pilisuk, Marc, Zazzi, Joanne and Larin, Lauren (2003) Understanding global violence and promoting world peace: networks and beliefs beyond disciplines. *Constructivism in the Human Sciences*, 8(1): 129–57.

Pinel, Elizabeth C. and Swann, William B. Jr. (2000) Finding the self through others: self-verification and social movement participation. In S. Stryker, T. J. Owens and R. W. White (eds.), *Self, identity, and social movements* (pp. 132–52). Minneapolis, MN: University of Minnesota Press.

Pines, Ayala M. (1994) The Palestinian intifada and Israelis' burnout. *Journal of Cross-Cultural Psychology*, 25: 438–51.

Pinkley, Robin L. (1992) Dimensions of conflict frame: relation to disputant perceptions and expectations. *International Journal of Conflict Management*, 3: 95–113.

Pitta, Dennis A., Fung, Hung Gay and Isberg, Steven (1999) Ethical issues across cultures: managing the differing perspectives of China and the USA. *Journal of Consumer Marketing*, 16: 240–56.

Piven, Jerry S. (2004) The psychosis (religion) of Islamic terrorists and the ecstasy of violence. *Journal of Psychohistory*, 32: 151–201.

Plante, Thomas G. and Canchola, Erika L. (2004) The association between strength of religious faith and coping with American terrorism regarding the events of September 11, 2001. *Pastoral Psychology*, 52: 269–78.

Polkinghorn, Brian and Byrne, Sean (2001) Between war and peace: an examination of conflict management styles in four conflict zones. *International Journal of Conflict Management*, 12: 23–46.

Pomerantz, J. (2001) Analysing the terrorist mind. *Drug Benefit Trends*, 113: 2–3.

Porter, Thomas W. and Lilly, Bryan S. (1996) The effects of conflict, trust, and task commitment on project team performance. *International Journal of Conflict Management*, 7: 361–76.

Post, J. M. (1987) The group dynamics of political terrorism. *Terrorism*, 10: 23–35.

(1990) Terrorist psycho-logic. In W. Reich (ed.), *Origins of terrorism: psychologies, ideologies, theologies, states of mind*. Cambridge: Cambridge University Press.

Post, Jerrold M. (1999) The psychopolitics of hatred: commentary on Ervin Staub's article. *Peace and Conflict: Journal of Peace Psychology*, 5: 337–44.

Post, J. M. (2000) Terrorist on trial: the context of political crime. *Journal of the American Academy of Psychiatry and the Law*, 28: 171–8.

Post, Stephen G., Underwood, Lynn G., Schloss, Jeffrey P. and Hurlbut, William B. (eds.) (2002) *Altruism and altruistic love: science, philosophy, & religion in dialogue*. Oxford: Oxford University Press.

Powell, Dayle E. (1991) Legal perspective. In V. A. Kremenyuk (ed.), *International negotiation: analysis, approaches, issues* (pp. 135–47). San Francisco: Jossey-Bass Inc., Publishers.

Powell, Larry and Self, William R. (2004) Personalized fear, personalized control, and reactions to the September 11 attacks. *North American Journal of Psychology*, 6: 55–70.

Pozgain, Ivan, Mandic, Nikola and Barkic, Jelena (1998) Homicides in war and peace in Croatia. *Journal of Forensic Sciences*, 43: 1124–6.

Prieto, Jose M. and Arias, Rosario Martinez (1997) Those things yonder are no giants, but decision makers in international teams. In P. C. Earley and M. Erez (eds.), *New perspectives on international industrial/organizational psychology* (pp. 410–45). San Francisco: The New Lexington Press/Jossey-Bass Inc., Publishers.

Princen, Thomas (1992) Mediation by a transnational organization: the case of the Vatican. In J. Bercovitch and J. Z. Rubin (eds.), *Mediation in international relations: multiple approaches to conflict management* (pp. 149–75). New York: St. Martin's Press, Inc.

(1997) Toward a theory of restraint. *Population and Environment: A Journal of Interdisciplinary Studies*, 18: 233–54.

Pruitt, Dean G. (1998) Social conflict. In Daniel T. Gilbert, Susan T. Fiske and G. Lindzey (eds.), *The handbook of social psychology* (4th edn., Vol. 2, pp. 470–503). Boston: McGraw-Hill.

Pruitt, Dean G. and Olczak, Paul V. (1995) Beyond hope: approaches to resolving seemingly intractable conflict. In B. B. Bunker and J. Z. Rubin (eds.), *Conflict, cooperation, and justice: essays inspired by the work of Morton Deutsch* (pp. 59–92). San Francisco: Jossey-Bass Inc, Publishers.

Pruitt, Dean G., Parker, John C. and Mikolic, Joseph M. (1997) Escalation as a reaction to persistent annoyance. *International Journal of Conflict Management*, 8: 252–70.

Pruitt, Dean G., Peirce, R. S., Zubek, J. M., McGillicuddy, N. B. and Welton, G. L. (1993) Determinants of short-term and long-term success in mediation. In S. Worchel and J. A. Simpson (eds.), *Conflict between people and groups: causes, processes, and resolutions* (pp. 60–75). Chicago: Nelson-Hall.

Punamaki, R. L. and Suleiman, R. (1990) Predictors and effectiveness of coping with political violence among Palestinian children. *British Journal of Social Psychology*, 29: 67–77.

Purdy, Jill M. and Gray, Barbara (1994) Case study: government agencies as mediators in public policy conflicts. *International Journal of Conflict Management*, 5: 158–80.

Putnam, Linda L. (2004) Transformations and critical moments in negotiations. *Negotiation Journal*, 20: 275–95.

Pynoos, R. S., Steinberg, A. M. and Goenjian, A. (1996) Traumatic stress in childhood and adolescence: recent trends and current controversies. In B. A. van der Kolk, A. C. McFarlane and L. Wiesaeth (eds.), *Traumatic stress: the effects of overwhelming experience on mind, body, and society* (pp. 331–58). New York: Guilford Press.

Pyszczynski, Tom, Solomon, Sheldon and Greenberg, Jeff (2003) *In the wake of 9/11: the psychology of terror.* Washington, DC: American Psychological Association.

Qin, J., Mitchell, K. J., Johnson, M. K., Krystal, J. H., Southwick, S. M., Rasmusson, A. M. and Allen, E. S. (2003) Reactions to and memories for the September 11, 2001 terrorist attacks in adults with post-traumatic stress disorder. *Applied Cognitive Psychology*, 17: 1081–97.

Qouta, S., Punamaki, R. L. and El-Sarraj, E. (2003) Prevalence and determinants of PTSD among Palestinian children exposed to military violence. *European Child and Adolescent Psychiatry*, 12: 265–72.

Qouta, Samir, Punamaki, Raija Leena and El-Sarraj, Eyad (1995) The impact of the peace treaty on psychological well-being: a follow-up study of Palestinian children. *Child Abuse and Neglect*, 19: 1197–208.

Quester, George H. (1990a) The psychological effects of bombing on civilian populations: unlimited and other future wars. In B. Glad (ed.), *Psychological dimensions of war* (pp. 310–15). Newbury Park, CA: Sage Publications, Inc.

(1990b) The psychological effects of bombing on civilian populations: wars of the past. In B. Glad (ed.), *Psychological dimensions of war* (pp. 201–14). Newbury Park, CA: Sage Publications, Inc.

Quintana, Stephen M. and Segura-Herrera, Theresa A. (2003) Developmental transformations of self and identity in the context of oppression. *Self and Identity*, 2: 269–85.

Qureshi, Sajda (1998) Supporting a network way of working in an electronic social space. *Group Decision and Negotiation*, 7: 399–416.

Rabow, Jerome, Hernandez, Anthony C. and Newcomb, Michael D. (1990) Nuclear fears and concerns among college students: a cross-national study of attitudes. *Political Psychology*, 11: 681–98.

Racy, J. (1970) Psychiatry in the Arab east. *Acta Psychiatrica Scandinavica*, 211: 1–171.

Radford, K. Jim, Hipel, Keith W. and Fang, Liping (1994) Decision making under conditions of conflict. *Group Decision and Negotiation*, 3: 169–85.

Rahim, M. Afzalur (ed.) (1990) *Theory and research in conflict management.* New York: Praeger Publishers.

Raiffa, Howard (1991) Contributions of applied systems analysis to international negotiation. In V. A. Kremenyuk (ed.), *International negotiation: analysis, approaches, issues* (pp. 5–21). San Francisco: Jossey-Bass Inc, Publishers.

Rakos, Richard F. (1991) Perestroika, glasnost, and international cooperation: a behavior analysis. *Behavior and Social Issues*, 1: 91–100.

Ramirez, J. Martin and Richardson, Deborah S. (eds.) (2001) *Cross-cultural approaches to research on aggression and reconciliation.* Huntington, NY: Nova Science Publishers.

Rangell, Leo (1991) The psychoanalyst in international relations: an exercise in applied analysis. *International Review of Psycho-Analysis*, 18: 87–96.

Rao, Mukunda (1990) International social welfare: global perspectives. In L. Ginsberg, S. Khinduka, J. A. Hall, F. Ross-Sheriff and A. Hartman (eds.), *Encyclopedia of social work: 1990 supplement* (pp. 189–202). Silver Spring, MD: National Association of Social Workers.

Rapoport, Anatol (1989) *The origins of violence: approaches to the study of conflict.* New Brunswick, NJ: Transaction Publishers.

Raundalen, Magne and Melton, Gary B. (1994) Children in war and its aftermath: mental health issues in the development of international law. *Behavioral Sciences and the Law,* 12: 21–34.

Raven, B. H. and Rubin, J. Z. (1983) *Social psychology* (2nd edn.). New York: Wiley.

Raviv, Amiram, Bar-Tal, Daniel, Koren Silvershatz, Leah and Raviv, Alona (1999) Beliefs about war, conflict, and peace in Israel as a function of developmental, cultural, and situational factors. In A. Raviv, L. Oppenheimer and D. Bar-Tal (eds.), *How children understand war and peace: a call for international peace education* (pp. 161–89). San Francisco, CA: Jossey-Bass/Pfeiffer.

Raviv, Amiram, Oppenheimer, Louis and Bar-Tal, Daniel (eds.) (1999) *How children understand war and peace: a call for international peace education.* San Francisco, CA: Jossey-Bass/Pfeiffer.

Raviv, Amiram, Sadeh, Avi, Raviv, Alona and Silberstein, Ora (1998) The reaction of the youth in Israel to the assassination of Prime Minister Yitzhak Rabin. *Political Psychology,* 19: 255–78.

Ravlo, Hilde, Gleditsch, Nils Petter and Dorussen, Han (2003) Colonial war and the democratic peace. *Journal of Conflict Resolution,* 47: 520–48.

Reagan, Patricia and Rohrbaugh, John (1990) Group decision process effectiveness: a competing values approach. *Group and Organization Studies,* 15: 20–43 [PsycINFO accession number AN 1990-14618-001].

Reardon, B. (1993) *Women and peace: feminist visions of global security.* Albany, NY: State University of New York Press.

Redfearn, J. W. T. (1990) Dreams of nuclear warfare: does avoiding the intrapsychic clash of opposites contribute to the concrete danger of world destruction? In N. Schwartz-Salant and M. Stein (eds.), *Dreams in analysis* (pp. 181–98). Wilmette, IL: Chiron Publications.

Reed, Richard, Lemak, David J. and Hesser, W. Andrew (1997) Cleaning up after the Cold War: management and social issues. *Academy of Management Review,* 22: 614–42.

Reich, K. Helmut and Paloutzian, Raymond F. (2002) Editor's note. *International Journal for the Psychology of Religion,* 12: 213–15.

Reich, W. (1990) *Origins of terrorism: psychologies, ideologies, theologies, states of mind.* Cambridge: Cambridge University Press.

Reich, Wilhelm (1972) *Character analysis.* New York: Farrar, Straus and Giroux.

Reid, W. H. (2003) Terrorism and forensic psychiatry. *Journal of the American Academy of Psychiatry and the Law,* 31: 285–8.

Reilly, Isobel, McDermott, Matt and Coulter, Stephen (2004) Living in the shadow of community violence in Northern Ireland: a therapeutic response. In N. B. Webb (ed.), *Mass trauma and violence: helping families and children cope* (pp. 304–26). New York: Guilford Press.

Reissman, Dori B., Klomp, Richard W., Kent, Adrian T. and Pfefferbaum, Betty (2004) Exploring psychological resilience in the face of terrorism. *Psychiatric Annals*, 34: 627–32.

Reiter, Dan (1999) Military strategy and the outbreak of international conflict: quantitative empirical tests, 1903–1992. *Journal of Conflict Resolution*, 43: 366–87.

Reiter, Dan and Tillman, Erik R. (2002) Public, legislative, and executive constraints on the democratic initiation of conflict. *Journal of Politics*, 64: 810–26.

Rempel, Martin W. and Fisher, Ronald J. (1997) Perceived threat, cohesion, and group problem solving in intergroup conflict. *International Journal of Conflict Management*, 8: 216–34.

Reuveny, Rafael and Maxwell, John W. (2001) Conflict and renewable resources. *Journal of Conflict Resolution*, 45: 719–42.

Ribas, Denys (1993) Ou projeter le haie, dans un monde federe par l'Eros? [Where can hatred be projected in a world governed by Eros?] *Revue Française de Psychanalyse*, 57: 1207–11.

Richman, Alvin (1991) Changing American attitudes towards the Soviet Union. *Public Opinion Quarterly*, 55: 135–48.

Richmond, Oliver P. (2003) Realizing hegemony? Symbolic terrorism and the roots of conflict. *Studies in Conflict and Terrorism*, 26: 289–309.

Richmond, Oliver (2004) Debating peace: new or old? *Peace and Conflict: Journal of Peace Psychology*, 10: 185–8.

Richter, H. E. (1996) Psychoanalysis and politics. *International Forum of Psychoanalysis*, 5: 295–300.

Ripley, Brian (1993) Psychology, foreign policy, and international relations theory. *Political Psychology*, 14: 403–16.

Ritov, Ilana and Drory, Amos (1996) Ambiguity and conflict management strategy. *International Journal of Conflict Management*, 7: 139–55.

Roach, Colleen (ed.) (1993a) *Communication and culture in war and peace.* Newbury Park, CA: Sage Publications.

(1993b) Information and culture in war and peace: overview. In C. Roach (ed.), *Communication and culture in war and peace* (pp. 1–40). Newbury Park, CA: Sage Publications, Inc.

Roberts, B. (1984) The death of machothink: feminist research and the transformation of peace studies. *Women's Studies International Forum*, 1: 195–200.

Robinson, Robert J. (1998) Power to the people: the use of 'forums' in conflict resolution in post-apartheid South Africa. *International Journal of Conflict Management*, 9: 51–71.

Roe, Micheal D., McKay, Susan A. and Wessells, Michael G. (2003) Pioneers in peace psychology: Milton Schwebel. *Peace and Conflict: Journal of Peace Psychology*, 9: 305–26.

Rofe, Yacov and Lewin, Isaac (1982) The effect of war environment on dreams and sleep habits. *Series in Clinical and Community Psychology: Stress and Anxiety*, 8: 67–79.

Rogers, James R. and Soyka, Karen M. (2004) Grace and compassion at 'Ground Zero', New York City. *Crisis*, 25: 27–9.

Rogers, John D., Spencer, Jonathan and Uyangoda, Jayadeva (1998) Sri Lanka: political violence and ethnic conflict. *American Psychologist*, 53: 771–7.

Rogers, Rita R. (1991) Common security: the only way. In J. Offerman-Zuckerberg (ed.), *Politics and psychology: contemporary psychodynamic perspectives* (pp. 231–7). New York: Plenum Press.

Rohrer, Tim (1991) To plow the sea: metaphors for regional peace in Latin America. *Metaphor and Symbolic Activity*, 6: 163–81.

Ronan, Kevin R. and Johnston, David M. (2001) Correlates of hazard education programs for youth. *Risk Analysis*, 21: 1055–63.

Ronen, T., Rahav, G. and Appel, N. (2003) Adolescent stress responses to a single acute stress and to continuous external stress: terrorist attacks. *Journal of Loss and Trauma*, 8: 261–82.

Ronen, T., Rahav, G. and Rosenbaum, M. (2003) Children's reactions to a war situation as a function of age and sex. *Anxiety, Stress and Coping*, 16: 59–69.

Rose, Fred (2000) *Coalitions across the class divide: lessons from the labor, peace, and environmental movements*. Ithaca, NY: Cornell University Press.

Rose, S. and Tehrani, N. (2002) *History, methods and development of psychological debriefing*. Leicester: British Psychological Society.

Rosenbaum, Michael and Ronen, Tammie (1997) Parents' and children's appraisals of each other's anxiety while facing a common threat. *Journal of Clinical Child Psychology*, 26: 43–52.

Ross, Jeffrey Ian (1996) A model of the psychological causes of oppositional political terrorism. *Peace and Conflict: Journal of Peace Psychology*, 2: 129–41.

Ross, Marc Howard (2000) 'Good enough' isn't so bad: thinking about success and failure in ethnic conflict management. *Peace and Conflict: Journal of Peace Psychology*, 6: 27–47.

Ross, William and LaCroix, Jessica (1996) Multiple meanings of trust in negotiation theory and research: a literature review and integrative model. *International Journal of Conflict Management*, 7: 314–60.

Rossin, A. David (2003) Marketing fear: nuclear issues in public policy. *American Behavioral Scientist*, 46: 812–21.

Roth, Kendall (1995) Managing international interdependence: CEO characteristics in a resource-based framework. *Academy of Management Journal*, 38: 200–31.

Rothbart, Myron (1993) Intergroup perception and social conflict. In S. Worchel and J. A. Simpson (eds.), *Conflict between people and groups: causes, processes, and resolutions* (pp. 93–109). Chicago: Nelson-Hall, Inc.

Rouhana, Nadim N. (1995) Unofficial third-party intervention in international conflict: between legitimacy and disarray. *Negotiation Journal*, 11: 255–70.

(2004) Group identity and power asymmetry in reconciliation processes: the Israeli–Palestinian case. *Peace and Conflict: Journal of Peace Psychology*, 10: 33–52.

Rouhana, Nadim N. and Kelman, Herbert C. (1994) Promoting joint thinking in international conflicts: an Israeli–Palestinian continuing workshop. *Journal of Social Issues*, 50(1): 157–78.

Rouhana, Nadim N. and Korper, Susan H. (1997) Power asymmetry and goals of unofficial third party intervention in protracted intergroup conflict. *Peace and Conflict: Journal of Peace Psychology*, 3: 1–17.

Rousseau, David L. (2002) Motivations for choice: the salience of relative gains in international politics. *Journal of Conflict Resolution*, 46: 394–426.

Rowland-Klein, Dani and Dunlop, Rosemary (1998) The transmission of trauma across generations: identification with parental trauma in children of Holocaust survivors. *Australian and New Zealand Journal of Psychiatry*, 32: 358–69.

Roy, Paul J. (2002) September 11, 2001 and beyond . . . *Journal of Transpersonal Psychology*, 34: 23–5.

Rubin, Jeffrey Z. (1991) Psychological approach. In V. A. Kremenyuk (ed.), *International negotiation: analysis, approaches, issues* (pp. 216–28). San Francisco: Jossey-Bass Inc., Publishers.

(1992) Conflict, negotiation, and peace: psychological perspectives and roles. In S. Staub and P. Green (eds.), *Psychology and social responsibility: facing global challenges* (pp. 121–44). New York: New York University Press.

Rubin, Jeffrey Z. and Levinger, George (1995) Levels of analysis: in search of generalizable knowledge. In B. B. Bunker and J. Z. Rubin (eds.), *Conflict, cooperation, and justice: essays inspired by the work of Morton Deutsch* (pp. 13–38). San Francisco: Jossey-Bass Inc, Publishers.

Rubin, Jeffrey Z., Pruitt, Dean G. and Kim, Sung Hee (1994) *Social conflict: escalation, stalemate, and settlement* (2nd edn.). New York: McGraw-Hill Book Company.

Rubin, Jeffrey Z. and Zartman, I. William (1995) Asymmetrical negotiations: some survey results that may surprise. *Negotiation Journal*, 11: 349–64.

Rubonis, A. and Bickman, L. (1991) Psychological impairment in the wake of disaster: the disaster psychopathology relationship. *Psychological Bulletin*, 109: 384–99.

Ruck, Hendrick W. and Mitchell, Jimmy L. (1993) Perceived need for and roles of uniformed behavioral scientists in the United States Air Force. *Military Psychology*, 5: 219–33.

Rudmin, Floyd W. (1991) Seventeen early peace psychologists. *Journal of Humanistic Psychology*, 31(2): 12–43.

Runyan, William McKinley (1993) Psychohistory and political psychology: a comparative analysis. In S. Iyengar and W. J. McGuire (eds.), *Explorations in political psychology* (pp. 36–63). Durham, NC: Duke University Press.

Russell, Gordon W. and Mustonen, Anu (1998) Peacemakers: those who would intervene to quell a sports riot. *Personality and Individual Differences*, 24: 335–9.

Sacco, K., Galletto, V. and Blanzieri, E. (2003) How has the 9/11 terrorist attack influenced decision making? *Applied Cognitive Psychology*, 17: 1113–27.

Said, Abdul Aziz and Funk, Nathan C. (2002) The role of faith in cross-cultural conflict resolution. *Peace and Conflict Studies*, 9(1): 37–50.

Salacuse, Jeswald W. (1999) Intercultural negotiation in international business. *Group Decision and Negotiation*, 8: 217–36.

Salib, E. (2003a) Effect of 11 September 2001 on suicide and homicide in England and Wales. *British Journal of Psychiatry*, 183: 207–12.

(2003b) Suicide terrorism: a case of folie à plusieurs? *British Journal of Psychiatry*, 182: 339–57.

Salomon, Gavriel (2002) The nature of peace education: not all programs are created equal. In G. Salomon and B. Nevo (eds.), *Peace education: the concept, principles, and practices around the world* (pp. 3–13). Mahwah, NJ: Lawrence Erlbaum Associates.

Salomon, Gavriel and Nevo, Baruch (eds.) (2002) *Peace education: the concept, principles, and practices around the world*. Mahwah, NJ: Lawrence Erlbaum Associates, Publishers.

Salter, Charles A. (2001) Psychological effects of nuclear and radiological warfare. *Military Medicine*, 166(12, Suppl. 2): 17–18.

Sample, Susan G. (1998) Military buildups, war, and realpolitik: a multivariate model. *Journal of Conflict Resolution*, 42: 156–75.

Samuels, Andrew (1993) *The political psyche*. London: Routledge.

Sandler, Todd (1999) Alliance formation, alliance expansion, and the core. *Journal of Conflict Resolution*, 43: 727–47.

Sandole, Dennis J. D. (2003) Virulent ethnocentrism and conflict intractability: puzzles and challenges for 3rd party intervenors. *Peace and Conflict Studies*, 10(1): 72–86.

Sanson, Ann, Prior, Margot, Smart, Diana and Oberklaid, Frank (1993) Gender differences in aggression in childhood: implications for a peaceful world. *Australian Psychologist*, 28: 86–92.

Santmire, Tara E., Wilkenfeld, Jonathan, Kraus, Sarit, Holley, Kim M., Santmire, Toni E. and Gleditsch, Kristian S. (1998) The impact of cognitive diversity on crisis negotiations. *Political Psychology*, 19: 721–48.

Saunders, Harold (1998) Whole-body politics and the role of psychoanalysts in the peace process. *Journal for the Psychoanalysis of Culture and Society*, 3: 106–7.

Saunders, Harold H. (1995) Possibilities and challenges: another way to consider unofficial third-party intervention. *Negotiation Journal*, 11: 271–5.

(2002) Two challenges for the new century: transforming relationships in whole bodies politic. *Political Psychology*, 23: 151–64.

Sawada, Aiko, Chaitin, Julia and Bar-On, Dan (2004) Surviving Hiroshima and Nagasaki – experiences and psychosocial meanings. *Psychiatry: Interpersonal and Biological Processes*, 67: 43–60.

Schafer, Mark and Walker, Stephen G. (2001) Political leadership and the democratic peace: the operational code of Prime Minister Tony Blair. In O. Feldman and L. O. Valenty (eds.), *Profiling political leaders: cross-cultural studies of personality and behavior* (pp. 21–35). Westport, CT: Praeger Publishers/Greenwood Publishing Group.

Scharfenberg, Joachim (1990) Der Mythos des 20. Jahrhunderts als Hindernis der Friedensfaehigkeit. [Twentieth-century myth as obstacle to inner peace.] *Zeitschrift für Psychoanalytische Theorie und Praxis*, 5: 228–37.

Scharoun, Kourtney and Dziegielewski, Sophia F. (2004) Bioterrorism and the emergency room: planning for the unexpected. *Stress, Trauma, and Crisis: An International Journal*, 7: 135–50.

Schatz, Robert T. and Fiske, Susan T. (1992) International reactions to the threat of nuclear war: the rise and fall of concern in the eighties. *Political Psychology*, 13: 1–29.

Schbley, A. (2003) Defining religious terrorism: a causal and anthropological profile. *Studies in Conflict and Terrorism*, 26: 105–34.

Scheer, Joern W. (1996) 'Congress' language, personal constructs, and constructive internationalism. In B. M. Walker and J. Costigan (eds.), *Personal construct theory: a psychology for the future* (pp. 129–49). Carlton South, Vic, Australia: Australian Psychological Society Ltd.

Schei, Vidar and Rognes, Jorn K. (2003) Knowing me, knowing you: own orientation and information about the opponent's orientation in negotiation. *International Journal of Conflict Management*, 14: 43–59.

Schein, Leon A., Spitz, Henry I., Burlingame, Gary M. and Muskin, Philip R. (eds.) (2005) *Psychological effects of terrorist disasters: group approaches to treatment*. Binghamton, NY: Haworth Press.

Schelling, Thomas C. (2000) Intergenerational and international discounting. *Risk Analysis*, 20: 833–8.

Scheye, Eric (1991) Psychological notes on Central Europe 1989 and beyond. *Political Psychology*, 12: 331–44.

Schindler, Ruben, Spiegel, Chya and Malachi, Esther (1992) Silences: helping elderly Holocaust victims deal with the past. *International Journal of Aging and Human Development*, 35: 243–52.

Schmidt, Rainer (1993) Kausalitaet und freiheit: gedanken zur friedensfaehigkeit des menschen aus tiefenpsychologischer sicht. [Causality and freedom: thoughts about the peace capability of man from the depth psychological point of view.] *Zeitschrift für Individualpsychologie*, 18(1): 26–36.

Schmuck, Peter (2003) The future of industrial civilization: are there ways out of the global crisis? *Peace and Conflict: Journal of Peace Psychology*, 9: 181–3.

Schouten, Ronald, Callahan, Michael V. and Bryant, Shannon (2004) Community response to disaster: the role of the workplace. *Harvard Review of Psychiatry*, 12: 229–37.

Schrodt, Philip A. (1990) A methodological critique of a test of the effects of the Maharishi technology of the unified field. *Journal of Conflict Resolution*, 34: 745–55.

(1991) Prediction of interstate conflict outcomes using a neural network. *Social Science Computer Review*, 9: 359–80.

Schrodt, Philip A. and Gerner, Deborah J. (1997) Empirical indicators of crisis phase in the Middle East, 1979–1995. *Journal of Conflict Resolution*, 41: 529–52.

Schuster, M. A., Stein, B. D., Jaycox, L. H., Collins, R. L., Marshall, G. N., Elliot, M. N., Zhou, A. J., Kanouse, D. E., Morrison, J. L. and Berry, S. H. (2001) A national survey of stress reactions after September 11 2001, terrorist attacks. *New England Journal of Medicine*, 345: 1507–12.

Schwebel, M. (1965) *Behavioral science and human survival*. Palo Alto, CA: Science and Behavior Books.

Schwebel, Milton (1993) What moves the peace movement: psychosocial factors in historical perspective. In V. K. Kool (ed.), *Nonviolence: social and psychological issues* (pp. 59–77). Lanham, MD: University Press of America.

——— (1999) Looking forward/looking backward: prevention of violent conflict. *Peace and Conflict: Journal of Peace Psychology*, 5: 297–302.

——— (2003) *Remaking America's three school systems: now separate and unequal.* Lanham, MD: Scarecrow Press.

Sciancalepore, Roseann and Motta, Robert W. (2004) Gender related correlates of post-traumatic stress symptoms in a World Trade Center tragedy sample. *International Journal of Emergency Mental Health*, 6: 15–24.

Scollon, Ron and Scollon, Suzie Wong (1994) Face parameters in East–West discourse. In S. Ting-Toomey (ed.), *The challenge of facework: cross-cultural and interpersonal issues* (pp. 133–57). Albany, NY: State University of New York Press.

Sears, David O. and Funk, Carolyn L. (1991) Graduate education in political psychology. *Political Psychology*, 12: 345–62.

Sederberg, Peter C. (1990) Away from goodness: problems of control in nuclear war. In B. Glad (ed.), *Psychological dimensions of war* (pp. 316–27). Newbury Park, CA: Sage Publications, Inc.

Seedat, Mohamed (1999) The construction of violence in South African newspapers: implications for prevention. *Peace and Conflict: Journal of Peace Psychology*, 5: 117–35.

Segal, David R. (2001) Is a peacekeeping culture emerging among American infantry in the Sinai MFO? *Journal of Contemporary Ethnography*, 30: 607–36.

Seidman, Laurence S. (1990) Crisis stability. *Journal of Conflict Resolution*, 34: 130–50.

Seifert, R. (1993) *War and rape: analytic approaches.* Geneva, Switzerland: Women's International League for Peace and Freedom.

Selth, Andrew (2004) Burma's Muslims and the war on terror. *Studies in Conflict and Terrorism*, 27: 107–26.

Semel, A. K. and Minix, D. A. (1979) *Psychological models and international politics.* Boulder, CO: Westview Press.

Senese, Paul D. (1997) Costs and demands: international sources of dispute challenges and reciprocation. *Journal of Conflict Resolution*, 41: 407–27.

Seo, Fumiko and Nishizaki, Ichiro (1994) Conflict resolution with robustness in international negotiations: a game theoretic approach. *Group Decision and Negotiation*, 3: 47–68.

Seo, Fumiko and Sakawa, Masatoshi (1990) A game theoretic approach with risk assessment for international conflict solving. *IEEE Transactions on Systems, Man, and Cybernetics*, 20: 141–8.

Sergeev, Victor M. (1991) Metaphors for understanding international negotiation. In V. A. Kremenyuk (ed.), *International negotiation: analysis, approaches, issues* (pp. 58–64). San Francisco: Jossey-Bass Inc., Publishers.

Sergeev, V. M., Akimov, V. P., Lukov, V. B. and Parshin, P. B. (1990) Interdependence in a crisis situation: a cognitive approach to modeling the Caribbean crisis. *Journal of Conflict Resolution*, 34: 179–207.

Shadmi, E. (2000) Between resistance and compliance, feminism and nationalism: women in black in Israel. *Women's Studies International Forum*, 23: 23–34.

Shalev, A. Y. (2000) Stress management and debriefing: historical concepts and present patterns. In B. Raphael and J. P. Wilson (eds.), *Psychological debriefing: theory, practice and evidence* (pp. 17–31). Cambridge: Cambridge University Press.

Shalev, Arieh Y., Yehuda, Rachel and McFarlane, Alexander C. (eds.) (2000) *International handbook of human response to trauma*. New York: Kluwer Academic/Plenum Publishers.

Shamai, Michal (2001) Parents' perceptions of their children in a context of shared political uncertainty. *Child and Family Social Work*, 6: 249–60.

Shamir, Jacob and Shamir, Michal (1996) Competing values in Israeli public opinion. *Megamot*, 37: 371–94.

Shapiro, Ilana (1999) New approaches to old problems: lessons from an ethnic conciliation project in four central and eastern European countries. *Negotiation Journal*, 15: 149–67.

Shapiro, Svi (2002) Toward a critical pedagogy of peace education. In G. Salomon and B. Nevo (eds.), *Peace education: the concept, principles, and practices around the world* (pp. 63–71). Mahwah, NJ: Lawrence Erlbaum Associates.

Sharkey, J. (1997) The greysteel massacre: the local effect on the prevalence of admissions with overdose. *Irish Journal of Psychological Medicine*, 14: 55–6.

Shaw, J. A. (2003) Children exposed to war/terrorism. *Clinical Child and Family Psychology Review*, 6: 237–46.

Shea, Dorothy (2002) *The South African Truth Commission: the politics of reconciliation*: Book review. *International Journal of Conflict Management*, 13: 198–200.

Shenkar, Oded and Yan, Aimin (2002) Failure as a consequence of partner politics: learning from the life and death of an international cooperative venture. *Human Relations*, 55: 565–601.

Sherif, M. and Sherif, C. W. (1953) *Groups in harmony and tension*. New York: Harper.

Shigemura, Jun and Nomura, Soichiro (2002) Mental health issues of peacekeeping workers. *Psychiatry and Clinical Neurosciences*, 56: 483–91.

Shimko, Keith L. (1992) Reagan on the Soviet Union and the nature of international conflict. *Political Psychology*, 13: 353–77.

Shiraev, Eric (1999) The post-Soviet orientations towards the United States and the West. In B. Glad and E. Shiraev (eds.), *The Russian transformation: political, sociological, and psychological aspects* (pp. 227–35). New York: St. Martin's Press.

Shoham, Efrat (1994) Family characteristics of delinquent youth in time of war. *International Journal of Offender Therapy and Comparative Criminology*, 38: 247–58.

Shomer, R. W., Davis, A. H. and Kelley, H. H. (1966) Threats and the development of coordination: further studies of the Deutsch and Krauss trucking game. *Journal of Personality and Social Psychology*, 4: 119–26.

Shuman, Michael H. (1991) Leader control: peace through participation. In D. Leviton (ed.), *Horrendous death and health: towards action* (pp. 205–26). New York: Hemisphere Publishing Corp.

Sidman, M. (2003) Terrorism as behavior. *Behavior and Social Issues*, 12: 83–9.

Siemienska, Renata (1994) Some determinants of Polish attitudes towards other nations during a period of transition. In R. F. Farnen (ed.), *Nationalism, ethnicity, and identity: cross national and comparative perspectives* (pp. 327–43). New Brunswick, NJ: Transaction Publishers.

Signorino, Curtis S. (1996) Simulating international cooperation under uncertainty: the effects of symmetric and asymmetric noise. *Journal of Conflict Resolution*, 40: 152–205.

Silke, A. (1998) Cheshire cat logic: the recurring theme of terrorist abnormality in psychological research. *Psychology, Crime and Law*, 4: 51–69.

(2001a) Terrorism. *The Psychologist*, 14: 580–1.

(2001b, November) Understanding suicidal terrorism. Paper presented at the Conferencia Internacional Sobre Seguridad Nacional Y Amenaza Terrorista, La Paz, Bolivia.

(2003a) Beyond horror: terrorist atrocity and the search for understanding: the case of the Shankill bombing. *Studies in Conflict and Terrorism*, 26: 37–60.

(2003b) *Terrorists, victims and society: psychological perspectives on terrorism and its consequences*. Chichester: Wiley.

Silver, E. (2001, 3 December) Bomber quit intelligence service to join Hamas two days before attack. *The Independent*, p. 2.

Silver, Roxane Cohen (2004) Conducting research after the 9/11 terrorist attacks: challenges and results. *Families, Systems, and Health*, 22: 47–51.

Simmons, Dale D., Binney, Stephen E. and Dodd, Brian (1992) Valuing 'a clean environment': factor location, norms, and relation to risks. *Journal of Social Behavior and Personality*, 7: 649–58.

Singer, Eric and Hudson, Valerie (1992a) Conclusion: political psychology/ foreign policy, the cognitive revolution, and international relations. In E. Singer and V. Hudson (eds.), *Political psychology and foreign policy* (pp. 247–64). Boulder, CO: Westview Press.

(eds.) (1992b) *Political psychology and foreign policy*. Boulder, CO: Westview Press.

Sjoestedt, Gunnar (1991) Trade talks. In V. A. Kremenyuk (ed.), *International negotiation: analysis, approaches, issues* (pp. 315–30). San Francisco: Jossey-Bass Inc., Publishers.

Skitka, Linda J., McMurray, Pamela J. and Burroughs, Thomas E. (1991) Willingness to provide post-war aid to Iraq and Kuwait: an application of the contingency model of distributive justice. *Contemporary Social Psychology*, 15: 179–88.

Skjelsbaek, Inger (2003) The role of gender in South Asian conflict zones. *Peace and Conflict: Journal of Peace Psychology*, 9: 387–9.

Slim, Randa M. (1992) Small-state mediation in international relations: the Algerian mediation of the Iranian hostage crisis. In J. Bercovitch and J. Z. Rubin (eds.), *Mediation in international relations: multiple approaches to conflict management* (pp. 206–31). New York: St. Martin's Press, Inc.

Slone, M. (2000) Responses to media coverage of terrorism. *Journal of Conflict Resolution*, 44: 508–22.

Slovic, Paul (ed.) (2000) *The perception of risk*. London: Earthscan Publications Ltd.

Sluzki, Carlos E. (2002) Seeding violence in the minds of children. *American Journal of Orthopsychiatry*, 72: 3–4.

(2004) The invention of peace: reflection on war and international order. *American Journal of Orthopsychiatry*, 74: 89.

Smith, Alan (2003) Citizenship education in Northern Ireland: beyond national identity? *Cambridge Journal of Education*, 33: 15–31.

Smith, Alastair (1996) To intervene or not to intervene: a biased decision. *Journal of Conflict Resolution*, 40: 16–40.

Smith, Alison (2000) Lessons from western Kosovo for the documentation of war crimes. *Psychiatry, Psychology and Law*, 7: 235–40.

Smith, Claggett G. (ed.) (1971) *Conflict resolution: contributions of the behavioral sciences*. Notre Dame, IN, and London: University of Notre Dame Press.

Smith, M. Brewster (1991) Political psychology and world order. *Contemporary Social Psychology*, 15: 150–2.

(1992) Nationalism, ethnocentrism, and the new world order. *Journal of Humanistic Psychology*, 32(4): 76–91.

(1999) Political psychology and peace: a half-century perspective. *Peace and Conflict: Journal of Peace Psychology*, 5: 1–16.

Smith, M. Brewster and Mann, Leon (1992) Irving L. Janis (1918–1990): Obituary. *American Psychologist*, 47: 812–13.

Smith, Roger W. (1999) Toward understanding and preventing genocide. *Peace and Conflict: Journal of Peace Psychology*, 5: 345–8.

Soeters, Joseph L. (1996) Culture and conflict: an application of Hofstede's theory to the conflict in the former Yugoslavia. *Peace and Conflict: Journal of Peace Psychology*, 2: 233–44.

Soeters, Joseph and Bos-Bakx, Miepke (2003) Cross-cultural issues in peacekeeping operations. In T. W. Britt and A. B. Adler (eds.), *The psychology of the peacekeeper: lessons from the field* (pp. 283–98). Westport, CT: Praeger Publishers/Greenwood Publishing Group.

Solomon, Sheldon, Greenberg, Jeff and Pyszczynski, Tom (2003) Why war? Fear is the mother of violence. In S. Krippner and T. M. McIntyre (eds.), *The psychological impact of war trauma on civilians: an international perspective* (pp. 249–56). Westport, CT: Praeger/Greenwood.

Solomon, Zahava, Neria, Yuval and Witztum, Eliezer (2000) Debriefing with service personnel in war and peace roles: experience and outcomes. In B. Raphael and J. P. Wilson (eds.), *Psychological debriefing: theory, practice and evidence* (pp. 161–73). New York: Cambridge University Press.

Somerfield, M. R. and McCrae, R. R. (2000) Stress and coping research. *American Psychologist*, 55: 620–5.

Sorensen, Bent (1992) Modern ethics and international law. In M. Basoglu (ed.), *Torture and its consequences: current treatment approaches* (pp. 511–19). Cambridge: Cambridge University Press.

Sorokin, Gerald L. (1994) Alliance formation and general deterrence: a game-theoretic model and the case of Israel. *Journal of Conflict Resolution*, 38: 298–325.

Sorokin, Pitirim (1954) *The ways and power of love: types, factors, and techniques of moral transformation.* Boston: Beacon Press. [Also, Chicago: First Gateway Edition, 1967.]

Soutter, Alison and McKenzie, Anne (1998) Evaluation of the dispute resolution project in Australian secondary schools. *School Psychology International*, 19: 307–16.

Spector, Bertram I. (1997) Analytical support to negotiations: an empirical assessment. *Group Decision and Negotiation*, 6: 421–36.

(1998) Deciding to negotiate with villains. *Negotiation Journal*, 14: 43–59.

Spink, Peter (1997) Paths to solidarity: some comments on 'Identification with the human species'. *Human Relations*, 50: 1005–14.

Sprang, Ginny (1999) Post-disaster stress following the Oklahoma City bombing: an examination of three community groups. *Journal of Interpersonal Violence*, 14: 161–75.

(2003) The psychological impact of isolated acts of terrorism. In A. Silke (ed.), *Terrorists, victims and society: psychological perspectives on terrorism and its consequences* (pp. 133–59). Chichester: Wiley.

Staab, Joachim F. and Wright, Claudia S. (1991) Media coverage in the Federal Republic of Germany of the conflict between the US and Libya in spring 1986. *Communications*, 16: 237–50.

Statement on the Iraq War (2003) [Psychologists for Social Responsibility, Washington, DC]. *Constructivism in the Human Sciences*, 8(1): 159–60.

Staub, Ervin (1996) Preventing genocide: activating bystanders, helping victims, and the creation of caring. *Peace and Conflict: Journal of Peace Psychology*, 2: 189–200.

(1999) The origins and prevention of genocide, mass killing, and other collective violence. *Peace and Conflict: Journal of Peace Psychology*, 5: 303–36.

(2001) Genocide and mass killing: their roots and prevention. In D. J. Christie, R. V. Wagner and D. D. Winter (eds.), *Peace, conflict, and violence: peace psychology for the 21st century* (pp. 76–86). Upper Saddle River, NJ: Prentice Hall.

(2002) From healing past wounds to the development of inclusive caring: contents and processes of peace education. In G. Salomon and B. Nevo (eds.), *Peace education: the concept, principles, and practices around the world* (pp. 79–86). Mahwah, NJ: Lawrence Erlbaum Associates.

(2003) Notes on cultures of violence, cultures of caring and peace, and the fulfillment of basic human needs. *Political Psychology*, 24(1): 1–21.

(2004) Justice, healing, and reconciliation: how the people's courts in Rwanda can promote them. *Peace and Conflict: Journal of Peace Psychology*, 10: 25–32.

Staub, Sylvia and Green, Paula (eds.) (1992) *Psychology and social responsibility: facing global challenges.* New York and London: New York University Press.

Steger, Manfred B. (2001) Peacebuilding and nonviolence: Gandhi's perspective on power. In D. J. Christie, R. V. Wagner and D. D. Winter (eds.), *Peace, conflict, and violence: peace psychology for the 21st century* (pp. 314–23). Upper Saddle River, NJ: Prentice Hall.

Stein, B. (1997) Community reactions to disaster: an emerging role for the school psychologist. *School Psychology International*, 18: 99–118.

Stein, Bradley D., Elliott, Marc N., Jaycox, Lisa H., Collins, Rebecca L., Berry, Sandra H., Klein, David J. and Schuster, Mark A. (2004) A national longitudinal study of the psychological consequences of the September 11, 2001 terrorist attacks: reactions, impairment, and help-seeking. *Psychiatry: Interpersonal and Biological Processes*, 67: 105–17.

Stein, Janice Gross (1991) Deterrence and reassurance. In P. E. Tetlock, J. L. Husbands, R. Jervis, P. C. Stern and C. Tilly (eds.), *Behavior, society, and nuclear war* (Vol. 2, pp. 8–72). New York: Oxford University Press.

(1999) Problem solving as metaphor: negotiation and identity conflict. *Peace and Conflict: Journal of Peace Psychology*, 5: 225–35.

Stein, R. (2003) Evil as love and as liberation: the mind of a suicidal religious terrorist. In D. Moss (ed.), *Hating in the first person plural: psychoanalytic essays on racism, homophobia, misogyny and terror* (pp. 281–310). New York: Other Press.

Steinberg, Blema S. (1991) Psychoanalytic concepts in international politics: the role of shame and humiliation. *International Review of Psycho-Analysis*, 18: 65–85.

Steinhausler, Friedrich (2003) What it takes to become a nuclear terrorist. *American Behavioral Scientist*, 46: 782–95.

Stephan, Cookie W. and Stephan, Walter G. (1992) Reducing intercultural anxiety through intercultural contact. *International Journal of Intercultural Relations*, 16: 89–106.

Stern, Paul C. (2000) Psychology and the science of human–environment interactions. *American Psychologist*, 55: 523–30.

Sternberg, R. J. (2003) A duplex theory of hate: development and application to terrorism, massacres and genocide. *Review of General Psychology*, 7: 299–328.

Sternberg, Robert J. and Frensch, Peter A. (eds.) (1991) *Complex problem solving: principles and mechanisms*. Hillsdale, NJ: Lawrence Erlbaum Associates.

Stevanovic, Ivana (1998) Violence against women in the Yugoslav war as told by women-refugees. *International Review of Victimology*, 6: 63–76.

Steven, G. (2002, November) Relationship between religious beliefs and motivation to join a terrorist group. Paper presented at the British Psychological Society, Aspects of Terrorism and Martyrdom seminar, Royal Holloway, University of London.

Stevens, Anthony (1995) Jungian approach to human aggression with special emphasis on war. *Aggressive Behavior*, 21: 3–11.

Stevens, Garth (2003) Academic representations of 'race' and racism in psychology: knowledge production, historical context and dialectics in transitional South Africa. *International Journal of Intercultural Relations*, 27: 189–207.

Stewart, Sherry H. (2004) Psychological impact of the events and aftermath of the September 11th, 2001, terrorist attacks. *Cognitive Behaviour Therapy*, 33: 49–50.

Stone, Brenda, Jones, Cindy and Betz, Brian (1996) Response of cooperators and competitors in a simulated arms race. *Psychological Reports*, 79: 1101–2.

Stone, Randall W. (2001) The use and abuse of game theory in international relations: the theory of moves. *Journal of Conflict Resolution*, 45: 216–44.

Stout, Chris E. (ed.) (2002) *The psychology of terrorism: clinical aspects and responses* (4 volumes). Westport, CT: Praeger/Greenwood.

Straker, G. (1992) *Faces in the revolution*. Cape Town, South Africa: David Philip.

Stringer, Maurice, Cornish, Ian M. and Denver, Sean (2000) The transition to peace and young people's perceptions of locations in Northern Ireland. *Peace and Conflict: Journal of Peace Psychology*, 6: 57–66.

Strozier, Charles B. and Flynn, Michael (eds.) (1996) *Genocide, war, and human survival*. Lanham, MD: Rowman and Littlefield.

Strozier, Charles B. and Simich, Laura (1991) Christian fundamentalism and nuclear threat. *Political Psychology*, 12: 81–96.

Stuhlmacher, Alice F., Gillespie, Treena L. and Champagne, Matthew V. (1998) The impact of time pressure in negotiation: a meta-analysis. *International Journal of Conflict Management*, 9: 97–116.

Suedfeld, Peter (1999) Toward a taxonomy of ethnopolitical violence: is collective killing by any other name still the same? *Peace and Conflict: Journal of Peace Psychology*, 5: 349–55.

   (2004) Harun al-Rashid and the terrorists: identity concealed, identity revealed. *Political Psychology*, 25: 479–92.

Suleiman, Ramzi (2002) Minority self-categorization: the case of the Palestinians in Israel. *Peace and Conflict: Journal of Peace Psychology*, 8: 31–46.

Sulfaro, Valerie A. and Crislip, Mark N. (1997) How Americans perceive foreign policy threats: a magnitude scaling analysis. *Political Psychology*, 18: 103–26.

Summerfield, D. (1996) *The impact of war and atrocity on civilian populations: basic principles for NGO interventions and a critique of psychological trauma projects*. [Relief and Rehabilitation Network, Network Paper 14.] London: Overseas Development Institute.

Susskind, Lawrence and Babbitt, Eileen (1992) Overcoming the obstacles to effective mediation of international disputes. In J. Bercovitch and J. Z. Rubin (eds.), *Mediation in international relations: multiple approaches to conflict management* (pp. 30–51). New York: St. Martin's Press, Inc.

Sutton, Robert I. and Kramer, Roderick M. (1990) Transforming failure into success: spin control in the Iceland arms control talks. In R. L. Kahn and M. N. Zald (eds.), *Organizations and nation-states: new perspectives on conflict and cooperation* (pp. 221–45). San Francisco: Jossey-Bass Inc., Publishers.

Swiss, S. and Giller, J. E. (1993) Rape as a crime of war: a medical perspective. *Journal of the American Medical Association*, 270: 612–15.

Sylvan, Donald A. and Thorson, Stuart J. (1992) Ontologies, problem representation, and the Cuban missile crisis. *Journal of Conflict Resolution*, 36: 709–32.

Tabachnick, B. Robert (1990) Studying peace in elementary schools: laying a foundation for the 'peaceable kingdom'. *Theory and Research in Social Education*, 18: 169–73.

Talentino, Andrea Kathryn (2003) Rethinking conflict resolution: matching problems and solutions. *Peace and Conflict Studies*, 10(1): 15–39.

Taliaferro, Jeffrey W. (2004) Power politics and the balance of risk: hypotheses on great power intervention in the periphery. *Political Psychology*, 25: 177–211.

Tang, Thomas Li Ping and Ibrahim, Abdul H. Safwat (1998) Importance of human needs during retrospective peacetime and the Persian Gulf war: mideastern employees. *International Journal of Stress Management*, 5: 25–37.

Tarar, Ahmer (2001) International bargaining with two-sided domestic constraints. *Journal of Conflict Resolution*, 45: 320–40.

Tatara, Mikihachiro (1998) The second generation of Hibakusha, atomic bomb survivors: a psychologist's view. In Y. Danieli (ed.), *International handbook of multigenerational legacies of trauma* (pp. 141–6). New York: Plenum Press.

Taylor, Bryan C. (1990) Reminiscences of Los Alamos: narrative, critical theory, and the organizational subject. *Western Journal of Speech Communication*, 54: 395–419.

Taylor, Bryan C. and Freer, Brian (2002) Containing the nuclear past: the politics of history and heritage at the Hanford plutonium works. *Journal of Organizational Change Management*, 15: 563–88.

Taylor, Carl E. (1998) How care for childhood psychological trauma in wartime may contribute to peace. *International Review of Psychiatry*, 10: 175–8.

Taylor, Donald M. and Moghaddam, Fathali M. (1994) *Theories of intergroup relations: International social psychological perspectives* (2nd edn.). Westport, CT: Praeger Publishers/Greenwood Publishing Group.

Taylor, Paul J. and Donald, Ian (2003) Foundations and evidence for an interaction-based approach to conflict negotiation. *International Journal of Conflict Management*, 14: 213–32.

Taylor, Rupert (2004) Peace building and theory building. *Peace and Conflict: Journal of Peace Psychology*, 10: 91–3.

Tehrani, N. (2002) Healing the wounds of the mind. *The Psychologist*, 15: 598–9.

Terr, L. C., Bloch, D. A., Michel, B. A., Shi, H., Reinhardt, J. A. and Metayer, S. (1999) Children's symptoms in the wake of Challenger: a field study of distant traumatic effects and an outline of related conditions. *American Journal of Psychiatry*, 156: 1536–44.

Terrorism and disaster: individual and community mental health interventions (2004) *Journal of Nervous and Mental Disease*, 192: 335.

Terry, Paul (2002) A commentary on the film *No Man's Land* for the PPOWP APS interest group. *Psychodynamic Practice: Individuals, Groups and Organisations*, 8: 532–6.

Tessler, Mark and Nachtwey, Jodi (1998) Islam and attitudes towards international conflict: evidence from survey research in the Arab world. *Journal of Conflict Resolution*, 42: 619–36.

Tessler, M., Nachtwey, J. and Grant, A. (1999) Further tests of the women and peace hypothesis: evidence from cross-national survey research in the Middle East. *International Studies Quarterly*, 43: 519–31.

Tetlock, Philip E. (1988) Monitoring the integrative complexity of American and Soviet policy rhetoric: What can be learned? *Journal of Social Issues*, 44(2): 101–31.

(1991) Learning in US and Soviet foreign policy: in search of an elusive concept. In G. W. Breslauer and P. E. Tetlock (eds.), *Learning in US and Soviet foreign policy* (pp. 20–61). Boulder, CO: Westview Press.

(1992) Good judgment in international politics: three psychological perspectives. *Political Psychology*, 13: 517–39.

(1997) Psychological perspectives on international conflict and cooperation. In D. F. Halpern and A. E. Voiskounsky (eds.), *States of mind: American and post-Soviet perspectives on contemporary issues in psychology* (pp. 49–76). New York: Oxford University Press.

(1998) Social psychology and world politics. In D. T. Gilbert, S. T. Fiske and G. Lindzey (eds.), *The handbook of social psychology* (Vol. 2, 4th edn., pp. 868–912). Boston: McGraw-Hill.

Tetlock, Philip E., Hoffmann, Stanley, Janis, Irving L., Stein, Janice Gross, Kressel, Neil J. and Cohen, Bernard C. (1993) The psychology of international conflict. In N. J. Kressel (ed.), *Political psychology: classic and contemporary readings* (pp. 312–416). New York: Paragon House Publishers.

Tetlock, Philip E., Husbands, Jo L., Jervis, Robert, Stern, Paul C. and Tilly, Charles (eds.) (1993) *Behavior, society, and international conflict, Vol. 3*. New York: Oxford University Press.

Tetlock, Philip E., McGuire, Charles B. and Mitchell, Gregory (1991) Psychological perspectives on nuclear deterrence. *Annual Review of Psychology*, 42: 239–76.

Thabet, Abdel Aziz and Vostanis, Panos (2000) Post traumatic stress disorder reactions in children of war: a longitudinal study. *Child Abuse and Neglect*, 24: 291–8.

Thies, Wallace J. (1991) Learning in US policy towards Europe. In G. W. Breslauer and P. E. Tetlock (eds.), *Learning in US and Soviet foreign policy* (pp. 158–207). Boulder, CO: Westview Press.

Thomas, Jeffrey L. and Castro, Carl Andrew (2003) Organizational behavior and the US peacekeeper. In T. W. Britt and A. B. Adler (eds.), *The psychology of the peacekeeper: lessons from the field* (pp. 127–46). Westport, CT: Praeger Publishers/Greenwood Publishing Group.

Thompson, James A. (1991) Perceptions of the Soviet Union and the arms race: a ten-nation cross-cultural study. In R. W. Rieber (ed.), *The psychology of war and peace: the image of the enemy* (pp. 155–67). New York: Plenum Press.

Thompson, Megan M. and Pasto, Luigi (2003) Psychological interventions in peace support operations: current practices and future challenges. In T. W. Britt and A. B. Adler (eds.), *The psychology of the peacekeeper: lessons from the field* (pp. 223–41). Westport, CT: Praeger Publishers/Greenwood Publishing Group.

Thrall, Charles A. and Blumberg, Herbert H. (1963) Attitudes of the American Protestant clergy towards issues of war and peace. *Fellowship*, 29(17): 3–9.

Thurston, Linda P. and Berkeley, Terry R. (2003) Peaceable school communities: morality and the ethic of care. In M. S. E. Fishbaugh, T. R. Berkeley, and G. Schroth (eds.), *Ensuring safe school environments: exploring issues – seeking solutions* (pp. 133–47). Mahwah, NJ: Lawrence Erlbaum Associates.

Tibon, Shira (2000) Personality traits and peace negotiations: integrative complexity and attitudes toward the Middle East peace process. *Group Decision and Negotiation*, 9: 1–15.

Tibon, Shira and Blumberg, Herbert H. (1999) Authoritarianism and political socialization in the context of the Arab–Israeli conflict. *Political Psychology*, 20: 581–91.

Tiffany, Donald W. and Tiffany, Phyllis G. (2000) *Power and control: escape from violence*. Lanham, MD: University Press of America.

Tilker, Harvey A. (1970) Socially responsible behavior as a function of observer responsibility and victim feedback. *Journal of Personality and Social Psychology*, 14: 95–100.

Tinckner, J. E. (1992) *Gender and international relations: feminist perspectives on achieving global security*. New York: Columbia University Press.

Ting-Toomey, Stella, Gao, Ge, Trubisky, Paula, Yang, Zhizhhong, Kim, H. S., Lin, S. and Mishida, T. (1991) Culture, face maintenance, and styles of handling interpersonal conflicts: a study in five cultures. *International Journal of Conflict Management*, 2: 275–96.

Ting-Toomey, Stella and Korzenny, Felipe (eds.) (1991) *Cross-cultural interpersonal communication*. Newbury Park, CA: Sage Publications.

Ting-Toomey, Stella and Kurogi, Atsuko (1998) Facework competence in intercultural conflict: an updated face-negotiation theory. *International Journal of Intercultural Relations*, 22: 187–225.

Tinsley, Catherine (1998) Models of conflict resolution in Japanese, German, and American cultures. *Journal of Applied Psychology*, 83: 316–23.

Tjosvold, Dean (1998) Cooperative and competitive goal approach to conflict: accomplishments and challenges. *Applied Psychology: An International Review*, 47: 285–342.

Tjosvold, Dean, Hui, Chun and Law, Kenneth S. (2001) Constructive conflict in China: cooperative conflict as a bridge between East and West. *Journal of World Business*, 36: 166–83.

Tjosvold, Dean, Hui, Chun and Yu, Ziyou (2003) Conflict management and task reflexivity for team in-role and extra-role performance in China. *International Journal of Conflict Management*, 14: 141–63.

Tjosvold, Dean, Leung, Kwok and Johnson, David W. (2000) Cooperative and competitive conflict in China. In M. Deutsch and P. T. Coleman (eds.), *The handbook of conflict resolution: theory and practice* (pp. 475–95). San Francisco: Jossey-Bass/Pfeiffer.

Tobin, Richard J. and Eagles, Munroe (1992) US and Canadian attitudes towards international interactions: a cross-national test of the double-standard hypothesis. *Basic and Applied Social Psychology*, 13: 447–59.

Tompkins, T. (1995) Rape as war crime. *Notre Dame Law Review*, 70: 845–90.

Tongren, Hale N., Hecht, Leo and Kovach, Kenneth (1995) Recognizing cultural differences: key to successful US–Russian enterprises. *Public Personnel Management*, 24: 1–17.

Torabi, Mohammad R. and Seo, Dong Chul (2004) National study of behavioral and life changes since September 11. *Health Education and Behavior*, 31: 179–92.

Tota, Anna Lisa (2004) Ethnographying public memory: the commemorative genre for the victims of terrorism in Italy. *Qualitative Research*, 4: 131–59.

Touval, Saadia (1992) The superpowers as mediators. In J. Bercovitch and J. Z. Rubin (eds.), *Mediation in international relations: multiple approaches to conflict management* (pp. 232–48). New York: St. Martin's Press, Inc.

(1995) Ethical dilemmas in international mediation. *Negotiation Journal*, 11: 333–7.

Townshend, C. (2002) *Terrorism: a very short introduction*. Oxford: Oxford University Press.

Trubisky, Paula, Ting-Toomey, Stella and Lin, Sung ling (1991) The influence of individualism-collectivism and self-monitoring on conflict styles. *International Journal of Intercultural Relations*, 15: 65–84.

Tsebelis, George (1990) Are sanctions effective? A game-theoretic analysis. *Journal of Conflict Resolution*, 34: 3–28.

Tucker, P., Pfefferbaum, B., Nixon, S. J. and Dickson, W. (2000) Predictors of post-traumatic stress symptoms in Oklahoma City: exposure, social support, peri-traumatic responses. *Journal of Behavioral Health Services and Research*, 27: 406–16.

Tudge, Jonathan, Chivian, Eric, Robinson, John P., Andreyenkov, Vladimir and Popov, N. (1990–1991) American and Soviet adolescents' attitudes towards the future: the relationship between worry about nuclear war and optimism. *International Journal of Mental Health*, 19(4): 58–84.

Tversky, Amos and Kahneman, Daniel (1980) Judgment under uncertainty: heuristics and biases. *Science*, 815: 1124–31.

Twemlow, Stuart W. (2004) Psychoanalytic understanding of terrorism and massive social trauma. *Journal of the American Psychoanalytic Association*, 52: 709–16.

Twemlow, Stuart W. and Sacco, Frank C. (1996) Peacekeeping and peacemaking: the conceptual foundations of a plan to reduce violence and improve the quality of life in a midsized community in Jamaica. *Psychiatry: Interpersonal and Biological Processes*, 59: 156–74.

2003 Gold Medal Award for Life Achievement in Psychology in the Public Interest (2003) [Title as author]. *American Psychologist*, 58: 551–3.

Tzeng, Oliver C. S. and Jackson, Jay W. (1994) Effects of contact, conflict, and social identity on interethnic group hostilities. *International Journal of Intercultural Relations*, 18: 259–76.

Ungar, Sheldon (1992) The rise and (relative) decline of global warming as a social problem. *Sociological Quarterly*, 33: 483–501.

United Nations (1995) *Platform for action*. New York: United Nations.

(1996) *Impact of armed conflict on children*. New York: United Nations. (Document A/51.306 & Add 1.) [Cited in Wessells (1998) AN 1998-03107-001.]

United Nations Children's Fund (UNICEF); Liberia and the US National Committee for UNICEF (1998, March) *The disarmament, demobilisation, and reintegration of child soldiers in Liberia, 1994–1997: the process and lessons learned*. New York: UNICEF.

United Nations High Commissioner for Refugees (1997) *The state of the world's refugees*. New York: Oxford University Press.

Ursano, Robert J., Fullerton, Carol S. and Norwood, Ann E. (eds.) (2003) *Terrorism and disaster: individual and community mental health interventions.* New York: Cambridge University Press.

Vaccaro, J. Matthew (1998) Creating a durable peace: psychological aspects of rebuilding and reforming the indigenous criminal justice system. In H. J. Langholtz (ed.), *The psychology of peacekeeping* (pp. 167–78). Westport, CT: Praeger Publishers/Greenwood Publishing Group, Inc.

Vandenplas-Holper, Christiane (1990) Children's books and films as media for moral education: some cognitive-developmentally orientated considerations. *School Psychology International,* 11: 31–8.

van der Dennen, Johan Matheus Gerardus (1995) *The origin of war: the evolution of a male-coalitional reproductive strategy,* 2 vols. Groningen, Netherlands: Origin Press.

van der Walt, Clint, Franchi, Vije and Stevens, Garth (2003) The South African Truth and Reconciliation Commission: 'race', historical compromise and transitional democracy. *International Journal of Intercultural Relations,* 27: 251–67.

van de Vliert, Evert (1995) Helpless helpers: an intergroup conflict intervention. *International Journal of Conflict Management,* 6: 91–100.

Van Ijzendoorn, M. H., Bakermans-Kranenburg, M. J. and Sagi-Schwartz, A. (2003) Are children of Holocaust survivors less well-adapted? A meta-analytic investigation of secondary traumatization. *Journal of Traumatic Stress,* 16: 459–69.

Van Lange, Paul A. and Liebrand, Wim B. (1991) The influence of other's morality and own social value orientation on cooperation in the Netherlands and the USA. *International Journal of Psychology,* 26: 429–49.

van Oudenhoven, Jan Pieter, Askevis-Leherpeux, Françoise, Hannover, Bettina, Jaarsma, Renske and Dardenne, Benoit (2002) Asymmetrical international attitudes. *European Journal of Social Psychology,* 32: 275–89.

van Oudenhoven, Jan Pieter, Mechelse, Lonneke and de Dreu, Carsten K. W. (1998) Managerial conflict management in five European countries: the importance of power distance, uncertainty avoidance, and masculinity. *Applied Psychology: An International Review,* 47: 439–55.

van Oudenhoven, Jan Pieter and van der Zee, Karen I. (2002) Successful international cooperation: the influence of cultural similarity, strategic differences, and international experience. *Applied Psychology: An International Review,* 51: 633–53.

Van Wyk, Koos and Radloff, Sarah (1993) Reciprocity and South Africa's dyadic foreign policy behavior. *Social Science Quarterly,* 74: 804–14.

Vasconcelos, Laercia A. (1992) Algumas caracteristicas da readaptacao de sobreviventes da bomba atomica em Hiroshima. [Some aspects of readaptation of atomic bomb survivors in Hiroshima.] *Psicologia: Teoria e Pesquisa,* 8: 113–22.

Veale, Angela and Dona, Giorgia (2002) Psychosocial interventions and children's rights: beyond clinical discourse. *Peace and Conflict: Journal of Peace Psychology,* 8: 47–61.

Veer, Guus van der (1998) *Counselling and therapy with refugees and victims of trauma: psychological problems of victims of war, torture, and repression* (2nd edn.). Chichester: John Wiley.

Verbeek, Peter and de Waal, Frans B. M. (2001) Peacemaking among preschool children. *Peace and Conflict: Journal of Peace Psychology*, 7: 5–28.

Vernez, Georges (1991) Current global refugee situation and international public policy. *American Psychologist*, 46: 627–31.

Vincent, Andrew and Shepherd, John (1998) Experiences in teaching Middle East politics via internet-based role-play simulations. *Journal of Interactive Media in Education*, 26(1): 29–48.

Volkan, V. D. (1999a) Psychoanalysis and diplomacy: part I, individual and large group identity. *Journal of Applied Psychoanalytic Studies*, 1: 29–55.

Volkan, Vamik D. (1999b) Psychoanalysis and diplomacy: part III, potentials for and obstacles against collaboration. *Journal of Applied Psychoanalytic Studies*, 1: 305–18.

Volkan, Vamik D. and Itzkowitz, Norman (2000) Modern Greek and Turkish identities and the psychodynamics of Greek–Turkish relations. In A. C. G. M. Robben and M. M. Suarez-Orozco (eds.), *Cultures under siege: collective violence and trauma* (pp. 227–47). New York: Cambridge University Press.

Volkema, Roger J. (1998) A comparison of perceptions of ethical negotiation behavior in Mexico and the US. *International Journal of Conflict Management*, 9: 218–33.

Voss, James F., Wolfe, Christopher R., Lawrence, Jeanette A. and Engle, Randi A. (1991) From representation to decision: an analysis of problem solving in international relations. In R. J. Sternberg and P. A. Frensch (eds.), *Complex problem solving: principles and mechanisms* (pp. 119–58). Hillsdale, NJ: Lawrence Erlbaum Associates, Inc.

Wadsworth, Martha E., Gudmundsen, Gretchen R., Raviv, Tali, Ahlkvist, Jarl A., McIntosh, Daniel N., Kline, Galena H., Rea, Jacqueline and Burwell, Rebecca A. (2004) Coping with terrorism: age and gender differences in effortful and involuntary responses to September 11th. *Applied Developmental Science*, 8: 143–57.

Wagner, Richard V. (1993) The differential psychological effects of positive and negative approaches to peace. In V. K. Kool (ed.), *Nonviolence: social and psychological issues* (pp. 79–84). Lanham, MD: University Press of America.

(2003) Foreword to Asian Peace Psychology. *Peace and Conflict: Journal of Peace Psychology*, 9: 191–3.

Walker, Kathleen, Myers-Bowman, Karen S. and Myers-Walls, Judith A. (2003) Understanding war, visualizing peace: children draw what they know. *Art Therapy*, 20: 191–200.

Walker, Stephen G., Schafer, Mark and Young, Michael D. (1999) Presidential operational codes and foreign policy conflicts in the post-Cold War world. *Journal of Conflict Resolution*, 43: 610–25.

Walker, Stephen G. and Watson, George L. (1992) The cognitive maps of British leaders, 1938–1939, the case of Chamberlain-in-cabinet. In E. Singer and V. Hudson (eds.), *Political psychology and foreign policy* (pp. 31–58). Boulder, CO: Westview Press.

(1994) Integrative complexity and British decisions during the Munich and Polish crises. *Journal of Conflict Resolution*, 38: 3–23.

Wall, James A. Jr., Sohn, Dong Won, Cleeton, Natalie and Jin, Deng Jian (1995) Community and family mediation in the People's Republic of China. *International Journal of Conflict Management*, 6: 30–47.

Wallensteen, Peter (1991) Is there a role for third parties in the prevention of nuclear war? In P. E. Tetlock, J. L. Husbands, R. Jervis, P. C. Stern and C. Tilly (eds.), *Behavior, society, and nuclear war* (Vol. 2, pp. 193–253). New York: Oxford University Press.

Walsh, Roger (1996) Toward a psychology of human and ecological survival: psychological approaches to contemporary global threats. In B. W. Scotton, A. B. Chinen and J. R. Battista (eds.), *Textbook of transpersonal psychiatry and psychology* (pp. 396–405). New York: Basic Books, Inc.

Walther, Joseph B. (1997) Group and interpersonal effects in international computer-mediated collaboration. *Human Communication Research*, 23: 342–69.

Walz, Tom and Ritchie, Heather (2000) Gandhian principles in social work practice: ethics revisited. *Social Work*, 45: 213–22.

Wang, Kevin H. (1996) Presidential responses to foreign policy crises: rational choice and domestic politics. *Journal of Conflict Resolution*, 40: 68–97.

Wangh, Martin (1994) Weitere klinische Ueberlegungen zum psychologischen Fallout der nuklearen Bedrohung. [Further clinical considerations of the psychological fallout of the nuclear threat.] *Psyche: Zeitschrift für Psychoanalyse und ihre Anwendungen*, 48: 387–95.

Wanis-St. John, Anthony (2003) Thinking globally and acting locally. *Negotiation Journal*, 19: 389–96.

Ward, Hugh (1993) Game theory and the politics of the global commons. *Journal of Conflict Resolution*, 37: 203–35.

Wardell, D. and Czerwinski, B. (2001) A military challenge to managing feminine and personal hygiene. *Journal of the American Academy of Nurse Practitioners*, 13: 187–93.

Wardi, Dina and Goldblum, Naomi (Trans.) (1992) *Memorial candles: children of the Holocaust*. London: Tavistock/Routledge.

Warner, Dorothy Anne (2001) The lantern-floating ritual: linking a community together. *Art Therapy*, 18: 14–19.

Watkins, Michael (1999) Negotiating in a complex world. *Negotiation Journal*, 15: 245–70.

Watkins, Michael and Lundberg, Kirsten (1998) Getting to the table in Oslo: driving forces and channel factors. *Negotiation Journal*, 14: 115–37.

Watkins, Michael and Rosegrant, Susan (1996) Sources of power in coalition building. *Negotiation Journal*, 12: 47–68.

(2002) Breakthrough international negotiation: how great negotiators transformed the world's toughest post-Cold War conflicts. *International Journal of Conflict Management*, 13: 95–104.

Watkins, Michael and Winters, Kim (1997) Intervenors with interests and power. *Negotiation Journal*, 13: 119–42.

Watson, Raymond K., Haines, Meredith and Bretherton, Di (1996) Effects of interpersonal communication process variables on outcomes in an international conflict negotiation simulation. *Journal of Social Psychology*, 136: 483–91.

Wayment, H. and Cordova, A. (2003) Mental models of attachment, social strain, and distress following a collective loss: a structural modelling analysis. *Current Research in Social Psychology*, 9(2).

Webb, Nancy Boyd (ed.) (2004) *Mass trauma and violence: helping families and children cope*. New York: Guilford Press.

Webber, Jane, Bass, Debra D. and Yep, Richard (eds.) (2005) *Terrorism, trauma, and tragedies: a counselor's guide to preparing and responding* (2nd edn.). Alexandria, VA: American Counseling Association Foundation.

Webel, Charles (2004) *Terror, terrorism, and the human condition*. New York: Palgrave Macmillan.

Weber, Steven (1991) Interactive learning in US–Soviet arms control. In G. W. Breslauer and P. E. Tetlock (eds.), *Learning in US and Soviet foreign policy* (pp. 784–824). Boulder, CO: Westview Press.

Weerts, Jos M. P., White, Wendy, Adler, Amy B., Castro, Carl A., Algra, Gielt, Bramsen, Inge, Dirkzwager, Anja J. E., Ploeg, Henk M. van der, Vries, Maaike de and Zijlmans, Ad (2002) Studies on military peacekeepers. In Y. Danieli (ed.), *Sharing the front line and the back hills: international protectors and providers: peacekeepers, humanitarian aid workers and the media in the midst of crisis* (pp. 31–48). Amityville, NY: Baywood Publishing Co.

Weine, Stevan M. (1999) Against evil. *Peace and Conflict: Journal of Peace Psychology*, 5: 357–64.

Weinstein, Monty M. (2004) Terrorism: the ongoing phenomenon. *Annals of the American Psychotherapy Association*, 7(1): 42.

Weisaeth, Lars (2003) The psychological challenge of peacekeeping operations. In T. W. Britt and A. B. Adler (eds.), *The psychology of the peacekeeper: lessons from the field* (pp. 207–22). Westport, CT: Praeger Publishers/Greenwood Publishing Group.

Weisinger, Judith Y. and Salipante, Paul F. (1995) Toward a method of exposing hidden assumptions in multicultural conflict. *International Journal of Conflict Management*, 6: 147–70.

Weiss, Joshua N. (2003) Trajectories towards peace: mediator sequencing strategies in intractable communal conflicts. *Negotiation Journal*, 19: 109–15.

Weissenberger, Stein (1992) Deterrence and the design of treaty verification systems. *IEEE Transactions on Systems, Man, and Cybernetics*, 22: 903–15.

Weldon, Elizabeth and Jehn, Karen A. (1995) Examining cross-cultural differences in conflict management behavior: a strategy for future research. *International Journal of Conflict Management*, 6: 387–403.

Wellman, James K. Jr. and Tokuno, Kyoko (2004) Is religious violence inevitable? *Journal for the Scientific Study of Religion*, 43: 291–6.

Welsh, Nancy A. and Coleman, Peter T. (2002) Institutionalized conflict resolution: have we come to expect too little? *Negotiation Journal*, 18: 345–50.

Welton, Gary L., Pruitt, Dean G., McGillicuddy, Neil B. and Ippolito, Carol A. (1992) Antecedents and characteristics of caucusing in community mediation. *International Journal of Conflict Management*, 3: 303–17.

Werner, Suzanne (1999) Choosing demands strategically: the distribution of power, the distribution of benefits, and the risk of conflict. *Journal of Conflict Resolution*, 43: 705–26.

Wessells, Michael G. (1993) Psychological obstacles to peace. In V. K. Kool (ed.), *Nonviolence: social and psychological issues* (pp. 25–35). Lanham, MD: University Press of America.

(1995) Comment on Blight and Lang's 'Burden of nuclear responsibility: reflections on the critical oral history of the Cuban missile crisis'. *Peace and Conflict: Journal of Peace Psychology*, 1: 265–73.

(1997) Child soldiers. *The Bulletin of the Atomic Scientists*, 53(6): 32–9.

(1998a) The changing nature of armed conflict and its implications for children: the Graca Machel/UN study. *Peace and Conflict: Journal of Peace Psychology*, 4: 321–34.

(1998b) Humanitarian intervention, psychosocial assistance, and peacekeeping. In H. J. Langholtz (ed.), *The psychology of peacekeeping* (pp. 131–52). Westport, CT: Praeger Publishers/Greenwood Publishing Group, Inc.

(1999) Systemic approaches to the understanding and prevention of genocide and mass killing. *Peace and Conflict: Journal of Peace Psychology*, 5: 365–71.

(2000) Contributions of psychology to peace and nonviolent conflict resolution. In K. Pawlik and M. R. Rosenzweig (eds.), *International handbook of psychology* (pp. 526–33). London: Sage.

Wessells, Michael G. and Bretherton, Di (2000) Psychological reconciliation: national and international perspectives. *Australian Psychologist*, 35: 100–8.

Wessells, Michael and Monteiro, Carlinda (2001) Psychosocial interventions and post-war reconstruction in Angola: interweaving Western and traditional approaches. In D. J. Christie, R. V. Wagner and D. D. Winter (eds.), *Peace, conflict, and violence: peace psychology for the 21st century* (pp. 262–75). Upper Saddle River, NJ: Prentice Hall.

(2003) Healing, social integration, and community mobilization for war-affected children: a view from Angola. In T. M. McIntyre and S. Krippner (eds.), *The psychological impact of war trauma on civilians: an international perspective* (pp. 179–91). Westport, CT: Praeger Publishers/Greenwood Publishing Group.

Wessells, Michael, Schwebel, Milton and Anderson, Anne (2001) Psychologists making a difference in the public arena: building cultures of peace. In D. J. Christie, R. V. Wagner and D. D. Winter (eds.), *Peace, conflict, and violence: peace psychology for the 21st century* (pp. 350–62). Upper Saddle River, NJ: Prentice Hall.

Westle, B. (1992) Strukturen nationaler identitaet in Ost- und Westdeutschland. [Structures of national identity in East and West Germany.] *Koelner Zeitschrift für Soziologie und Sozialpsychologie*, 44: 461–88.

Wetzel, Janice W. (1992) Profiles on women: a global perspective. *Social Work in Health Care*, 16(3): 13–27.

'What are some typical misperceptions and stereotypes Westerners hold about Islam and the Middle East, and vice versa?' (28 November 2004). http:// www.pbs.org/wgbh/globalconnections/mideast/questions/types/
Wheeler, C. E. and Chinn, P. (1991) *Peace and power: handbook of feminist process* (3rd edn.). New York: National League for Nursing.
White, Ralph K. (ed.) (1986) *Psychology and the prevention of nuclear war*. New York: New York University Press.
(1990) Why aggressors lose. *Political Psychology*, 11: 227–42.
(1994) Empathizing with Saddam Hussein – updated. In H. H. Blumberg and C. C. French (eds.), *The Persian Gulf War: views from the social and behavioral sciences* (pp. 171–89). Lanham, MD: University Press of America.
(1995) When does intervention make sense? *Peace and Conflict: Journal of Peace Psychology*, 1: 85–95.
(1996) Why the Serbs fought: motives and misperceptions. *Peace and Conflict: Journal of Peace Psychology*, 2: 109–28.
(2000) Psychological aspects of the Kosova crisis. *Peace and Conflict: Journal of Peace Psychology*, 6: 49–55.
Whiting, Allen S. (1991) Soviet policy towards China, 1969–1988. In G. W. Breslauer and P. E. Tetlock (eds.), *Learning in US and Soviet foreign policy* (pp. 504–50). Boulder, CO: Westview Press.
Whitman, J. (2001) Those that have the power to harm but would do none. In D. S. Gordon and F. H. Toase (eds.), *The military and humanitarianism: aspects of peacekeeping* (pp. 101–14). London: Frank Cass.
Whittaker, D. J. (2002) *Terrorism: understanding the global threat*. Harlow: Pearson Education.
Wilkenfeld, Jonathan and Kaufman, Joyce (1993) Political science: network simulation in international politics. *Social Science Computer Review*, 11: 464–76.
Wilkenfeld, Jonathan, Young, Kathleen, Asal, Victor and Quinn, David (2003) Mediating international crises: cross-national and experimental perspectives. *Journal of Conflict Resolution*, 47: 279–301.
Williams, Kristen P. (2004) Achieving peace in the post-Cold War world. *Peace and Conflict: Journal of Peace Psychology*, 10: 189–92.
Wilson, M. A. (2000) Toward a model of terrorist behavior in hostage-taking incidents. *Journal of Conflict Resolution*, 44: 403–24.
Winslow, Donna (1998) Misplaced loyalties: the role of military culture in the breakdown of discipline in peace operations. *Canadian Review of Sociology and Anthropology*, 35: 345–67.
Winter, Deborah Du Nann (1998) War is not healthy for children and other living things. *Peace and Conflict: Journal of Peace Psychology*, 4: 415–28.
(2000) Some big ideas for some big problems. *American Psychologist*, 55: 516–22.
(2003) Nurturing a hopeful environmental peace psychology. *Peace and Conflict: Journal of Peace Psychology*, 9: 327–31.
(2006) The psycho-ecology of armed conflict. *Journal of Social Issues*, 62: 19–40.
Wirth, H. J. (2003) 9/11 as a collective trauma. *Journal of Psychohistory*, 30: 363–88.

Wisher, Robert A. (2003) Task identification and skill deterioration in peace-keeping operations. In T. W. Britt and A. B. Adler (eds.), *The psychology of the peacekeeper: lessons from the field* (pp. 91–109). Westport, CT: Praeger Publishers/Greenwood Publishing Group, Inc.

Withers, B. (2003) Terrorism and war: unconscious dynamics of political violence. *Journal of Analytical Psychology*, 48: 513–14.

Wollman, Neil and Wexler, Michael (1992) A workshop for activists: giving psychology away to peace and justice workers. *Journal of Humanistic Psychology*, 32(4): 147–56.

Woodhouse, Tom (1998) Peacekeeping and the psychology of conflict resolution. In H. J. Langholtz (ed.), *The psychology of peacekeeping* (pp. 153–66). Westport, CT: Praeger Publishers/Greenwood Publishing Group, Inc.

Worchel, Stephen and Simpson, Jeffry A. (eds.) (1993) *Conflict between people and groups: causes, processes, and resolutions*. Chicago, IL: Nelson-Hall.

World Vision (1996) *The effects of armed conflict on girls: a discussion paper prepared by World Vision for the UN study on the impact of armed conflict on children*. Monrovia, CA: World Vision.

Wright, Sue (2002) Language education and foreign relations in Vietnam. In J. W. Tollefson (ed.), *Language policies in education: critical issues* (pp. 225–44). Mahwah, NJ: Lawrence Erlbaum Associates.

Wronka, Joseph (1993) Teaching human rights in the social sciences. In V. K. Kool (ed.), *Nonviolence: social and psychological issues* (pp. 259–68). Lanham, MD: University Press of America.

Wurmser, Leon (2004) Psychoanalytic reflection on 9/11, terrorism, and genocidal prejudice: roots and sequels. *Journal of the American Psychoanalytic Association*, 52: 911–26.

Wylie, Gillian (2003) Women's rights and 'righteous war': an argument for women's autonomy in Afghanistan. *Feminist Theory*, 4: 217–23.

Xu, Xinyi (1994) People's conciliation: a mode of conflict management of civil disputes in China. *International Journal of Conflict Management*, 5: 326–42.

Yawney, Ruta (1995) Music therapy in Gaza: an occupational hazard? *Canadian Journal of Music Therapy*, 3(1): 1–17.

Yedidia, Tova and Itzhaky, Haya (2004) A drawing technique for diagnosis and therapy of adolescents suffering traumatic stress and loss related to terrorism. In N. B. Webb (ed.), *Mass trauma and violence: helping families and children cope* (pp. 283–303). New York: Guilford Press.

Yoon, Mi Yung (1997) Explaining US intervention in Third World internal wars, 1945–1989. *Journal of Conflict Resolution*, 41: 580–602.

Youngs, Gillian (2003) Private pain/public peace: women's rights as human rights and Amnesty International's report on violence against women. *Signs*, 28: 1209–29.

Yu, Xuejian (1995) Conflict in a multicultural organization: an ethnographic attempt to discover work-related cultural assumptions between Chinese and American co-workers. *International Journal of Conflict Management*, 6: 211–32.

Zaitseva, Lyudmila and Hand, Kevin (2003) Nuclear smuggling chains: suppliers, intermediaries, and ends-users. *American Behavioral Scientist*, 46: 822–44.

Zartman, I. William (1991) Regional conflict resolution. In V. A. Kremenyuk (ed.), *International negotiation: analysis, approaches, issues* (pp. 302–14). San Francisco: Jossey-Bass Inc, Publishers.

(1992) International environmental negotiation: challenges for analysis and practice. *Negotiation Journal*, 8: 113–23.

Zartman, William (2003) An open letter to the authors of *Narrative mediation*. *Peace and Conflict: Journal of Peace Psychology*, 9: 189–90.

Zelizer, Craig (2003) The role of artistic processes in peacebuilding in Bosznia-Herzegovina. *Peace and Conflict Studies*, 10(2): 62–75.

Zeng, Dajun and Sycara, Katia (1998) Bayesian learning in negotiation. *International Journal of Human Computer Studies*, 48: 125–41.

Ziller, Robert C., Moriarty, Dahlie S. and Phillips, Stephen T. (1999) The peace personality. In A. Raviv, L. Oppenheimer and D. Bar-Tal (eds.), *How children understand war and peace: a call for international peace education* (pp. 78–90). San Francisco, CA: Jossey-Bass/Pfeiffer.

Zimbardo, P. G. (1969) The human choice. *Nebraska Symposium on Motivation*, 17: 237–307.

Zisk, Kimberly M. (1990) Soviet academic theories on international conflict and negotiation: a research note. *Journal of Conflict Resolution*, 34: 678–93.

Zong, Guichun (2002) Can computer mediated communication help to prepare global teachers? An analysis of preservice social studies teachers' experience. *Theory and Research in Social Education*, 30: 589–616.

Index

Isolated instances of words such as peace and psychology have not been indexed. Entries for names represent a name index, not a person index. Thus the entries for two people whose name appears the same in different publication records will be interfiled; and the records for one person whose name appears in different ways – perhaps with or without a middle initial, for example – may be indexed separately, though in some instances records that obviously refer to the same person have been combined.